# A BIBLICAL THEOLOGY OF THE DOCTRINES OF SOVEREIGN GRACE

# A BIBLICAL THEOLOGY OF THE DOCTRINES OF SOVEREIGN GRACE

Exegetical Considerations of
Key Anthropological, Hamartiological,
and Soteriological Terms and Motifs

*by*

George J. Zemek

*Wipf & Stock*
PUBLISHERS
*Eugene, Oregon*

*Most Scripture quotations are the author's translations.*

The Hebrew Text employed throughout this work is:
  *Biblical Hebraica Stuttgartensia,* ed. K. Elliger; W. Rudolf;
  Stuttgart, 1984.

The Greek Text employed throughout is:
  *The Greek New Testament,* ed. B. Aland; K. Aland;
  J. Karavidopoulos; C. M. Martin; B. M. Metzger;
  Deutsche Bibelgesellschaft: United Bible Societies, 1993.

Some English translations (as specifically noted) taken from:
  *New American Standard Bible,* copyright The Lockman
  Foundation 1960, 1962, 1963, 1968, 1971, 1972, 1973,
  1975, 1977.

  *Holy Bible: New International Version,* copyright 1973, 1978,
  1984 by the International Bible Society; published by
  Zondervan.

The original languages software program used is:
  *Linguist's Software, Inc.*
  Foreign Language Fonts
  PO Box 580
  Edmonds, Wa. 98020-0580
  75507.1157@compuserve.com

A BIBLICAL THEOLOGY OF THE DOCTRINES OF SOVEREIGN
GRACE
By George J. Zemek

ISBN: 1-59752-379-8

# CONTENTS

## DEDICATION

To my dear "foundation" friends whose generosity
has made possible the publication and circulation of my books. I would
especially like to commend Ken and Elouise Fuller for their hands-on
labors of love in the typing of my virtually indecipherable hand-written
manuscripts. All of these friends are "fellow workers for the truth"
found in God's marvelous Word (3 John 8).

# LIST OF ABBREVIATIONS

AB          Anchor Bible

*AOT*       H. W. Wolff, *Anthropology of the Old Testament;* Philadel-
            phia: Fortress, 1974.

*APC*       L. Morris, *Apostolic Preaching of the Cross;* Grand Rapids:
            Eerdmans, 1983.

BAG         W. Bauer; W. F. Arndt; F. W. Gringrich; *Greek-English
            Lexicon of the New Testament;* Chicago, 1957.

BAGD        W. Bauer; W. F. Arndt; F. W. Gringrich; F. W. Danker;
            *Greek-English Lexicon of the New Testament;* Chicago,
            1979.

BDB         F. Brown; S. R. Driver; C. A. Briggs; *Hebrew and English
            Lexicon of the Old Testament;* Oxford, 1907.

*BDT*       *Baker's Dictionary of Theology,* ed. E. F. Harrison; Grand
            Rapids: Baker, 1960.

*BETS*      *Bulletin of the Evangelical Theological Society*

*BHS*       *Biblia Hebraica Stuttgartensia,* ed. K. Elliger; W. Rudolf;
            Stuttgart, 1983.

*B Sac*     *Bibliotheca Sacra*

*EBC*       *The Expositor's Bible Commentary,* ed. F. E. Gaebelein, 12
            vols.; Grand Rapids: Zondervan, 1976 ff.

*EDNTW*     W. E. Vine, *Expository Dictionary of New Testament Words,*
            ed. M. F. Unger; W. White; Nashville: Nelson, 1996.

*EDOTW*     W. E. Vine, *Expository Dictionary of Old Testament Words;*
            ed. M. F. Unger; W. White; Nashville: Nelson 1996.

| | |
|---|---|
| *EGT* | *Expositors Greek Testament,* 5 vols., ed. W. R. Nicoll; Grand Rapids: Eerdmans, reprint 1970. |
| *EQ* | *Evangelical Quarterly* |
| *GELSD* | J. P. Louw; E. A. Nida; *Greek-English Lexicon of the New Testament based on Semantic Domains,* 2 vols.; UBS, 1989. |
| *GGBB* | D. B. Wallace, *Greek Grammar Beyond the Basics;* Grand Rapids: Zondervan, 1996. |
| *GTJ* | *Grace Theological Journal* |
| *GWHM* | D. Hill, *Greek Words and Hebrew Meanings;* Cambridge, 1967. |
| *Int* | *Interpretation* |
| *ISBE* | *International Standard Bible Encyclopedia,* ed. J. Orr, 5 vols.; Grand Rapids: Eerdmans, 1939. |
| *ISBE* | *International Standard Bible Encyclopedia,* ed. G. W. Bromiley, 4 vols.; Grand Rapids: Eerdmans, 1979. |
| *JETS* | *Journal of the Evangelical Theological Society* |
| *JTS* | *Journal of Theological Studies* |
| KB | L. Koehler; W. Baumgartner; *Lexicon in Veteris Libros,* 2 vols.; Leiden: Brill, 1958. |
| KD | C. F. Keil; F. Delitzsch; *Commentary on the Old Testament in 10 Volumes;* Grand Rapids: Eerdmans. |
| *LASNTG* | B. M. Metzger, *Lexical Aids for Students of New Testament Greek;* Princeton, 1971. |
| LXX | Septuagint |
| MM | J. H. Moulton; G. Milligan; *The Vocabulary of the Greek Testament;* Grand Rapids: Eerdmans, 1972. |

NASB    The New American Standard Bible

NCBC    New Century Bible Commentary

NICNT   The New International Commentary on the New Testament, ed. F. F. Bruce; Grand Rapids: Eerdmans.

*NIDNTT*  *The New International Dictionary of New Testament Theology*, ed. C. Brown, 4 vols.; Grand Rapids: Zondervan, 1971.

*NIDOTTE* *The New International Dictionary of Old Testament Theology and Exegesis,* ed. W. A. Van Gemeren, 5 vols.; Grand Rapids: Zondervan, 1997.

NIV     New International Version

NTC     W. Hendriksen, New Testament Commentary; Grand Rapids: Baker, 1953ff.

*NTT*     D. Guthrie, *New Testament Theology*; Downers Grove: IVP, 1981.

*PAT*     R. Jewett, *Paul's Anthropological Terms: A Study of Their Use in Conflict Settings*; Leiden: Brill, 1971.

*POT*     H. Ridderbos, *Paul: An Outline of His Theology*; Grand Rapids: Eedermans, 1975.

*PVM*     W. D. Stacey, *The Pauline View of Man*; London: Macmillan, 1956.

*RTR*     *Reformed Theological Review*

*SSF*     E. D. Burton, *Spirit, Soul, and Flesh*; Chicago, 1918.

*TDNT*    *Theological Dictionary of the New Testament,* ed. G. Kittel; G. Friedrich, 10 vols.; Grand Rapids: Eerdmans, 1976.

*TDOT*    *Theological Dictionary of the Old Testament,* ed. G. J. Botterweck; H. Ringgren; Grand Rapids, 1974ff.

TLNT      C. Spicq, *Theological Lexicon of the New Testament*, 3 vols.; Peabody, MA: Hendrickson, 1994.

TLOT      *Theological Lexicon of the Old Testament*, ed. E. Jenni; C. Westermann, 3 vols.; Peabody, MA: Henrickson, 1997.

TNT       G. E. Ladd, *A Theology of the New Testament;* Grand Rapids: Eerdmans, 1974.

TNTC      Tyndale New Testament Commentary

TWOT      *Theological Wordbook of the Old Testament*, ed. R. L. Harris: G. L. Archer; B. K. Waltke; 2 vols.; Chicago: Moody, 1980.

UBS 4     *The Greet New Testament*, 4th edition; ed. B. Aland; K. Aland; J. Karavidopoulos; C. M. Martini; B. M. Metzger; UBS, 1993.

VE        *Vox Egangelica*

VT        *Vetus Testamentum*

WBC       Word Biblical Commentary

WEC       Wycliffe Exegetical Commentary; Chicago: Moody.

WP        A. T. Robertson, *Word Pictures in the New Testament*, 6 vols.; Nashville: Broadman, 1930.

# TRANSLITERATIONS TABLES

| Hebrew | | Greek | |
|---|---|---|---|
| **Consonants:** | **Vowel "points":** | **Alphabet:** | **Rough breathing, Double consonants, Dipthongs:** |
| א = ʾ | ָ = ā | α = a | ʿ = h |
| ב = b | הָ = â | β = b | ῥ = rh |
| ג = g | ַ = a | γ = g | γγ = ng |
| ד = d | ֳ = ᵃ | δ = d | γκ = nk |
| ה = h | ֵ = ē | ε = e | γξ = nx |
| ו = w | ֵי = ê | ζ = z | γχ = nch |
| ז = z | ֶ = e | η = ē | αι = ai |
| ח = ḥ | ְ (vocal) = ᵉ | φ = th | αυ = au |
| ט = ṭ | ֱ = ᵉ | ι = i | ει = ei |
| י = y | ִ = i | κ = k | ευ = eu |
| כ, ך = k | ִי = î | λ = l | οι = oi |
| ל = l | ֹ = ō | μ = m | ου = ou |
| מ, ם = m | וֹ = ô | ν = n | υι = ui |
| נ, ן = n | ָ = o | ξ = x | ηυ = ēu |
| ס = s | ֳ = ᵒ | ο = o | ᾳ = ā |
| ע = ʿ | וּ = û | π = p | ῃ = ē |
| פ, ף = p | ֻ = u | ρ = r | ῳ = ō |
| צ, ץ = ṣ | | σ, s = s | |
| ק = q | | τ = t | |
| ר = r | | υ = u | |
| שׂ = ś | | φ = ph | |
| שׁ = š | | χ = ch | |
| ת = t | | ψ = ps | |
| | | ω = ō | |

# PREFACE

The topics covered in this volume constitute the stuff of the Christian's rebirth and renewal. I have tried to handle the biblical materials as inductively as possible. My goal has been to review the salient scriptural data bases of the doctrines of man, sin, and salvation and then to express them systematically, hopefully not beyond what the exegetical evidences would allow.

Those who have studied both the biblical languages and theology are probably asking, "What's new in the following pages?" Well, probably very little or possibly nothing. However, my particular handling and packaging of the various words and issues may prove to offer some fresh insights to stimulate profitable thinking, whether you agree or disagree with me at any given juncture. Editors often provide some different angles from which their readers obtain new perspectives on old subjects. And, needless to say, the subject matter at hand is of preeminent importance.

Would that we all enter into this biblical survey of the doctrines of sovereign grace with the theological outlook of Isaiah when he was commissioned by our LORD (cf. Isaiah 6). As a result of the prophet's experience, two great givens were indelibly impressed upon his mind, the awesome holiness of God (v. 3) and the utter sinfulness of man (v. 5).

In biblical context these two truths consistently manifest themselves as contrasting corollaries. When focusing on the Sovereign One (cf., e.g., Isaiah 6:1) who is KING of kings and LORD of lords (cf., e.g., 6:5) we too should be overwhelmed by God's transcendent holiness (cf., e.g., 6:1, 3) while at the same time being convicted by our own alienating sinfulness (cf., e.g., 6:5 again).

Consequently, as we approach these studies on man, sin, and salvation, we ought to bear in mind both the brilliant and the black backdrops of our salvation. A prerequisite understanding of theology proper will allow us to comprehend and to appreciate, all the more, our unworthiness and His unfathomable mercy. Furthermore, as the redeemed draw near to the holy ground of the doctrines of sovereign grace, various exhortations seem appropriate. Indeed, the ones put forth by the author of Hebrews are especially fitting as we launch out into our study:

> Make every effort to live in peace with all men and to be holy;
> without holiness no one will see the Lord. See to it that no

one misses the grace of God and that no bitter root grows up to cause trouble and defile many. See that no one is sexually immoral, or is godless like Esau. ...

You have not come to a mountain that can be touched and that is burning with fire; to darkness, gloom and storm; to a trumpet blast or to such a voice speaking words, so that those who heard it begged that no further word be spoken to them, because they could not bear what was commanded: "If even an animal touches the mountain, it must be stoned." The sight was so terrifying that Moses said, "I am trembling with fear."

But you have come to Mount Zion, to the heavenly Jerusalem, the city of the living God. You have come to thousands upon thousands of angels in joyful assembly, to the church of the firstborn, whose names are written in heaven. You have come to God, the judge of all men, to the spirits of righteous men made perfect, to Jesus the mediator of a new covenant, and to the sprinkled blood that speaks a better word than the blood of Abel.

See to it that you do not refuse him who speaks. If they did not escape when they refused him who warned them on earth, how much less will we, if we turn away from him who warns us from heaven? At that time his voice shook the earth, but now he has promised, "Once more I will shake not only the earth but also the heavens." The words "once more" indicate the removing of what can be shaken—that is, created things—so that what cannot be shaken may remain.

Therefore, since we are receiving a kingdom that cannot be shaken, let us be thankful, and so worship God acceptably with reverence and awe, for our God is a consuming fire (Hebrews 12:14-16a, 18-29; NIV).

# PART I

# BIBLICAL ANTHROPOLOGY

# An Introduction To Biblical Anthropology

Just as it is a priority to keep in mind God's holiness and righteous-ness as we examine the doctrines of sovereign grace (cf. PREFACE), it is also a priority to begin this study with a survey of biblical anthropology. For example, we will find it exegetically beneficial to get a glimpse of the created dignity of pre-fall man prior to examining the ethically grotesque picture of the race in its post-fallen estate. Such a foundational study will enable us to understand better the Bible's teachings about sin and salva-tion. Furthermore, it will prevent us from becoming theologically eccen-tric when it comes to thinking through many general and specific hamartiological and soteriological issues.

From cover to cover the Bible reveals that man is a very special cre-ation of God. The LORD by divine intention made him the crowning capstone of the six days of creation.[1] Genesis 1:26–28 is an important piece of documentation concerning this fact.

> Then God said, "Let us make man (or, mankind, humanity) in our image (בְּצַלְמֵנוּ [bᵉsalmēnû]), according to our likeness[2] (כִּדְמוּתֵנוּ [kidmûtēnû]), and let them have dominion (i.e. rule) over the fish of the sea and the birds of the sky and the animals and over the whole earth, even over every creeping thing that moves about upon the earth." So God created man in His im-age; in the image of God He created *him;* male and female He created *them.*[3] Then God blessed them and said to them, "Be fruitful and multiply; fill the earth and subdue it. Now exercise dominion over the fish of the sea and the birds of the sky and over every living thing that moves about on the earth."

---

[1] On the literality of the six days of creation, cf., e.g., Genesis 1 as the pattern for *our* week of "days" in Exodus 20:11.

[2] Or, "similitude, resemblance" (BDB, 198); cf. the basic idea of a "copy" (Jenni, *TLOT*, 1:340).

[3] Emphasis added: note the singular "him" followed by the plural "them," in this context referring to a "male" image-bearer and a "female" image-bearer. Although both bear the image and likeness of God by creation (*not* culture; cf., e.g., 1 Corinthians 11:3), the LORD has established *functional* distinctions including an economic order of headship for families (cf. even the functional hierarchy within the Trinity). This is also immediately implied in the expansion account of Genesis 2:18–25. For some commentary on this passage that is foundational to the Bible's teaching about marriage see APPENDIX A: "An Excursus on the Inviolability of the 'One-flesh' Relationship of Marriage."

The terms "image" (i.e. צֶלֶם [selem]) and "likeness" (i.e. דְּמוּת [dᵉmût]) are important building blocks when constructing a biblical anthropology. Except for a few idioms in the Old Testament, the preponderance of occurrences of these two Semitic roots exhibits some sort of connection to concrete or physical exemplars.[4] This is not brought into view to argue necessarily for a physical dimension of the "image" and "likeness" of God in mankind,[5] but as a mild corrective to the tradition which *assumes* there can be absolutely no association with any kind of physical aspect in reference to the *imago dei*. Nevertheless, the primary significance of man as image bearer is metaphysical.

Before a few of the historically suggested interpretations of this *imago dei* are mentioned, it would be profitable to sharpen our focus on the biblical data found in the early chapters of Genesis. First, concerning the terms צֶלֶם (selem) and דְּמוּת (dᵉmût), they "are best regarded as essentially synonymous."[6] Also, two creation verbs, בָּרָא (bārā') and עָשָׂה ('asâ), normally rendered respectively "to create" and "to make," are both used with these two *imago* nouns. These two verbs are also virtually synonymous. To state the obvious, this "image" or "likeness" was the product of God's sovereign creative act. Furthermore, concerning the prepositions ־בְּ (bᵉ־) and ־כְּ (kᵉ־), respectively translated "in" and "according to" in Genesis 1:26 and 5:1, 3, they seem to be used quite interchangeably with the *imago* terms. Therefore, Sawyer justifiably concludes that "there is no semantic distinction between בִּדְמוּת [bidmût] and כִּדְמוּת [kidmût] …the same is probably true of the other pair בְּצֶלֶם [bᵉselem] and כְּצֶלֶם [kᵉselem], although there is no corresponding pair of sentences to prove this in Genesis i–xi."[7]

Now we can move on to some major views on the nature of this image or likeness of God in man,[8] but not without an up-front concession.

---

[4] Cf. the sub-thesis of Trevor Craigen, "צלם and דמות: an Exegetical Interaction" (unpublished seminar paper, Grace Theological Seminary, 1980). See a table of these terms in APPENDIX B.

[5] Although it might be tempting to extrapolate theologically in this area, e.g., by holding up the preincarnate God-man as especially the Divine Archetype for the creation of mankind in God's "image" and "likeness," and by holding Him up, after His historical incarnation, as the special Divine Model for the re-creation of believers into His "Image" (cf., e.g., 2 Corinthians 3:18; Ephesians 4:24; Colossians 3:10; etc.). Indeed, at glorification which graciously results in our moral perfection there will also come the blessing of a resurrection body, also patterned after Christ (cf., e.g., 1 Corinthians 15; Philippians 3:21; etc.).

[6] John J. Davis, *Paradise to Prison: Studies in Genesis* (Winona Lake: BMH, 1975), 81; cf. Wildberger, *TLOT*, 3:1084.

[7] John F. A. Sawyer, "The Meaning of בְּצֶלֶם אֱלֹהִים ('In the Image of God') in Genesis I–XI," *JTS*, 25 n.s. (October 1974): 421.

[8] For a good survey of the main interpretations, see: Millard J. Erickson, *Christian Theology* (Grand Rapids: Baker, 1985), 498–517.

Henry posts this important concession with the following words: "The Bible does not define for us the precise content of the original *imago*."[9]

A view popular among Old Testament exegetes and theologians is that the image of God in man refers functionally to humanity's dominion over the rest of creation. Man is regarded as God's vice-regent (cf. Genesis 1:28; note the context of 1:26ff.).[10]

Another major interpretation of the significance of the *imago dei* is also basically functional in nature. This interpretation is usually dubbed the relational view. It is popular among, although not restricted to, existentialists. Yet it is obvious (just as it was in the case of the former functional view) that relationship is more a *consequence* of bearing God's image; it is not the total stuff of it.

This leads us to the interpretation with the most longevity, the traditional or so-called analogical view. It is primarily ontological in nature. By analogy, it is argued that man as originally created was endowed with the communicable attributes of God, and it is this core of characteristics that constitutes the *imago dei*.[11]

Regarding these views, it seems best to begin with the strengths of the traditional view supplementing it with the consequential functions attending it (i.e. like those of dominion and relationship). After all, a more comprehensive impression of the *imago* suggests that it is "a cohesive unity of interrelated components that interact with and condition each other."[12]

A biblical understanding of the image and likeness of God in man is important not only for theological reasons, but also for methodological ones.[13] It is exceedingly important to understand that although the *imago dei* was beaten up nearly to the point of death at the fall of mankind, it did not "pass away." Genesis 9:6 and James 3:9 unequivocally substantiate this truth that has created great tension.[14] Henry describes

---

[9] Carl F. Henry, *God, Revelation, and Authority* (Waco: Word Books, 1976), 2:125.

[10] For some typical argument concerning the image pointing to the divine "investiture" of the race, cf. Wildberger, *TLOT*, 3:1083–1084.

[11] For some short-comings concerning the analogical view, cf., e.g., G. C. Berkovwer, *Man: The Image of God*, translated by D. W. Jellema (Grand Rapids: Eerdmans, 1962) 72–74; and Sawyer, "The Meaning of בְּצֶלֶם אֱלֹהִים," 422. For a brief consideration of the 'propagation' of this image and likeness subsequent to the divine creation of it in Adam, see APPENDIX C: "Traducianism or Creationism: What Model Aligns Best with the Biblical Data?"

[12] Henry, *God, Revelation, and Authority*, 2:125.

[13] Cf., e.g., evangelism.

[14] Concerning the background of Genesis 9:6 one should remember that both pre-and post-flood people are evaluated by God as being totally depraved (cf., e.g., Genesis 6:5 and 8:21). Nevertheless, the divine mandate for capital punishment is grounded upon the fact that all human beings have been created in the "image" of God. Concerning the retention of the "likeness" of God in man in James 3:9, the perfect participle emphasizes abiding results (τοὺς καθ' ὁμοίωσιν θεοῦ γεγόντας [*tous kath homoiōsin theou gegontas*]). Both "image" and "likeness" indeed persist, even in fallen mankind.

the tension as follows: "However much the moral earthquake of the fall impaired the *imago*, it did not wholly demolish it. …The *imago* content is reduced, distorted and even falsified as it is incorporated into conjectural philosophical and religious perspectives, yet it is never wholly eradicated."[15] Similarly, Halsey argues that "one who holds to scriptural teaching concerning the depravity of man must maintain that the faculties are corrupt and defiled, but this doctrine does not imply their complete annihilation."[16]

Consequently, for example, based upon the retention of the image of God in man, relationships and communications are possible, both on the horizontal and the vertical plane. From the anthropological perspective, all men share common ground ontologically or metaphysically. Turner well summarizes the methodological impact of this truth as applied especially to the preaching of the Gospel; he argues that

> the common ground between believers and unbelievers lies not in a supposed common epistemology but in a common bearing of God's image. This metaphysical common ground, involving as it does the *sensus deitatis*, becomes the proper point of contact in apologetics and evangelism. Men are accessible to the gospel because they are God's image-bearers and live in God's universe which constantly testifies to them of God.[17]

Without this persistence of the image and likeness of God in fallen people, any communication of the Good News would be absolutely futile. Anthropologically there would be no basis for regeneration nor the process of renewal into God's moral likeness.

---

[15] *God, Revelation, and Authority*, 1:406–06.

[16] Jim S. Halsey, *For a Time Such as This: An Introduction to the Reformed Apologetic of Cornelius Van Til* (Philadelphia: Presbyterian and Reformed, 1976), 30.

[17] David L. Turner, "Cornelius Van Til and Romans 1:18–21: A Study in the Epistemology of Presuppositional Apologetics, " *GTJ*, 2 (Spring 1981): 57. As true and significant as Turner's synopsis is, later it will become crystal clear that from the hamartiological perspective this "'point of contact' is the 'point of conflict.' …Conflict is inevitable because of human depravity and sin" (this is one of Geisler's accurate assessments of biblical presuppositionalism: Norman Geisler, *Christian Apologetics* [Grand Rapids: Baker 1976], 57).

# CHAPTER 1

# BIBLICAL ANTHROPOLOGY: THE TERMINOLOGY OF IT

It is hard to imagine another area of theology that is as thoroughly consistent throughout both testaments as biblical anthropology. An exegetically derived anthropology is also exceedingly clear in reference to its major focus. As the data from the "whole counsel of God" will demonstrate, the nature of biblical anthropology is indisputably wholistic.

## Old Testament Terminology

### Words for "Man"

As might be expected both Old Testament Hebrew and New Testament Greek exhibit terms that translate into English as "man, men, mankind," etc. Semantically, these are anthropological words.

## אָדָם (*'ādām*)

The first and most generic term is אָדָם (*'ādām*). Many lexicographers posit that the Hebrew root from which this noun is derived conveys the idea of redness, i.e. a reddish brown color.[18] Often support for this etymological conjecture is conscribed from Genesis 2:7a: "Now Yahweh God had formed (or shaped; i.e. יָצַר [*yāṣar*], the potter word-group) the man (הָאָדָם [*hā'ādām*]) of dust from the ground (הָאֲדָמָה [*hā'a dāmâ*])...."[19] Whether this etymological connection is valid or not, the really important thing (as is the case in any word-group) is how it *is used* in various contexts.

---

[18] Cf., e.g., Maass' etymological survey in *TDOT*, 1:78–79.
[19] Some appeal to 1 Corinthians 15:47a as secondary support for this particular etymological association.

We have already been exposed to the primary usages of אָדָם (*'ādām*) in the "Introduction," namely, "Adam" (i.e. the first "man"), "man" (i.e. an individual image-bearer), "mankind" (i.e. the race coming from Adam), etc. The inextricable connection between "'the one'" (i.e. "Adam") and "'the many'" (i.e. the race, all humanity) cannot be over-emphasized.[20]

Concerning generic and collective usages of אָדָם (*'ādām*) in the Old Testament, besides the translations "man" or "mankind," sometimes "a person" or "people"[21] would be appropriate renderings in certain contexts. To round out this category of usage, it is important to note the anthropological occurrences of the important phrases בֶּן־אָדָם (*ben-'ādām*) and בְּנֵי־אָדָם (*bᵉnê- 'ādām*), respectively, "son of man" and "sons of man." This combination evidences yet another instance of the idiomatic use of בֶּן־ / בְּנֵי־ (*ben-/bᵉnê*) indicating *sameness of nature*. All *descendants* of the race, i.e. "sons of men" are indeed "men" (i.e., like begets like kind). In many contexts these phrasal idioms for humanity put the spotlight on man's fraility and/or his finiteness, and they are also sometimes found in settings speaking of his fallenness.[22] The emphasis on finiteness and frailty often associated with בֶּן־אָדָם (*ben-'ādām*) provides a fitting transition to the next anthropological term for "man."


## אֱנוֹשׁ  (*'ᵉnôš*)


Etymologically, "scholars assume that the original meaning was 'to be weak' or 'to be sociable.'"[23] Many of the noun's forty-two Hebrew and Aramaic occurrences in the Old Testament do seem to be set in contexts which emphasize man's frailty and/or his finiteness. As McComiskey puts it, "the word *'enosh* reminds man of his transience and of his lowly position before the Almighty."[24] This conclusion is especially born out in the wisdom literature, as Westermann appropriately notes:

---

[20] As we will see, this connection is vital not only for the sake of understanding biblical anthropology but also for its applications to hamartiology and soteriology.

[21] Westermann, *TLOT*, 1:33.

[22] Cf., e.g., Genesis 11:5; Numbers 23:19; 1 Samuel 26:19; Psalms 8:4; 11:4; 12:2 [v. 1, Eng]; 14:2; 33:13; 57:5 [v. 4, Eng]; 90:3; 146:3; Ecclesiastes 9:3; etc.

[23] Maass, *TDOT*, 1:346. Remember that it is this word group which some lexicographers put forth as the root standing behind the word אִשָּׁה (*'issa*), "woman" (cf. the previous discussion on Genesis 2:23).

[24] *TWOT*, 1:59; on אֱנוֹשׁ (*'ᵉnôš*) stressing mankind's lowliness before God, cf., e.g., Job 4:17a; 15:14; 25:4; etc.

"The sense of the human being as mortal, frail, and limited predominate in Job and Psalms."[25] Just a few examples will demonstrate how significant this biblical perspective on "man," "men," or "mankind" as אֱנוֹשׁ (*'enôš*) really is. Psalm 90:2–3 starkly depicts the radical difference between the eternal Creator (v. 2) and transient mankind (v. 3). Verse 3 reads, "You [i.e. the Creator] turn man (אֱנוֹשׁ [*'enôš*]) back into dust, and say, 'Return, Sons of man!'" (i.e. בְּנֵי־אָדָם [*bᵉnê -'ādām*]).[26] Now listen to the testimony of Psalm 103:15–16: "Man (אֱנוֹשׁ [*'enôš*])—his days are like grass; like a flower of the field, so he flourishes. Indeed (or, "When…) wind blows upon it and (or, "then…) it is gone [literally it is not] and its place does not acknowledge *it* any more." Psalm 144:3–4 is especially graphic in this regard: "Yahweh, what is man (or mankind, humanity; אָדָם [*'ādām*]) that you should regard him, son of man בֶּן־אֱנוֹשׁ [*ben⁻'ᵉnôš*]) that You should be mindful of him? Man (אָדָם [*'ādām*]) is like a vapor (or breath); his days are like a passing shadow."[27] The psalmist apparently wants the worshipping community, made up of human beings who are "here today and gone tomorrow," to stand in awe of God's concern and care for them.

## גֶּבֶר (*geber*)

If we placed this term for "man" and the previous one along a semantical spectrum their hues would shine forth on opposite ends of it. Basically the colors would shift from man as puny (אֱנוֹשׁ [*'enôš*]) to man as macho (גֶּבֶר [*geber*]). The force of the root גבר (*gbr*) is "to be superior, strong."[28] Consequently, "a *gebher* without power is a self-contradiction, and is as good as dead (Psalm 88:5f. [4f.])."[29] Oswalt summarizes the anthropological significance of this word-group when he concludes that "it depicts humanity at its most competent and capable level."[30] Quite commonly this word-group refers to men of military might.[31]

---

[25] *TLOT*, 1:33.

[26] Note the parallelism between אֱנוֹשׁ (*'enôš*) and בְּנֵי־אָדָם (*bᵉnê-'ādām*).

[27] The synonymous parallelisms and appositional phrasing are especially arresting. The truth of v. 4 is picked up by James in the New Testament (cf. James 4:14b).

[28] Kühlewein, *TLOT*, 1:299.

[29] Kosmala, *TDOT*, 2:377.

[30] *TWOT*, 1:148–49.

[31] Cf. the adjective גִּבּוֹר (*gibbôr*) and especially the phrase גִּבּוֹר חַיִל (*gibbôr ḥayil*), e.g., in Judges 6:12; 11:1; 1 Samuel 2:4; 9:1; 1 Kings 11:28; Job 16:14; etc.

## אִישׁ (*'îš*)[32]

Unlike the previous word-groups for man, אִישׁ (*'îš*) is almost never used generically. As McComiskey puts it, "the word *'ish* connotes primarily the concept of man as an individual and thus differs in that regard from the more general concepts."[33] Its fundamental usages are "man" as an individual male,[34] "husband" in actual or logical parallelisms with אִשָּׁה (*'iššâ*), "woman" or "wife,"[35] and "each," e.g., in the idiom "*each* to the *other*" or "*one* to *another*."

### Aspects of Man

Very few Old Testament or New Testament terms for the aspects of man individuate.[36] Biblical anthropology is essentially synthetic and perspectival not analytical and compartmentalized. Dimensionally or functionally the vast majority of the following anthropological terms are scripturally presented as facets of the *whole* man.

As we now approach the biblical data it is imperative that we keep in mind Erickson's warning:

> In considering the makeup of man, we must be particularly careful to examine the presuppositions we bring to our study. Because there are nonbiblical disciplines which also are concerned about man, the possibility that some of their conceptions might affect our theological construction looms large. Whether it be an ancient Greek dualism, or a modern behavioristic monism, we need to be on guard against reading a nonbiblical presupposition into our understanding of Scripture.[37]

---

[32] For the most part, the plural of אִישׁ (*'îš*) is supplied by the root אֱנֹשׁ (*'nš*, i.e. אֲנָשִׁים [*"nāšîm*]).

[33] *TWOT*, 1:38.

[34] With approximately the more nuanced force of זָכָר (*zākār*).

[35] With approximately the more nuanced force of בַּעַל (*ba'al*). In this vein, Kühlewein argues that "the word's basic meaning is 'man' (the mature male in contrast to the woman). This meaning establishes a natural semantic field in which man and woman stand in contrast" (*TLOT*, 1:99).

[36] I.e. treat him like a hunk of this and a piece of that. Man biblically viewed is not a mosaic of multiple pieces each of which is totally distinct.

[37] Erickson, *Christian Theology*, 520.

# בָּשָׂר (bāśār)

With the arrival of this first term comes the first test of our anthropological presuppositions. When we hear the word "flesh" most of us automatically think of its main meaning in English, i.e., physical stuff, e.g., the "*meat* on one's bones." However, this usage of "flesh in the strict sense"[38] is not prominent in the Old Testament.[39] The same is true of flesh "in an extended sense,"[40] i.e., the material substance standing for the whole body.[41]

בָּשָׂר (bāśār) is also used metaphorically in the Old Testament to indicate intimate relationship, be it a blood relationship or the marital relationship.[42] In the Old Testament we also encounter the prepositional phrase כָּל־בָּשָׂר (kol-bāśār) which idiomatically refers to all animal life and/or all humanity.[43] However, the usages of בָּשָׂר (bāśār) "in a transferred sense"[44] are the most significant theologically. For example, by synecdoche "in poetic passages בָּשָׂר is coupled with נֶפֶשׁ or לֵב or both to denote the whole person even when the things affirmed are strictly true only of the inner man."[45] Note the telling parallelisms in Psalms 63:2 [v. 1, Eng.] and 84:3 [v. 2, Eng.]:

God, You are my God; I am seeking You; my soul (נַפְשִׁי [napšî]) thirsts for You; my flesh (בְשָׂרִי [bᵉśārî]) longs for You in a dry and weary land without water.

My soul (נַפְשִׁי [napšî]) has yearned and has also longed for the courts of the LORD; my heart and my flesh (לִבִּי וּבְשָׂרִי [libbî ûbᵉśārî]) are crying out to the living God.

---

[38] Baumgartel's semantical heading, *TDNT*, 7:105.

[39] Although, cf. the physical "flesh" of a man in Genesis 2:21 and of animals in Exodus 21:28; Numbers 11:4ff.; Deuteronomy 12:15; Ezekiel 4:14.

[40] *TDNT*, 7:106.

[41] Cf. Leviticus 16:4; 2 Kings 9:36–37; Job 7:5.

[42] Cf. respectively, Genesis 37:27 and 2:24.

[43] Cf. Genesis 6:12–13; Isaiah 40:5–7. Gerleman, wisely notes regarding כָּל־בָּשָׂר (kol-bāśār) that it indicates "an expansion of meaning toward the abstract"( *TLOT*, 1:284).

[44] *TDNT*, 7:107.

[45] Ernest DeWitt Burton, *Spirit, Soul, and Flesh: the Usages of Πνεῦμα, Ψυχή and Σάρξ in Greek Writings and Translated Works from the Earliest Period to 180 A. D.; and of Their Equivalents* רוּחַ, נֶפֶשׁ, *and* בָּשָׂר *in the Hebrew Old Testament* (Chicago: University of Chicago Press, 1918), 69. Although this work is old, it is superb for its exegetical contributions to anthropology and hamartiology.

This anthropological phenomenon will prove to be a key to a proper understanding of "flesh" as associated with sin in the Bible.[46]

Furthermore, by extended synecdoche, בָּשָׂר (*bāsār*) often stands for the whole race, i.e. "man,"[47] "humankind,"[48] etc. This usage is common and exceedingly important in that it is almost always associated with man's "frailty and impotence."[49] On this association listen to the unified voice from some selected passages:

Then the LORD said, My Spirit shall not strive with man (בָּאָדָם [*bā'ādām*]) forever; in their wandering they are flesh (בָּשָׂר [*bāsār*]). Now his days will be 120 years (Genesis 6:3).[50]

In God (whose) word I praise, in God I have trusted; I will not fear. What can flesh (בָּשָׂר [*bāsār*]) do to me? (Psalm 56:5 [v. 4, Eng]).[51]

He [i.e. God] remembered that they were flesh (בָּשָׂר [*bāsār*]), a passing wind that does not return (Psalm 78:39).

Thus says the LORD, "Cursed is the man (הַגֶּבֶר [*haggeber*][52]) who trusts in mankind (i.e. אָדָם ['ādām]) and who makes flesh (בָּשָׂר [*bāsār*]) his arm [i.e. his strength[53]] and whose heart (i.e. לֵב [*lēb*]) departs from the LORD (Jeremiah 17:5).[54]

In view of these and other similar passages, "a person as flesh is recognized as weak and lacking in strength."[55] Consequently, Wolff boils down the anthropological significance of בָּשָׂר (*bāsār*) to "man in his infirmity."[56]

---

[46] For a quite comprehensive consideration of this issue, see my "Σάρξ in the New Testament with Special Emphases on its Background and its Occurrences in Hamartiological Contexts," unpublished Th. M. thesis (Winona Lake: Grace Theological Seminary, 1977).

[47] Bratsiotis, *TDOT*, 2:319.

[48] Chisholm, *NIDOTTE*, 1:777. Cf., e.g., the prepositional phrase כָּל־בָּשָׂר (*kol-bāsār*) mentioned above when it contextually designates the human race.

[49] Baumgartel, *TDNT*, 7:107.

[50] Note the frequently attending feature of transience associated with man as בָּשָׂר (*bāsār*); cf. the interpretive rendering of "mortal" in the NIV, and also note the force of כָּל־בָּשָׂר (*kol-bāsār*) in Isaiah 40:5–7.

[51] Note אֱנוֹשׁ ('ᵉnôš) in v. 2 (v. 1 Eng.) and especially the echo of v. 5 (v. 4), but employing אָדָם ('ādām), in v. 12 (v. 11).

[52] Using the term that could be nuanced as (*macho*) man; cf. above.

[53] Cf. NASB, NIV, etc. for this common Old Testament word-picture.

[54] Cf. a similar assessment applied to Sennacherib and his military forces in 2 Chronicles 32:8: "With him is only the arm of flesh, but with us is the LORD our God to help us and to fight our battles."

[55] William Dyrness, *Themes in Old Testament Theology* (Downers Grove: InterVarsity Press, 1970), 88.

[56] *AOT*, 26–31.

Just prior to pressing on to the next anthropological facet of man, a *preliminary* word needs to be offered in reference to occurrences of a "flesh"/"spirit" antithesis in the Bible. Jacob's brief generalization about this phenomenon in its Old Testament context will be proven true as more data comes to bear upon it:

> The antithesis of flesh and spirit is found occasionally in the Old Testament, Genesis 6:1–8; Isaiah 31:3. It is not, however, the antithesis of two principles but of man's weakness and God's strength....[An internal] dualism...is never found in the Old Testament and would deny the very foundations of Old Testament anthropology.[57]

Even more concisely and comprehensively, Mork commendably confronts the neo-platonic thinking which separates man into two warring parts (i.e. the physical part vs. the metaphysical part): "Man divided against himself is straight Platonism, it is never the thought of revelation."[58]

## נֶפֶשׁ *(nepeš)*

Without a doubt "soul" is the most misunderstood anthropological term in both testaments. This is so not only because of the powerful influence of the prevalent English usage but also because of the fact that most systematic theologies throughout the history of the church have canonized that prevalent English denotation. The biblical usages of both Old Testament נֶפֶשׁ (*nepeš*) and New Testament ψυχή (*psuchē*), "soul," almost never denote the metaphysical "'part'" of man in contrast with his physical "'part'" (i.e. his "body").[59] As we will see later, נֶפֶשׁ (*nepeš*) and ψυχή (*psuchē*) do not function in an individuating manner like רוּחַ (*rûaḥ*) and πνεῦμα (*pneuma*) do. A salient review of the exegetical data pertaining to the primary images of the Old and New Testament terms

---

[57] *TDNT*, 9:630, 623.

[58] Don Wulstan Mork, *The Biblical Meaning of Man* (Milwaukee: Bruce Publishing Company, 1967), 14.

[59] The LXX also adds its contribution to an exegetical corrective. As Lys has credibly observed and concluded, "the LXX never goes in the direction in which 'soul' would be understood as opposite to 'body' (as in Platonic dualism)" (D. Lys, *VT*, 16 [1966]:227). Waltke adds, "in its most synthetic use *nepesh* stands for the entire person. . . . The substantive must not be taken in the metaphysical, theological sense in which we tend to use the term 'soul' today" (*TWOT*, 2:590).

will demonstrate how eccentric the church's thinking has been in this strategic area of anthropology.

That one ought to be far more careful so as not to put נֶפֶשׁ (*nepeš*) into one semantic box is obvious even from a cursory survey of its various nuances. Lexicographers have documented a whole range of meanings. Consider, for example, BDB: "*soul, living being, life, self, person, desire, appetite, emotion, and passion*";[60] or KB: "*throat, neck, breath, living being, people, personality* (i.e. oneself, every person, etc.), *life, soul* (i.e. as the center of feelings and perceptions), *dead soul* (i.e. deceased person, corpse)."[61]

It will prove helpful to sub-categorize some of these usages in order to sharpen our anthropological focus on נֶפֶשׁ (*nepeš*). Burton groups a wide array of its occurrences under the following heading: "soul, the seat of appetite, emotion, and the like, with no implication of a separate entity, or of the possibility of separate existence."[62] Sometimes נֶפֶשׁ (*nepeš*) indicates "the seat of will and moral action,"[63] and "rarely" it references "the seat of mentality."[64] Most significantly, נֶפֶשׁ (*nepeš*) is very frequently identified "with the entire person."[65] Westermann appropriately affixes the following label to this exceedingly important sub-category: "Living being/person: (a) in laws, (b) in enumerations, (c) general expressions, (d) pronominal usage."[66] It is illuminating to examine just a few samples of נֶפֶשׁ (*nepeš*) indicating a "person" (or, in the plural, "people"): Genesis 14:21; Exodus 1:5; 12:15; Leviticus 17:12; Lamentations 3:25. Concerning its usages wherein "it has the force of a reflexive or personal pronoun,"[67] consider the following samplings: Genesis 27:4, 19, 25, 31; Leviticus 11:43;[68] Psalm 63:1;[69] Proverbs 11:17; Isaiah 3:9; Jeremiah 17:21; 18:20; Habakkuk 2:10. All of this data points in the same direction: "נֶפֶשׁ is the usual term for a man's total nature, for what he is and not just what he has."[70]

---

[60] BDB, 659.

[61] KB, 2:712–13.

[62] Burton, *SSF*, 63; concerning an emphasis on appetite, cf., e.g., Deuteronomy 12:20; on emotion, cf., e.g., Job 30:25; Psalm 86:4; Song of Solomon 1:7.

[63] Ibid., 64; cf., e.g., Deuteronomy 6:5 (note the important parallelisms with לֵב [*lēb*] and מְאֹד [*mᵉʾōd*]); 1 Chronicles 28:9 (again note the parallel with לֵב [*lēb*]).

[64] Ibid., 65; cf., e.g., Esther 4:13.

[65] Fredericks, *NIDOTTE*, 3:133.

[66] *TLOT*, 2:744; some of the translations that would appertain herein would be "living being, person, individual, self, someone," etc.

[67] Burton, *SSF*, 67.

[68] Note the parallelism of נַפְשֹׁתֵכֶם (*napšōtêkem*) with the following reflexive verb in v. 44 (i.e. וְהִתְקַדִּשְׁתֶּם [*wᵉhitqaddištem*]).

[69] Cf. comments above on בָּשָׂר (*bāśār*) in this verse; the same wholistic emphasis is obviously also conveyed by נֶפֶשׁ (*nepeš*).

[70] Jacob, *TDNT*, 9:620. Wolff corroborates this credible conclusion with similar words: "man does not have n. [i.e. *nepeš*], he is n., he lives as n." (*AOT*, 10).

# רוּחַ (rûaḥ)

רוּחַ (rûaḥ) also exhibits a wide spectrum of usages, e.g., "wind, breath, transitoriness, volition, disposition, temper, spirit, Spirit."[71] The occurrences of רוּחַ (rûaḥ) merely as "breath" are not that significant anthropologically;[72] however, when the term speaks, either explicitly or implicitly, of the breath of life, its importance is self-evident.[73]

More significant yet is the association of רוּחַ (rûaḥ) with man's emotionality, rationality, and volitionality.[74] Albertz and Westermann are careful to nuance the occurrences falling under this broad category of usage with these qualifying words:

> rûaḥ is assimilated to the anthropological terms derived from names for organs (esp. lēb "heart") to mean the center of human volition and action. Its original dynamic character is thus largely attenuated; it persists only to the extent that the entire Old Testament anthropological understanding is dynamic. Only in this derived semantic context can rûaḥ indicate the human "spirit" a few times, not so much as a component but as a human capacity. On the one hand rûaḥ means the innermost aspect of the human being; on the other hand it means the entire existence; thus in poetic language it can become a synonym for "I."[75]

Another important category of usage is the "divinely effected רוּחַ."[76] For Wolff, because רוּחַ is primarily associated with God, he considers it to be so frequently "a theo-anthropological term."[77] Therefore, he argues that its anthropological significance should be "man as he is empowered."[78] This provides a (not the) key to an understanding of the rare flesh/spirit antithesis in the Old Testament. Isaiah 31:1–3 is a paradigm passage. God's people must not rely on human alliances and/or contrivances for their power base (cf. vv. 1–2). Why? Well, the parallelisms and

---

[71] Van Pelt; Kaiser; Block, NIDOTTE, 3:1073.
[72] Cf., e.g., Job 9:18; 19:17.
[73] Cf., e.g., Genesis 6:17; Isaiah 42:5.
[74] Cf., e.g. Judges 8:3; Job 7:11; Psalm 51:14 (v. 12, Eng.); Proverbs 18:14; Isaiah 26:9; 29:24; 57:15; Ezekiel 11:5.
[75] TLOT, 3:1211.
[76] Baumgartel's label (TDNT, 6:362); cf., e.g., Exodus 28:3; Ezra 1:1; Job 10:12; 32:8; Ezekiel 11:19.
[77] AOT, 32.
[78] Ibid.

principles of v. 3 provide the answer: "But the Egyptians are men (אָדָם ['ādām]) and not God; their horses are flesh (בָּשָׂר [bāśār]) and not spirit (רוּחַ [rûaḥ]). When the LORD stretches out his hand [i.e. a power idiom], he who helps will stumble, he who is helped will fall; both will perish together" (Isaiah 31:3; NIV). Burton comments:

> In Isaiah 31:3 רוּחַ is used qualitatively with special reference to its powerfulness in contrast with the flesh as weak....While the term does not refer specifically to the spirit of God, the idea of power associated with it is probably derived from the use of רוּחַ in reference to the divine spirit.[79]

Consequently, Jacob is on target when he argues,

> The antithesis of flesh and spirit...is not...the antithesis of two principles but of man's weakness and God's strength. These two are not irreconcilable, for the God who has made man...also does all that is needed to transfer something of His strength to man. Flesh and spirit are incompatible only when flesh forgets to trust in the God who is Spirit and trusts in itself, Jeremiah 17:5ff; 2 Chronicles 32:8.[80]

## לֵב / לֵבָב (lēb/lēbāb)

"Heart" in the Bible could well be regarded as the king of anthropological terms. Most often Old Testament לֵב (lēb) and New Testament καρδία (kardia) relate to man's mission-control center. As Payne puts it, the heart is the "symbol for the focus of life."[81] So, although references to לֵב (lēb) as a physical, blood-pumping organ are virtually non-existent,[82] the figurative sense of "the innermost part of man"[83] permeates all portions of the Old Testament.

When speaking of the figurative use of לֵב (lēb), we must *not* go first to our number one metaphorical employment of the English term

---

[79] Burton, SSF, 55.

[80] TDNT, 9:630; his conclusions will be corroborated from the New Testament when we get to such passages as Romans 8:4ff.

[81] J. Barton Payne, The Theology of the Older Testament (Grand Rapids: Zondervan, 1962), 225.

[82] The closest association with anything physical is found in Hosea 13:8 (לֵב [lēb]=the illustration of a female bear robbed of her cubs tearing open people's chests).

[83] Baumgartel, TDNT, 3:606.

"heart" with its common *emotional* associations. Although feelings s.
as anxiety, tranquillity, joy, etc., are seen as sometimes arising from the
לֵב (*lēb*),[84] the emotional function of the heart in the Old Testament is
definitely in the background. Also in the background is the function of
"desire and longing."[85] What is conspicuously in the foreground, by a
large majority, are the term's respective emphases on man's rationality
and his volitionality.

Very significantly, "the heart [is] the seat of rational functions."[86]
This category is so determinative that Wolff's chapter title for לֵב (*lēb*) is
"Reasonable Man."[87] Documenting passages abound, among which
Deuteronomy 8:5, Joshua 23:14, Job 12:3,[88] Isaiah 6:10 serve as examples. Furthermore, "from the heart comes planning and volition."[89]
Consider, for example, the force of לֵב (*lēb*) in passages like Exodus
35:5; Numbers 16:28; 1 Kings 8:18; 2 Chronicles 24:4; Proverbs 16:1,
9. In this regard the parallelisms of Isaiah 10:7 are especially enlightening; of Assyria and/or its arrogant king, God says: "Yet he [or it] does
not so intend (or devise, i.e. a Piel from דמה [*dmh*]), nor does his heart
(i.e. לְבָבוֹ [*l<sup>e</sup>bābô*]) so plan (from the root חשב [*ḥšb*]), but (it is) in his
heart (בִּלְבָבוֹ [*bilbābô*]) to destroy and to cut down not just a few
nations."[90]

One more usage of לֵב (*lēb*) needs to be mentioned before summarizing its overall anthropological/ethical significance. In certain
contexts לֵב (*lēb*) conveys the connotation of conscience[91] (cf., e.g., 1
Samuel 24:5; 2 Samuel 24:10; Job 27:6). So when this function of
conscience is added to that of thinking and/or planning, the לֵב (*lēb*) is
recognized scripturally as "the organ which wills or decides, thinks,
knows, and judges between right and wrong."[92] Consequently, being
"such a major anthropological term," it "serves to describe the
relationship between God and person."[93] Indeed, the "heart" is the

---

[84] Cf., e.g., Psalm 25:17; Proverbs 14:30; 17:22.
[85] Wolff, *AOT*, 45–46; cf., e.g., Psalm 21:2; Proverbs 6:25; 13:12.
[86] Baumgartel, *TDNT*, 3:606.
[87] *AOT*, 40.
[88] Cf. also having "heart" or not having "heart" in the sense of possessing or lacking *intelligence* (or discernment) in Proverbs 6:32; *et al.*
[89] Baumgartel, *TDNT*, 3:607.
[90] Since the last clause contains twin purpose infinitives, its force is: "his purpose is to destroy, to put an end to many nations" (NIV).
[91] In such settings it carries the semantic freight of New Testament συνείδησις (*suneidēsis*).
[92] Paul Heinisch, *Theology of the Old Testament,* translated by W. Heidt (Collegeville, MN; Liturgical Press, 1950), 160.
[93] Stolz, *TLOT*, 2:640.

nly of man's sinful culpability[94] but also of his spiritual
,[95]

Oth..       ns

There are other less frequently mentioned organs of the body that also function synecdochically in the Old Testament. These "'parts'" often stand for the whole man and usually contextually emphasize some characteristic of personality such as rationality or emotionality. Take "bones" (עֲצָמוֹת ["ᵃṣāmôt]), for example, in texts such as Psalm 6:3 [vs. 2, Eng.]; 35:10; Jeremiah 20:9 (note the parallelism with לֵב [lēb] and ultimately the "I" of the verb forms); 23:9 (cf. the same kinds of parallelisms); etc. "Bones" in such settings stands for "one's whole being."[96]

The "kidneys" (כְּלָיוֹת [kᵉlāyot]) in the Old Testament sometimes function rationally. In such settings they convey approximately the same sense as does לֵב (lēb) with its mental moorings. Two prominent passages especially illustrate this function quite clearly, i.e. Psalm 16:7 and Jeremiah 17:10 (note the parallelism with the לֵב [lēb] of v. 9).

A person's "belly" (or inner "bowels") is quite often associated with his core of being. Notice, for example, בֶּטֶן (beten) in Proverbs 20:27, and קֶרֶב (qereb) in Jeremiah 31:33 (once again, in parallelism with לֵב [lēb]). Sometimes this inner core of the person is noted as functioning emotionally (cf., e.g., בֶּטֶן [beten] in Habakkuk 3:16 and קֶרֶב [qereb] in Isaiah 16:11).[97]

## New Testament Terminology

### Words for "Man"

#### ἄνθρωπος (anthrōpos)

Answering quite consistently to אָדָם ('ādām) in the Old Testament is New Testament ἄνθρωπος (anthropos). This term's generic employments

---

[94] Cf., e.g., Jeremiah 3:17; 17:9; Ezekiel 2:4; etc.

[95] As Baumgartel (TDNT, 3:607) puts it, "religious and moral conduct is rooted in the heart"; cf., e.g., Deuteronomy 6:5; 10:16 [cf. the divine initiative in 30:6]; 1 Samuel 12:20; Psalm 7:11 [v. 10, Eng.] 51:12 [v. 10, Eng.]; etc.

[96] BDB, 782.

[97] On these and other bodily "'parts'" and their anthropological significance, see Wolff, AOT, 63–66; but beware of some of his pressed associations.

predominate. It is hard to improve upon Vine's sub-classifications of its major usage sphere:

> *ANTHRŌPOS* (ἄνθρωπος) is used (a) generally, of a human being, male or female, without reference to sex or nationality, e.g., Matthew 4:4; 12:35; John 2:25; (b) in distinction from God, e.g., Matthew 19:6; John 10:33; Galatians 1:11; Colossians 3:23; (c) in distinction from animals etc., e.g., Luke 5:10; (d) sometimes in the plural, of men and women, people, e.g., Matthew 5:13, 16; ... (e) in some instances with a suggestion of human frailty and imperfection, e.g., 1 Corinthians 2:5; ... (j) as equivalent simply to 'a person,' or 'one,' whether man or woman, e.g., Acts 19:16; Romans 3:28; Galatians 2:16; ... or again ... "a man," e.g., Matthew 17:14; Luke 13;19.[98]

Although on rare occasions ἄνθρωπος (*anthrōpos*) may refer contextually to an adult male or a husband (cf. respectively, Matthew 11:8 and 19:5, 10), these specific, connotations are reserved most frequently for the next term.

## ἀνήρ (anēr)

Ἀνήρ (*anēr*) like its Old Testament counterpart, אִישׁ ('*îš*), emphasizes manliness. It usually refers to an adult male[99] (cf., e.g., Matthew 14:21; Acts 8:3, 12; 1 Corinthians 11:3) and/or a husband (cf., e.g. Matthew 11:16, 19; Ephesians 5:22ff.; 1 Timothy 3:2, 12, 5:9). Generic usages do not occur except possibly in the case of one *metaphorical/salvific* application (i.e. Ephesians 4:13).

## Aspects of Man

A general note of comparison needs to be posted before proceeding from the Old Testament to the New. There are many more Greek anthropological terms which express the same facets and functions of the Hebrew terms mentioned above. The New Testament terminology at

---

[98] *EDNTW*, 388.
[99] In these settings it takes on the semantically particularized color of ἄρσην (*arsēn*; cf. Old Testament זָכָר [*zākār*]).

times is more semantically specific, advancing precision; however, it is built solidly upon an Old Testament anthropological foundation.[100] Nevertheless, in the case of a few terms in certain New Testament contexts a tendency toward individuation is observable. The first anthropological aspect that follows should be considered Exhibit A in this regard.

## σῶμα (sōma)

Although anthropological occurrences of σῶμα (sōma) periodically show up in metaphorically expanded settings in the New Testament, the term is rarely employed with a full-blown synecdochical sense for the whole person.[101] Σῶμα (sōma) predominately individuates. The LXX helps in providing some background since both σῶμα (sōma) and σάρξ (sarx) are used to render בָּשָׂר (bāsār). When σῶμα (sōma) is used, the setting of בָּשָׂר emphasizes man's "individual corporeality."[102] Nevertheless, in contrast with pagan Greek perversions,[103] there is not one shred of evidence of "an anthropological dualism in the Old Testament canon which would oppose the soul or mind to the body as something of higher value."[104]

Now with this generalization and implicit warning in mind, we need to examine some categories of New Testament usages:[105]

1. "dead body" or "corpse" (e.g., Matthew 27:58–59; Luke 17:37; Jude 9)

2. "the living body" (e.g., Matthew 5:29–30; Romans 1:24)

3. "with and in contrast to πνεῦμα [pneuma]" (e.g., 1 Corinthians 7:34; James 2:26)

---

[100] This will also prove to be the case in connection with the other doctrines of sovereign grace. Concerning this prevalent phenomenon on the semantic level, the thesis of Hill's treatise is well documented: David Hill, *Greek Words and Hebrew Meanings* (Cambridge: University Press, 1967).

[101] Contrast the main thesis of John A. T. Robinson, *The Body*, Studies in Biblical Theology, 5 (London: SCM Press, 1952). For a monograph that demonstrates more balance on this crucial issue, see: Robert H. Gundry, *Sōma in Biblical Theology with Emphasis on Pauline Anthropology*, Society for New Testament Studies, Monograph Series, 29 (Cambridge University Press, 1976).

[102] Using Wibbing's phraseology, but not his overall argumentation: *NIDNTT*, 1:233.

[103] Such as σῶμα σῆμα (sōma sēma), "the body is a tomb"; or, such as "the body is the prison-house of the soul."

[104] Wibbing, *NIDNTT*, 1:233.

[105] The following categories and sub-categories are the anthropologically significant ones adapted from BAGD, 799–800.

4. "with and in contrast to ψυχή [*psuchē*]" (e.g., Matthew 6:25; 10:28)

5. "the body is the instrument of human experience and suffering" (e.g., Romans 12:1; 2 Corinthians 4:10; Galatians 6:17; Philemon 1:20)

The individuation of the physical aspect of man is self-evident in categories 3 and 4 above. James 2:26 is especially telling: "For just as the body (τὸ σῶμα [*to sōma*]) apart from (or without) the spirit (πνεύματος [*pneumatos*]) is dead, so also faith apart from (or without) works is dead." A more graphic and understandable *illustration* of James' main point is inconceivable. Σῶμα (*sōma*) indeed most frequently references the physical body. In *purely* anthropological contexts in the New Testament this presents no hermeneutical problem.

However, σῶμα (*sōma*) as found in anthropological/hamartiological settings often tests the fiber of the interpreter. Will he put on his neo-platonic hermeneutical lenses? Or, maybe, to avoid this unbiblical option, will he grab his exclusively wholistic glasses? After all, the second prescription seems to have been written on the synecdochical prescription pad of Old Testament anthropology. As appealing as this latter option is, it is not the right choice in most cases. It would sometimes, for example, rob σῶμα (*sōma*) of its full metaphorical power in certain contexts.

Then how are we to understand σῶμα (*sōma*) in such challenging settings? Essentially by observing that the physical body in these contexts is an *instrument* not a personal agent.[106] Scripturally considered σῶμα (*sōma*) may be the instrument (i.e. the vehicle of expression) of personal sin, or contrastingly, of personal obedience in holiness. Let me take two paradigmatic passages out of Romans as examples.

In Romans 6:1–14[107] Paul is urging professing believers respectively to be and to behave as who they are in Christ (i.e. positionally and corporately "new man") and not to behave as who they were (i.e. positionally and corporately "old man"). Formerly they were "slaves of sin" (e.g., v. 6); now they are to be slaves of Christ and His righteousness based upon their vital union with Him. In this context σῶμα (*sōma*) occurs in verses 6 and 12. For those that would like to accuse the physical body of being the agent of sinful acts, the use of σῶμα (*sōma*) in v. 6 seems to provide them with a good proof-text. However, when Paul says

---

[106] In category #5 above, the choice of the descriptive word "instrument" in BAGD is commendable.
[107] This is a key passage that we will consider more deeply later in connection with salvation and sanctification.

that "our old man was co-crucified [i.e. was crucified (with Christ)] in order that the body of sin (τὸ σῶμα τῆς ἁμαρτίας [*to sōma tēs hamartias*]) might become idle, so that we should no longer serve sin" (Romans 6:6), he is not allowing his readers to pass the buck of blame regarding personal sin on to their physical bodies. First, throughout Romans 6:1–14 every challenge and command is presented to *persons* who are responsible for thinking through and, accordingly, acting upon the realities being surveyed by Paul. Consequently, this graphic illustration of the physical body stresses instrumentality, while at the same time, by a degree of synecdoche, σῶμα (*sōma*) extends itself in its close association with the responsible, personal agents being addressed. Also, this passage cannot be properly understood apart from grasping its significant contribution to the biblical presentation of salvation history.[108] Moo briefly but skillfully puts these important pieces together:

> Paul's point is that the real, though forensic, inclusion of the believer with Christ in His crucifixion means that our solidarity with and dominance by, Adam, through whom we are bound to the nexus of sin and death, has ended. And the purpose of this was that *the body as a helpless tool of sin* might be definitely defeated. What this means for the Christian life, though inherent in what Paul has already said, is spelled out in the concluding clause: "that we should no longer serve sin."[109]

Because of who believers are in Christ, they should be progressively and more consistently manifesting, through their physical instrument, the body, Christlikeness. The flip side of this Adam-theology[110] coin is emphasized in v. 6. Since their "old man" is dead and gone positionally, those who are "in Christ" should not go on manifesting through that same highly visible, physical instrument, i.e. "the body," sinful behavior. The goal is that their physical σῶμα (*sōma*) should end up in the unemployment line.[111]

The admonitions of verses 12–13 continue to build upon the truth of v. 6:

---

[108] For a good synopsis of this phenomenon in Romans 6:1–14, see James D. G. Dunn, *Romans 1–8*, WBC, 38a (Dallas: Word, 1988), 303–340.

[109] Douglas Moo, *Romans 1–8*, The Wycliffe Exegetical Commentary (Chicago: Moody Press, 1991), 393; emphasis added.

[110] A discussion of Adam theology is forthcoming, especially in connection with Romans 5:12ff.

[111] One of the extra-biblical usages of the verb καταργέω (*katargeo*) conveys the idea "to be unemployed"; cf. Delling, *TDNT,* 1:452.

Therefore do not allow sin to rule as a king in your mortal body (ἐν τῷ θνητῷ ὑμῶν σώματι [*en tō thnētō humōn sōmati*]) so that you keep on obeying its lusts, and do not go on presenting your members [i.e. the parts of your body] as weapons of unrighteousness for sin; but present yourselves to God as living ones from the dead and your members as weapons of righteousness for God.

As in the case of the use of σῶμα (*sōma*) in v. 6, there is in the context of v. 12 an intricate balance between its physicality and instrumentality along with a synecdochical extension.[112] Yet, the vitality of Paul's metaphors of "body" and "members" in vv. 12–13 depends largely upon his emphasis on their instrumentality. As Gundry puts it: "Paul writes quite straightforwardly about the Christian's responsibility to put his physical body into the service of righteousness."[113]

The theology and argument of Romans 6:12–13 anticipates Paul's booster-rocket launching of the more exclusively ethical portion of his epistle. In Romans 12:1–2 the apostle writes:

Therefore, I am urging you, brothers, through the tender mercies of God to present your bodies a sacrifice, living, holy, well pleasing to God, which is your spiritual service (or worship). And do not be molded after this age, but rather be transformed by the renewal of the mind so that you may test (with a view toward approval) what the will of God is, what is good and well pleasing and perfect.

Once again although many commentators vie for the wholistic interpretations of σῶμα (*sōma*) in verse 1,[114] the main illustration of the apostle's exhortation turns on the hinge of instrumentality:

---

[112] It seems that the occurrence of "members" (τὰ μέλη [*ta melē*] ) in v. 13 reinforces the physical instrumentality of the σῶμα (*sōma*) of v. 12, while the "yourselves" (ἑαυτοὺς [*heautous*]) parallelism of v. 13 highlights the synecdochical dimension of the previous reference to "body."

[113] Gundry, *Sōma*, 31; cf. his whole argument in chapter 5, "The Alternation of *Sōma* with Personal Pronouns in Pauline Literature," 29–33. In a few places, however, his argument over-corrects appropriate synecdochical colorings of σῶμα (*sōma*).

[114] If there is some synecdochical influence of σῶμα (*sōma*) in Romans 12:1, the term is not being used in an unqualified wholistic sense; cf., e.g., Dunn's nuancing of it: "the point to be emphasized... is that σῶμα denotes not just the person, but the person in his corporeality, in his concrete relationships within this world" (*Romans 1–8*, 709).

Paul uses *sōmata* precisely because he wishes to stress the sanctification of that part of our being which is the place and means of concrete activity in the world. . . . Disparagement of the body in the Hellenistic world necessitated such an emphasis by Paul. Substitution of the reflexive personal pronoun reduces the emphasis and leaves a wrong impression concerning the meaning of *sōma*. Of course, the offering to God of the physical vehicle of life in the world implies also an inner consecration to God. . . . The body may be the instrument of the mind and emotions without being equated with them.[115]

So, in review of the *predominant* anthropological impression of σῶμα (*sōma*) in the New Testament, it refers to "the body as a whole, the instrument of life."[116] Its normal tendency is to individuate since "the body is not the man, for he himself can exist apart from his body."[117] Therefore, since man's personhood inheres to his metaphysical dimension, not his physical dimension, the body is not the source of sin.[118] It is a vehicle which may be used to serve sin or to glorify God.

## σάρξ  (sarx)

Unlike σῶμα (*sōma*), New Testament σάρξ (*sarx*), "flesh," hardly ever individuates in a purely physical sense.[119] But when σάρξ (*sarx*) does *exceedingly infrequently* approximate "body," (cf., Matthew 26:41; 1 Corinthians 5:5 [?]; Hebrews 9:13), it is "quite neutral."[120] Indeed the semantical roots of σάρξ (*sarx*) are most firmly planted in the soil of Old Testament בָּשָׂר (*bāsār*). Consequently, in settings emphasizing sin, it may well be regarded as "the involuntary accomplice to the act of sin but not the criminal."[121]

---

[115] Gundry, *Sōma*, 35, 36.

[116] Vine, *EDNTW*, 72.

[117] Ibid., 137. Such an observation does not deny the fact that σῶμα (*sōma*) in a few contexts may also exhibit synecdochical influences. However, in such rare settings it should be regarded as concretely and visibly *representing* the whole person, not as *being* the whole person (cf., e.g., Gundry, *Sōma*, 29–30).

[118] For extensive exegetical support of this conclusion, see J. A. Schep, *The Nature of the Resurrection Body* (Grand Rapids: Eerdmans, 1964); his polemic against platonism is superb.

[119] Nor is it frequently used to indicate physical substance in general, i.e. meat (cf. a couple of rare occurrences with this denotation in Luke 24:39 and 1 Corinthians 15:39).

[120] William Barclay, *The Mind of St. Paul* (New York: Harper & Brothers, 1958), 195.

[121] W. D. Davies, *Paul and Rabbinic Judaism* (London: S.P.C.K., 1948), 19.

The semantical foundation stones of New Testament σάρξ (*sarx*) as laid upon the anthropological footing of Old Testament בָּשָׂר (*bāśār*) are strategically important for a correct understanding of a wide range of hermeneutically challenging occurrences of this term in the New Testament. For example, σάρξ (*sarx*) is true to its roots in that it is used to connote mankind as weak, fragile, transitory, etc.[122] Peter's quote of the Isaiah 40:6–8 passage in 1 Peter 1:24 is an excellent example. Σάρξ (*sarx*), used in this sense, focuses on some sort of human limitation.[123] The same is true of the combination σάρξ καὶ αἷμα (*sarx kai haima*; or, vice versa).[124]

A second crucial connection of σάρξ (*sarx*) to its Old Testament predecessor, בָּשָׂר (*bāśār*), involves the fact that "by synecdoche" it stands for "the totality of all that is essential to manhood."[125] The LXX has helped to pave the way for this phenomenon. This early Greek version "translates the Hebrew *bāśār* especially with *sarx*, referring to the whole living creature. . . ."[126]

These general connotations of σάρξ (*sarx*), especially its limitation and tendency to stand for the whole man, are exceedingly relevant factors when examining the several, significant occurrences of the term in hamartiological contexts. The finiteness of the human creature is *not* the reason for his falleness, *nor* is his physical "flesh" the high-handed agent of sin. In such contexts the term's physical connotation is overwhelmed by a whole-man-apart-from-God-and/or-His-resources significance. Take, for example, the occurrences of σάρξ (*sarx*) in Romans 7 (i.e. vv. 5, 18, 25). As Spicq notes about these particular references in Paul:

> This is not to say that what we call the body is corrupt. *Sarx* is almost personified. ... It is the "whole person" that is corrupt, a perverse mind and will. Just as the arm and the hand are considered as autonomous and responsible for actions in

---

[122] For some good discussion on this connection, see: Bo Reicke, "Body and Soul in the New Testament," *Studia Theologica*, 19 (1965): 200–212; Ridderbos, *POT*, 94; Stacey, *PVM*, 157; Guthrie, *NTT*, 172.

[123] For an eye-catching example, cf. its application to the incarnation of Christ in John 1:14.

[124] Cf., e.g., Matthew 16:17; Ephesians 6:12.

[125] Vine, *EDNTW*, 242.

[126] Spicq, *TLNT*, 3:233. Another evidence of continuity with Old Testament בָּשָׂר (*bāśār*) is the New Testament employment of σάρξ (*sarx*) to indicate intimate relationship, e.g., biological descent or marriage (cf. Matthew 19:5–6; Romans 1:3; 9:5).

which they are really just instruments, Paul treats the flesh…as the locus of the passions and covetousness.[127]

What is involved concerning any physical emphasis of σάρξ (*sarx*) in hamartiological contexts is instrumentality, not agency.[128]

In view of the above tendencies, consider some of the more credible definitions of σάρξ (*sarx*) in settings with hamartiological connections:

Our fallen, ego-centric human nature and all that belongs to it.[129]

Mere human nature … apart from divine influence, and therefore prone to sin and opposed to God.[130]

Flesh is…the whole nature of man, turned away from God, in the supreme interest of self, devoted to the creature. …The ruling principle of the flesh is undoubtedly selfishness.[131]

The self reliant attitude of the man who puts his trust in his own strength, and in that which is controllable by him.[132]

---

[127] Ibid., 3:238. Burton well notes that in such settings "the strictly material sense is left behind several steps before we reach the distinctly ethical meaning" (*SSF*, 195).

[128] Cf. σῶμα (*sōma*) in similar contexts. For exegetical support, see: Murray, *Romans,* 1: 256–273. Furthermore, in settings such as Romans 7 Paul continues to develop his aeon theology. The significance of this factor also helps to correct any neo-platonic hangover on the part of the interpreter. Commenting on Romans 7:14 (note the adjective σαρκινoś [*sarkinos*] therein), Dunn carefully observes, based upon the larger context, that "Paul does not take what to many would have been the easy way out; he does not attempt to distinguish the 'I' from 'the flesh,' to exonerate the willing 'I' from any blame for its impotence by depicting it as imprisoned within the flesh. He does not, in other words, opt for a dualism which understands the 'I' as an element of a higher world incarcerated within the lower world of matter. He is confused and frustrated by his powerlessness (v. 15), but he understands well enough that he himself is the subject performing the actions he himself abhors (vv. 15–16). That is why we must speak of a split in the 'I' rather than of a split between the 'I' and the flesh. Paul is talking about himself in his belongingness to the world of flesh, the old epoch. However much he may also rejoice in his belongingness with Christ to the life beyond the resurrection, the new epoch, he recognizes with all seriousness that he is still flesh; that is still inextricably bound up with the fallen world, an attachment which only death will sever, when the believer's identification with Christ's death has worked itself out completely" (Dunn, *Romans 1–8*, 408).

[129] Cranfield, *Romans* 1:372.

[130] Joseph Henry Thayer, *Greek-English Lexicon of the New Testament* (Grand Rapids: Zondervan, n.d.), 571; cf. Marvin R. Vincent, *Word Studies in the New Testament* (New York: Scribners, 1908), 3:76.

[131] John Peter Lange, *The Epistle of Paul to the Romans* (Grand Rapids: Zondervan, 1949), 236.

[132] Rudolf Bultmann, *Theology of the New Testament,* translated by K. Grobel (New York: Scribners, 1954), 1:240; this definition bears an impress of the language of Jeremiah 17:5.

Now, via review, it would do us well to tune in to excerpts from Thiselton's synopsis of σάρξ (*sarx*) especially as it leads up to a summary of its anthropological significance in hamartiological contents:

> Since the meaning of *sarx* varies radically from context to context, several distinct points must be made about the hermeneutics of the term. . . . In some contexts . . . *sarx* calls attention to man's creatureliness and frailty; to the fact that he is fragile, fallible, and vulnerable. ...The biblical writers ... give a warning against any false hope and consequent disillusionment brought about by putting undue confidence and trust in man as a fallible and frail creature. ...The Bible also calls attention to man's creatureliness before God, and distance from him in his otherness and transcendence. ...In time of oppression or persecution, the believer is encouraged not to fear an enemy who is mere flesh. ...The physical nature of *sarx* has positive significance in terms of the bodily obedience of the Christian. Paul is far from endorsing the verdict of Seneca, his contemporary, that the flesh is "useless"....The life of Jesus is to be manifested "in our mortal flesh" (2 Corinthians 4:11). Here Paul's use of flesh overlaps with that of *sōma*, body (2 Corinthians 4:10). The believer still lives "in" the flesh (*en sarki*) although not "according to" the flesh (2 Corinthians 10:3). . . . A quite different use of *sarx* appears in the major theological passages in Paul such as Romans 8:5–8. ...In this passage the mental outlook of the flesh (*to phronēma tēs sarkos*) is hostile to God. "Flesh" here evaluates man as a sinner before God. The outlook of the flesh is the outlook oriented towards self, that which pursues its own ends in self-sufficient independence of God.[133]

## ψυχή *(psuchē)*

New Testament ψυχή (*psuchē*), by and large, still echoes some of the main fields of usage of Old Testament נֶפֶשׁ (*nepeš*); however, in certain settings it does individuate by placing an emphasis on the non-physical

---

[133] *NIDNTT*, 1:678–680.

aspect of man.[134] Nevertheless, the *platonic* conception of the immortality of the ψυχή (*psuchē*)[135] is not the governing feature of the term in New Testament revelation. Furthermore, the New Testament never glorifies man's ψυχή (*psuchē*) while at the same time depreciating his "body" or physical "flesh," as is the case in much of pagan thinking.

For a quick survey of ψυχή (*psuchē*) in the New Testament consider Burton's usage categories:[136]

1. Life, the loss of which is death; used only of men (cf. Matthew 2:20; 6:25; etc.).

2. The soul of man as distinguished from the body and existing separately or capable of so doing (cf. Matthew 10:28; Revelation 6:9; 20:4).[137]

3. Soul as a constituent element of man's nature, the seat of vitality, thought, emotion, will; the human mind in the larger sense of the word; most frequently with special reference to its religious capacities and experiences (cf. Matthew 22:37;[138] Luke 2:35; Acts 14:2; Hebrews 12:3; 3 John 2).

4. More frequently ψυχή alone denotes a human person.

This last category perpetuates an Old Testament precedent in that, like נֶפֶשׁ (*nepeš*), New Testament ψυχή (*psuchē*) often indicates "a person, an individual man" (cf., e.g., Acts 2:43; Romans 2:9; 13:1; etc.).[139] It is similarly used "in enumerations" (cf., e.g., Acts 2:41; 7:14; 1 Peter 3:20; etc.).[140] Furthermore, very much in accord with an Old Testament emphasis, ψυχή (*psuchē*) functions "with possessive limitation, for self" (cf., e.g., Matthew 12:18; Luke 1:46; 12:19; etc.).[141]

---

[134] Cf., e.g., Johannes P. Louw and Eugene A. Nida, *Greek-English Lexicon of the New Testament* (New York: United Bible Societies, 1989), 1:106, 262, 321–22. The LXX slightly nudged the term in this direction. It was used over 900 times mostly for נֶפֶשׁ (*nepeš*), but it also renders לֵב (*lēb*) 25 times and רוּחַ (*ruah*) two times (cf. Harder, *NIDNTT*, 3:679–80).

[135] Cf., e.g., the popularization of this emphasis as the term's major usage in Plato and his philosophical successors as discussed in *TLNT*, 3:232; *NIDNTT*, 3:679, 681; etc.

[136] Excerpted from *SSF*, 183–84; cf. BAG, 901–902.

[137] This sense is very rare in the New Testament.

[138] One must be careful of Burton's terminology of "constituent element," especially in situations like Matthew 22:37 (cf. Deuteronomy 6:5). Our Lord is not breaking human beings down into distinguishable metaphysical parts, i.e. καρδία (*kardia*), ψυχή (*psuchē*), and διάνοια (*dianoia*), but His purpose is to show that a person *with his whole being* should *unreservedly* love God.

[139] Burton, *SSF*, 184.

[140] Ibid.

[141] Ibid.

Therefore, in conclusion, "*psuchē* appears under more or less similar conditions as in the Old Testament."[142] Yet,

> there is disparity of concept between the Old Testament *nepeš* and the New Testament *psychē*. The basic difference lies in the fact that the *nepeš*, unlike the *psychē*, is not a spiritual entity which exists apart from the body. ...To the Hebrew, man was not a "body" and a "soul," but rather a "body-soul." ...The *nepeš* is then simply the individual in his totality. ...The New Testament, although it continues the idea of the soul (*psychē*) as the life-principle...which becomes personified (Acts 2:43), yet also views it as a spiritual entity which continues to exist after death.[143]

## πνεῦμα *(pneuma)*

Speaking of metaphysical individuation, that seems to be the primary characteristic of πνεῦμα (*pneuma*). The New Testament functions of this term are virtually identical to those of Old Testament רוּחַ (*ruah*). For example, πνεῦμα (*pneuma*) in the New Testament is used in the following ways:[144]

1. As "wind" or "breath" (e.g., John 3:8;[145] 2 Thessalonians 2:8).
2. As indicating "the spirit of man separated from the body after death" (e.g., 1 Corinthians 5:5; Hebrews 12:23).
3. As the "embodied...human spirit, that element of a living man by virtue of which he lives, feels, perceives, and wills."

---

[142] J. I. Marais, *ISBE* (Grand Rapids: Eerdmans, 1939), 5:2837.

[143] R. Laurin, *Baker's Dictionary of Theology*, edited by Everett F. Harrison (Grand Rapids: Baker, 1960), 491–92.

[144] Excerpted from Ernest DeWitt Burton, *The Epistle to the Galatians: A Critical Exegetical Commentary* (Edinburgh: T&T Clark, 1988), 486ff.

[145] Notice how πνεῦμα (*pneuma*) as "wind" is illustrative of the effects of the Spirit (i.e. πνεῦμα [*pneuma*]).

This last category is exceedingly significant and may be broken down into sub-categories; for example, πνεῦμα (*pneuma*) is viewed:[146]

1. As the seat of life, or that in man which constitutes him a living being (cf., e.g., Matthew 27:50; Luke 8:55; James 2:26).

2. As the seat of emotion and will, especially of the moral and religious life, including thought as concerned with religion (cf., e.g., Mark 8:12; John 11:33; Acts 17:16; 19:21; 20:22; Romans 12:11; 2 Corinthians 2:13).

3. As the seat of consciousness and intelligence (cf., e.g., Mark 2:8; 1 Corinthians 2:11).

Used with these senses, πνεῦμα (*pneuma*) does seem to parallel ψυχή (*psuchē*) in settings where "soul" individuates metaphysically. In this vein Stacey has noted that "there is a personal πνεῦμα, the natural possession of every man...and [it] is not easily distinguished from ψυχή."[147] Yet, πνεῦμα (*pneuma*) is nuanced by an overarching phenomenon. Dunn does a good job of identifying this special coloring of "spirit" in its mega setting: "*pneuma* denotes that power which man experiences as relating him to the spiritual realm. ...At one end of *pneuma*'s spectrum of meaning it denotes the human spirit, or perhaps better, man in so far as he belongs to the spiritual realm and interacts with the spiritual realm."[148]

These valid observations also constitute an important piece to the hermeneutical puzzle of the "spirit"/ "flesh" antithesis which shows up periodically in Paul's writings. Stacey commendably walks us safely through this interpretive mine field:

> From a superficial point of view, flesh and spirit are antithetical. In Greek thought, they represented the tangible and the intangible, the base and the lofty, the contaminated and the pure, the bound and the free. ...Paul's contrast was between man as a human being seeking to live a godless life, and man as a child of God seeking fellowship with Him. "The contrast between 'flesh' and 'spirit,' therefore, is not the contrast between matter and spirit; it is a contrast between human nature, of which sin has taken possession, and the Spirit of God."

---

[146] Exerpted from Burton, *SSF*, 178–179.

[147] *PVM*, 129.

[148] *NIDNTT*, 3:693. The adjective πνευματικός (*pneumatikos*) in contrast with ψυχικός (*psuchikos*) in 1 Corinthians 15:44 may be used to illustrate this nuance in application to the resurrection body; i.e., it is especially suitable to the *spiritual* realm.

...Spirit stands for the divine life and power as manifested to men. ...The flesh stands for the weakness and frailty of man which entertains evil and so separates from God and leads to death. ...Paul...is...being practical and ethical, in the true Hebrew tradition.[149]

After sifting through all the data, Dickson concurs; he concludes, "In the case of πνεῦμα, the predominant element in St. Paul's thought was the divine power issuing from God and operative in the believer, so we find in the case of σάρξ the predominant thought of man standing by himself or left to himself over against God."[150]

## καρδία  *(kardia)*

Although there are several Greek terms that could translationally specify certain key functions of לֵב (*lēb*) in the Old Testament,[151] καρδία (*kardia*) often perpetuates its predecessor's multi-faceted employment. This phenomenon will conspicuously reveal itself through a brief usage survey of "heart" in the New Testament. Exceedingly rare is "the thought of the heart as the central organ of the body and the seat of physical activity."[152] Overwhelmingly predominant is the impression "that the heart is the center of the inner life of man and the source or seat of all the forces and functions of soul and spirit. . . . "[153] For example, "in the heart dwell feelings and emotions, desires and passions."[154] This broad field of usage is very similar to metaphysical applications of "heart" in English. However, in alignment with Old Testament precedents, "the heart is the seat of understanding, the source of thought and reflection,"[155] and "the heart is the seat of the will, the source of resolves."[156]

---

[149] *PVM*, 174–178. In other words, this antithesis is not an internal, anthropological warring of the physical aspect of man with his metaphysical aspect; it is an anthropological/cosmological or eschatological tension.

[150] William P. Dickson, *St. Paul's Use of the Terms Flesh and Spirit* (Glasgow: Maclehose, 1883), 271.

[151] Cf. two of these terms which immediately follow this discussion of καρδία (*kardia*).

[152] Behm, *TDNT*, 3:611; he restricts this sense to Luke 21:34; Acts 14:17; and James 5:5. Even these three occurrences could be taken in other ways such as term for the total man (e.g., "'yourselves'").

[153] Ibid.

[154] Ibid., 612. Citing many passages, Behm documents that καρδία (*kardia*) is intimately associated with joy, pain, sorrow, love, desire, lust, etc.

[155] Ibid.; cf., e.g., occurrences of καρδία (*kardia*) in Matthew 9:4; 13:15 [quoting Isaiah 6:10]; Mark 2:6–8; 7:21; Luke 1:51; 2:19; etc.

[156] Ibid.; cf., e.g., Acts 5:4; 11:23; 1 Corinthians 4:5; 2 Corinthians 9:7; Hebrews 4:21; etc.

In view of these characterizing emphases, "καρδία comes to stand for the whole of the inner being of man."[157] It "is supremely the one center in man...which determines moral conduct."[158] Therefore, like Old Testament לֵב (*lēb*) New Testament καρδία (*kardia*) most significantly is the moral mission-control center of man. Sorg aptly summarizes the main usages of "heart" in the New Testament especially as they impact the term's anthropological significance:

> The New Testament use of *kardia* coincides with the Old Testament understanding of the term. . . . The meaning of the heart as the inner life, the center of the personality and as the place in which God reveals himself to men is even more clearly expressed in the New Testament than in the Old Testament.... It...frequently denotes the seat of intellectual and spiritual life, the inner life in opposition to external appearance....The powers of the spirit, reason, and will have their seat in the heart....The heart stands for man's ego. It is simply the person ("the hidden person of the heart," 1 Peter 3:4)....The most significant instances of *kardia* in the New Testament occur in those passages which speak of man's standing before God....It is the seat of doubt and hardness as well as of faith and obedience. A striking feature of the New Testament is the essential closeness of *kardia* to the concept *nous*, mind....Thus it is the person, the thinking, feeling, willing ego of man, with particular regard to his responsibility to God, that the New Testament denotes by the use of *kardia*. Sin marks, dominates and spoils...man's innermost being, his heart...."The heart is deceitful above all things, and desperately corrupt; who can understand it?" Jeremiah's complaint (17:9) voices the view of the New Testament also....Just as the heart is the seat of faithlessness, it is also the seat of faith (Romans 10:6–10)....Conversion of the heart to faith is not achieved through the will or desire of the human heart (1 Corinthians 2:9), but solely because God opens a man's heart (Acts 16:14) and lets his light illuminate the heart (2 Corinthians 4:6). ...The heart of man...is the place...where...faith proves its reality in obedience and patience.[159]

---

[157] Ibid.
[158] Ibid.
[159] *NIDNTT*, 2:182–83.

So "heart," לֵב (*lēb*) in the Old Testament and καρδία (*kardia*) in the New Testament, statistically and ethically are the most prominent terms for man's mission-control center.

## νοῦς (*nous*)[160]

Although לֵב (*lēb*) in the Old Testament is the multi-functional, work-horse term,[161] and although καρδία (*kardia*) is still used in the New Testament to emphasize man's thinking and planning functions, other Greek terms are also employed more restrictively to specify many of these particularized functions. Prominently among them stands the νοῦς (*nous*) word-group. The noun is used with several senses which often overlap one another. For example, νοῦς (*nous*) denotes:[162]

1. "mind" or "disposition" (cf., e.g., Romans 1:28; 12:2; Ephesians 4:17, 23; 1 Timothy 6:5; Titus 1:15).

2. "practical reason" (i.e. "the moral consciousness as it concretely determines will and action"; cf., e.g., Romans 7:23, 25; 1 Corinthians 1:10).

3. "understanding" (cf., e.g., Luke 24:45; 2 Thessalonians 2:2; Revelation 17:9).

4. "thought," "judgment," "resolve"; in the senses of "opinion" or "decree"[163] (cf. respectively, Romans 14:5 and 1 Corinthians 2:16a).

Most basically, νοῦς (*nous*) refers to "the total inner man viewed from the mental perspective, which consciously acts in making practical

---

[160] This noun is part of an exceedingly significant word-group with important applications not only to anthropology but also to hamartiology and soteriology. The *noetic* impact (an English adjective built upon the Greek noun, i.e., having to do with the *mind*) of this family of words, will become clearer through discussions in the next two parts of this work. Furthermore, close cousins to this word-family will significantly add their weight to the discussions. For general surveys, see: *EDNTW*, 408–409; *NIDNTT*, 2:616–620; 3:122–133.

[161] Although the LXX uses καρδία (*kardia*) mainly for לֵב (*lēb*), νοῦς (*nous*) is employed six times to render it (cf. the Behm's discussion in *TDNT*, 4:953).

[162] Excerpted from Behm, *TDNT*, 4:958–59.

[163] BAG, 547.

moral judgments."[164] Because of this rational-ethical emphasis, man's "mind" in the New Testament is especially pictured as a nucleus *of* sin and the target *for* salvation: "Νοῦς [*nous*] ...occurs in various contexts as depraved (i.e. ἀδόκιμος [*adokimos*], Romans 1:28), futile (i.e. ματαίοτης [*mataiotēs*], Ephesians 4:17), self-centered (cf. Colossians 2:18), and corrupt or defiled (cf. 1 Timothy 6:5; 2 Timothy 3:8; Titus 1:15). Therefore, it stands in desperate need of divine intervention (cf. διανοίγω [*dianoigō*] + νοῦς [*nous*] in Luke 24:45) and renewal (cf. Romans 12:2; Ephesians 4:23). The only cure for mankind's inflated and perverted νοῦς [*nous*] is the νοῦν Χριστοῦ [*noun Christou*] (1 Corinthians 2:16; note the polemic against self-aggrandizement in chapters 1–3)."[165]

## συνείδησις *(suneidesis)*

We have already observed that one of the contextual connotations of לֵב (*lēb*) in the Old Testament is *conscience*.[166] However, συνείδησις (*suneidēsis*) in Greek literature specifically *denotes* the human "conscience." Conceptionally there are some commonalities between "'conscience'" in the Old Testament, extra-biblical occurrences of συνείδησις (*suneidēsis*), and certain usages of the Greek term in the New Testament. Yet, not unexpectedly, some correctives and advancements show up when this term's thirty-one sure occurrences are examined in the setting of New Testament revelation. For example, Paul's uses of συνείδησις (*suneidēsis*) transcend both Stoic and popular Greek employments.[167] Furthermore, although "the conscience is part of the *equipment*, as it were, given to us by God,"[168] in the New Testament it is never viewed as functioning as a perfect moral guide. It is not an infallible Jiminy

---

[164] Donald Eggleston, "The Biblical Concept of νοῦς: The Noetic Effects of the Fall and Regeneration," unpublished M. Div. thesis (Grace Theological Seminary, 1979), 82. For a superb treatment, see: Theo J. W. Kunst, "The Implications of Pauline Theology of the Mind for the Work of the Theologian," unpublished Th. D. dissertation (Dallas Seminary, 1979). Also, one needs to remember that the New Testament usages of νοῦς (*nous*) have nothing to do with its employments in the Greek philosophical writings. For example, in the New Testament "there is no connection with the...mystico-religious use. Noῦς is not the divine or the divinely related element in man" (*TDNT*, 4:958; cf. *NIDNTT*, 3:127).

[165] George J. Zemek, "Aiming the Mind: A Key to Godly Living," *GTJ*, 5:2 (Fall 1984): 211–212. Parts II and III of this current work will pick up the harmartiological significance and the soteriological importance of the "mind."

[166] Cf. above under לֵב (*lēb*).

[167] Cf., e.g., Guthrie, *NTT*, 171.

[168] B. F. Harris, *WTJ* (May 1962): 186; cf. pp. 173–186 (this whole article is quite good).

Cricket. Nor, on the other hand, even as a result of the fall, is it viewed as always errant in its monitorings. As an anthropological term, in and of itself, it is neutral. Various adjectives and/or contextual nuancings "combine both positive and negative ideas with conscience" in the New Testament Scriptures.[169]

So, concerning the relationship of "conscience" to the noetic faculties and functions, "mind and conscience are distinct. ... νοῦς is that which creates a purpose or act: συνείδησις is that which judges a purpose or act."[170] Without impugning the *basic* credibility of such a generalization, the concept of conscience in the New Testament is quite complex. Brown's survey which meanders through most of the term's New Testament settings is very helpful:

> At best conscience is a check....Conscience can be a highly defective guide, if one relies solely on the absence of the pain that we call conscience as a guide to conduct....To say this, however, does not mean that the New Testament writers urge that conscience should be ignored. Christ died to make the conscience clean (Hebrews 9:14; 10:22; cf. 8:9; 10:2; 1 Peter 3:21). But the conscience is only part of our moral make-up. Its work is largely negative. As the pain we feel when we do something wrong, it acts like a red warning light. It serves as a sort of moral double-check on our actions....It needs to be educated and carefully tended. But as such, it is very important (Acts 23:1; 24:16; Romans 2:15; 9:1; 13:5; 1 Timothy 1:5, 19; 3:9; 2 Timothy 1:3; 1 Peter 2:19; 3:16; 2 Corinthians 1:12). When we speak of conscience in English, our meaning seems to oscillate between conscience in the narrow sense as the pain, or the instrument which makes us feel pain, when we transgress the moral law, and the wider sense of moral consciousness. The latter involves the whole person, viewed as a responsible moral being. It is not just a pain which works retrospectively in the light of past actions and which by extension might enable us to forecast what future actions might cause us pain. It includes the power of discernment and rational reflection which enables the mind to analyze situations and actions, to discern moral values and principles, the capacity to hear and apply the Word of God to our lives, and also conscience in the

---

[169] Ibid., 179.
[170] Ibid., 178.

narrower sense. For the Christian, guidance belongs to the realm of moral consciousness in this wider sense which includes *syneidesis* in the narrower sense, but is by no means confined to it.[171]

Paul's usages are particularly significant; the apostle "made *syneidēsis* into the interior faculty for the personal discernment of good and evil, the practical rule of conduct and motive for action."[172]

## ἔξω / ἔσω ἄνθρωπος *(exō/esō anthrōpos)*

These phrases appear only in Paul (Romans 7:22; 2 Corinthians 4:16; Ephesians 3:16). Most simply put, the ἔξω ἄνθρωπος *(exō anthrōpos)* points to the "man" people may observe, for example, as winding down in his capabilities, while the ἔσω ἄνθρωπος *(esō anthrōpos)* refers to the inner person who is not readily observable to the eye of on-lookers. As Jeremias puts it, "'the outer man'" emphasizes man "according to his physical and mortal side."[173] On the other hand, "the inward man is the true self, yearning for the life of the Spirit."[174] Second Corinthians 4:16 is especially significant, since the two phrases appear in the same immediate context as contrasting perspectives on the person. Because of this tension, "the major problem regarding 'inner/outer man' is the extent to which the dualism inherent in the terms themselves is carried over into Paul's anthropology."[175] Jewett correctly argues that there is some sort of anthropological dichotomy manifested through this antithesis; however, it did not emerge from a Greek philosophical lower/higher nature of man assumption.[176] In Paul's biblical thinking ἔξω ἄνθρωπος *(exō anthrōpos)* is a person viewed anthropologically, or possibly, to some degree, anthro-

---

[171] *NIDNTT*, 1:351–53.

[172] Spicq, *TLNT*, 3:335. In view of the larger picture, I would prefer substituting "an"... "a" for "the" ... "the" in this summary statement.

[173] *TDNT*, 1:365.

[174] Stacey, *PVM*, 212. Stacey also said of ἔσω ἄνθρωπος *(esō anthrōpos)*, "One cannot resist the idea that here...is a term for the essential self, apart from any particular aspect. The inward man is the real self that passes from the body of flesh to the body of resurrection" (ibid., 211).

[175] Robert Jewett, *Paul's Anthropological Terms. A Study of Their Use in Conflict Settings* (Leiden: E. J. Brill, 1971), 395.

[176] Ibid., 391–95.

pologically/hamartiologically. Ἔσω ἄνθρωπος (*Esō anthrōpos*) would therefore be the same person viewed anthropologically/soteriologically. Contrasting processes (of physically winding down and of spiritually winding up) are going on in true believers.

It must also be clearly noted that these phrases, "outer man" and "inner man," are in no way parallel with the biblical designations of "old man" and "new man."[177] For this reason Berkouwer in his volume on anthropology states, "We do not further include the distinction between the old man and the new man, since that obviously does not concern an anthropological distinction within man's general humanness, but refers rather to man from a historical-soteriological viewpoint."[178]

---

[177] Cf., e.g., Jeremias, *TDNT*, 1:365–66.

[178] Berkouwer, *Man: The Image of God*, 198. The "old man" and "new man" antithesis will be discussed later on in Part III.

# CHAPTER 2

# BIBLICAL ANTHROPOLOGY: THE THEOLOGY OF IT

Needless to say, biblical anthropology differs radically from the secular teachings of modern evolutionary and sociological anthropology.[179] Furthermore, as already witnessed by the data surveys of chapter one, biblical anthropology also greatly differs from ancient anthropologies, especially from the analytical and compartmentalized Greek conceptions about man. Indeed the Bible generally views man wholistically. Old Testament revelation about man is particularly consistent regarding this tendency, and the teachings of the New Testament very frequently perpetuate it. One reason why this is so is touched upon by Vorlander: "The New Testament is not interested in an isolated self-contained anthropology any more than the Old Testament. Statements about man are always partly theological pronouncements."[180]

So concerning the aspects of man, the biblical evidence shows that synthesis is the norm but separation is the exception. As Berkouwer warns, "We can never gain a clear understanding of the mystery of man if, in one way or another, we abstract mere components of the whole man."[181] Therefore, consider the following summary-conclusions about the nature of man in progressive revelation.

## *Synthesis: The Norm*

Wolff well capsulizes the essence of the Semitic conception of man in the Old Testament when he notes:

> Concepts like heart, soul, flesh, and spirit...are not infrequently interchangeable in Hebrew poetry. In poetic parallelism, they can be used by turns for the whole man, almost like

---

[179] For some major differences, cf. G. W. Bromiley, *ISBE* (Grand Rapids: Eerdmans, 1979), 1:131.
[180] *NIDNTT*, 2:565.
[181] *Man: The Image of God*, 194.

pronouns (Psalm 84:2). ...This has been well characterized as the "stereometry of expression."...Stereometric thinking thus simultaneously presupposes a synopsis of the members and organs of the human body with their capabilities and functions. It is synthetic thinking....[182]

The evidence from the New Testament points in a similar direction. Guthrie's generalizations are right on target:

> The New Testament view of man must be deduced from a wide range of apparently disparate material. In fact, the New Testament does not set out in so many words what man is. It does not supply a psychological account....There is little support for an analytical approach to man's nature....Of all the New Testament writers Paul gives the fullest expression to a doctrine of man....The main ideas which Paul uses to describe various aspects of man are soul (*psychē*), spirit (*pneuma*), flesh (*sarx*), body (*sōma*), heart (*kardia*) and mind (*nous*). To those may be added the important concept of conscience (*synēidesis*) and the characteristically Pauline idea of the inner man....The foregoing evidence has demonstrated the wide variety of Paul's terms for aspects of man and the impossibility of constructing a consistent psychology. Indeed psychology is the wrong word to use, since Paul is so strongly influenced by the Hebrew idea of the whole man that Greek notions of separate functions have only a minimum impact on Paul's thinking.[183]

Consequently, "Paul, a Hebrew of the Hebrews, is primarily and characteristically Hebrew in his anthropology, and...even where his ideas (in this realm) come nearest to a Greek form or are clothed in a Greek terminology, they are a legitimate outcome of Old Testament conceptions."[184] More fully and very credibly, Stacey concludes:

> Paul's approach to anthropology was synthetic, not analytic. ...A second feature of Paul's use of anthropological terms, following from the one above, is the looseness of his terminology....Paul uses some words with exactly the same

---

[182] *AOT*, 7–8.
[183] *NTT*, 186, 163, 164, 176.
[184] H. W. Robinson, "Hebrew Psychology in Relation to Pauline Anthropology," *Mansfield College Essays* (London: Hodder & Stoughton, 1909), 268.

meaning as their Old Testament equivalents, without change or development....Other terms, which Paul developed, and to which he added his own original sense, have an Old Testament basis. ...Paul used some words that were Greek, with no Hebrew synonym, but he used them, not in the pure Greek sense, but in the sense in which they were used in the intertestament literature, that is to say, in a Hebrew setting.[185]

## Separation: The Exception

Although the overwhelming majority of the anthropological data from special revelation bears witness to the fact that the physical and metaphysical aspects of human beings are perspectives on the whole man, a few passages allude to a state[186] or condition in which the conscious metaphysical core of man may exist *temporarily* apart from his physical dimension.[187] At first glance this might seem to parallel platonic thinking after all. However, this state *is* indeed *temporary*. Man during this interim awaits a resurrection body. Paul's statements in 2 Corinthians 5:1–10 are exceedingly informative.

Now we know that if the earthly tent we live in is destroyed, we have a building from God, an eternal house in heaven, not built by human hands. Meanwhile we groan, longing to be clothed with our heavenly dwelling,[188] because when we are clothed, we will not be found naked. For while we are in this tent, we groan and are burdened, because we do not wish to be unclothed but to be clothed[189] with our heavenly dwelling, so that what is mortal may be swallowed up by life. Now it is God who has made us for this very purpose and has given us the Spirit as a deposit, guaranteeing what is to come.[190]

---

[185] *PVM*, 222–225.

[186] In the terminology of systematic theology, this is the "intermediate state."

[187] Any biblically partitive perspectives about man fall into two wide-sweeping categories, his physical characteristics and his metaphysical attributes. For a brief survey of the systematic-theological positions of dichotomy and trichotomy, see APPENDIX D: Dichotomy, Trichotomy, or What?

[188] That the metaphors of "tent," "building," "house," and "dwelling" in this context refer to the human "body" is certain from the several appearances of σῶμα (*sōma*) in vv. 6–10.

[189] Note that Paul's viewpoint is antithetical to the pagan concept of σῶμα σῆμα (*sōma sēma*), "the body is a tomb." Platonic thinking longed for a bodiless state. That is why the resurrection was so offensive to Greeks (cf., e.g., Acts 17:18, 31–34; 1 Corinthians 1:23; etc.)

[190] Part of what is to come is the resurrection body suited to new environments (cf. 1 Corinthians 15:12ff., especially vv. 35ff.).

Therefore we are always confident and know that as long as we are at home in the body we are away from the Lord. We live by faith, not by sight. We are confident, I say, and would prefer to be away from the body and at home with the Lord. So we make it our goal to please him, whether we are at home in the body or away from it. For we must all appear before the judgment seat of Christ, that each one may receive what is due him for the things done while in the body, whether good or bad (2 Corinthians 5:1–10, NIV).

Erickson, labels the anthropological state of man in relation to this intermediate condition "contingent monism."[191] The gist of his argument is that:

the pictures of man in Scripture seem to regard him for the most part as a unitary being. Seldom is his spiritual nature addressed independently of or apart from the body. Having said this, however, we must also recall those passages…which point to an immaterial aspect of man which is separable from his material existence. Scripture indicates that there is an intermediate state involving personal conscious existence between death and resurrection. This concept of an intermediate state is not inconsistent with the doctrine of resurrection. For this intermediate (i.e. immaterial or disembodied) state is clearly incomplete or abnormal (2 Corinthians 5:2–4). In the coming resurrection (1 Corinthians 15) the person will receive a new or perfected body. The full range of the biblical data can best be accommodated by the view which we will term "conditional unity." According to this view, the normal state of man is as a materialized unitary being.[192]

Such a careful walking of the biblical balance beam of anthropology is commendable. Scripturally, anthropological synthesis is indeed the norm while separation is the exception.

---

[191] Erickson, *Christian Theology*, cf. 519–539.
[192] Ibid., 536–537.

# PART II

# BIBLICAL HAMARTIOLOGY

# An Introduction To Biblical Hamartiology

Jonathan Edwards very perceptively labeled hamartiology "that great important doctrine."[193] More fully, he affirmed:

> For, if the case be such indeed, that all mankind are by nature in a state of total ruin,...then doubtless the great salvation by Christ stands in direct relation to this ruin, as the remedy to the disease; and the whole gospel or doctrine of salvation, must oppose it; and all real belief, or true notion of that gospel must be built upon it.[194]

One degree off course here, according to the massive hamartiological compass of God's Word, will result in missing the theological destination of an understanding of biblical salvation by a million miles. And, not only will one be off course theologically because of his defective hamartiology, but also he will be errant in his ministerial methodology. As Horne puts it, "If this doctrine of total depravity is not clearly understood in its full Biblical delineation, then one's apologetic system is bound to be woefully defective."[195]

As an indication of just how important is the connection between man's spiritually terminal condition and God's merciful provision of the cure in Christ, pay careful attention to how various passages from His Word juxtapose our helpless estate with His merciful deliverance. Paul is especially fond of reminding us about who we were in sin versus who we now are in Christ. Declarations about the inexplicable benefits of our salvation in Christ are most often given in settings which bring to remembrance our former enslavement to sin. The normal order is to give a reminder about our B. C. (i.e. before Christ and His applied Crosswork) condition followed by a rehearsal of blessings related to our A. C. (i.e. after Christ and His applied Crosswork) position.[196]

---

[193] Jonathan Edwards, *Original Sin*, edited by C. A. Holbrook (New Haven & London: Yale University Press, 1970), 102.

[194] Ibid., 103.

[195] Charles M. Horne, "A Biblical Apologetic Methodology," unpublished Th. D. dissertation (Winona Lake: Grace Theological Seminary, 1963), 83. For a fuller discussion of this crucial methodological connection, see my *Doing God's Business God's Way: A Biblical Theology of Ministry* (P.O. Box 428, Mango, FL 33550–0428).

[196] Cf., e.g., Romans 1:18–3:20 with 3:21ff.; Ephesians 2:1–3 with vv. 4–10; Titus 3:3 with vv. 4–7; etc.

# CHAPTER 3

# BIBLICAL HAMARTIOLOGY:
# THE TERMINOLOGY OF IT

A procedure similar to the previous development of the biblical terminology relating to anthropology will be followed here in the arena of hamartiology. I will commence with the respective Hebrew and Greek words that are *semantically* equivalent to the general word for "sin" in English. Then I will follow up with some salient *theological* terms which develop the doctrine of sin in the Old and New Testaments.

## *Old Testament Terminology*[197]

### The Root חטא *(ḥṭ')*[198]

Judges 20:16 provides a non-moral picture of the basic idea undergirding this Hebrew root: "among all these soldiers there were seven hundred chosen men who were left-handed, each of whom could sling a stone at a hair and not *miss*" (NIV).[199] These warriors could sling stones and *not miss* their marks, not even by a hair's breadth. If they "missed" their mark, it would be said that they had "failed" to hit the target. Therefore, when this Hebrew root is brought into ethical settings, any failure to hit God's moral mark is a *miss*, i.e. a sin.[200] As Knierim says, "The transition from the literal to the figurative usage in the sense of a perverted life-style is clear."[201]

---

[197] Right up front, it should be noted that "the vocabulary for sin in the Old Testament is notably rich because of the strong spiritual and moral sense of the biblical faith" (A. Luc, *NIDOTTE*, 2:87).
[198] This Hebrew root exemplifies a phenomenon that will also show up in the case of other word-groups for sin. The *same* root may speak of the condition or offense of sin, while in other contexts it may signal the divinely prescribed method for propitiating such sin(s). Of this particular word group, Luc observes, "The root *ḥṭ'* with all its derivatives occurs a total of 593 times and possesses the broadest range of meaning, covering sin, sinner, sin offering, etc." (ibid.). For an excellent survey of "sin-offering(s)" in the Bible, see R. E. Averbeck in *NIDOTTE*, 2:93–103.
[199] My emphasis on the translation of the imperfect verb form of חָטָא *(ḥāṭā')*.
[200] Cf., e.g., G. H. Livingston, *TWOT*, 1:277; Luc, *NIDOTTE*, 2:87–88; etc.
[201] *TLOT*, 1:407.

Verbs, verbals and nouns from this word group are found in a variety of situations throughout the Old Testament.[202] In many passages other more strongly nuanced terms for sin stand in parallelism alongside of occurrences from the חטא(*ht'*) word family, but these additions most often function illustratively to expose the heinous nature of *falling short* of God's standard (cf., e.g., Job 34:37).[203] So the root חטא(*ht'*) conveys the most generic and inclusive perspective on sin in the Old Testament.

In a few contexts the verb is beefed up by a certain prepositional complement (i.e. חָטָא לְ־ [*ḥāṭā' lĕ*]; cf., e.g., 1 Kings 8:46; Psalm 51:6 [v. 4, English]). However, let it be known that any sin, whether indicated by a member of the חטא(*ht'*) word group or one of the other terms to follow, brings death apart from the merciful intervention and gracious provisions of a Holy God. Even inadvertent or unintentional "sins" called for sacrifice in the Old Testament (cf. תֶחֱטָא [*teḥĕṭā'*], e.g., in Leviticus 4:2ff.).[204]


## The Root תעה *(t'h)*


Like חטא (*ht'*), the non-moral usages of the root תעה (*t'h*) illustrate the hamartiological significance of this word family. These literal usages include physically wandering around (e.g., Genesis 21:14; 37:15; Exodus 23:4; Job 38:41) and staggering about from drunkenness (e.g., Job 12:25; Isaiah 28:7).[205] Needless to say, such images graphically depict sin as moral wandering. Therefore, in ethical settings this word group focuses on "erring" or "going astray."[206] Two very familiar passages which employ this hamartiological metaphor are Psalm 58:4b (v. 3b, English) and Isaiah 53:6 which respectively read:

---

[202] Cf., e.g., selected verbs and verbals in Genesis 39:9; Leviticus 5:5; Numbers 15:27–28; Deuteronomy 39:9; Joshua 7:20; 1 Samuel 12:10; 2 Samuel 24:10; 1 Kings 16:2; Psalm 78:32; Isaiah 1:4; 64:5 (v. 4, English); Daniel 9:8; etc. Also note some sample noun forms: Genesis 18:20; Leviticus 26:21; Numbers 16:26; 27:3; Deuteronomy 9:18; 24:16; 1 Samuel 2:17; 1 Kings 8:34; 15:3; Nehemiah 1:6; Psalms 25:7; 51:4, 5, 11 (vv. 2, 3, 9; English); Jeremiah 14:10; Lamentations 4:22; Daniel 9:20; Hosea 9:9; Micah 6:13; etc.

[203] Adam not only missed or failed in his disobedience, he also (especially because of the explicit divine command of Genesis 2:17) high-handedly rebelled against God.

[204] See Knierim's references to "'errors'" and "'misdeeds'" (*TLOT*, 1:408–411, *passim*).

[205] BDB, 1073.

[206] Cf., e.g. Psalms 95:10 (note this wandering is centered in the "heart" [לְבָב/*lēbāb*]); 119:110; Proverbs 14:22; 21:16; Isaiah 29:24 (note the center of ethical erring is in the "spirit," i.e. the "mind" [רוּחַ/*rûaḥ*]); 32:6 (a noun form); Ezekiel 14:11; 44:10, 15; 48:11; etc.

The wicked are estranged from the womb; These who speak lies go astray (תָּעוּ [tāʿû]) from birth (Psalm 58:3, NASB).

We all, like sheep, have gone astray (תָּעִינוּ [tāʿînû]), each of us has turned to his own way; and the LORD has laid on him the iniquity of us all (Isaiah 53:6, NIV).[207]

Such sinful wanderings are often exposed as deliberate or high-handed, but this is not always the case.[208] Two related word groups in Hebrew perpetuate the basic wandering imagery of the תעה (tʿh) family; however, they usually occur in contexts wherein the sin is serious but not intentional.[209] Nevertheless,

a sin of error does not signify diminished guilt or culpability but only a preferential offer of atonement. The act of atonement is lesser or greater in accord with the status of the wrong doer....The danger of unknown but no less fully responsible error demonstrates that people are totally dependent on God's disclosure (Psalm 19:13; 119:66f.), guidance (119:10) and judgment or forgiveness (Psalm 119:21, 118). Openness to the disclosure of error thus becomes an important concern of biblical anthropology. According to Ecclesiastes 5:5 one who excuses oneself by referring to an "error" incurs God's wrath.[210]

Man is totally accountable before an absolutely holy God for all wanderings.

---

[207] Martens well notes of Isaiah 53:6, "The prophet captures the human dilemma of a bent toward waywardness that spells disorientation and lostness. The metaphor is significant as a way of illuminating sin and how destitute humanity is without salvation" (NIDOTTE, 4:319–320).

[208] "The straying may be listless wandering from the known and the true or it may be deliberate departure from the good for something other, such as idols" (ibid., 319). For a good example of the former scenario, cf. Psalm 119:176 in its mega-context.

[209] The Hebrew roots שגג (šgg) and שגה (šgh) are most often employed to signal so-called sins of inadvertence. For helpful treatments of these two word groups, see: Hamilton, TWOT, 2:903–905; and Hill, NIDOTTE, 4:42–44.

[210] Knierim, TLOT, 3:1303–1304.

## The Verb סוּר *(sûr)*

This word depicts a certain kind of wandering, a veering off course. Its basic meaning is "to turn aside," usually implying a departure from the way:[211]

> For the most part *swr* has to do with the moral/spiritual direction someone is taking. Persons turn from the right road. ...To turn from the way God commanded is to invite a curse (Deuteronomy 11:28) and worse (Jeremiah 17:13).[212]

On such moral detours which beg for divine judgment compare especially Jeremiah 17:5: "Thus says Yahweh, 'Cursed is the man who trusts in mankind, and makes flesh his arm, but, from Yahweh, his heart *turns aside*'" (i.e. יָסוּר [*yāsûr*]). Also notice this verb's role in the sweeping indictments regarding the *deviations* that characterize depravity in Psalm 14:1–3.[213] Verse 3 reads: "The whole (lot of them) in solidarity has (morally) *turned aside* (סָר [*sār*][214]); they have turned sour (i.e. they have become morally putrefied); there is not one who does good; there is not even one." This primary focus on deviation, [215] especially when explicitly complemented by the preposition מִן (*min*, i.e. "from"), looks upon sin as apostasy.[216]

## The Verb עָבַר *('ābar)*

This word also has non-moral movements standing behind its hamartiological employments. In spatial settings it frequently means to "pass over, through, by," etc.[217] For example, it is used for the crossing of a river,[218] the passing through a region or country, the traversing

---

[211] BBD, 693. On literal, i.e. non-moral, turnings aside, cf., e.g., Exodus 3:3; Judges 18:3; 19:15; Jeremiah 15:5; etc. For an excellent moral application, see Deuteronomy 9:12b.

[212] Thompson and Martens, *NIDOTTE*, 3:238–239.

[213] Note Paul's application to the *whole* race in Romans 3:10ff.

[214] It is interesting that the parallel statement of Psalm 53:4 (v. 3, English) most likely reads סָג (*sāg*) instead of סָר (*sār*). Nevertheless, the root סוג (*swg*) perfectly echoes its cousin סור (*swr*). For a good survey of סוג (*swg*) including its hamartiological significance, see Wakely's article in *NIDOTTE*, 3:229–233. The occurrence of וְנָסוֹג (*wᵉnāsōg*) in Isaiah 59:13 is particularly telling in reference to sin as departure and desertion.

[215] Cf. Schwertner, *TLOT*, 2:796–797.

[216] From the perspective of human responsibility, this calls for a reverse 'apostasy' (cf., e.g., Job 28:28; Psalm 34:15 [v. 14, English]; 37:27; Proverbs 3:7; 16:6, 17; etc.).

[217] BDB, 716.

[218] Cf. even the feminine noun (i.e. עֲבָרָה [*ᵃbārâ*]) from this root which means "ford."

within a land, etc.[219] From these literal situations several metaphorical extensions easily developed.[220]

The most important one of these for our purposes is the moral usage of עָבַר (*'ābar*). Concerning this term's "'movement'" from the literal domain into the ethical-metaphorical one (pun intended!), Girdlestone well captures the basic hamartiological significance of its occurrences in ethical contexts when he argues that עָבַר (*'ābar*) refers to the "crossing over the boundary of right and entering the forbidden land of wrong."[221] The boundary marker, if you will, God's line drawn in the sand, is almost always His covenant with its stipulations.[222] Sin in this sense is therefore portrayed as "overstepping" or "contravening" the LORD's law.[223] Deuteronomy 17:2–7 is exemplary. In this casuistic scenario, the protasis of vv. 2–4 speaks of a man or a woman who *transgresses* (i.e. v. 2) God's covenant. In this case the specific transgression involves idolatry (v. 3); therefore, if there proves to be documented evidence for such a transgression (vv. 4, 6–7), the person must be stoned to death (cf. the apodosis of v. 5). Another good example dramatizing the exceedingly serious nature of stepping across the line of God's Word is found in the historical episode about Achan. עָבַר (*'ābar*) is used to characterize his sin in Joshua 7:15.[224] Among many other occurrences of this verb which portray high-handed sin, especially note the presence of עָבַר (*'ābar*) in Numbers 14:41; Joshua 23:16; 1 Samuel 15:24; Isaiah 24:5; and Daniel 9:11. Permit me to add just one more text as a theological punctuation mark for this discussion of עָבַר (*'ābar*): "But they, like Adam, transgressed (i.e. עָבְרוּ [*'ābŕû*]) the covenant[225]; there they dealt treacherously against Me" (Hosea 6:7).

# The Root פָּשַׁע *(pŝ')*

Words deriving from this root most often depict spiritual rebellion in the Old Testament. Consider its noun forms (meaning "rebellion, re-

---

[219] For a survey, cf. Harman, *NIDOTTE*, 3:314.

[220] For a survey, cf. Van Groningen, *TWOT*, 2:641–642.

[221] Robert Baker Girdlestone, *Synonyms of the Old Testament*, reprinted (Grand Rapids: Eerdmans, 1973), 79.

[222] Cf. Harman, *NIDOTTE*, 3:315.

[223] KB, 2:779. Cf., e.g., the force of παραβαίνω (*parabainō*) in the New Testament; furthermore, this is the Greek term of choice for עָבַר (*'ābar*) in the LXX.

[224] Furthermore, because of solidarity, the nation was also said to have "transgressed" God's "covenant" in v. 11.

[225] Remember Genesis 2:17 and the fall of Adam as recorded in chapter 3.

volt, transgression"[226]) as found, for example in Leviticus 16:16, 21 (notice the Day of Atonement context); Joshua 24:19; Job 31:33 (notice, once again, Adam is used as a bad example); Psalms 32:1, 5; 36:2 (v. 1, English); 51:3, 5 (vv. 1, 3; English); 89:33 (v. 32, English); 103:12; Proverbs 12:13; 28:13; Isaiah 53:5, 8; Lamentations 1:14; etc. Verbs and verbals show up, for example, in Isaiah 1:2, 28; 53:12; Jeremiah 2:29; 3:13; Ezekiel 2:3b; 20:38; Hosea 7:13; Zephaniah 3:11; etc. Furthermore, noun *and* verb forms are found in tandem in 1 Kings 8:50 and Ezekiel 18:31.

In many of the passages cited above along with the other occurrences of this root in the Old Testament, פשע (*pš'*) is frequently found in parallelism with other hamartiological terms. Sometimes it further specifies חטא (*ḥṭ'*) by adding the concept of rebellion to failure, but more often it links up with similar terms which convey man's sin as moral mutiny. Two significantly analogous roots are מרד (*mrd*)[227] and its close cousin מרה (*mrh*).[228] Listen to the condemning testimony found in two key verses.

> He said, "Son of Man, I am sending you to the Israelites, to a rebellious [הַמּוֹרְדִים (*hammôrᵉdîm*) from מרד (*mrd*)] nation that has rebelled against me [מָרְדוּ־בִי (*marᵉdû-bî*) also from מרד (*mrd*)]; they and their fathers have been in revolt [פָּשְׁעוּ (*pāšᵉ'û*) from פשע (*pš'*)] against me to this very day" (Ezekiel 2:3; the Hebrew was added to the NIV rendering).

> We (emphatic) have rebelled [פָּשַׁעְנוּ (*pāša'nû*) from פשע (*pš'*)] and revolted [וּמָרִינוּ (*ûmārînû*) from מרה (*mrh*)]; You [also emphatic for an even stronger contrast] have not pardoned (Lamentations 3:42).

From just this brief survey, it is obvious that "*pešaʿ* is a theological term because the deeds it describes affect Yahweh or his sovereignty and consequently require his judgment and forgiveness."[229] Such rebellious deeds are often defined as breaches of the stipulations of the Mosaic covenant.[230]

---

[226] Livingston, *TWOT*, 2:741.

[227] For מרד in parallelism with other terms for high-handed sin, cf. it as the fourth member of five hamartiological descriptives in Daniel 9:5; also cf. its stand alone occurrence in Daniel 9:9.

[228] Cf. this root as the term of choice for ethical anarchy in Isaiah 1:20. Sometimes מרה (*mrh*), which expresses observable rebellion, is yoked with an occurrence of the root סרר (*srr*) which also speaks of rebellion and/or the stubborn attitude standing behind it (cf. Psalm 78:8). For סרר (*srr*) apart from מרה (*mrh*), cf. Isaiah 30:1; Jeremiah 6:28.

[229] Knierim, *TLOT*, 2:1036.

[230] Cf., e.g., Carpenter and Grisanti's discussion in *NIDOTTE*, 3:707.

# The Root מעל (m'l)

The harmartiological common denominator of words built upon this root is spiritual infidelity.[231] On the horizontal plane of relationships,[232] "the combination of the verb with the noun occurs in Numbers 5:12, 27, where it refers to a woman's infidelity in the marriage relationship."[233] This kind of picture then extends vertically (i.e. heavenward) with many scriptural indictments of an individual's or the nation's unfaithfulness to God.[234] At this juncture, Knierim asserts about מעל (m'l), "Thus it is by nature an explicitly theological term."[235] He then goes on to note, "Characteristic is the formula m'l (ma'al) byhwh 'to commit unfaithfulness against Yahweh' (Leviticus 5:21 [6:2, English]; 26:40; Numbers 5:6; Deuteronomy 32:51; 1 Chronicles 10:13; 2 Chronicles 12:2; 26:16; 28:19, 22; 30:7; cf. Joshua 22:16; Ezra 10:2; Nehemiah 13:27; 1 Chronicles 5:25)."[236] Of course, the standards for identifying and exposing acts of infidelity against the LORD once again are His covenant stipulations.[237]

A very close relative of the מעל (m'l) family is the בגד (bgd) word group. Like מעל (m'l), the verb בָּגַד (bāgad):

> is used to denote unfaithfulness in several different relationships. It is used in connection with unfaithfulness in marriage. The object of this faithlessness may be the wife (Exodus 21:8, a slave wife; Malachi 2:14, wife of one's youth), or the husband.[238]

The Malachi 2:14 passage is particularly germane since it shows that if one is dealing treacherously with the wife of his youth, he is also dealing treacherously, i.e. acting faithlessly or deceitfully with the LORD (vv. 10–11, 16). Especially condemning references concerning the history of

---

[231] KB, 2:613, gives "disloyalty" or "infidelity" for major meanings of the noun; for a quite complete list of similar nuances, see Wakely, *NIDOTTE*, 2:1020.

[232] Knierim convincingly argues that "*m'l* refers, then, to the legally definable relationship of trust that exists between two persons" (*TLOT*, 2:681).

[233] Wakely, *NIDOTTE*, 2:1020.

[234] Cf. ibid., 2:1020–1025.

[235] *TLOT*, 2:681.

[236] Ibid.

[237] Hamilton is quick to note that "in almost all the biblical references *mā'al* is used to designate the breaking or violation of religious law as a conscious act of treachery" (*TWOT*, 1:519–520).

[238] Goldberg, *TWOT*, 1:90; for other scenarios of human infidelity as conveyed by this word group, see Klopfenstein, *TLOT*, 1:198–199; and Wakely, *NIDOTTE*, 1:582–593, *passim*.

Israel's infidelity against Yahweh are found in Psalm 78:57 and Hosea 5:7; 6:7ff. Needless to say, the larger context of Hosea adds the graphic image of harlotry to the treachery conveyed by the root בגד (*bgd*).[239] Such a state of faithlessness and treachery most obviously warrants divine retribution (cf. Proverbs 2:22).[240]

## The Root עקב (*'qb*)

Moving from concrete acts of treachery to fallen humanity's natural tendency to treachery brings us to the עקב (*'qb*) word group. In Hebrew and several of its cognate languages various forms derived from this root develop, but all are somehow related to the noun meaning "heel."[241] Quite illustratively, the name "Jacob" comes from this root. From his birth when he came out of the womb second holding on to his twin brother's "heel" (Genesis 25:26), he historically demonstrated a drive "to supplant." Compare, for example, Esau's retrospective lament in Genesis 27:36: "Then he [i.e. Esau] said, 'Is he not rightly named Jacob [i.e. יַעֲקֹב (*ya'ăqōb*) from עקב (*'qb*)], for he supplanted me [i.e. וַיַּעְקְבֵנִי (*wayya'q'bēnî*), a verb form from עקב (*'qb*)] these two times? He took away my birthright, and behold, now he has taken away my blessing'" (Hebrew words added to the NASB translation). The key verb in this verse from עקב (*'qb*) could also be rendered "he has deceived me" (cf. NIV). The historical accounts not only confirm the *fact* that Jacob took Esau's place, but they also thoroughly document *how* he did it. Indeed, he was a dean of *deception*.

But Jacob does not stand alone as an unethical trickster. Consider also, for example, Jehu in 2 Kings 10. Listen to vv. 18–19:

> Then Jehu brought all the people together and said to them, "Ahab served Baal a little; Jehu will serve him much. Now

---

[239] Cf. also similar occurrences of the root בגד (*bgd*) in Jeremiah 3:7, 10; the basic metaphor being developed is one of marital infidelity (vv. 6ff). Isaiah 48:8 is even more concise: "You have not heard nor understood; even from of old your ear has not been open. Surely I knew that you would act very treacherously (בָּגוֹד תִּבְגּוֹד [*bāgôd tibgōd*], i.e. 'you would always be gross infidels') and be called a rebel (i.e. עַ פֹּשֵׁ [*pōšēa'*]) from the womb."

[240] And yet, as Wakely observes with amazement (i.e., the amazement of "amazing grace"), "Yet even in the face of Israel's unrelenting obstinacy and recalcitrance, God's forbearance persevered, his will remained intent on good, and his resolve to transform blind and deaf Israel into a fit instrument to fulfill his purpose continued steadfast" (*NIDOTTE*, 1:588).

[241] Cf. Luc, *NIDOTTE*, 3:506; for conjectures on how this basic idea of "heel" relates to various literal and metaphorical employments of the different forms of this word group in the Old Testament; cf. also, Payne, *TWOT*, 2:691–692.

summon all the prophets of Baal, all his ministers and all his priests. See that no one is missing, because I am going to hold a great sacrifice for Baal. Anyone who fails to come will no longer live." But Jehu was acting deceptively [בְּעָקְבָּה ($b^e$ '$oqb\bar{a}$), a noun form from עָקַב ('$qb$), literally translated "in deceitfulness" or "with deception"; cf. "in cunning," NASB] in order to destroy the ministers of Baal (the Hebrew phrase added to the NIV rendering of 2 Kings 10:18–19).

However, this tendency to treachery did not stop when Jacob and Jehu passed off the historical scene. Unfortunately, the whole of Adam's fallen race is characterized by a Jacob/Jehu "heart."

The adjective derived from this particular Hebrew root is scarce but exceedingly significant when it comes to synthesizing a biblical hamartiology. And this descriptive's appearance in Jeremiah 17:9 seems to say it all: "The heart[242] is more deceitful (עָקֹב [ '$\bar{a}q\bar{o}b$]; i.e. insidious, sly, devious, crafty, manipulative, cunning, etc.) than all,[243] and it is incurably sick.[244] Who can understand it?"[245] Laetsch commendably captures the hamartiological significance of this key verse when he comments:

> In point of deceitfulness, treachery, the human heart exceeds all things. …Just because of its inherent incurable treachery no man can fully fathom the depths of the depravity of man's heart. The Lord is not speaking here of particularly wicked degenerates. He describes the human heart, the life seat of every human being. And the diagnosis of the searcher of man's heart, the greatest Psychologist, is: Incurably wicked![246]

## The Root חמס *(hms)*

Quite frequently, words from the חמס (*hms*) word family emphasize an epidemic of wrong-doing (cf., e.g., the noun form, usually translated "violence," in such contexts as Genesis 6:11–13 [*anarchy* might be a

---

[242] I.e. that mission-control center wherein man thinks and plans.

[243] I.e. the heart of man is more deceptive than *anything and everything* imaginable.

[244] Humanity's spiritual heart disease, apart from a heart transplant by the Great Physician, is terminal.

[245] The obvious answer to this rhetorical question is no mere man. Only God can see into its murky depths (cf. v. 10).

[246] Theodore Laetsch, *Bible Commentary: Jeremiah* (St. Louis: Concordia, 1952), 163.

good paraphrase here]; Ezekiel 7:11; Habakkuk 1:3; etc.). Sometimes the word group is applied to specific covenant violations (cf. e.g., Jeremiah 22:3b; Ezekiel 22:26; etc.). As Stoebe notes, "*ḥāmās* characterizes the diminution of another's rights and living space as a violation of duty to the neighbor and encompasses the entire range of antisocial behavior (Amos 3:10) in opposition to justice and righteousness (Jeremiah 22:3; Ezekiel 45:9)."[247] Furthermore,

> crimes described by *hms/hamas* are directed ultimately against Yahweh and provoke his judgment, which is carried out without human intervention on the basis of his holiness and righteousness (Genesis 6:13; 49:7; Judges 9:24; Psalm 7:16 [17]; Jeremiah 51:35; Ezekiel 7:11; Amos 6:7; Obediah 10; Micah 6:13–15; Habakkuk 2:17). For this reason the victims of *hamas* in the Psalms are also sure that God will hear their passionate appeal for deliverance (Psalm 7:10–13 [11–14]; 55:16–19 [17–20]).[248]

Needless to say, חמס (*hms*) is not a hamartiological problem restricted to antiquity; our contemporary headlines reflect the fact that the world is still overflowing with it.[249]

# The Root רעע (*r‘‘*)

The most basic idea of this root is "to be bad."[250] As Livingston argues:

> The essential meaning of the root can be seen in its frequent juxtaposition with the root *ṭôb*. Thus Moses concluded, "See I set before you today life and what is good [*ṭôb*], death and what is evil/bad [*ra‘*] (cf. Micah 3:2). Frequently they occur in the merism that one distinguishes "good and evil/bad" (II Samuel 14:17; 19:35 [H 36]; I Kings 3:9; Isaiah 7:15; cf. here "tree of good and evil," Genesis 2:9, 17).[251]

---

[247] *TLOT*, 1:439; previously, he noted that "*ḥāmās*...violates an order established or guaranteed by God" (ibid., 437). Cf. also Swart and Van Dam, *NIDOTTE*, 2:178.

[248] *NIDOTTE*, 2:179.

[249] Harris aptly argues that חמס (*hms*) "is often a name for extreme wickedness" (*TWOT*, 1:297); notice the explicit parallelism in Ezekiel 7:11.

[250] Stoebe, *TLOT*, 3:1249.

[251] *TWOT*, 2:854.

Furthermore, and very importantly,

> The root can have either a passive or active connotation: "mis-
> fortune, calamity," and "wickedness" respectively. It can occur
> in profane contexts, "bad," "repulsive," and moral contexts,
> "evil" "wickedness."[252]

Almost always, what separates occurrences of the רעע (r$^{cc}$) word group
into those which are passive/non-moral[253] versus those which are active/
moral are the criteria of who is doing a given act labeled רַע (ra$^c$) and/or
who is evaluating a particular act as רַע (ra$^c$).[254]

Of course, our special interest lies in the hamartiological settings of
members from this family. And we are not short-changed regarding the
biblical data that fall into this ethical category. As Baker notes,

> Most commonly, the adjective [i.e. רַע (ra$^c$)] is applied to
> people and their activities in contexts that indicate moral
> turpitude....An individual such as Haman is vile (ra$^c$) because
> of his despicable plot to harm others (Esther 7:6; 9:25; cf. 1
> Samuel 30:22). The very heart of humankind is now evil
> (Jeremiah 3:17; 7:24), as are their inclinations (yēṣer; Genesis
> 8:21). Humanity's way of life is evil (Psalm 119:101; Proverbs
> 4:14) as are his methods, deeds, and practices (1 Kings 13:33;
> Nehemiah 9:35; Proverbs 8;13; Ecclesiastes 4:3; Isaiah 32:7;
> Jeremiah 18:11; Zechariah 1:4). Humankind in groups is also
> evil, whether as a community (Numbers 14:27), a nation
> (Jeremiah 8:3; 13:10; Ezekiel 7:24), or a generation (Deut-
> eronomy 1:35). As a result of humanity's wickedness and
> wicked nature, the good but holy and righteous God will send
> judgment, which, from the perspective of the one who is its
> object, is dreadful (ra$^c$) (Ezekiel 14:21; cf. Exodus 33:4;
> Deuteronomy 6:22).[255]

---

[252] Ibid.

[253] For some examples that fit into this basic box of usage, cf. Baker, *NIDOTTE*, 3:1154. Some of
the translations falling into this broad category would be "wild" (of an animal), "misery, sorrow,
adversity, trouble, distress, calamity," etc. (BDB, 947–949; Gridlestone, *Synonyms*, 80.)

[254] A good illustration here may be found in different applications of the phrase "in the eyes of," i.e.
"'in the estimation'" of a finite and fallen man, or as ethically evaluated by the holy and righteous
God. For discussions, see *NIDOTTE* 3:1155; and *TLOT*, 3:1250.

[255] *NIDOTTE*, 3:1155. Livingston adds: "Left to himself, an evil person has no chance of survival"
(*TWOT*, 2:855); he commendably follows up with the importance of repenting from רעע (r$^{cc}$), citing passages such as Psalm 37:27; Proverbs 3:7; Amos 5:14–15; etc.

So, mankind is pictured in the Old Testament as "evil" (i.e. רַע [ra ʿ]) to the core of his being.

## The Root רשע (rš ʿ)

Like the previous word group wherein רַע (ra ʿ; "evil") was often given definition standing antithetically with טוֹב (tôb; "good"), "the root rš ʿ appears in the Old Testament as the most important antonym of ṣdq"[256] (i.e. "wickedness" in contrast with "righteousness"). "The use of rš ʿ always includes the idea of wickedness, evil intent, and injustice against God or persons."[257] Furthermore, the noun form of this word group "is used in parallel with almost every Hebrew word for sin, evil, and iniquity."[258]

Members of this word family frequently show up in legal contexts thereby emphasizing criminality. "However, it is more than a legal term. It connotes the inner nature of the guilty person when evil has become a habitual feature of one's disposition and actions."[259] As Livingston puts it, "the inner lives of the wicked correspond to their actions. They are vicious, haughty, treacherous, vile, polluted, and unstable."[260]

## The Noun אָוֶן ('āwen)[261]

The wide-ranging meanings of this word are all negative in nature; for example, "disaster, (looming) disaster, sin, injustice, deception, false, idolatrous cult."[262] Yet, two basic trends are observable in the Old Testa-

---

[256] Van Leeuwen, TLOT, 3:1262; cf. this antithesis, e.g., in such key passages as Deuteronomy 25:1 (note the perversion in Proverbs 17:15); Psalms 1:5, 6; 37:28–29; 68:3, 4 (vv. 2, 3; English); especially throughout Proverbs; etc.

[257] Carpenter and Grisanti, NIDOTTE, 3:1201.

[258] Livingston, TWOT, 2:863; e.g., cf. Solomon's paradigm prayer of confession in 1 Kings 8:47.

[259] Carpenter and Grisanti, NIDOTTE, 3:1204. Vine provides a highly condensed character sketch of רָשָׁע (rāšā ʿ) people when he writes, "The 'wicked' does not seek God (Psalm 10:4); he challenges God (Psalm 10:13). In his way of life the 'wicked' loves violence (Psalm 11:5), oppresses the righteous (Psalm 17:9), does not repay his debts (Psalm 37:21), and lays a snare to trap the righteous (Psalm 119:110)" (EDOTW, 287).

[260] TWOT, 2:864.

[261] Knierim, argues that "the Hebrew noun 'āwen 'harm, disaster' usually derived from a root 'wn 'to be strong, powerful'..., seems to have cognates only in NW Semitic....The chief meaning of the term largely reflects its etymology: destructive power" (TLOT, 1:60, 61). Carpenter and Grisanti add, "Consequently, 'āwen could highlight a negative aspect of power, i.e., the abuse of power that brings harm and destruction" (NIDOTTE, 1:310).

[262] KB, 1:22.

ment, "a stress on trouble which moves on to wickedness, and an emphasis on emptiness which moves on to idolatry."[263] In either case, the end of the line is hamartiologically relevant.[264]

Consider the following excerpts from Carpenter and Grisanti:

> *'āwen* can signify wicked conduct in the realms of worship (Isaiah 1:13; Zechariah 10:2), politics (Isaiah 31:2), legal relationships (10:1; 29:20), or warfare (Psalm 56:7 [8]). . . . The parallel or contextual proximity of *'āwen* with several other words for sin demonstrates its moral perversity: *ḥāmās* (violence, Isaiah 59:6; Habakkuk 1:3,...), *'awel* (iniquity, Job 11:14; Proverbs 22:8 ..., ...), *rāʻ* (wickedness, Psalm 28:3; 36:3 [4]; 94:23; 141:4; Proverbs 6:18; 12:21; Isaiah 31:2; 59:7; Jeremiah 4:14; Ezekiel 11:2; Micah 2:1, ...), *rāʻâ* (wicked, Psalm 64:2 [3]; 94:16; Proverbs 17:4; Isaiah 31:2, ...), and *rāšāʻ* (wicked, Psalm 28:3; 53:3 [4]; 92:7 [8]; 101:8; Proverbs 11:7; 12:21; 19:28; Isaiah 55:7, ...).[265]

The high-handed, heinous nature of sin as אָוֶן (*'āwen*) is especially illustrated by the prophets' use of the term.[266] For example, it is used as a scathing substitute for Bethel (i.e. "Bethel," בֵּיתְאֵל [*bêt'ēl*], 'House of God', was renamed, by the dark nature of the things that took place in association with this place, בֵּית אָוֶן [*bêt 'āwen*], house of iniquity).[267] It is no wonder why Livingston closes his treatment of אָוֶן (*'āwen*) with these words of amazement and admonition:

> Generally, biblical theologians have given little attention to *'āwen* as a contributor to an understanding of sin. Since the word stresses the planning and expression of deception and points to the painful aftermath of sin, it should be noted more.[268]

---

[263] Livingston, *TWOT*, 1:23.

[264] Kniermin puts it this way, "...every type of *'āwen*-act or *'āwen*-sphere is implicitly or explicitly ungodly" (*TLOT*, 1:62).

[265] *NIDOTTE*, 1:310.

[266] For a brief survey, see Bernhardt, *TDOT*, 1:143–144.

[267] Cf., e.g., Hosea 4:15; 5:8; 10:5.

[268] *TWOT*, 1:23–24.

# The Root עול (ʿwl)

All kinds of wrong-doing are encompassed by the occurrences of this word family in the Old Testament.[269] Concerning its prevalent noun forms,[270] "the basic meaning of the term is usually rendered 'injustice, unrighteousness, perversity, crime.'"[271] These noun forms sometimes occur with a verb of *doing* or performing (e.g., "those who commit injustice"; "those who practice perversity"; etc.).[272] As might be expected with meanings such as "injustice" and "unrighteousness," these nouns are often situated in legal settings.[273] And furthermore, as it also might be expected, the Law of God is the norm or standard by which such deeds of injustice are exposed and measured.[274]

Occurrences from this word group often stand in parallelisms with a host of other high-handed hamartiological terms.[275] Furthermore, parallel-passage parallelisms between near synonyms provide a vivid illustration of the nasty nature of עָוֶל (ʿāwel): "The complete contrast to anything godly is shown by 'wickedness' being an action of an atheist in Psalm 53:1 [2], one who denies God's very existence. In the parallel Psalm 14:1 ʿāwel is replaced by ʿᵃlîlâ, describing ruthless and wanton behavior."[276]

# The Root עוה (ʿwh)

The force of this root is evidenced by its verbal thrusts:

> The basic meaning of the verb, "to bend, twist, distort," can be seen in its concrete, non-theological uses:...(Psalm 38:7 [v. 6, English]) ...(Isaiah 24:1). From this primary notion it de-

---

[269] Later Semitic texts in Hebrew and cognate languages indicate that the primary idea standing behind the root is "to deviate" (cf., e.g., Knierim, *TLOT*, 2:849).

[270] Denominative verbs in the Old Testament occur only in Psalm 71:4 and Isaiah 26:10.

[271] Ibid., 850.

[272] Cf., e.g., Livingston, *TWOT*, 2:653.

[273] Cf., Knierim, *TLOT*, 2:849–850.

[274] Herein, Livingston affirms that "the basic meaning of this root means to deviate from a right standard, to act contrary to what is right" (*TWOT*, 2:652). He goes on to supplement his argument by showing that nouns from the עול (ʿwl) word group are found regularly in antithetical parallelisms with members of the צדק (ṣdq) family (ibid., 653). However, the ultimate antithesis *par excellence* is the character of God (ibid.; cf., e.g., Deuteronomy 32:4 [contrast Deuteronomy 25:16]; 2 Chronicles 19:7; Job 34:10; etc.).

[275] See a good summary paragraph by Baker in *NIDOTTE*, 3:342.

[276] Ibid., 343.

rives the sense "to distort, to make crooked, to pervert": ...
(Lamentations 3:9) ... (Job 33:27) ... (Proverbs 12:8). When
the distortion pertains to law, it means "to sin, to infract, to
commit a perversion/iniquity."[277]

Therefore, the high-frequency noun עָוֹן (*ʿāwôn*),[278] generally portrays sin
as being morally crooked or ethically perverted. Waltke notes that "the
derivative noun *ʿāwōn* occurs with only the derived, abstract theological
notion of the root: 'infraction, crooked behavior, perversion, iniquity,
etc.'"[279] He also passes along this important observation:

> Moreover,...it [i.e. עָוֹן (*ʿāwôn*)] denotes both the deed and its
> consequences, the misdeed and its punishment. Both notions
> are present, but sometimes the focus is on the deed ("sin"),
> and at other times on the outcome of the misdeed ("punish-
> ment"), and sometimes on the situation between the deed and
> its consequence ("guilt")....The remarkable ambivalence be-
> tween the meanings "sin as an act" and "penalty" shows that
> in the thought of the Old Testament sin and its penalty are
> not radically separate notions as we tend to think of them.
> Rather in the Old Testament the action of man and what hap-
> pens to him are presupposed to be directly related as one pro-
> cess within the basic divine order. This connection has been
> called a "synthetic view of life" (Von Rad, G., *Theology of the
> Old Testament I*, p. 205).[280]

As we have seen many times before, these hamartiological terms are
further defined by the (bad) company they keep. In the case of עָוֹן
(*ʿāwôn*), it stands besides both חטא (*ḥṭ'*) and פשע (*pšʿ*) thirteen times (cf.,
e.g., Leviticus 16:21–22). As terrible as these perversities, sins, and rebellions are, amazingly they do not stand beyond atonement as Leviticus
16 makes clear. Luc rejoices in this inexplicable reality of divine forgiveness when he says,

---

[277] Schultz, *TWOT*, 2:650; cf. also Vine, *EDOTW*, 231.

[278] Knierim (*TLOT*, 2:863) tabulates 231 occurrences.

[279] Waltke, editor's addition to *TWOT*, 2:650.

[280] Ibid., 650, 651. Waltke gives some sample references for each of these phases of the עָוֹן (*ʿāwôn*)
spectrum; however, remember how fluid these nuances are. We have already observed a similar,
though not identical, phenomenon in the case of both the חטא (*ḥṭ'*) and the אשם (*'šm*) word
groups. For more (probably too much) on this phenomenon as applied to עון (*ʿwn*), see Knierim,
*TLOT*, 2:862–866, *passim*.

...in Exodus 34:7, the phrase "wickedness, rebellion, and sin" is used in God's proclamation of his mercy to forgive. While this phrase is used to signify the totality of sins against God, it also directs our attention to the completeness of God's forgiveness for those who repent.[281]

There are other Hebrew terms and a variety of figurative expressions which also contribute to the very extensive hamartiology developed throughout the pages of the Old Testament Scriptures.[282]

Now just prior to pressing on to the New Testament terminology, a review of the data from the Old Testament would be helpful. Since clusters of hamartiological terms in certain passages seem to paint the darkest pictures of sin, it is suggested that APPENDIX E: "Some Selected Dirges on Sin in the Old Testament" be surveyed at this time.

## New Testament Terminology

### ἁμαρτάνω / ἁμαρτία  (hamartanō/hamartia)[283]

In background and usage this New Testament word group is quite similar to the חטא (ht‘) family in the Old Testament. For example, in early Greek ἁμαρτάνω (hamartanō) meant "not to hit," i.e. "to miss." However, in ancient Greek this word family did not have a predominately ethical focus.[284] The moral association would come into the New Testament through the channel of the LXX.[285] Furthermore, Günther notes that "following the prominent use of hamartanō and its cognates in the LXX, the New Testament uses them as a comprehensive expression of everything opposed to God."[286]

An analysis of the most commonly occurring noun form will give us good insight into the significance of this word group. Preliminarily, it needs to be understood that "hamartia is always used in the New Testa-

---

[281] NIDOTTE, 3:351.

[282] Most of these can be obtained by synthesizing the lists of related terms found at the ends of the articles from the various word books previously cited.

[283] Very obviously this word group provides the name for the division of theology dealing with sin, i.e. hamartiology.

[284] Stählin, TDNT, 1:293. At its worst in secular settings, the word group sometimes carried an intellectual sense of to "'be mistaken'" (Günther, NIDNTT, 3:575).

[285] E.g. Stählin observes that "only by its use for חטא in the LXX did ἁμαρτία itself become a distinctly religious term" (ibid.). Remember that this septuagintal phenomenon of impregnating a Greek term with theological meaning is wide-spread.

[286] NIDNTT, 3:579.

ment of man's sin which is ultimately directed against God."[287] There are, nonetheless, several *general* categories of usage. Vine suggests four; ἁμαρτία (*hamartia*):

> . . . is used of sin as (a) a principle or source of action, or an inward element producing acts, e.g., Romans 3:9; . . . 6:1,2; 7:7 . . . 7:8 (twice), 9, 11, 13, . . . (b) a governing principle or power, e.g., Romans 6:6 . . . 7:11, 14, 17, 20, 23, 25; . . . (c) a generic term (distinct from specific terms..., yet sometimes inclusive of concrete wrong doing . . . ); . . . Romans 8:3 . . . Hebrews 9:26; 10:6, 8, 18; 13:11; 1 John 1:7, 8; 3:4 . . . (d) a sinful deed, an act of sin, e.g. Matthew 12:31; Acts 7:60; . . . James 2:9. . . . "[288]

His first two categories (i.e. a & b) obviously are closely related, except that the second one lends itself to sin being considered as a *seemingly* independent power within the world. The fourth category is the most easily recognizable; however, concrete deeds of sin in the New Testament are not as significant as the overall concept of sin for the development of a biblical hamartiology. Concerning Vine's third category, it would seem that the two hamartiological terms mentioned in Romans 5:12–14 illustrate it best. Sin viewed generically (cf. ἁμαρτία [*hamartia*] and ἁμαρτάνω [*hamartanō*] in vv. 12 a, b, c; 13 a, b; and the first term of v. 14) takes on a tone of explicit infraction (cf. παράβασις [*parabasis*], the second term of v. 14) when the specific ordinances of God come into play.[289] Nevertheless, any and every category of usage of the ἁμαρτία (*hamartia*) word group is exceedingly important when it comes to developing a panoramic picture of sin in the New Testament.

## πλανάω/πλανή (*planaō/planē*)

Standing in the background of this hamartiologically significant word group is a long history of literal wanderings or strayings off course.[290] In the LXX, "*planaō* most frequently stands for *tā'āh*."[291] As a

---

[287] Ibid.
[288] *EDNTW*, 576–577.
[289] Cf. further discussion under παραβαίνω (*parabainō*)/παράβασις (*parabasis*) below. The principle of hamartiological advancement in the realm of specificity is analogous to the one previously cited in Job 34:37 (cf. and contrast חטא [*ḥṭ'*] with פשע [*pš'*]).
[290] For a survey of some of these, see Braun, *TDNT*, 6:229–230, 234.
[291] Günther, *NIDNTT*, 2:458.

matter of fact, πλανάω (*planaō*) so renders תָּעָה (*tāʿâ*) in Isaiah 53:6, that illustrative passage about the sheep nature of human sinners. Concerning this important imagery as it carries over into the New Testament, Günther has well noted that "the primary, spatial sense is seen most clearly where the picture of sheep is expressly introduced (Matthew 18:12ff.; 1 Peter 2:25), or in combination with *hodos*, way (2 Peter 2:15;...). It is never, however, spatial and nothing more: There is always a theological meaning associated with its use."[292]

Jude, using a word play on this group, adds yet another vivid picture. He warns about false teachers saying,

> Woe to them! They have taken the way [from ὁδός (*hodos*)] of Cain; they have rushed for profit into Balaam's error [i.e. from πλανή (*planē*)]; they have been destroyed in Korah's rebellion. These men are blemishes at your love feasts, eating with you without the slightest qualm—shepherds who feed only themselves. They are clouds without rain, blown along by the wind; autumn trees, without fruit and uprooted—twice dead. They are wild waves of the sea, foaming up their shame; wandering stars [ἀστέρες πλανῆται (*asteres planētai*)],[293] for whom blackest darkness has been reserved forever (Jude 11–13, NIV).

Throughout the New Testament, the verb is used both actively and passively in settings emphasizing the sin of wandering or straying. A good example illustrating both usages is found in 2 Timothy 3:13: "But evil men and impostors will proceed from bad to worse, deceiving [πλανῶντες (*planōntes*; active voice)] and being deceived [πλανώμενοι (*planōmenoi*; passive voice)]" (2 Timothy 3:13, NASB). And, as already intimated, the most common, feminine noun from this family moves from the literal background of "wandering" or "roaming" to "*wandering* from the path of truth," i.e. "error, delusion, deceit, deception."[294] Second Peter 3:17 is exemplary in that it warns the flock of God about "the error [πλάνη (*planē*)] of unprincipled men."[295] Needless to say, sin as πλανή (*planē*) is a highly culpable offense.

---

[292] Ibid., 459.

[293] Such *literal movement* in space (cf., e.g., the English word "planet" deriving from the πλανάω [*planaō*] word group) provides another illustration of what sinners, conceived as *ethical wanderers* are like.

[294] BAG, 671.

[295] Ibid.

# παραβαίνω / παράβασις (parabainō/parabasis)[296]

Vine immediately takes off from the etymological constituents of this word family: "Literally to go aside (para), hence to go beyond,...chiefly used metaphorically of 'transgressing'...."[297]

In secular Greek the word group was used when some law was broken by an individual, *stepping over the line* drawn by that law.[298] The idea of 'stepping over' also stands behind later usages in the papyri.[299] More importantly, in the LXX this family is often employed to indicate the violations of God's Law. For example, "man becomes guilty in respect of God's commandments and ordinances, Exodus 32:8:...cf. also Deuteronomy 9:12, 16."[300]

Similarly, as we move into the New Testament, the noun:

> denotes "sin in its relation to law, i.e., to a requirement or obligation which is legally valid or has legal force." Paul in Romans 2:23 alleges that the Jew dishonors God by transgressing the Law. In Romans 4:15 he declares that there is transgression only where there is law.[301]

Romans 4:15 is illuminated more fully by a passage which comes after it in the next chapter of Romans.[302] Vine's survey of παράβασις (parabasis) shows how important the context of the fifth chapter of Romans really is for a proper understanding of this word family in the New Testament; this noun is:

> primarily "a going aside," then "an overstepping"... used metaphorically to denote transgression (always a breach of law): (a)

---

[296] This word group is the first of three, the different stems of which have the same prefixed preposition, i.e. παρά (para). This preposition exhibits two basic "root meanings": 1) "beside, near"; 2) "violation, transgression, neglect" (Bruce M. Metzger, *Lexical Aids for Students of New Testament Greek* [Princeton: Theological Book Agency, 1971], 84). These basic colorings will help us to grasp the hamartiological impact of the following terms.

[297] *EDNTW*, 639; cf. Schneider: intransitively, "'to go by or beside'"; transitively in a transferred sense, "'to overstep,' 'to transgress,' 'to offend,' strictly 'to pass by someone without noticing'" (*TDNT*, 5:736).

[298] Schneider, *TDNT*, 5:736.

[299] Ibid., 737.

[300] Ibid.

[301] Ibid., 739–740.

[302] I.e. a passage previously mentioned under my treatment of the ἁμαρτάνω (hamartanō) word group.

of Adam, Romans 5:14; (b) of Eve, 1 Timothy 2:14; (c) nega-
tively, where there is no law, since transgression implies the
violation of law, none having been enacted between Adam's
transgression and those under the Law, Romans 4:15; (d) of
transgressions of the Law, Galatians 3:19, where the statement
"it was added because of transgressions" is best understood
according to Romans 4:15; 5:13 and 5:20; the Law does not
make men sinners, but makes them transgressors; hence sin becomes "exceedingly sinful," Romans 7:7,13.[303]

Let James 2:9 also lend its voice to the basic force of sin further
specified as *transgression*: "Now if you show personal favoritism,[304] you
are committing sin, being convicted by the Law[305] as transgressors
(παραβάται [*parabatai*])." Consequently, this word group points to
high-handed breaches of God's will as it is revealed in His Word.[306]

## παράπτωμα *(paraptōma)*

The etymology of this compound noun also helps to crystallize its
main thrust. For example, Michaelis observes that the verb form of this
word group in early Greek "means 'to fall beside or aside.'"[307]

Usage wise, the noun form παράπτωμα (*paraptōma*) in the LXX often renders מַעַל (*ma'al*, "treachery"), פֶּשַׁע (*peša'*, "rebellion") and עָוֶל
(*'āwel*, "wrongdoing"),[308] all of which (as previously noted) indicate
highly accountable sins in the Old Testament.[309] This picture of culpability continues on into the New Testament. Bauder's survey is helpful:

> Apart from the Pauline writings, the noun is only found in the
> New Testament in Matthew 6:14f. par. Luke 11:25f. As in the
> Old Testament, it is used as one of several words for sin, but
> emphasizes strongly the deliberate act (only in Romans 5:20 is

---

303 *EDNTW*, 640.

304 Or, "show partiality"; literally, "if you face-take."

305 James likely had some application of Leviticus 19:18 in mind; he had just quoted it in v. 8.

306 A very low frequency word group that parallels the basic thrust of the παραβαίνω (*parabainō*)
family in the New Testament is παρανομέω/παρανομία (*paranomeō/paranomia*). Its basic thrust is
*overstepping the law*. One verb and one noun occurrence appear respectively in Acts 23:3 ("violate,"
NIV) and 2 Peter 2:16 ("transgression," NASB).

307 *TDNT*, 6:170.

308 Ibid.

309 Cf. Bauder, *NIDNTT*, 3:585–586.

it used of a universal fact) with its fateful consequences. Hence, figuratively it means an action through which man falls and loses the position that God gave him. Thus trespasses committed by one man against another directly affect man's relation to God and in the final judgment provide the standard by which he is judged (Matthew 6:14f. par. Luke 11:25f.).[310]

I feel compelled to stress how parallel παράβασις (*parabasis*) and παράπτωμα (*paraptōma*) are in Romans 5:12ff.[311] The flagrant sin (i.e. ἁμαρτία [*hamartia*]/ἁμαρτάνω [*hamartanō*]; cf. Romans 5:12, 13, 14, 16, 20) of Adam, the father of our fallen race, is further exposed as both παράβασις (*parabasis*) in verse 14 and παράπτωμα (*paraptōma*) in verses 15, 16, 17, 18, and 20.[312] No wonder the whole lot of humanity is described as "being dead in reference to our transgressions and sins" (τοῖς παραπτώμασιν καὶ ταῖς ἁμαρτίαις ὑμῶν [*tois paraptōmasin kai tais hamartiais humōn*]) (Ephesians 2:1).[313]

## παρακούω / παρακοή  (*parakouō/parakoē*)

This word family also develops in relation to the general force of its constituent parts, i.e. a "bad hearing."[314] Kittel asserts that this basic impression involves an "unwillingness to hear...therefore in the guilty sense of disobedience."[315] Conceptually, the force and fruition of this Greek word group echoes the Old Testament idiom of "not listening to," i.e. "not obeying" the LORD.[316] In view of all these things, "*parakoē* expresses above all a refusal to listen, turning a deaf ear."[317] Based upon its occurrence in Romans 5:19, Spicq dubs παρακοή (*parakoē*) "the original human transgression, punishable by death."[318]

---

[310] Ibid., 586.

[311] I.e. a passage of great theological significance for anthropology and hamartiology.

[312] παρακοή (*parakoē*), our next word to be considered, also enters the picture in v. 19.

[313] At one point in his argument, Michaelis affirms that παράτωμα (*paraptōma*) "refers directly to the disruption of man's relation to God through his fault" (*TDNT*, 6:172).

[314] Kittel, *TDNT*, 1:223.

[315] Ibid.

[316] I.e. קוֹל + בְּ / לְ + שָׁמַע + לֹא (*lō' + šāmaʿ + lᵉ / bᵉ + qōl*); lit., "not listening to the voice of" the LORD.

[317] Spicq, *TLNT*, 3:29.

[318] Ibid., 28. Such heinous disobedience is even brought into sharper contrast in the presence of the "obedience" of Christ, the 'Second' or 'Last Adam' (cf. again Romans 5:19 in its context). Also, the semantic contrast between "disobedience" (παρακοή [*parakoē*]) and "obedience" (ὑπακοή [*hupakoē*]) is brought out in 2 Corinthians 10:6.

Erickson's conclusion about its hamartiological significance is on target: "Thus the sin of παρακοή is either the failure to listen and heed when God is speaking, or the disobedience which follows upon failure to hear aright."[319]

## ἀπειθέω/ἀπείθεια/ἀπειθής  *(apeitheō/apeitheia/apeithēs)*

This word group and the four to follow have alpha privatives affixed to their respective stems, meaning that the force of each stem's meaning is negated or reversed.[320] In connection with this phenomenon, Vine characterizes the force of the ἀπειθέω *(apeitheō)* group as "literally, the condition of being unpersuadable (*a*, negative, *peithō*, to persuade)," denoting "'obstinacy, obstinate rejection of the will of God'; hence 'disobedience.'"[321] Indeed, since classical times the verb has meant "to be disobedient."[322] Turning to biblical Greek, "in the LXX it is used for various Hebrew words, especially מרה and סרר. Here already it is a significant theological term inasmuch as it denotes the sinful attitude of the people, which in the Old Testament is essentially understood as disobedience against God."[323]

In the majority of this word group's occurrences in the New Testament, the contexts suggest "disobedience to God, mostly in contrast with faith."[324] For example,

> such ἀπειθεῖν can be asserted of either Jews[325] (Romans 11:31, 15:31; Acts 14:2;...19:9) or Gentiles, or without regard to the nationality of those concerned (1 Peter 2:...8; 3:1; 4:17; John 3:36...). In this sense ἀπειθεῖν can be used in the absolute (Romans 11:31; 15:31; Acts 14:2;...19:9; ...), or we have ἀπειθεῖν τῷ λόγῳ (1 Peter 2:8; 3:1), τῷ εὐαγγελίῳ (1 Peter 4:17), τῷ υἱῷ (John 3:36 ...).[326]

---

[319] *Christian Theology,* 2:567.
[320] E.g. "righteousness" becomes "*un*righteousness" when the alpha privative is prefixed to it.
[321] *EDNTW,* 173.
[322] Cf. Bultmann, *TDNT,* 6:10.
[323] Ibid.
[324] Becker, *NIDNTT,* 1:593. In this regard Bultmann aptly observes that "ἀπειθεῖν often stands in antithesis to πιστεύειν, Acts 14:1f.; 1 Peter 2:7f; John 3:36. It is also synonymous with ἀπιστία" (*TDNT,* 6:11).
[325] Herein also cf. the noun ἀπείθεια *(apeitheia)* in Romans 11:30, 32; Hebrews 4:6, 11.
[326] Bultmann, *TDNT,* 6:11; respectively, "disobedience" unqualified; then "disobedience" "to the Word," "to the Gospel," "to the Son."

A couple of comments on two different verses wherein members of this word family make their presence known will elucidate the high-handed nature of this hamartiological group. Turning first to the close parallelism between "disobedience" and "unbelief" in Hebrews 3:18, 19,[327] Hughes argues that

> the juxtaposition of unbelief and disobedience indicates the close connection between the two. As Wescott says, "unbelief passed into action." And this is always the case. It is what happened when man first fell from God; it was repeated in the wilderness; and the same disastrous sequence was now threatening the community to whom this letter was sent.[328]

Now concerning John 3:36, consider the hamartiological impact of Godet's credible comment on the substantive participle ὁ ἀπειθῶν (*ho apeithōn*), "he who disobeys brings out the voluntary side in unbelief, that of revolt."[329]

## ἀνομία / ἄνομος (*anomia/anomos*)

The alpha privative in the case of the ἀνομία (*anomia*) word group most basically carries the force of "against," i.e. "against the (a) law."[330] The noun occurs in the LXX, for example, in Exodus 34:7; Leviticus 16:21; 2 Samuel 14:9; Ezra 9:6, 7, 13; Job 7:21; Isaiah 1:5; Lamentations 4:6, 22; Ezekiel 3:19; etc.[331] The descriptive adjective crops up in 1 Kings 8:32; Proverbs 21:18; Isaiah 1:4, 28; Ezekiel 3:19; Daniel 12:10; etc.[332] By looking at the settings of these occurrences, its juxtapositions with other words for sin, and the variety of heavy-duty, hamartiological terms that it renders, we can discern that the emphasis of this word group in the

---

[327] I.e. between ἀπειθήσασιν (*apeithēsasin*) and ἀπιστίαν (*apistian*).

[328] Philip E. Hughes, *A Commentary on the Epistle of Hebrews* (Grand Rapids: Eerdmans, 1977), 154.

[329] Frederick L. Godet, *Commentary on the Gospel of John* (Grand Rapids: Zondervan, reprinted, n.d.), 1:413.

[330] Gutbrod, *TDNT*, 4:1085.

[331] "ἀνομία is common in the LXX, though there is no fixed Hebrew equivalent. It corresponds most frequently to עָוֹן (some 60 times), אָוֶן (some 25 times, especially in Psalms), פֶּשַׁע (some 20 times), תּוֹעֵבָה (some 25 times, especially in English).... It also corresponds to about 20 other Hebrew terms, but in most cases only once each" (Gutbrod, *TDNT*, 4:1085).

[332] "In the LXX ἄνομος is used some 30 times for רָשָׁע, but elsewhere it occurs for about 25 other Hebrew terms, in most cases only once each" (ibid).

Greek Old Testament is on exceedingly serious sin(s). This helps to inform its very condemning references in the Greek New Testament.

BAG breaks down the New Testament occurrences of the noun ἀνομία (*anomia*) into two broad categories of usage, "lawlessness...as a frame of mind" and as "a lawless deed."[333] Obviously, these general categories often overlap, especially as sin regularly manifests itself in observable actions. Even a casual reading of the verses in which the noun form is found will reveal its culpable nature (cf. Matthew 7:23; 13:41; 23:28; 24:21; Romans 4:7; 6:19; 2 Corinthians 6:14; 2 Thessalonians 2:7; Titus 2:14; Hebrews 1:9; 8:12; 10:17; 1 John 3:4). Vine, choosing a couple of key passages, characterizes the hamartiological impact of ἀνομία (*anomia*) in New Testament revelation:

> *anomia*..., "lawlessness"...is most frequently translated "iniquity;" in 2 Thessalonians 2:7, RV, "lawlessness" (KJV, "iniquity"); ...the display of "lawlessness" by the "lawless" one (v. 8)[334] will be the effect of the attempt by the powers of darkness to overthrow the divine government. In 1 John 3:4, the RV adheres to the real meaning of the word, "every one that doeth sin (a practice, not the committal of an act) doeth also lawlessness: and sin is lawlessness." This definition of sin sets forth its essential character as the rejection of the law, or will, of God and the substitution of the will of self.[335]

Sticking with Vine, he also selects a good paradigm passage to illustrate the main thrust of the adjective when it occurs in contexts controlled by the standard of "God's moral law":[336]

> *anomos*..., "without law," also denotes "lawless".... In 2 Peter 2:8 [it is used] of deeds (KJV, "unlawful'), where the thought is not simply that of doing what is unlawful, but of flagrant defiance of the known will of God.[337]

Consequently, this is yet another graphic word group that describes people and their sinful defiance.

---

[333] BAG, 71.

[334] Carefully note how the noun in v. 7 is followed up by the personal embodiment of supreme lawlessness in the satanic henchman identified in v. 8. This certainly helps us to understand how highly offensive to God sin viewed as ἀνομία (*anomia*) really is.

[335] *EDNTW*, 357.

[336] Cf. also, BAG, 71.

[337] *EDNTW*, 357.

# ἀδικέω/ἀδικία (adikeō/adikia)

Alpha privatives prefixed to words built upon the stem -δικ- (-dik-) "denote the opposite of the positive concepts" of righteousness, justice, etc.[338] In order to distinguish between "righteousness" and "unrighteousness" some sort of standard or norm must be present.[339] As Günther notes, "the definition of the content of the concept is usually dependent on the norm of justice that obtains at any particular time and to which it is related....But above all, the concept of *adikia* is rooted in legal thinking...."[340] Concerning this word group's forensic function, Spicq observes that "this latter meaning predominates in the LXX" and that "the New Testament knows only this meaning."[341] Now returning to the idea of what is righteous or unrighteous according to some custom or norm, the ultimate *Standard* in biblical Greek is the Person and/or precepts of God.

With this background in mind, Günther illuminatingly informs us about the use of the ἀδικέω (*adikeō*) word complex in the Greek Old Testament:

> The LXX uses these words to translate a variety of Hebrew equivalents; the Hebrew vocabulary is here far more complex and varied than the Greek. The most important are these: *adikeō* translates twenty-four Hebrew words; proportionately the most frequent (twelve times) is the qal of ʿāšaq, act unjustly, oppress, extort. ... By far the commonest of these words in the LXX is *adikia* (c. 250 times). It represents thirty-six different Hebrew words; most often it translates ʿāwôn, offense, guilt, punishment (c. eighty times), but occasionally also ʿawlâh, perversity, wickedness (e.g. Hosea 10:13), ḥāmās, violent act, injustice (e.g. Psalm 7:16 (17)), and šeqer, lie (e.g. Psalm 119:104).[342]

Such is a sampling of this word group's ethically lurid legacy which continues on into the New Testament.

---

[338] Günther, *NIDNTT*, 3:573; the common denominator of the root of this stem, i.e. δεικ [*deik*], in ancient Greek was "'to give direction,' 'to show,' 'to indicate,' 'to posit,' 'to establish.'... When applied specifically in the legal sphere, the word means 'what is laid down by law'" (Schrenk, *TDNT*, 2:180).

[339] Cf., Hill's discussion of the δικ (*dik*) word group (*GWHM*, 98ff); cf. also Seebass and Brown, *NIDNTT*, 3:352; etc.

[340] *NIDNTT*, 3:573–574.

[341] *TLNT*, 1:320.

[342] *NIDNTT*, 3:574.

Concerning the verb ἀδικέω (*adikeō*) in the New Testament, its two occurrences in Revelation 22:11 are paradigmatic both by precedent[343] and by parallelism:[344] "Let the one who practices unrighteousness continue to do unrighteousness,[345] ... and [logically 'however' in such a setting of stark contrast,] let the righteous one continue to do righteousness...." In reference to the noun ἀδικία (*adikia*), Schrenk categorizes its main settings as follows:[346]

1. a. It is an antonym to δικαιοσύνη. ...In Romans 1:29 ἀδικία is put first in the list of offenses as "violation of the divine law and its norm"....It is in Romans 6:13 however — ὅπλα ἀδικίας/ ὅπλα δικαιοσύνης — that we reach the height of contrast to the solemn basic concept of the δικαιοσύνη θεοῦ. ...b. It is also opposite of ἀλήθεια....[347]

2. a. We find...the relationship to ἀσέβεια....In the thesis of Paul in Romans 1:18: ἀποκαλύπτεται γὰρ ὀργὴ θεοῦ ἐπὶ πᾶσαν ἀσέβειαν καὶ ἀδικίαν ἀνθρώπων, which stands at the head of two sections vv. 19–23... and vv. 24–32..., a distinction is made between them.... b. ἀδικία is also defined as "sin against God".....In 1 John 1:9 ἀδικία is expressly linked with ἁμαρτία as unrighteousness against God. A definition along these lines is given in 1 John 5:17: πᾶσα ἀδικία ἁμαρτία ἐστίν. Thus in 3:7ff. ποεῖν τὴν ἁμαρτίαν is the opposite of ποεῖν τὴν δικαιοσύνην.

3. The term is also used apocalyptically. . . . In 2 Thessalonians 2:10 mention is made of the ἀπάτη ἀδικίας in depiction of the operation of antichrist. . . . In 2 Peter 2:13 ἀδικούμενος μισθὸν ἀδικίας means being harmed by the reward "paid for unrighteousness." . . .

4. We find the Hebrew gen. of definition...in [Luke] 18:6 κριτὴς τῆς ἀδικίας = a judge who "perverts justice."

Just a cursory survey indeed reveals that this word group represents bold sinning. Consider, for example, how Günther characterized this

---

[343] Note the present tense, characterizing participle ἀδικῶν (*ho adikōn*).
[344] I.e. through a contrasting parallelism with positive counterparts. Cf. adjectives in antithetical parallelism in Matthew 5:45 and Acts 24:15.
[345] Vine labels this "the retributive and permanent effect of a persistent course of unrighteous-doing" (*EDNTW*, 653).
[346] Excerpted from *TDNT*, 1:155–157.
[347] Cf. e.g. 1 Corinthians 13:6; 2 Thessalonians 2:12; etc.

word family as he brings it alongside of the most generic hamartiological group: "In comparison with *hamartia, adikia* describes more forcibly the outwardly visible characteristics of that which stands under the power of sin."[348]

## ἀσεβέω/ἀσέβεια/ἀσεβής  (*asebeō/asebeia/asebēs*)

"Derivatives of the stem σεβ⁻ are used commonly in Greek and are a typical expression of Greek piety."[349] So when the negating alpha privative is glued on, for example, to the noun, its basic meaning becomes "*im*piety."[350] In the LXX the verb ἀσεβέω (*asebeō*) renders primarily רָשַׁע (*rāša'*) and פָּשַׁע (*pāša'*) which, as we have already observed, indicate flagrant oppositions to the LORD and/or His Law. Concerning this word group's noun form in the Greek Old Testament, Foerster credibly stresses the fact that

> ἀσέβεια is not a subjective disposition but an objective fact....The objective state of affairs which the group ἀσεβ- denotes in the LXX is the violation of the will of God, in whose territory it also occurs. Since the Law regulates all men's conduct, all bad deeds are ἀσέβειαι.[351]

Flipping over to the Greek New Testament, the verb ἀσεβέω (*asebeō*) "signifies (a) 'to be or live ungodly,' 2 Peter 2:6; (b) 'to commit ungodly deeds,' Jude 15."[352] The noun ἀσέβια (*asebeia*), "'impiety, ungodliness,' is used of (a) general impiety, Romans 1:18; 11:26; 2 Timothy 2:16; Titus 2:12; (b) 'ungodly' deeds, Jude 15 RV, 'works of ungodliness'; (c) of lusts or desires after evil things, Jude 18. It is the opposite of *eusebeia*, 'godliness.'"[353] Although possibly open to a modicum of semantic criticism, Vine's footnote is basically credible and generally helpful: "*Anomia* is disregard for, or defiance of, God's laws;

---

[348] *NIDNTT*, 2:575.

[349] Foerster, *TDNT*, 7:168; importantly, however, he notes that "the LXX...is very restrained in its use of it" (ibid.). It is illuminating to compare σεβάζομαι (*sebazomai* [Romans 1:25]), σέβομαι (*sebomai*), and σέβασμα (*sebasma*) in the New Testament; of a total of thirteen occurrences approximately one-half of them indicate some kind of improper worship.

[350] Here Forerster observes that "the LXX is not so restrained in relation to ἀσεβής, ἀσέβεια, and ἀσεβέω ..." (Ibid., 169).

[351] Ibid., 188.

[352] Vine, *EDNTT*, 651.

[353] Ibid.

*asebeia* is the same attitude towards God's person." The descriptive adjective ἀσεβής (*asebēs*) in the New Testament means "'impious, ungodly'..., 'without reverence for God,' not merely irreligious, but acting in contravention of God's demands, Romans 4:5; 5:6; 1 Timothy 1:9; 1 Peter 4:18; 2 Peter 2:5 (v. 6 in some manuscripts) 3:7; Jude 4, 15 (twice)."[354] No wonder, for example, 2 Peter and Jude describe "great sinners of all ages up to the end as transgressors, *ungodly*, and sinners."[355]

## ἄγνοια *(agnoia)*

Erickson summarizes the etymological significance of this noun in the following way: "One of the New Testament words stressing a cause of sin is ἄγνοια. A combination of a Greek verb meaning 'to know' (γινώσκω, from γνόω) and the alpha privative, it is related to the English word *agnostic*."[356] The history of this word family in secular Greek is generally quite benign,[357] but in the theological mega-setting of the LXX it often takes on various degrees of culpability. For example,

> In Daniel 9:15 it[358] is used beside *hamartanō*, to sin. Similarly *agnoēma* (in the New Testament only in Hebrews 9:7) is used not merely for error but also for an offense done in ignorance....In legal settings *agnoia* means ignorance of the law; *kat' agnoian* means unwittingly (e.g. Leviticus 5:18). The LXX used *agnoia* (mostly for Hebrew *'āšām*) concretely in the sense of *agnoēma*, also meaning (unintentional) guilt, offense, error, generally (e.g., Leviticus 5:18).[359]

The verb ἀγνοέω (*agnoeō*) in the New Testament exhibits the following basic nuances:[360]

---

[354] Ibid. Erickson (*Christian Theology* 2:565) over-corrects those who, like Vine, insist on retaining the more high-handed emphasis of this word group in the New Testament. Foerster's comments (*TDNT*, 7:190) on Romans 1:18; 4:5; 5:6, 8; etc. help to correct the leanings of correctors such as Erickson.

[355] *TDNT*, 7:191, emphasis added; cf. Foerster's full discussion (ibid., 190–191).

[356] *Christian Theology*, 2:565.

[357] Cf., e.g., Bultmann, *TDNT*, 1:115ff.

[358] I.e. the verb ἀγνοέω (*agnoeō*).

[359] Schütz, *NIDNTT*, 2:406.

[360] Ibid., 406–407.

a) Not to understand in the sense of not being able to grasp (Mark 9:32 and Luke 9:45, in each case of a passion prediction by Jesus).

b) Not to know, not be informed (e.g., 2 Peter 2:12...).[361]

c) An ignorance that leads astray....[362]

d) A failure to know in the sense of a disobedient closing of the mind to the revealing word of God (Acts 13:27; Romans 10:3). This is not simply a lack of knowledge, but "a false understanding, a false path in knowing and thinking" (O. Michel, *Der Brief an die Römer*, KEK 4, 1966, on Romans 10:3). Ignorance and disobedience are here used as parallels; ignorance is the guilty turning away from the revelation of God in Jesus Christ....

e) To be unknown....[363]

Furthermore, in reference to the adjective ἄγνωστος (*agnōstos*) in the phrase "to an *unknown* god" followed by the attention-arresting relative clause "what you worship *without knowing* it" (i.e. ἀγνοοῦντες [*agnoountes*])[364] in Acts 17:23, Bahnsen, after wandering down many illuminating exegetical and theological side roads, correctly asserts that "the unbeliever is fully responsible for his mental state, and this is a state of *culpable ignorance*. This explains why Paul issued a call for *repentance* to the Athenians (v. 30); their ignorant mindset was immoral."[365]

With this usage background based upon other members of the immediate family of ἄγνοια (*agnoia*),[366] the noun's use as a hamartiological term in the New Testament starts to take on some definition. Bultmann well speaks of "the guilty aspect of ἄγνοια."[367] The force

---

[361] Schütz includes Paul's famous "do you not know" challenges (e.g. Romans 6:3; 7:1) under this subheading; however, rightly he is quick to qualify such occurrences with the following words: "...a present knowledge is presupposed which implies a need to respond to the gospel. Almost all the passages cited above deal with a partial recognition of faith in Christ, as the object of *agnoeō*. It never means merely a lack of intellectual knowledge which can be removed by a neutral statement of facts" (ibid., 407).

[362] Schütz cites 1 Timothy 1:13 and Hebrews 5:2 as examples (ibid).

[363] Schütz cites 2 Corinthians 6:9 as an example (ibid).

[364] Rendering of BAG, 11; emphasis added.

[365] Greg L. Bahnsen, *Always Ready: Directions for Defending the Faith*, edited by Robert Booth (Atlanta: American Vision, 1996), 256.

[366] Note the New Testament occurrences of ἄγνοια (*agnoia*): Acts 3:17; 17:30; Ephesians 4:18; 1 Peter 1:14.

[367] *TDNT*, 1:118.

and function of this noun in its setting in Acts 3:17 are captured by Bruce when he comments:

> We may think that Peter's words were surprisingly lenient to people like Caiaphas and his fellow-members of the chief-priestly families, who were so determined to have Jesus put to death. But however that may be, here is a proclamation of divine generosity, offering a free pardon to all who took part in the death of Christ if only *they realize their error, confess their sin, and turn to God in repentance.*[368]

In the middle of v. 18 of Ephesians 4 Paul says of the Gentiles,[369] they stand "alienated from the life of God because of the ignorance which dwells in them."[370] Lincoln's comments on this Pauline portion provide for us a great service in reference to our "'ignorance'" of the hamartiological significance of ἄγνοια (*agnoia*):

> This ignorance does not provide an excuse for the broken relationship with God. In the tradition of Jewish apologetic of which it is a part..., Gentile ignorance is viewed as culpable, and elsewhere in Jewish thought ignorance is linked with sin....This is certainly also the perspective of the more extended and profound analysis of Romans 1:18–23, where knowledge of God becomes futility and folly and therefore, in effect, ignorance, because of a failure to honor God as God. Here in Ephesians, the Gentiles' responsibility for their own ignorance comes out more explicitly in the following characterizations, but is perhaps hinted at in the formulation "the ignorance that is in them." The ignorance cannot be blamed on other factors; it has its roots within them....[371]

---

[368] F. F. Bruce, *Commentary on the Book of Acts*, NICNT (Grand Rapids: Eerdmans, 1971), 90; italics added to show the culpability of all such "ignorance." Cf. a similar force and function of the noun but in a Gentile setting in Acts 17:30.

[369] Herein=non-Christians.

[370] Schnackenburg's dynamic rendering (Rudolph Schnackenburg, *Ephesians: A Commentary*, translated by H. Heron [Edinburgh: T&T Clark 1991], 194).

[371] Andrew T. Lincoln, *Ephesians*, WBC (Dallas: Word, 1990), 278.

Consequently, whether expressed in biblical Greek or by an old English proverb, "Ignorance is no excuse!"

## ὀφείλημα *(opheilēma)*

The non-moral background of the ὀφείλημα (*opheilēma*) word group is situated in the realm of business and finance.[372] The common semantical denominator of all members from this word family is "to owe someone something."[373] Foundationed upon this commercial imagery, in the context of Scripture these words often extend into the moral realm. Respectively of the verb and noun, Louw and Nida provide the following renderings and comments: "to commit a sin against someone and thus incur moral debt"; "the moral debt incurred as the result of sin—'offense, sin, transgression, guilt.'"[374] Surprisingly, "the Old Testament does not make use of the concept of legal debt in order to depict obligation to Yahweh."[375] However, "Later Judaism, which views the relation to God as a legal and business relation, often applies the metaphor of indebtedness to the ethical and religious relation between man and God."[376]

The synoptic parallels of Matthew 6:12 and Luke 11:4 illustrate the New Testament's depiction of *sin* as IOU along with man's fundamental need, namely, a divine pardoning of our debts.[377] As Tiedtke and Link put it, "The concept of debt (*opheilēma*) is linked by Jesus not with achievements or demands concerning payments of arrears, but with forgiveness."[378] Our "failure before God,"[379] our moral indebtedness, can only be paid off in full with the credit of Christ and His crosswork.

---

[372] Cf., e.g., *GELSD*, 1:582; MM, 468–469; etc.

[373] Hauck, *TDNT*, 5:559.

[374] *GELSD*, 1:774.

[375] Tiedtke and Link, *NIDNTT*, 2:667.

[376] Hauck, *TDNT*, 5:561. Nevertheless, the nature of Judaism's metaphorical extensions is quite different from most of the New Testament's teachings about sin as a debt owed (cf., e.g., Tiedtke and Link, *NIDNTT*, 2:667–668). Romans 4:4ff. addresses the difference very pointedly.

[377] Vine well notes that "sin as a debt...demands expiation" (*EDNTW*, 150).

[378] *NIDNTT*, 2:667; their example of "the parable of the unmerciful servant" (Matthew 18:23–35) is especially illustrative (ibid.).

[379] Guelich's common denominator for ὀφειλήματα (*opheilēmata*), whether rendered literally as "debts," or figuratively as "sins" or "trespasses" (Robert A. Guelich, *The Sermon on the Mount* [Waco: Word, 1982], 312).

## κακός /κακία  (kakos/kakia)[380]

Since the adjective κακός (*kakos*) and the feminine noun κακία (*kakia*) are such high-frequency terms not only throughout Greek literature but also in the New Testament, most of our attention will be devoted to their occurrences in morally malignant settings.[381] "*Kakos* is found from Homer on in a large variey of associations. It means bad in the sense of lacking something, always in contrast to *agathos*, good."[382]

In the LXX,[383] as might be expected, this word group's morality quotient rises. Conceptually,

> κακός is one of the LXX words which in the main correspond to a specific Hebrew stem, namely, רַע. In numerous cases it is used for synonymous or generally related terms. If it thus misses the particular nuances of the original, it brings out even more strongly the one-sidedness and impressiveness of the moral and religious judgment which Judaism pronounces on evil and wickedness.[384]

Especially significant are the morally freighted occurrences of this word group in Psalms, Proverbs, and the prophets.[385] These ethically pregnant portions of the Old Testament have much to say about *doing* or *not doing* that which is *bad* or *evil*.[386] At this juncture Achilles well notes that "the Old Testament very seldom speaks theoretically of evil. It

---

[380] This word group along with the one to follow generally look upon sin as being morally bad or evil. On the essential synonymity of these two word groups, see Achilles' introductory paragraph under "Evil, Bad, Wickedness" (*NIDNTT* 1:561). The synoptic parallelism of Matthew 15:19 and Mark 7:2 is especially telling.

[381] Notice, for example, how BAG sorts out these usage-settings: κακία (*kakia*) "1. in the moral sense... a. *depravity, wickedness, vice* generally opposed to virtue...b. a special kind of moral inferiority...*malice, ill-will, malignity*" "2. *trouble, misfortune*"; κακός, ή, όν (*kakos,- ē, - on*) "1. In the moral sense *bad, evil*"... "2. *evil, injurious, dangerous, pernicious...*" "3. Certain passages fall between 1 and 2; in them the harm is caused by evil intent, so that 1 and 2 are combined: *evil, harm, wrong*" (BAG, 397–399).

[382] Achilles, *NIDNTT*, 1:561.

[383] Statistically, "there are 371 instances of κακός in the LXX. In 227 cases it is a rendering of רַע (293 in the Masora) or רָעָה (346 in the Masora), for which κακία or more often πονηρός (266) is also used" (Grundmann, *TDNT*, 3:477).

[384] Ibid., 476; beware, however, of Grundmann's unacceptable assumptions when he throws around such statements as "Judaism pronounces."

[385] For a survey, cf. ibid., 476–479, *passim;* but again, read the data through your revelational prescription lenses, not through Grundmann's glasses.

[386] Achilles, *NIDNTT*, 1:562.

describes it concretely and concentrates on the case at hand."[387] A good way to illustrate this fact is by pointing to a couple of compounds from the κακός (*kakos*) word family, κακοποιός (*kakopoios*) and κακοῦργος (*kakourgos*). For example, "in Proverbs 2:15, the *kakourgos* is the 'doer of iniquity' (Hebrew *pō'ēl 'awen*) and is contrasted with the just person, who practices equity."[388]

Such septuagintal emphases prepare the hamartiological way for the impact of this word complex in the New Testament. Excerpts from Achilles' article aptly highlight the significance of κακός (*kakos*) and its semantical kin in the New Testament:

> *kakos* is used in the New Testament with the meaning evil, bad, destructive, damaging, unjust. It is found 50 times, 26 of these being in Paul (Romans 15 times, but only 7 times in the synoptics)....The noun *kakia* is often used synonymously with the neuter adjective *kakon* as evil, badness, wickedness, and denotes the source of the bahavior of a *kakos*, an evil person, or *kakopoios*, evil-doer (cf. Acts 8:22; Romans 1:29; 1 Corinthians 5:8)....The verb *kakoō* means to do evil, cause damage, handle badly or harm (1 Peter 3:13, and often in Acts), stir up, embitter (Acts 14:2, RSV poison); and *kakopoieō* behave badly, do wrong (1 Peter 3:17; 3 John 11), harm (cf. Mark 3:4 parallel)....*kakos* is used attributively and as a noun of persons (Matthew 21:41; 24:48; Philippians 3:2; Titus 1:12; Revelation 2:2) and attributively of things (Mark 7:21; Romans 13:3; 1 Corinthians 15:33; Colossians 3:5; Revelation 16:2). Otherwise it is always a neuter noun meaning evil or the evil in the sense of misfortune, wrong, suffering...or an evil act, a sin (cf. Matthew 27:23 parallel; Acts 23:9; 3 John 11), especially in Paul (cf. Romans 7:19, 21; 12:21; 13:4; 16:19).[389]

Just prior to pressing on to the πονηρός (*poneros*) word group which is a very close semantical sibling to the κακός (*kakos*) family,[390] a clarification needs to be brought in concerning the roots of the antithesis of

---

[387] Ibid.

[388] Spicq, *TLNT*, 2:241.

[389] *NIDNTT*, 1:563–564.

[390] As previously noted, the two word groups should be regarded as essentially synonymous, although "*kakos* is the wider term and often covers the meaning of *poneros*"... "*Kakos* has a wider meaning, *poneros* a stronger meaning. *Poneros* alone is used of Satan and might well be translated 'the malignant one'" (Vine, *EDNTW*, respectively, 211, 49).

"good" and "evil" as found in the Bible. The New Testament does not imbibe any kind of Zoroastrian dualism such as that which apparently made its way into the teachings at Qumran:

> Though numerous dualistic notes may be heard in the New Testament ..., one can never find a dualism in which evil has the same power as good. Equally the thought is rejected that the root of evil could lie in God; "for God is untouched [literally cannot be tempted] by evil" (James 1:13, NEB). Evil comes rather from a man's heart in the form of evil thoughts which find expression in acts (Mark 7:21f. par.; cf. Matthew 15:19 *poneros*)....[391]

## πονηρός/πονηρία (*poneros/poneria*)

As in the case of so many of these Greek word groups that contribute biblically to a huge arsenal of hamartiological terms, their background in classical Greek literature was normally quite benign.[392] However, when we examine their usages in the LXX these word groups indicate a high degree of moral culpability. This is transparently clear in the case presently at hand. As a matter of observation, "the use of πονηρός for רַע and derivates of רָעַע remains within the sphere of the Hebrew original."[393] This also pertains to the noun πονηρία (*poneria*) which renders רָעָה.[394] It is obviously the *ethical* sub-categories of these general semantical equivalencies that become exceedingly significant as background for the many moral occurrences of πονηρός (*poneros*) and πονηρία (*poneria*) in the New Testament. For example, "רַע or πονηρός is used generally of men in the sense of 'morally bad,' 'culpable.'"[395] More specifically,

> the inner part of man is evil, the will has turned aside from God....The organs at the disposal of the will and thoughts are also morally evil....[396] The ὁδός [397] is evil and culpable....[398]

---

[391] Achilles, *NIDNTT*, 1:563–564.
[392] For a sample survey of such hamartiologically anemic usages in secular Greek, cf., e.g. Harder, *TDNT*, 6:546–548.
[393] Ibid., 549.
[394] Ibid., 563.
[395] Ibid., 551; Harder lists Psalm 139:2; Isaiah 25:4; 31:2 as examples.
[396] Remember the synecdochical and instrumental emphases of Old Testament anthropology.
[397] I.e. man's "way" of life.
[398] Ibid., 551; consider some of Harder's documentations for these summaries of usage: Isaiah 3:9; Jeremiah 3:17; 11:19; 18:11; 23:10, 14; Ezekiel 11:2; 13:22; etc.

All of this constitutes a foundation for New Testament revelation. Rare are the occurrences of the adjective πονηρός (*ponēros*) "in the physical sense."[399] Concerning the noun πονηρία (*ponēria*) in the New Testament, it "occurs only in a moral sense, especially in a very generalized way, as in lists of vices, e.g. Romans 1:29."[400] Achilles' survey of the main moral usages of the adjective provides a helpful hamartiological synopsis of the whole word group; πονηρός (*ponēros*):

> is used ethically in the sense of being opposed to God. (a) Jesus used it as an adjective of men in general, whom he called evil (cf. Matthew 7:11 par.). God alone is good, in contrast to them (Mark 10:18). The Pharisees were evil in the sense of being hardened (Matthew 12:34), just as the Jews were the evil generation (Matthew 12:39; 16:4; Luke 11:29), who showed their character in their opposition to Jesus. So too anyone is evil who decides against Jesus (cf. 2 Thessalonians 3:2; 2 Timothy 3:13). Out of the evil treasure of his heart he brings forth evil (Matthew 12:35 par.)....Thoughts also can be evil (Matthew 15:19). In James 2:4 the *dialogismōn ponēron* means the evil reflections by which judges may be led astray....In Colossians 1:21 and 2 Timothy 4:18 it is used with *ergon* to denote human actions....[401]

It should be remembered that the substantive, masculine, singular usage of πονηρός (*ponēros*) often occurs as a designation for Satan, the archetype of moral malignancy. Indeed, this word group portrays the devil, his henchmen, and men as evil to the core.

By now it may seem like a broken record, but there are many other Greek terms and a variety of figurative expressions which also significantly contribute to a very extensive hamartiology in the New Testament. For a few samplings of the breadth and depth of the New Testament teachings on sin, it is suggested that APPENDIX F, "Some Selected Dirges on Sin in the New Testament," be perused at this time.

---

[399] BAG, 697; i.e., "in the sense of bad, harmful, unserviceable, useless" (Harder, *TDNT*, 6:554).
[400] *TDNT*, 6:565.
[401] *NIDNTT*, 1:565–566.

# CHAPTER 4

# BIBLICAL HAMARTIOLOGY: THE THEOLOGY OF IT

By taking the previous terminological data and supplementing it with more biblical input, the time has come to consider some important systematic theological issues. First, most generally and via review, anyone who has a defective hamartiology will necessarily also be errant in his soteriology. An exceedingly important point in my "Introduction to Biblical Hamartiology" was the fact that "the very nature of the cure for sin is grounded in the nature of the disease of sin."[402] And since sin is a spiritually *terminal* disease, i.e. apart from the merciful intervention of the Great Physician, we need to understand through biblical insight that the prognosis of man, in and of himself, is hopeless and helpless.

Furthermore, based on biblical anthropology and hamartiology, sin was not part of the "stuff" of human beings as originally created in the image and likeness of God. It indeed is a dark *reality*, but its origin and continuance may not be attributed to the physical dimension of our human existence. Sin's attributes and associations are metaphysical, not physical in nature. This truth especially surfaced when the relationship of "flesh" and "sin" in *biblical contexts* was examined. Again, by way of review, we concluded that "sin is not traced back to *sarx*, but has an independent position in the universe."[403] Gundry corroborates with this brief synopsis, "sin dwells within the flesh and the flesh weakly submits to it. On both counts the flesh as a physical entity with 'members' is distinguishable from sin."[404] This is so mainly because Paul, for example, "insists on the responsibility of the individual for his sin...."[405] People sin;

---

[402] John J. Davis, "Regeneration in the Old Testament," unpublished Th. M. thesis (Grace Theological Seminary, 1964), 76.

[403] Reicke, "Body and Soul in the New Testament," 203.

[404] Gundry, "*Sōma*," 40.

[405] Davies, *Paul and Rabbinic Judaism*, 34. For a brief survey of the differences between Rabbinic Judaism and Jesus or Paul in the New Testament, see: Günther, *NIDNTT*, 3:579–582.

*physical* bodies and *physical* "members" don't. From all of this we conclude with McDonald:

> The fact is that sin is not conceived of in the Bible as a spiritual bacillus hiding in the blood of the mother and received into the veins of the child. Sin is essentially moral and spiritual, not material and tangible. The Church has always set itself against all Manichaean ideas which regard sin as identifiable with the material substance of our being. Sin is not an essential part of the stuff of manhood; it is an intruder.[406]

Then how did sin enter human existence originally, and how is it that this "intruder" has persisted throughout the history of the race? These exceedingly difficult and hotly debated issues will occupy our thinking as we turn to the related topics of the fall of mankind and original sin.

## The Fall and Original Sin

### The Fall of Man

In order to explore the beginning of sin, we must turn back to the Book of Beginnings, i.e. Genesis. Furthermore, if we are going to mine out anthropological and hamartiological truths from it, we must do so with the presupposition that we indeed are handling *Truth*.[407] Therefore, as we dig into Genesis 2–3 our understanding is that we are dealing with God's truth and historical facts. Now proceeding with this biblically valid presupposition, a survey of the salient exegetical data from these two chapters will provide many stones for the building of a solid hamartiological footing and foundation.

Genesis 2 sets the background for the spiritual catastrophe chronicled in chapter 3. The historical setting of the fall was in a real garden lavishly landscaped by God Himself (Genesis 2:8ff.). The special test for the original couple was to obey a clearly articulated divine command:

> And the LORD God commanded the man, saying, "From any tree of the garden you may indeed eat, but from the tree of the knowledge of good and evil you shall not eat from it, be-

---

[406] H. D. McDonald, *Jesus—Human and Divine* (Grand Rapids: Zondervan, 1968), 38.

[407] Old-line liberalism would look upon Genesis, especially its early chapters, as containing no facts, i.e. no truth. Concerning Neo-orthodoxy's presuppositions, the regarding of chapters 2–3 as "'true myth,'" is hardly an advancement.

cause on the day that you eat from it you[408] will surely die" (Genesis 2:16–17).

This was the special test given by God to the man and the woman in the Garden of Eden.[409]

It is nearly universally agreed upon in the history of Christian interpretation that the tempter was Satan possessing the body of a serpent (cf., e.g., Genesis 3:1, 14; Romans 16:20; 2 Corinthians 11:3; Revelation 12:9; etc.). His attack focused on God's limitation; he deliberately avoided mentioning all the things that God had provided and permitted. By employing untruths (Genesis 3:4)[410] and "'half-truths'" (Genesis 3:5),[411] he sowed his seeds of doubt. These seeds sprouted in the soil of the heart of the first couple, and the fall of mankind took place in time, space, and history (Genesis 3:6–7).

Catastrophic results followed. The serpent was judged and condemned (Genesis 3:14; cf. Isaiah 65:25). Because of Eve's role in the fall, women experience the curse of labor pains (Genesis 3:16).[412] Concerning the man who had been appointed vice-regent over the planet, all of nature was divinely adjusted because of its now fallen head (Genesis 3:17–18; cf. Romans 8:19–22). In addition, our first parents were expelled from the garden (Genesis 3:23–24). However, the spiritual results of the fall were of the greatest magnitude—separation from God, the marring of the "image," the guilt of sin, etc.[413]

---

[408] Both the command and the outcome, should this divine mandate be broken, are emphatically crystal clear in the Hebrew text of Genesis 2:17. It is a moot point to try to argue, as some do, that Adam and Eve had no clue about the consequences of disobedience since they had had no empirical knowledge of death. The way the command and consequence were stated made them aware of the exceedingly serious nature of this divine communication.

[409] Systematic theologians usually refer to the state of Adam and Eve before the fall by such descriptions, e.g., as untested, unconfirmed creature holiness.

[410] The satanic serpent here in Genesis 3:4 took the words of God at the end of 2:17 and negated them with an emphatic לֹא (lō'), "not." Concerning the *serpentine* interpreters who agree with the devil by reasoning that Adam and Eve did not die instantaneously *physically*, may it be noted that the data of vv. 7ff. exhibit the clear symptoms of *spiritual* death (i.e. separation and alienation from God). Later the obituary column of Genesis 5 confirms the fact that physical death ultimately resulted.

[411] Indeed, Adam and Eve's eyes were opened so that they came to know both good *and evil* empirically. However, the price tag of that knowledge was astronomically high, namely, an overwhelmingly consuming guilt.

[412] Many interpreters look upon Genesis 3:16 as containing two curses; however, "contextual evidence...indicates that the woman's desire for the man and his rule over her are not the punishment but the conditions in which the woman will suffer punishment" (Irv Busenitz, "Woman's Desire for Man: Genesis 3:16 Reconsidered," *GTJ*, 7 [Fall 1986]: 203; cf. his whole article, 203–212).

[413] Yet in the midst of the darkness of Genesis 3 a candle glimmered, Genesis 3:15 (cf. Romans 16:20 and Galatians 3:16) the so-called *"protevangelium."*

So the first Adam flunked God's test.[414] As we will see shortly in reference to Adam's sin and our sin, there are crucial factors of continuity and discontinuity concerning the one and the many. Young in dealing with the tragedy of Genesis 3 draws our attention to an important factor of discontinuity:

> Adam went through a unique experience....When Adam sinned, he fell from an estate of being good into an estate of being evil. He was created by God as a creature of whom it could be said that he was "very good." From this estate in which he was created by God he fell into an estate of sin and misery and by his disobedience plunged all men into that same estate of sin and misery. That is not true of me. My sin has not plunged all men into an estate of sin and misery. Furthermore, by my sin I did not fall from an estate of being "very good" into an estate of evil. I and all men like me were born into that miserable estate of sin, and when we sinned we simply showed that we were in such an estate. By sinning Adam became a sinner; by sinning we do not become sinners, we are already sinners. Sin does not cause us to fall from the estate wherein we were created, for we were born into a fallen estate. With Adam, however, the case was quite different. His sin brought him into a fallen estate. By disobedience he fell; by disobedience we simply show that we are already fallen.[415]

This is a great time for a transition to the topic of original sin. Romans 5:12ff. will be our exegetical resource.

## Original Sin

Just prior to camping out for awhile in Romans 5, we must first keep in mind that the Bible connects man's actual sin to his sinful nature (cf., again, e.g. Psalm 51:7 [v. 5, English]; Matthew 7:16–18; Ephesians 2:1, 3; etc.). Concerning Psalm 51:7 (v. 5, English), consider the following exegetical excerpts from Dalglish:

---

[414] When we think about soteriology and its basis, we see how the "Last Adam" passed God's test with flying colors, even after having been tempted in a similar, but far more intense, fashion (cf., e.g., Genesis 3:4ff; 1 John 2:16; etc. with Matthew 4:1–11).

[415] E. J. Young, *Genesis 3* (London: Banner of Truth, 1966), 60–61.

The Psalmist frankly acknowledges his congenital sinfulness....
In Psalm li.7 the Psalmist is relating his sinfulness to the very
conception of life; he traces his development beyond his
birth...to the genesis of his being in his mother's womb—even
to the very hour of conception....He is certainly not concerned
here with the confession of his mother's sin. She is relevant only
as the agent whom initiated his life, the point where sinful humanity and the individual self of the penitent met, where the inheritance of the race became his vital endowment.[416]

Furthermore, our actual sin cannot be regarded as merely something
"acquired" or "learned." Simpson commenting on Ephesians 2:1–3,
eloquently makes this point when he argues:

As the history of humanity abundantly proves, *all* mankind
without exception turns aside to its own way. We are sinners *in
grain*; every mother's son learns to be naughty without book.
Nor will either impulse or example suffice to account for the
anomaly of wrongdoing co-extensive with an entire species of
moral agents, whilst our fellow-lodgers, the animal creation,
fulfill their instinctive ends without fail. To confine sin to outward acts is merely resorting to a hollow euphemism; for
whence these uniformly corrupt fruits save from a corrupt
tree? Deny original sin and the state of our world becomes
harder to construe than if you embrace the tenet. The evil
principle lurks beneath the surface, seated in the hidden
heart.[417]

Focusing on the impact of Ephesians 2:3c which contains the important
qualifier φύσει (*phusei*; i.e. "by nature"), Salmond credibly comments:[418]

The clause means, therefore, that in their pre-Christian life
those meant by the ἡμεῖς πάντες [419] were in the condition of
subjection to the Divine wrath; and that they were so not by
deed merely, nor by circumstance, nor by passing into it, but

---

[416] Edward R. Dalglish, *Psalm Fifty-one in the Light of Ancient Near Eastern Patternism* (Leien: E. J. Brill, 1962), 118, 121.
[417] Simpson, *Ephesians and Colossians, NICNT*, 49–50.
[418] "Ephesians," *EGT*, 3:286–287.
[419] I.e. "we all."

by nature. Their universal sin has been already affirmed. This universal sin is now described as sin by nature. Beyond this Paul does not go in the present passage. But the one is the explanation of the other. Universal sin implies a law of sinning, a sin that is of the nature; and this, again, is the explanation of the fact that all are under the Divine wrath. For the Divine wrath operates only where sin is. Here is the essential meaning of the doctrine of *original sin*.

Now, going one level deeper and one step farther back, the Bible also connects man's actual sin and his sinning nature to the first sin of Adam. This is where Romans 5:12–21 fills in some theological blanks. The Adam theology[420] of these verses moves hamartiologically from the one (i.e. Adam) to the many (i.e. the whole race), and soteriologically from the One (i.e. Christ) to "those who receive" (v. 17, i.e. believers). Each one (i.e. Adam and Christ) stands representatively as the head of a respective constituency; reciprocally each constituency (i.e. all humanity and believers[421]) stands in solidarity with its respective head.

Before we look at some of the salient data from these hamartiologically strategic verses, the passage must be set into its larger context. This portion of Paul's epistle[422] launches with a "therefore."[423] This connection plugs Romans 5:12ff back into the argument of the previous verses. But how far back? Specifically, to the death of Christ and the life God has provided by His death (Romans 5:6–11), but also generally to the blessings bestowed through Christ upon those justified by grace through faith in Him (Romans 5:1ff). But Romans 5:1–11 also begins with a "therefore"[424] linking it with Paul's previous argument. In that Romans 5:1 begins with the words "therefore having been justified by faith" NASB),[425] this phase of argument summarizes and builds upon the apostle's whole synopsis of justification by grace through faith (Romans 3:21–4:25). However, the backward connections of Romans 5:12–21 do not stop there in that when Paul introduced the grand theme of his letter in Romans 1:16ff, the Gospel of God's sovereign grace, he did not

---

[420] The great resurrection chapter of 1 Corinthians 15 also especially emphasizes the importance of Adam theology (cf. vv. 21–22, 45–47).

[421] Scripturally, "believers" are God's elect whom He draws to faith (cf., e.g., Acts 13:48b).

[422] Romans could well be regarded as a God-breathed tract on the Gospel of God's sovereign grace.

[423] I.e. Διὰ τοῦτο (*Dia touto*), literally "on account of this," "for this reason," etc., idiomatically conveying the sense of "therefore" in contexts such as this.

[424] In this case Paul's most frequently used "therefore," i.e. οὖν (*oun*).

[425] With the force of "since we have been justified through faith" (NIV) in view of what Paul says in vv. 1b ff.

immediately jump into his presentation of the Good News of "the righteousness of God being revealed from faith to faith" (Romans 1:17). He prepared the way for revealing how good that Good News really is by showing how bad the bad news of "the wrath of God" against all sinful humanity is (i.e. Romans 1:18–3:20). So Romans 5:12–21 with its respective emphases on sin and salvation picks up all these theological threads adding to them the terrible truth about the connection of the actual sins of the many (Romans 1:18–3:20, especially 3:9–20) to the original sin of the one, i.e. Adam, the head of the race. Between the one and the many there is some sort of solidarity in sin.

Rather than even attempting an exegetical analysis of the entire passage[426] I prefer to select some salient data which should provide sufficient insight for an accurate interpretation. Romans 5:12ff. is quite unique structurally. Immediately after the opening "therefore" we are confronted with a "just as" (i.e. ὥσπερ [hōsper]) clause. The interpretive challenge of this protasis of Romans 5:12a is where is the apodosis which completes the comparison? Is it found immediately in 5:12b? Not likely, since that clause begins with καὶ οὕτως (kai houtōs) rather than a οὕτως καὶ (houtōs kai).[427] Technically, a directly matching apodosis is not to be found in what follows. It is best, therefore, to regard Romans 5:12a as an example of anacolouthon. However, the basic substance of this protasis is repeated in vv. 15a and 18a along with corresponding apodoses.[428] So what is the significance of the syntax and structure of Romans 5:12–21? Milne provides a credible answer to this important question when he argues that the analogy between the first and the Last Adam, i.e. between Adam and Christ, is "begun in v. 12…explained in v.13f., delimited in v.15ff., and finally completed in v. 18f."[429] Paul's argument indeed turns on facets of this analogy.[430]

Now I would like to put the spotlight on three key prepositions which find themselves in the service of this analogy. The first is the preposition διά (dia; i.e. with the genitive case) meaning "by" or

---

[426] This passage has attracted more exegetical and theological attention than most others in the New Testament. Monographs, theses, dissertations, etc. on it abound. Most commentaries on Romans illustrate its importance. This passage has prompted a variety of theological positions, and many of these positions are naunced in different ways by different interpreters. However, very generally, the history of its interpretation has resulted in the formation of three basic camps: 1) the strictly realistic view (i.e. seminal headship); 2) the strictly representational view (i.e. "federal" headship); and 3) the mediate imputation view.

[427] On this point of grammar, cf. BAG, 908; ATR, Grammar, 438; etc.

[428] Cf. e.g., Moo's discussion (Romans 1–8, 330–331).

[429] "Genesis 3 in Romans," RTR, 39:13; cf. John Murray, The Imputation of Adam's Sin (Grand Rapids: Eerdmans, 1959), 8, 19–21, etc.

[430] Paul also points out factors of disanalogy (cf., e.g., vv. 15a, 16).

"through."[431] It emphasizes the channel or agency by which something has come about. In Romans 5:12ff. compare especially vv. 12a, 12b, 16a, 17a, 17b, 18a, 18b, 19a, 19b. The second preposition of special note is ἐκ (*ek*) meaning "out of," "from," etc.[432] It often emphasizes the *source* of something or some action (cf. Romans 5:16a, 16b). The third load-bearing preposition is εἰς (*eis*) meaning "toward," "to," "unto," "into," etc.[433] It is obviously direction oriented[434] and therefore is a suitable indicator of *results* (cf. especially Romans 5:16a, 16b, 18a, 18b). These little prepositions make a significant contribution to the main theological points of Paul's analogy. Newell in chart form summarizes these main points like this:[435]

## THE TWO MEN

$\left.\begin{array}{l} Adam \\ Christ \end{array}\right\}$ Verse 14

## THE TWO ACTS

*Adam*—one trespass: verses 12, 15, 17, 18, 19
*Christ*—one righteous act (on the cross): verse 18

## THE TWO RESULTS

*By Adam*—Condemnation, guilt, death: verses 15, 16, 18, 19
*By Christ*—Justification, life, kingship: verses 17, 18, 19

A couple more observations need to be added to this exegetical mixture before coming to a final conclusion theologically. First is the issue of the meaning and significance of the prepositional phrase that stands near the end of v. 12. Much ink has been spilt over this ἐφ' ᾧ (*eph hō*) clause.[436] But the position that makes the most sense with the least diffi-

---

[431] Cf. BAG, 179.
[432] Ibid., 233.
[433] Thayer, *Lexicon*, 183.
[434] Furthermore, "no one has ever questioned that *eis* can express metaphorical direction" (Murray, *NIDNTT*, 3:1186).
[435] William R. Newell, *Romans: Verse by Verse* (Chicago: Grace, 1945), 176.
[436] For a brief survey of the most frequently held views, see Cranfield, *Romans*, 1:274–279. See also, e.g. Wallace, *GGBB*, 342–343.

culties in this context treats this phrase idiomatically as a causal conjunction: "Death spread unto all men *because* all have sinned." Does that
mean that Romans 5:12ff. is really about actual sin rather than original
sin? Not really. It does mean, however, that Paul wants to make sure that
we do not forget about the culpability of all humans throughout history
due to their own sinfulness (i.e. Romans 1:18–3:20, especially 3:9–20).
So he sets this reminder about the sin of the many into a context which
now focuses on the original transgression of our racial head with whom
we find ourselves in solidarity hamartiologically. Obviously, there is a
seminal (i.e. a genetic or biological) connection of every human being
ever born to the original couple (cf., e.g., Genesis 3:20),[437] but that
physical connection is not the mechanism of the so-called "transmission
of the sin nature." Physical lineage is very important,[438] but it is certainly
not Paul's burden in Romans 5:12ff.

His burden, as already seen, is carried along by the two men and
their antithetical actions. The prepositions previously surveyed indicate
some sort of a forensic rather than a physical connection between the respective heads and their constituencies. This imputational connection is
very clear in the case of Christ and the elect who come to believe in Him
(note, esp. vv. 17b, 18b, 19b). Paul is obviously building upon the doctrine of justification which he has been emphasizing since 3:21ff. By parallelism and by analogy should we not expect the same mechanism of
connection between Adam, the original transgressor and the sinful race
(e.g., vv. 17a, 18a, 19)? Besides the weight of the parallelisms of vv.
15ff., the two appearances of the verb καθίστημι (*kathistēmi*) in v. 19
lend support. This verb is most frequently found in legal or forensic settings.[439] "'To constitute' someone something" captures its thrust in Romans 5:19. Consider Wibbing's dynamic rendering of v. 19 along with
his conclusion about its significance in this context:

> Adam's act of disobedience has binding results for all;
> they stand there (*katestathēsan*) as sinners. Through
> Christ's obedience they are to be reckoned (*katasta-
> thēsontai*) as righteous. In v. 19 this contrasted pair of

---

[437] Here we need to warm up the material that was put on the back burner from APPENDIX C,
"Tradcuianism or Creationism."

[438] Cf., e.g., John Murray, who rightly does not minimize the significance of Adam's seminal
headship nor of the race's actual sin (*The Imputation Of Adam's Sin*, [Grand Rapids: Eerdmans.
1959], 26).

[439] Cf., e.g., Oepke, *TDNT*, 3:445; MM, 313; etc.

facts is thus in each case described by *kathistēmi*. Paul
uses this verb to describe God's judgment on man....
Adam here is a representative of "man" used to illustrate the fact of man's being a "sinner" because of disobedience.[440]

Consequently, "Romans chapter 5...reveals the true starting point of
his[441] hamartiology."[442]

In review,

the context of Romans 5 over and over again relates our sin
and guilt to the act of *one man*.... In v. 12 the apostle makes
the point that *all* die because *all* have sinned. In the following
verses, vv. 13–19 (including both the parenthesis of vv. 13–17
and the apodosis of vv. 18–19), he makes the point that *all* die
because *one* sinned. Can the apostle be dealing with two different things? Hardly. The one fact may be expressed in the
terms of both plurality and singularity....There must be some
kind of solidarity.[443]

For those who would cry "foul" or "not fair" concerning the imputation of Adam's sin to the whole race, McClain's answer phrased in the
form of a question is a good one: "You may say you do not think it is right
that we should die for Adam's sin. But by the same token, is it right for
God to give you righteousness when you do not have any?"[444] If anyone
wants to accuse God of injustice, this is the only place he could do so. But
what believer, having experienced the mercy and grace of God in Christ,
would dare protest the death of the absolutely righteous One on behalf of
"the many" who by position and practice were unrighteous?

---

[440] *NIDNTT*, 1:472.
[441] I.e., Paul's.
[442] Milne, "Genesis 3 in Romans," 11.
[443] S. Lewis Johnson, Jr., "Romans 5:12—an Exercise in Exegesis and Theology," *New Dimensions in New Testament Study*, ed. by Longenecker and Tenney (Grand Rapids: Zondervan, 1974), 310, 313.
[444] Alva J. McClain, *Romans: The Gospel of God's Grace*, ed. by Herman Hoyt (Chicago: Moody, 1973), 137.

# Total Depravity and Total Inability

## Total Depravity

In order to document this doctrine fully, we would have to bring in the seemingly inexhaustible reservoir of evidences from virtually every page and paragraph of Scripture. Total depravity is indeed "total" in that the Bible, over and over again, depicts both the breadth and the depth of humanity's sin. Corporately, the whole race is depraved, and individually, all human faculties have been radically affected (i.e. depravity is total in that it deeply touches each person noetically, volitionally, and emotionally).

Concerning the breadth of total depravity, we could muster into service such passages as Genesis 6:5a; 1 Kings 8:46; Job 4:17; 14:4; 15:14–16; 25:4–6; Psalm 14:1–3; 53:1–3; 58:1–5 (vv. 2–6, Hebrew); 130:3; 143:2b; Proverbs 20:9; Ecclesiastes 7:20, 29; 9:3b; Isaiah 53:4–6; 64:6 (v. 5, Hebrew); Jeremiah 17:5–10; Matthew 12:34; Luke 11:13; John 3:19; Romans 1:18–32; 3:9–18; 5:6–10[445]; 6:17–28, 20; Galatians 3:22a; etc.[446] Turning to the depth of total depravity, a few of the passages that come to mind immediately are Genesis 6:5b; 8:21; Matthew 15:19–20; Ephesians 4:17–19; Colossians 1:21[447]; etc.

## Total Inability

The practical bottom line of the breadth and depth of human depravity is total inability. Steele and Thomas connect the theological dots with these words:

> Originally, Adam's will was free from the dominion of sin; he was under no natural compulsion to choose evil, but through his fall, he brought spiritual death upon himself and all his posterity. He thereby plunged himself and the entire race into spiritual ruin and lost for himself and his descendants the ability to make right choices in the spiritual realm. His descendants are still free to choose—every man makes choices

---

[445] I.e. the concessive or temporal parts of these verses describing our condition when God saved us.

[446] For exegetical-theological commentary, see my dissertation: "Exegetical and Theological Bases for a Consistently Presuppositional Approach to Apologetics" (Grace Theological Seminary, 1982), 15–32, 47–186.

[447] "Mankind has a perpetual mind-set of active hostility towards God and the things of God" (ibid., 122).

throughout life—but inasmuch as Adam's offspring are born with sinful natures, they do not have the ABILITY to choose spiritual good over evil. Consequently, man's will is no longer free (i.e., free from the dominion of sin) as Adam's will was free before the fall. Instead, man's will, as the result of inherited depravity, is in bondage to his sinful nature.[448]

Two passages, one from each testament, help to get a biblical handle on this terrorizing truth. Jeremiah 13:23 reads: "Can the Ethiopian change his skin or the leopard his spots? Neither can you do good who are accustomed to doing evil" (NIV). The punch-line of this verse is built upon two illustrations of an unwavering precedent from nature. The point that Jeremiah is making is well captured by Laetsch who comments:

This sin is not merely an acquired habit, which they might give up at any time they choose to do so. They can relinquish their sinful nature as little as the Ethiopian can rid himself of his skin or the leopard his spots. Ever since Adam's fall, all children of Adam are, like their father, sinful, every imagination of the thoughts of their hearts being only evil continually (Genesis 6:5; 8:21; Jeremiah 17:9; Romans 5:19; Ephesians 2:1–2). To make man willing to yield himself to God and his members as instruments of righteousness unto God is a miracle even greater than changing an Ethiopian's skin and a leopard's spots, a miracle possible only to the almighty grace of the Lord Jehovah (Jeremiah 31:18, 20, 31–34; 33:8).[449]

It is noteworthy that Jesus took Nicodemus down a similar road in John 3. The work of the Holy Spirit on the human spirit is absolutely necessary for new birth to take place, since "that which is born of the flesh is flesh, and that which is born of the Spirit is spirit" (John 3:6).[450]

---

[448] David N. Steele, and Curtis C. Thomas, *Romans: An Interpretive Outline* (Phillipsburg, NJ: Presbyterian and Reformed, 1963), 153.

[449] Theo Laetsch, *Bible Commentary: Jeremiah* (St. Louis: Concordia, 1952), 141–142.

[450] Kent comments, "Jesus made the assertion that spiritual birth requires the action of God's Spirit, on the principle that all forms of life reproduce after their kind. Natural life ("flesh") is capable of reproducing itself but nothing higher. Thus the Spirit of God must intervene if man is to be born again with spiritual life" (Homer A. Kent, Jr., *Light in the Darkness: Studies in the Gospel of John* [Winona Lake: BMH, 1974], 60.) Cf. also the testimony of John 1:13 in its context.

The contribution of 1 Corinthians 2:14 to the doctrine of total inability is patently transparent. The first half of this condemning verse reviews the unbeliever's resistance to spiritual things.[451] Paul writes, "But a natural (i.e. an unspiritual[452]) man[453] does not receive the things of the Spirit of God, because they are foolishness[454] to him" (1 Corinthians 2:14a). The key verb[455] in this clause which is preceded by an objective negation "has an air of welcoming about it, being the usual word for receiving a guest. Thus the point is that the natural man does not welcome the things of the Spirit; he refuses them, he rejects them."[456]

As we move on to the second part of the verse, "the words: *he cannot know them* are still stronger, since they do not merely refer to what the natural man attempts but what is objectively true about him; they refer to his condition."[457] The unregenerate person's total inability is succinctly confirmed by the words οὐ δύναται γνῶναι (*ou dunatai gnōnai*), "he is not able to comprehend"[458] the spiritual things that bring eternal life. Since spiritual truths must be "investigated in a spiritual manner,"[459] a natural or unspiritual person "lacks the equipment necessary to examine spiritual things....He is like a blind man in an art gallery, like a deaf man at a symphony."[460]

In view of all that the Word of God has to say about total depravity and total inability, man's only hope of deliverance is the sovereign grace of a merciful God. In and of himself, man is spiritually hopeless and helpless apart from divine intervention.[461] With this pitch dark reality in mind, we should be able to appreciate all the more the brilliant facets of God's great salvation about to be sketched out next in Part III.

---

[451] It is important to note the shift in person and number from earlier first person plurals to third person singulars. It makes these assertions about the unspiritual person aphoristic; as Grosheide puts it, "verses 14 and 15 give a general characterization" (F.W. Grosheide, *Commentary on the First Epistle to the Corinthians*, NICNT [Grand Rapids: Eerdmans, 1953], 73.)

[452] BAG, 902.

[453] Or, generically "person."

[454] I.e., μωρία (*mōria*); they are *moronic* or silly to him.

[455] I.e. δέχομαι (*dechomai*).

[456] Leon Morris, *The First Epistle of Paul to the Corinthians: An Introduction and Commentary*, TNTC (Grand Rapids: Eerdmans, 1958), 60.

[457] Grosheide, *First Corinthians*, 73.

[458] I.e. such an unspiritual person "'cannot even begin to know'" spiritual things (James L. Boyer, *For a World Like Ours: Studies in 1 Corinthians* [Winona Lake: BMH, 1971], 41).

[459] Orr and Walter's translation of the last causal clause of 1 Corinthians 2:14 (William F. Orr and James Arthur Walter, *1 Corinthians*, AB [Garden City, NY: Doubleday, 1976], 158).

[460] Boyer, *For a World Like Ours*, 41.

[461] On the humbling ramifications of biblical hamartiology for Christian ministry, see my *Doing God's Business God's Way*.

# PART III

# BIBLICAL SOTERIOLOGY

# AN INTRODUCTION TO BIBLICAL SOTERIOLOGY

## *Preliminary Terminological Studies*

The precedent of surveying terminology before synthesizing theology will be perpetuated as we launch out into the huge data bank of biblical soteriology. However, since the doctrine of soteriology is so multifaceted, this procedure may be applied only *generally* at the outset of the more extensive investigation which will follow. Here we will restrict ourselves to the most comprehensive terms pertaining to salvation.

### General Word Groups in the Old Testament

It is best logically to begin with the two primary semantical equivalents then to move on to some of the conceptual parallels. The two most general word groups denoting "salvation" and "to save" in Old Testament Hebrew are respectively ישׁע (*yšʿ*) and נצל (*nṣl*).

### The ישׁע (*yšʿ*) Group

Normally the etymology of this word family is viewed as indicating "'to be roomy, broad' as opposed to narrowness, restriction, etc." [462] Concerning actual usage, members of the ישׁע (*yšʿ*) family present a panoramic picture of salvation in the Old Testament. [463] "There is nothing in the word *yashaʿ* which indicates the mode or which limits the extent

---

[462] Fohrer, *TDNT*, 7:973; cf. BDB, 446: "give width and breadth to, liberate." Often in the Psalms the plight of the petitioning psalmist is pictured as being tightly confined by his "straits" (i.e. " his distresses"); therefore he cries out to God for deliverance, i.e. for salvation (cf., e.g., occurrences of members of the צרר [*ṣrr*] word complex in association with those of the ישׁע [*yšʿ*] family). For some appropriate commentary on this phenomenon, see: Hartley, *TWOT*, 1:414–415.

[463] Cf., e.g., Exodus 14:30; 1 Chronicles 16:35; Psalms 3:9 (v. 8; English); 20:7, 10 (vv. 6, 9; English); 79:9 [note the parallel terms]; 119:94; Isaiah 43:3, 11; Jeremiah 31:7; Hosea 1:7 [note especially the context]; Zecheriah 9:9, 16; etc. Cf. Hubbard, *NIDOTTE*, 2:556–562, for an adequate usage survey. At the outset of his survey, he rightly stresses the fact that ישׁע (*yšʿ*) "is almost exclusively a theological term with Yahweh as its subject and his people as its object" (ibid., 556).

of salvation. It includes divinely bestowed deliverance from every class of spiritual and temporal evil to which mortal man is subjected." [464]

Before moving on to the next Old Testament word group, it will prove to be important for New Testament studies in the semantics of soteriology that we note how the LXX renders the יָשַׁע (*yš‘*) word group. Over 60% of these renderings of יָשַׁע (*yš‘*) in the Old Testament were conveyed in Greek by the σώζω (*sōzo*) word complex.[465]

Appropriately corresponding verb forms of σώζειν (*sōzein*) are used to translate the 14 Niphal and 144 Hiphil occurrences of the verb יָשַׁע (*yāša‘*).[466] Concerning the nouns "savior" and "salvation," σωτήρ (*sōtēr*) and σωτήριον (*sōterion*) are respectively employed. No wonder as we move on into the New Testament the name "Jesus" carries with it so much soteriological significance. Rengstorf's comments are noteworthy:

> According to Matthew 1:21 and Luke 1:31, Jesus' name was determined by heavenly instruction.... Matthew in this context also gives an interpretation of the name Jesus. In passing, it describes the future task of Mary's son as to "save his people from their sins." This interpretation is certainly connected with the meaning of the name *Yᵉhôšua‘* (formed from the divine name and *šua‘*, from the root *yš‘*) which, as we have shown, has a continuing life in the Greek *Iēsous*: "Yahweh is our help" or "Yahweh" is our helper.[467]

So for early Hebrew Christians reading through the original Greek text of Matthew 1:21, when they got to the words Ἰησοῦν (*Iēsoun*), "Jesus," and σώσει (*sōsei*), "he shall save," the cognate combination of יְהוֹשֻׁעַ (*yᵉhôšua‘*) . . . יְהוֹשִׁיעַ (*yᵉhôšia‘*) was flashing in their minds like a neon sign.

---

[464] Girdlestone, *Synonyms*, 125. A trend however is clearly discernible. In the Old Testament, the percentage of temporal applications is much higher, while in the New Testament, spiritual applications predominate.

[465] Less frequently occurring renderings come from the βοηθεῖν (*boēthein*), the ῥύεσθαι (*rhuesthai*), and the λυτροῦν (*lutroun*) word groups.

[466] The compound form διασώζειν (*diasozein*) also occurs although certainly not as frequently.

[467] Rengstorf, *NIDNTT*, 2:332.

# The נצל (*nṣl*) Group

The etymology of this word group probably has to do with "snatching away or separating."[468] Consequently, the frequently occurring Hiphil verb means to "snatch away, deliver," i.e. to "deliver from: *enemies and troubles... from death... from sin and guilt.*"[469] It is obvious that נצל (*nṣl*) "indicates removal or liberation from all types of restrictions."[470] "Quite often, however, a literal personal salvation or deliverance (often physical but not without spiritual overtones or application) is involved."[471] Also, as might be expected, "Consistent with other usage with Yahweh as its subject, the verb hi.[472] portrays Yahweh as the deliverer par excellence."[473]

Now it is time to move on to some conceptual equivalents. These have been drawn out of a pool of other Hebrew roots and metaphors, all which shed light upon the basic idea of salvation in the Old Testament.

# The פלט / מלט (*plṭ/mlṭ*) Group[474]

"The root *plṭ*, to escape and to save, is widely attested in Semitic languages, especially its west Semitic branches."[475] Furthermore, these "West Semitic comparative materials suggest that *mlṭ* derives from *plṭ*, to save." [476] The former root manifests itself in key verb forms, and several nouns also derive from it.[477] Interestingly, no noun forms have developed from מלט (*mlṭ*).

---

[468] Fisher, *TWOT*, 2:594; cf. 2 Samuel 14:6 which speaks of no one having been available to snatch apart two fighting brothers.

[469] BDB, 664–665; for some sample occurrences, cf. Exodus 3:8; 18:9–10; 1 Samuel 17:37; 2 Kings 18:29ff.; Psalms 39:9 (v. 8; English); 71:2 [note the parallels ; Fisher wisely suggests that "a comparison of the distinctives of other Hebrew synonyms of the concepts 'deliver, save, preserve, escape' will better delineate the semantic range from our root" (*TWOT*, 2:594)]; Jeremiah 20:13; 39:17; etc.

[470] Bergmann, *TLOT*, 2:760.

[471] Fisher, *TWOT*, 2:594. Concerning a semantic bridge to Greek renderings of verb forms of נצל (*nṣl*), the LXX employs ῥύεσθαι (*rheusthai*) 83 times and ἐξαιρεῖν (*exairein*) 80 times. It is interesting that σώζειν (*sozein*) comes in a distant third being used only 16 times.

[472] I.e. Hiphil verb forms of נצל (*nṣl*).

[473] Hubbard, *NIDOTTE*, 3:145.

[474] These words have been grouped together because of their close synonymity largely due to the fact that two of their three consonants line up: פלט/מלט. Ruprecht therefore suggests, "*mlṭ pi./hi.* is so similar to *plṭ pi./hi.* in meaning and construction that a single treatment of the two verbs is justified" (*TLOT*, 2:986; note his treatment of them on pp. 986–990).

[475] Hubbard, *NIDOTTE*, 3:621.

[476] Hubbard, *NIDOTTE*, 2:950.

[477] E.g. פַּלֵּט (*pallēṭ*), "deliverance"; מִפְלָט (*miplāṭ*), "place of escape"; פָּלִיט (*palîṭ*), "escaped one, fugitive"; etc. (cf. BDB, 812; for some commentary on such nouns, cf. Fohrer, *TDNT*, 7:978–979).

"The verb *palaṭ* in the sense of 'rescue, deliver' is limited to poetry in the Old Testament. In the Psalter the verb is always on the lips of the Psalmist addressed to God either in the form of a testimony of praise for deliverance or, *palaṭ* is in the form of an imperative, seeking God's deliverance."[478] Concerning various verb forms built upon the root מלט (*mlṭ*), "the most common use of this word is to express the 'escaping' from any kind of danger, such as an enemy (Isaiah 20:6), a trap (2 Kings 10:24), or a temptress (Ecclesiastes 7:26)."[479] One of the most soteriologically significant occurrences of מלט (*mlṭ*) is found in Joel 3:5 (2:32; English): "Then it will come to pass that each one who calls upon the name of Yahweh will be delivered (יִמָּלֵט [*yimmālēṭ*]), for on Mt. Zion and in Jerusalem there will be an escaped remnant (note the noun פְּלֵיטָא [*pᵉlêṭā'*] from the root פלט [*plṭ*]) just as Yahweh has promised [literally, said], indeed from among the survivors whom Yahweh calls."[480] Speaking of such kinds of occurrences of מלט (*mlṭ*), Carr has appropriately noted:

> The usual emphasis is on the role of Yahweh in deliverance.... He is the protecting, delivering God. By contrast, escape is not found in the strength of a horse (Psalm 33:17), the might of another nation (Isaiah 21:6), riches (Job 20:20), or in one's own understanding.[481]

## The פדה / גאל (*pdh/g'l*) Group

These are the major roots which develop the concept of redemption in the Old Testament. The parallelism found in Psalm 69:19 (v. 18; English) illustrates their essential synonymity: "Draw near to my soul [i.e. to me]; redeem it (גְאָלָהּ [*gᵉ'ālāh*] from the root גאל [*g'l*]); because of my enemies, ransom me" (פְּדֵנִי [*pᵉdēnî*] from the root פדה [*pdh*]).

Although these two roots exhibit much semantical overlap, the different images underlying their respective backgrounds beautifully nuance them. On the one hand, גאל (*g'l*), to "*redeem*, with God as sub-

---

[478] Hamilton, *TWOT*, 2:725; cf., e.g., Psalms 17:13; 18:44 (v. 43; English); 31:2 (v. 1; English); 37:40; 43:1; 71:2, 4; 82:4; etc.

[479] Vine, *EDOTW*, 71.

[480] The soteriological importance of this promise is magnified by Paul's employment of these words in Romans 10:13.

[481] *TWOT*, 1:507.

ject" is based upon the imagery of the kinsman-redeemer.[482] On the other hand, פדה (*pdh*), to ransom is built upon the imagery of the emancipation of slaves from bondage by the payment of a price.[483] Harris notes of גאל (*g'l*) in comparison and contrast with פדה (*pdh*) that "the primary meaning of this root [i.e. of גאל (*g'l*)] is to do the part of a kinsman and thus to redeem his kin from difficulty or danger.... One difference between this root and the very similar root *pādâ* 'redeem,' is that there is usually an emphasis in *gā'al* on the redemption being the privilege or duty of a near relative."[484] Similarly, Girdlestone argues:

> The word which specifically indicates redemption is *Gaal* (גאל), best known in the form *Goel*, redeemer.... In most of the passages...redemption may be considered as synonymous with deliverance, but always with the idea more or less developed that the Redeemer enters into a certain relationship with the redeemed—allies Himself in some sense with them, and so claims the right of redemption.... A parallel to *gaal*, namely, *padah* (פדה; Assyrian *padû*, "to spare")...rendered by the words deliver, redeem, ransom, and rescue...is used...of the first-born, who were regarded as representatives of those who had been spared when the first-born of Egypt were destroyed.... *Padah* is often adopted to represent the deliverance of a servant from slavery.... The word *padah* is not used in the peculiar technical senses which *gaal* expresses, but...it especially refers to the deliverance from *bondage*.[485]

As might be expected,

> the semantic development of *pādâ* is one of great significance to Christian theology. Originally, it had to do with the payment of a required sum for the transfer of ownership, a com-

---

[482] BDB, 145. Note some sample occurrences: Genesis 48:16; Exodus 6:6; 15:13; Ruth 2:20; 3:9, 12; 4:1ff. [these occurrences in Ruth depict the ancient near eastern imagery of the kinsman redeemer very nicely]; Job 19:25; Psalms 72:14; 103:4; 119:154 [note the parallels]; Isaiah 41:14; 43:1; 44:22–23; Hosea 13:14 [note the parallel here is with פדה]; etc.

[483] Cf., e.g., BDB, 804. For some sample occurrences, see: Exodus 13:15; Deuteronomy 7:8; 2 Samuel 7:23; 1 Kings 1:29; Job 33:28; Psalms 26:11; 31:6 (v. 5, English); 130:8; Micah 6:4; etc.

[484] *TWOT*, 1:144.

[485] *Synonyms*, 117–120; on the "peculiar technical" sense which גאל (*g'l*) sometimes displays, it should be noted that the LXX occasionally uses ἀγχιστεύω (*anchisteuō*), "to act the neighbor," to render it. However, most frequently, both גאל (*g'l*) and פדה (*pdh*) are translated by appropriately corresponding forms from the λυτρόω (*lutroō*) word group. Also, ῥύομαι (*rhuomai*) is used for both. Much more infrequently, σώζω (*sōzō*) shows up, but for פדה (*pdh*) only.

mercial term.... The word was given special religious significance by the Exodus.... Israel had been delivered, ransomed
from servitude in Egypt by the hand of God. This fact was to
color Hebrew thought through the centuries to come.... The
concept of redemption continued to broaden.[486]

# The Root חיה *(ḥyh)*

"All instances of the root may be grouped rather closely around the
concept 'life.'"[487] Verbs from this family fall into one of two general categories of usage: 1) the giving of life, i.e. "to make alive"; and 2) the
preservation of life, i.e. "to revive."[488] As Delitzsch stated it, "הֶחֱיָה and
חִיָה always signify either to keep that which is living alive, or to restore to
life that which is dead."[489] Instances having to do with the sustaining of
life (i.e. "revival") abound. Although it is more difficult to find
unambivalent examples pertaining to the granting of life, especially as
connoting the impartation of spiritual life, when some are identified,
they become quite significant.[490]

Psalm 119 provides us with much data for a good case study of the
root חיה (*ḥyh*). After looking at some selected occurrences of the חיה
(*ḥyh*) word group in this great wisdom poem, Brensinger concludes,
"According to Psalm 119, the Lord gives life, sustains life, renews life,
and gives life meaning."[491] The psalmist was obviously preoccupied with
the priority of "fullness of life in divine favor."[492] Listen to how Hill very
ably analyzes and synthesizes the nature and impact of חיה (*ḥyh*) in the
Old Testament:

> Man's life...is more than simply length of days and abundance
> of possessions.... We recall the utterance of Deuteronomy 8:3,
> "Man lives (יִחְיֶה) by everything which proceeds from the

---

[486] Coker, *TWOT*, 2:716. The movement of redemption terminology from secular settings into sa-
cred settings will also be observable when we consider corresponding Greek words.

[487] Gerleman, *TLOT*, 1:413.

[488] Cf., e.g., BDB, 311; Smick, *TWOT*, 1:279–282; etc.

[489] F. Delitzsch, *Isaiah, Commentary on the Old Testament in Ten Volumes* (Grand Rapids:
Eerdmans, 1969), 380.

[490] Cf., e.g., Psalm 119:93 in its context. This verse is well translated: "I will never forget your precepts, because You gave me life by means of them" (Zemek, *The Word of God in the Child of God*
[PO Box 428, Mango, FL 33550], 215); for commentary, see Ibid., 216, 224.

[491] *NIDOTTE*, 2:111.

[492] BDB, 311.

mouth of the Lord": in the promulgation of the law, Moses sets before Israel life (חַיִּים) and good, death and evil (Deuteronomy 30:15ff.); and Deuteronomy 30:20 "...loving the Lord your God, obeying his voice and cleaving to him, that is your life (חַיֶּיךָ) and the length of your days." . . . Only by faithfulness, that is, by loyalty to Yahweh and his covenant, will the righteous man live (Habakkuk 2:4). In these instances the verb חָיָה connotes not only physical survival in a time of disaster, but also living in right relation to God....

In conclusion we may reiterate what is perhaps the most significant aspect of the Hebrew understanding of "life," namely, its dependence on God.... Life here and now, life after death, are given and sustained by Him.[493]

So the LORD is pictured, not only in the New Testament, but also in the Old Testament as the Bestower of the "abundant life."

# A General Word-Group in the New Testament

Salvation as presented most generally in the New Testament is conveyed by members of the σῴζω (*sōzō*) word family. We always need to keep in mind its special Old Testament connection:

The Greek representative of *yasha'* in the New Testament is σῴζω. The doctrine of salvation in the New Testament derives its name from a word which was ingrained in the history and language of Israel from the period of the deliverance of the people out of Egypt up to the time of their restoration from captivity. The word *yasha'* (יָשַׁע), to save, which generally answers to the Greek σῴζω, has given a name not only to Joshua, but to Jesus, who should save His people from their sins.... The Messiah was to be the embodiment of the Divine help and salvation.[494]

We also need to keep in mind the respectively differing proportional emphases on temporal and spiritual salvation in the Old and New Testaments. In the New Testament the σῴζω (*sōzō*) word complex is "used of

---

[493] *GWHM*, 165, 168.

[494] Girdlestone, *Synonyms*, 125, 124.

both temporal and spiritual deliverance, though the latter sense strongly predominates."[495]

More fully, Spicq expresses it in the following way:

> The specifically religious meaning is dominant...first of all of deliverance from sins (Matthew 1:21; Luke 1:68, 69, 71, 77) and "the wrath to come" (Romans 5:9; cf. 1 Corinthians 3:15; 5:5; 1 Thessalonians 5:9).... It has to do with salvation of the soul (Mark 8:35; 1 Peter 1:9), which is already actual (...Romans 8:24...Titus 3:5) and continues to become effective (...1 Corinthians 1:18; 2 Corinthians 2:15), but will not be complete and definite until entrance into heaven: eternal life (1 Timothy 1:16; 6:12), which is still an object of hope (Romans 8:24; Titus 3:7; Hebrews 6:18; 1 Peter 1:3).[496]

Verb forms of this word complex are well attested throughout the pages of the New Testament.[497] The same is true of the noun σωτηρία (sōtēria) which means "deliverance, preservation, salvation," etc.[498] The adjective σωτήριος (sōtērios), "saving, delivering, preserving, bringing salvation,"[499] occurs five times. Four of these five occurrences are neuter substantives. In Luke 2:30 and 3:6 the substantive adjectives personify the salvation embodied in the incarnate Son. In Titus 2:11 it "describes the grace of God,"[500] also by virtually personifying it. Rounding off this word group is the noun σωτήρ (sōtēr).[501] It "occurs 24 times in the New Testament, and in 16 of these instances it is applied to Christ."[502]

---

[495] Ibid., 125.

[496] *TLNT*, 3:349–350

[497] "The vb. *sōzō* is found...106 times" (Schneider, *NIDNTT*, 3:211); cf., e.g., Matthew 1:21; Mark 8:35; John 3:17; 5:34; Acts 16:30–31; Romans 5:9–10; 10:9; 1 Corinthians 1:18, 21; 15:2; Ephesians 2:5, 8; 1 Thessalonians 2:16; 1 Timothy 1:15; 2:4; Titus 3:5; Hebrews 7:25; James 1:21; 2:14; 1 Peter 3:21; etc. The compound verb διασώζω (*diasōzō*) which occurs 8 times exhibits temporal applications (cf., e.g., Vine, *EDNTW*, 548).

[498] Vine, *EDNTW*, 545; cf., e.g., Luke 1:69, 71, 77; John 4:22; Acts 4:12; 13:26, 47; Romans 1:16; 10:10; 13:11; 2 Corinthians 6:2; Ephesians 1:13; Philippians 2:12; 1 Thessalonians 5:9; 2 Thessalonians 2:13; 2 Timothy 2:10; 3:15; Hebrews 2:3; 5:9; 9:28; 1 Peter 1:9–10; Jude 3; Revelation 7:10; etc.

[499] BAG, 809.

[500] Vine, *EDNTW*, 545.

In summary,

> *sōzō* and *sōtēria* gained a central importance through their application to Christ as the basis, content and goal of the gospel. They are used to sum up the essential characteristic of his mission.... In Acts 4:12 Peter declares to the assembled religious leaders that "there is salvation in no one else, for there is no other name under heaven given among men by which we must be saved.". . . The apostolic kerygma which was addressed first to the Jews (Acts 13:26) and then to the Gentiles (Acts 16:17 etc.) excludes every other way of salvation..., for salvation can be gained only by faith in Christ (Acts 16:31).... In him God is personally present in a saving way.[503]

## *Preliminary Theological Syntheses*

Although it may seem a bit incongruous to put forth some basic soteriological conclusions in an introduction, I would like to do just that prior to digging into more of the exegetical data of both testaments. Taking in a panoramic view of the whole theological forest will hopefully keep things in perspective as we move on to examine more carefully its trees, branches, twigs, and leaves. I have chosen to use Horne's wide-angle snapshots of salvation. His syntheses are based upon extensive soteriological investigations in both the Old and New Testaments.

---

[501] This noun in the context of secular Greek literature was applied with several different nuances to various human benefactors (cf., e.g., Foerster's survey: *TDNT*, 7:1004–1012); however, it obviously took on a religious sense in Biblical Greek.

[502] Schneider and Brown, *NIDNTT*, 3:219; cf., e.g., Luke 1:47; 2:11; John 4:42; Acts 5:31; 13:23; Ephesians 5:23; Philippians 3:20; 1 Timothy 1:1, 2:3; 4:10; 2 Timothy 1:10; Titus 1:3, 4; 2:10, 13; 3:6; 2 Peter 1:1; 2:20; 3:18; 1 John 4:14; Jude 25, etc. On the Christological connections of Titus 2:13 and 2 Peter 1:1, see: Murray J. Harris, *Jesus as God* (Grand Rapids: Baker, 1992), 173–185; 229–238.

[503] Brown, *NIDNTT*, 3:213.

# A Preliminary Synthesis of Old Testament Soteriology

Notice first these excerpts taken from Horne's general conclusions about salvation in the Old Testament:

> In the majority of Old Testament references salvation is seen to be the work of a sovereign God (Isaiah 43:11). It is Yahweh who saves His people from Egypt (Psalm 106:7–10); from Babylon (Jeremiah 30:10); from trouble (Jeremiah 14:8).
>
> Salvation is accomplished in history. The first occurrence of *yasha'* is found in Exodus 14:30. In this reference there is the account of Israel's deliverance from Egyptian bondage: "Thus the LORD saved Israel that day from the hand of the Egyptians." This national deliverance made the deepest impression on the Hebrew mind, an impression which was to be maintained by the annual Passover feast (Deuteronomy 16:1). This deliverance of Israel from Egypt is the supreme Old Testament sign of Yahweh's saving grace.[504]
>
> Salvation is deliverance from enemies. Among these enemies were death and its fear (Psalms 6:4–5; 107:13, 14); the lion's mouth (Psalm 22:21); the battlefield (Deuteronomy 20:4); the wicked (Psalm 59:2); sickness (Isaiah 38:21); trouble (Jeremiah 30:7); and sins (Psalms 51:14; 130:8; Ezekiel 36:29). In the Old Testament times God was conceived to be the Savior from all foes, both spiritual and physical.
>
> Salvation is deliverance to the Lord. Yahweh not only delivered His people from that which would destroy them, but He also brought them to Himself. His salvation was not merely a rescue from a dangerous situation but it was also a rescue for a special purpose, that purpose being that those rescued should worship, praise and glorify Him through lives dedicated to obeying Him in all of life (1 Chronicles 16:23; Isaiah 43:11, 12; 49:6, 7; Zacheriah 8:13).[505]

---

[504] For them, at that stage in the historical revelation of God's redemptive dealings, the sign of God's grace in the Exodus event would have been fairly analogous to what the Cross has come to symbolize for us.

[505] At this point Horne takes off on an important theological-ethical issue, the presence of the indicative/imperative motif (i.e. God's 'done' and His people's responsibility to 'do') in the Old Testament.

Salvation is appropriated solely by faith in God apart from any reliance upon supposed merit of human effort. This was true salvation both on a national and individual scale (Psalms 44:3; 55:16; 86:2; 138:7; etc.).[506]

To this photo album of deliverance in the Old Testament, Walters adds the striking portrait of Messiah, noting, "The Old Testament doctrine of salvation reaches its zenith in the portrayal of the suffering Servant (e.g. Isaiah liii); in this respect the Old Testament sets the scene for, and adumbrates, the New Testament salvation."[507]

# A Preliminary Synthesis of New Testament Soteriology

Now turning to a panoramic picture of salvation in the New Testament, we will observe points of continuity with the Old Testament but also areas of significant advancement. Once again, Horne's synopsis is very helpful:

The whole initiative of salvation is with God. "For God has not destined us for wrath, but to obtain salvation through our Lord Jesus Christ" (1 Thessalonians 5:9). See also John 3:16, 17; 2 Thessalonians 2:13; 1 Timothy 1:15; 2 Timothy 1:9; Titus 3:5; Revelation 7:10; 19:1.

Jesus is the center of God's saving work; in no one else is there salvation (Acts 4:12; Hebrews 2:10; 5:9). Without Him and His work there is no *soteria*.

Salvation in the New Testament sense of spiritual deliverance means a total salvation. God saves fallen man—body and soul. Specifically, *soteria* is salvation from physical illness (Matthew 9:21; Luke 8:36), from lostness (Matthew 18:11; Luke 19:10), from sin (Matthew 1:21), from wrath (Romans 5:9).

Salvation is eschatological. Although [one] begins to enjoy his salvation here and now there is yet a time coming when he will realize it in all its fullness. That time will be at the Second

---

[506] Charles M. Horne, "Salvation," *Zondervan Pictorial Encyclopedia*, 5:222.
[507] "Salvation," *New Bible Dictionary*, 1127.

Coming of Christ, a day when He will be enthroned as King of the world (Romans 13:11; 1 Corinthians 5:5; 2 Timothy 4:18; Hebrews 9:28; 1 Peter 1:5; Revelation 12:10).

In summary, *soteria* is the rescue of fallen man through Christ from all that would ruin his soul in this life and in the life to come.[508]

With these generalizations in mind we need to press on to more focused studies. The chapters to follow are dedicated to this purpose, namely, the exploration of specific soteriological terms, topics, and tensions.

---

[508] Horne, *Zondervan Pictorial Encyclopedia*, 5:222.

# CHAPTER 5

# BIBLICAL SOTERIOLOGY

In this chapter, I will concentrate on the issues relating primarily to salvation proper. By the designation "salvation proper" I mean the things theologically pertaining to, but certainly not blindly restricted to, our initial salvation.[509] In chapter 6, the focus will narrow to some important issues relating more explicitly to our Christian life, i.e. sanctification.

## *The Divine Motive*

First, we must never forget that "the whole Biblical concept and the attendant demands of salvation find their sole basis in the fact that man is helpless apart from the grace of God."[510] Furthermore, "pointedly put, *salvation by grace* and *the sovereignty of God in salvation* are interchangeable terms."[511] An illustrative text that glues these important concepts together is Exodus 33:19b: "I will be gracious (וְחַנֹּתִי [*weḥannōtî*]) to whom I will be gracious (אָחֹן [*'āḥōn*]), and I will have compassion (וְרִחַמְתִּי [*weriḥamtî*]) on whom I will have compassion (אֲרַחֵם [*'ᵃraḥēm*])." These succinct clauses capture the very essence of sovereign grace.[512] It will become increasingly more obvious as we continue to investigate biblical soteriology that "salvation belongs to the LORD." This incontestable scriptural attestation of Psalm 3:9a (v. 8a, English) is rendered both literally and interpretively by Alexander like this: "*To the LORD, Jehovah, the salvation,* which I need and hope for, is or belongs,

---

[509] As we will see, it is not always possible to pigeon-hole all the soteriological data systematically into bins conveniently labeled initial salvation, progressive salvation (i.e. sanctification), or future salvation (i.e. glorification). In many cases the context of various bytes of biblical data will allow such pigeon-holing; however, in some cases the biblical bytes spill out and over into another bin, or even into both of the others. After all, the whole garment of salvation is ultimately of one piece.

[510] Davis, "Regeneration in the Old Testament," 76.

[511] R. B. Kuiper, "Scriptural Preaching," *The Infallible Word*, ed. by Stonehouse and Woolley (Philadelphia: Presbyterian Guardian, 1946), 233.

[512] For some documenting scriptural argumentation concerning sovereign grace, see how Paul uses Exodus 33:19b in the larger context of his quote found in Romans 9:15.

as to its only author and dispenser."[513] Simpson referring back to the axiomatic truth of Psalm 3:9a (v. 8a, English) rightly labels the LORD's salvation "His august monopoly."[514]

But why is it that God would save anyone? Sovereign grace! But in view of His holiness and righteousness, and because of our own sinfulness, it is a mystery why God is gracious to anyone.[515] Yet in point of fact, our awesome God does manifest His mercy to people deserving damnation. Logically, God's operations of sovereign grace are quite inscrutable; however, *theo*-logically, for the blessed beneficiaries of His undeserved mercy, these truisms held in tension are matters of revelational fact and the greatest of all delights. Consequently, although we may not ever be able to fully fathom sovereign grace, we are eternally privileged to exalt and worship its Author.

## The Terminology of Sovereign Grace

At this juncture it should prove helpful to survey the semantics of grace in the Bible. In the Old Testament, "grace" is linguistically denoted by members of the חנן (*ḥnn*) word family (cf., e.g., Genesis 6:8; Exodus 33:19; 2 Kings 13:23; Psalm 84:12 [v. 11, English]; Isaiah 30:18–19; Amos 5:15; etc.). As already intimated, the occurrences of this word group in Exodus 33:19 and 34:6 are exceedingly formulative theologically. Treating these verses in reverse order, Freedman and Lundbom reason:

> Graciousness is a divine attribute. The adjective *ḥannûn* is used almost exclusively of Yahweh in the Old Testament, and almost always it is joined by other adjectives in liturgical con-

---

[513] J. A. Alexander, *The Psalms Translated and Explained* (New York: Baker and Scribner, 1850), 1:25. Note: It is admitted that proportionally there is more of an emphasis on temporal deliverance in the Old Testament. However, some passages seem to function as all inclusive maxims. The affirmation of Psalm 3:8 seems to have been driven by a personal crisis calling for a particular kind of rescue, but the basic truth of the first part of the verse is far more comprehensive, potentially including temporal and/or spiritual needs, whether experienced individually or corporately, etc. For some discussion on the respective primary and secondary applications of salvation in the Old and New Testaments, cf. Geoffrey W. Grogan, "The Experience of Salvation in the Old and New Testaments," *VE* 5 (1967): 4–26. On some important attendant points dealing with this issue, also see John S. Feinberg, "Salvation in the Old Testament," in *Tradition and Testament*, ed. by J.S. Feinberg and P. D. Feinberg (Chicago: Moody, 1981).

[514] *Ephesians and Colossians*, 54.

[515] Stoebe, e.g., comments, "Because the difference between God and people is immeasurable, the nuance of free grace assumes prominence when God is counterpart" (*TLOT*, 1:444).

cert. Yahweh is gracious and merciful, slow to anger, and abounding in steadfast love and faithfulness (Exodus 34:6; Joel 2:13; Jonah 4:2; Psalms 86:15; 103:8; 111:4; 116:5; 145:8; Nehemiah 9:17, 31; 2 Chronicles 30:9). After the apostasy of the golden calf, and in response to Moses' specific request, Yahweh reveals his essential qualities and character: he is first of all *raḥúm weḥannún* (Exodus 34:6).... The *idem per idem* constructions of Exodus 33:19 use *ḥanan* and *riḥam*: "I will be gracious to whom I will be gracious, and will show mercy on whom I will show mercy.... Here in Exodus 33:19 the form has normally been taken to express Yahweh's supreme authority in dispensing grace and mercy, when, where, how, and as he pleases.[516]

More succinctly put, "God's grace is...finally rooted, not in what people do, but in his disposition to be gracious in ways beyond any human formula or calculation (Exodus 33:19; 34:6)."[517]

But beside the semantical equivalency of the חנן (*ḥnn*) word group in the Old Testament, stands an even more significant *conceptual* equivalent for grace. This theological parallel is found in the Old Testament noun חֶסֶד (*ḥesed*). As Ryrie notes, "The meaning of this word is difficult to convey in English. It even defies exact description in the original, though it occurs about 250 times in the Old Testament. However, it is a word which is related to the New Testament word for grace, *charis*, even more than *chen*."[518] Studies on חֶסֶד (*ḥesed*) keep coming out like water from a hydrant.[519] One of the most careful and credible siftings of the biblical data and commentaries on it comes from the pen of Harris:

> חֶסֶד (*ḥesed*) kindness, lovingkindness, mercy and similar words (KJV). (RSV usually has steadfast love, occasionally loyalty, NASB lovingkindness, kindness, love, NIV unfailing love.)... The question is, do the texts ascribe his *ḥesed* to his[520] covenants[521] or to his everlasting love?... A prominent early usage

---

[516] *TDOT*, 5:30.

[517] Fretheim, *NIDOTTE*, 2:205.

[518] Charles Ryrie, *The Grace of God* (Chicago: Moody 1963), 15–16; cf. also C. H. Dodd, *The Bible and the Greeks* (London: Hodder and Stoughton, 1954), 63–63. For a superb synopsis of how it was that χάρις (*charis*) came to supersede ἔλεος (*eleos*) in Biblical Greek as the primary term for characterizing God's salvific acts, see Andrew T. Lincoln, *Ephesians*, WBC, 42:102–103.

[519] For interactions with much of this material, see: Zobel, *TDOT*, 5:44–64; Stoebe, *TLOT*, 2:449–464; and Baer and Gordon, *NIDOTTE*, 2:211–218.

[520] I.e. God's.

[521] *Ala* Glueck, *et.al.*

is in God's declaration of his own character: Exodus 20:6 parallel to Deuteronomy 5:10 and also Exodus 34:6–7.... The phrase *ḥesed* and *'emet* "truth"... is thought by some to argue for the concept of loyalty or fidelity in *ḥesed*.[522] It occurs some twenty-five times with about seven more in less close connection. Most agree it is a hendiadys and one noun serves to describe the other. Therefore, the phrase means "faithful love" or "true kindness" or the like.... Another pair of nouns is covenant, *bᵉrît*, and *ḥesed* used seven times with some other instances of use in near contexts. The main instance is Deuteronomy 7:9, 12 which has echoes in 1 Kings 8:23; 2 Chronicles 6:14; Nehemiah 1:5; 9:32; and Daniel 9:4.... It should be mentioned that *ḥesed* is also paired about fifteen times with nouns of mercy like *raḥûm*, e.g. Psalm 103:4; Zechariah 7:9; (and cf. Exodus 34:6–7 above), *ḥen*, e.g. Genesis 19:19; Psalm 109:12, *tanḥûm*, Psalm 94:15–19, etc. ...The implication is that *ḥesed* is one of the words descriptive of the love of God.... It is obvious that God was in covenant relation with Israel, also that he expressed this relation in *ḥesed*, that God's *ḥesed* was eternal (Note the refrain of Psalm 136)—though the *ḥesed* of Ephraim and others was not (Hosea 6:4). However, it is by no means clear that *ḥesed* necessarily involves a covenant or means fidelity to a covenant.... It is a kind of love, including mercy, *ḥannûn*, when the object is in a pitiful state.[523]

Now pushing on to the Greek New Testament, the primary words for mercy and compassion are ἔλεος (*eleos*) and οἰκτιρμός (*oiktirmos*).[524] For a brief synopsis of the divine ἔλεος (*eleos*), the following excerpts from Spicq help to call attention to its magnificence:

As for God, his mercy is revealed in the coming of the messianic salvation and is sung by the Virgin Mary and the priest Zechariah in terms borrowed from the Old Testament.[525] It is a gratuitous favor, a grace that presupposes God's love and the

---

[522] On the dynamic of this Old Testament duo, cf., its conceptual migration into the New Testament, e.g., in key passages like John 1:14.

[523] Harris, *TWOT*, 1:305–307.

[524] Also, the verb σπλαγχνίζομαι (*splanchnizomai*) is sometimes used in the gospels to characterize Jesus' attitude of tender care and compassion (e.g. Matthew 9:36; Mark 1:41; Luke 7:13; etc.).

[525] The documentation Spicq cites in his footnote is "Luke 1:50 (=Psalm 102:17); 1:54 (Psalm 97:3); 1:72 (=Micah 7:20); 1:78, διὰ σπλάγχνα ἐλέους θεοῦ ἡμῶν" (*TLNT*, 1:478, n. 28).

intervention of his omnipotence.... It extends to all believers (Galatians 6:16) and together with Christ's mercy becomes the content of the apostle's wish for a whole church: "Grace, mercy, and peace from God the Father and Christ our Savior" (1 Timothy 1:2; 2 Timothy 1:2; Jude 2; 2 John 3).... It is thanks to his[526] intercession that believers can "approach the throne of grace to receive mercy and find grace to help in time of need" (Hebrews 4:16).... God is free to grant or deny his favors and his forgiveness (Romans 9:15–18; cf. Exodus 33:19).... St. Paul's innovation in the biblical theology of *eleos* is to locate God's mercy at the beginning and at the end of the plan of salvation: "Formerly you were disobedient to God; now you have obtained mercy.... God has consigned all people to disobedience so as to show mercy to all" (Romans 11:30–32).... Mercy extends to Gentiles as well as Jews (Romans 15:9) and consists in the forgiveness of sins.[527]

The οἰκτιρμός (*oiktirmos*) word group adds its weight to the description of our compassionate God. He is dubbed ὁ πατὴρ τῶν οἰκτιρμῶν (*ho patēr tōn oiktirmōn*), "the Father of mercies" (2 Corinthians 1:3), being by nature πολυσπλαγχνός (*polusplanchnos*), "very compassionate" and οἰκτίρμων (*oiktirmōn*), "merciful" (James 5:11). Returning again to Romans 9:15 (a quote of Exodus 33:19), the verb οἰκτίρω (*oiktirō*), "to have compassion," joins forces with ἐλεέω (*eleeō*), "to have mercy on," emphasizing the sovereign basis of God's salvific interventions. It is spiritually reasonable that the begraced beneficiaries of the undeserved mercies should be motivated to live holy lives to His honor and glory (cf., e.g., Romans 12:1ff; Philippians 2:1ff.). His heart of compassion should be creating in us one of like kind (cf., e.g., Colossians 3:12).

Having considered the marvelous mercy and compassion of our great Savior leads us to the ultimate New Testament term for His unmerited favor, namely His χάρις (*charis*), "grace." Conzelmann captures its great theological significance when he notes that "in Paul χάρις is a central concept that most clearly expresses his understanding of the salvation event. Specifically Pauline is the use of the word to expound the structure of the salvation event. The linguistic starting-point is the sense of ...showing free unmerited grace."[528] Similarly, Esser argues that χάρις (*charis*) "is the essence of God's decisive saving act in Jesus Christ, which

---

[526] I.e. Jesus'.
[527] Spicq, *TLNT*, 1:478–479.
[528] *TDNT*, 9:393, 394.

took place in his sacrificial death, and also of all its consequences in the present and future (Romans 3:24ff.)."[529] These generalizations are thoroughly documented by the New Testament's usages of various members of the "grace"[530] and "mercy" word groups.

## Selected Texts Emphasizing Sovereign Grace

Rather than becoming frustrated by the process of choosing many occurrences of the key terms for sovereign grace and leaving many more excellent ones out, it seems best to point to a couple of paradigm passages which eloquently publish this exceedingly important doctrine with great contextual clarity. Since we have already spent some time in a text which at its beginning emphasizes the helplessness and hopelessness of sinners in their fallen estate, Ephesians 2:1ff. becomes an excellent candidate. Ephesians 2:1–10 is a *sola gratia* passage par excellence. We have already concluded from the first three verses that the provisions of God's sovereign grace are undeserved in the light of our *background*. As the passage continues (i.e. vv. 4–10) we are left with the distinct impression that the provisions of God's sovereign grace are unfathomable in view of our *blessings*. Samples of those blessings are found in vv. 5–6, namely, we were "made alive together with Christ," "raised up with," and even "seated with" Him in the heavenlies. But notice how God's mercy and grace are sprinkled in and around these verses as the divine motive standing behind His beneficent interventions: "But God, being rich in mercy" (i.e. ἔλεος [*eleos*]), "on account of His great love with which He loved us" (v. 4)... "by grace (i.e. χάρις [*charis*]) you have been saved" (v. 5b)... "for by grace (again, χάρις [*charis*]) you have been saved through faith, and this[531] not of yourselves—(it is) the gift of God—(it is) not of works in order that no one should boast" (v. 9). The major message is that salvation, from start to finish,[532] is *sola gratia*.

---

[529] *NIDNTT*, 2:119. Similarly, Spicq intimately associates grace with "the gratuitousness and generosity of the salvation granted in the New Testament" (*TLNT*, 3:520).

[530] For an adequate survey of χάρις (*charis*), χαρίζομαι (*charizomai*), *et.al*, see Esser's article in *NIDNTT*, 2:118–123.

[531] The pronoun τοῦτο (*touto*) is neuter, and is best explained as referring back "to the concept of a grace-by-faith salvation" (Wallace, *GGBB*, 335).

[532] Even in this passage the twice repeated affirmation about our salvation is not merely a historical reference to initial deliverance. The ἐστε σεσωσμένοι (*este sesōsmenoi*) found in vv. 5b and 8a is a perfect periphrastic construction. Furthermore, the participle is passive—in this context, quite obviously, a divine passive (cf., e.g., Wallace, *GGBB*, 438). The idea of the whole construction therefore is that because of God's merciful intervention we "were saved and continue to be so" (Salmond, "Ephesians," *EGT*, 3:288).

Among the many New Testament passages magnifying the grace of God in salvation, Titus 3:3–7 stands out as one of the most comprehensive. I have already stressed the hamartiological significance of Titus 3:3 which pertains to our formerly hopeless condition. On the heels of that B. C. picture of spiritual darkness comes a condensed synopsis of our brilliant blessings in Christ, and of course, these spiritual benefits are ours only by the grace of God:

> But when God our Savior's kindness and love for mankind appeared, not based upon works which we had righteously done but rather according to His mercy, He saved us, through the washing of regeneration and renewal of the Holy Spirit, whom He richly poured out upon us through Jesus Christ, our Savior, in order that, having been justified by that One's grace, we might become heirs according to the hope of eternal life (Titus 3:4–7).

A few very brief comments may be helpful. These verses show the involvement of every member of the Trinity in our salvation.[533] Nevertheless, it is the Father who is the subject of the leading verb at the core of this passage: "He *saved* us."[534] The most obvious characteristic of this passage, however, is its magnification of the mercy of God.[535] Norbie comments:

> Paul is writing of God's marvelous grace in saving sinners. This great salvation flows out freely from the fountainhead of God's kindness and love. Its source is…found…in the very nature and attributes of God. In fact, by nature and practice man merited only the burning wrath of God who hates sin…. The condemned are pardoned because God is a God of mercy.[536]

Indeed, the divine motive standing behind salvation, from beginning to end, is the "amazing grace"[537] of God. Micah, long before Newton wrote the words to "Amazing Grace," concluded his book with an inscripturated hymn about sovereign grace. Its title is found in the opening line of his prophecy's concluding anthem. In wonder and worship,

---

[533] Cf. the spotlight on God the Father in vv. 4ff., the agency of the Spirit in v. 5, and the work of Christ in v. 6b.

[534] For other syntactical and exegetical comments, see my "Exegetical and Theological Bases for a Consistently Presuppositional Approach to Apologetics," 147–148.

[535] Note especially God's "kindness" (v. 4), His "love for mankind" (i.e. φιλανθρωπία [*philanthrōpia*; cf. "philanthropy" in English], v. 4), the strong denial of good works on our part as the basis for salvation (v. 5a), His "mercy" (v. 5b), and the "grace" of Christ (v. 7).

[536] Donald L. Norbie, "The Washing of Regeneration," *EQ* 34 (January-March, 1962): 36.

[537] Borrowing the title of John Newton's grand hymn.

the prophet asks rhetorically: "Who is a God like Thee, who pardons iniquity….?" (Micah 7:18a; NASB).

# The Divine Grounds

By grace alone, not only the eternal plan of God but also the historical out-workings of it are shown to be a "done deal" in Scripture. The Bible unequivocally teaches that "God the Father is…the sovereign architect of a spiritual blueprint drawn up in eternity past which includes the provision, means, and application of salvation."[538] The Word of God also informs us that the ground of salvation is atonement and that atonement was strategically and prominently included in our merciful Master's plan (cf., e.g., Revelation 13:8b[539]). However, before we are tempted to prematurely synthesize a position on the atonement, it is necessary that a fairly thorough survey of the vocabulary of atonement be conducted.

## The Terminology of Atonement

### The Old Testament Root כפר (cpr)

There is only one word group used for "atonement" in the Old Testament, namely, כפר (cpr). Many people for years have built theologies upon etymologies, and כפר (cpr) most likely stands as Exhibit A in regard to this hazardous procedure.[540] More inductively, Herrmann raised the issue, examined the data, and has come to a credible conclusion:

> "The question of the etymological meaning of the Hebrew root כפר is obscure."…The various Semitic analogies do not permit us to make a definitive distinction between "to cover" and "to wash away." There are Semitic analogies for regarding forgiveness of sins both in terms of covering and in terms of

---

[538] Zemek, *Doing God's Business God's Way*, 52; cf., e.g., Isaiah 53; Ephesians 1:3–14; 2 Timothy 1:8–10; etc.

[539] I.e. οὐ οὐ γέγραπται τὸ ὄνομα αὐτοῦ ἐν τῷ βιβλίῳ τῆς ζωῆς τοῦ ἀρνίου τοῦ ἐσφαγμένου ἀπὸ καταβολῆς κόσμου (*hou ou gegraptai to onoma autou en tō bibliō tēs zōes tou arniou tou esphagmenou apo katabolēs kosmou*); the NIV's primary (i.e. not marginal) rendering is preferred; "all whose names have not been written in the book of life belonging to the Lamb that was slain from the creation of the world."

[540] Cf. Harris' challenge to the most popular version concerning כפר (cpr): "It has been suggested that the Old Testament ritual symbolized a covering over of sin until it was dealt with in fact by the atonement of Christ. There is, however, very little evidence for this view" (*TWOT*, 1:452). Cf., also Maass, *TLOT*, 2:625. Some offer a third view concerning the fundamental idea undergirding this root, i.e. ransom (cf. Averbeck's survey of this view and the other two [*NIDOTTE*, 2:692–693]).

washing away.... All in all, the solution of the problem is perhaps that the root leaves etymological play for both "to cover" and "to wash away."[541]

Concerning the actual usages of this theologically important word group,[542] they seem to fall into two major spheres, those which are connected to the cultus (i.e. the sacrificial rituals mediated by priests) and those which are not. Of the former, more significant group, consider some illuminating excerpts from Herrmann's discussion:

> About three quarters of all the occurrences of כִּפֶּר are in connection with specific sacrifices.... There can be no doubt...that expiation is linked with the manipulation of blood.... At this point we may legitimately address the well-known text Leviticus 17:11[543].... Here expiation is made with the blood that Yahweh has given for the altar, and this is brought about by the fact that in the blood is the נֶפֶשׁ, the soul or the life.... In the fourfold ritual of the sin-offering in Leviticus 4 (for the priest, the congregation, the prince and the ordinary Israelite) the climax of the action is incontestably the manipulation of the blood of the sin offering by the priest.... It is here that we find the statements concerning the purpose and result of the sacrifice: "and the priest shall make an atonement for him, and it shall be forgiven him" (vv. 20, 26, 31, 35)[544].... It is only

---

[541] *TDNT*, 3:302.

[542] The statistics of verb forms are as follows: "The verb occurs 101 times in the Old Testament, 92 times piel (Leviticus 49 times, Numbers 15 times, Exodus 7 times, Ezekiel 6 times), 7 times pual (Isaiah 4 times) and 1 time each hithpael (1 Samuel 3:14) and niphal (Deuteronomy 21:8)" (Maass, *TLOT*, 2:626). The noun "form *koper*...occurs 13 times..." and "the abstract term *kippurim*, atonement, occurs 8 times (Exodus 29:36; 30:10, 16; Leviticus 23:27, 28 [the only anarthrous use]; 25:9; Numbers 5:8; 29:11) and *kapporet*, place of atonement, mercy seat, or cover...occurs 26 times" (Averbeck, *NIDOTTE*, 2:690, 691). For general meaning for these various members of the כפר (*cpr*) family also see Averbeck (*NIDOTTE*, 2:689). For a handy chart of this word group's association with the various kinds of sacrifices in the Old Testament, see: Lang, *TDOT*, 7:299.

[543] For an excellent consideration of this key verse in its context, see Averbeck (*NIDOTTE*, 2:693ff.). Also note Lang's expanded translation: "'For the life of the flesh is in the blood; and I [God] Myself have given it for you upon/for the altar, that it may make atonement for you personally...; for it is the blood that makes atonement by virtue of the life... [that is in it]'" (*TDOT*, 7:291).

[544] These verses and others just like them must be allowed to mean what they say. Christian exegetes and theologians, for example, should not employ a superficially synthesized theology, e.g., selectively and subjectively excerpted from the Epistle to the Hebrews to evacuate the clear meaning of Old Testament passages such as Leviticus 4. The main argument of Hebrews, e.g., is that Christ, as "a vicarious sacrificer, a vicarious sacrifice, and a vicarious place of sacrifice" (*NIDOTTE*, 2:709), has *once-and-for-all* atoned for sin. Never demeaning that ultimate Sacrifice of all sacrifices, passages like Leviticus 4 nevertheless speak of "'effected atonement'" (Maass, *TLOT*, 2:627; note his discussion of כפר (*kipper*) + עַל (*'al*), 626–627). For some other syntactical connections, see Lang *TDOT*, 7:290–291.

natural that there should be no mention of expiation in the ritual meal offering in Leviticus 2.... The concepts of purification, cleansing and consecration are all found in the ritual of the great Day of Atonement (Leviticus 16)[545].... It is quite evident...that expiation is here linked with the sin offerings.... How strongly the idea of expiation permeated the whole culture may be seen not only from the fact that the great Day of Atonement has come to have such overwhelming significance amongst the Israelite feasts but also from the fact that in the calendar of sacrifices in Numbers 28 and 29, which is supplementary to the calendar of feasts in Leviticus 23, the expiatory sin offering (Numbers 28:22, 30; 29:5) is now offered along with the burnt offering, not just at the daily and Sabbath offerings, but at all others.... Through cultic ordinances Yahweh Himself has provided the possibility of expiating what needs expiation.... The disturbed relationship between God and the community can always be restored, both on a small scale and on a great, by the fulfillment of the laws of expiation which Yahweh Himself has given.[546]

Earlier in his discussion Herrmann stated the bottom-line of atonement: "If God does not atone, if He does not make or grant expiation, if He does not forgive, the sinful man must die (Jeremiah 18:23; Isaiah 22:14). If God atones, man lives (Psalm 78:38) and is saved (Psalm 79:9)."[547]

Speaking of the important association of this word group with sacrifice and substitution, Harris has appropriately argued that

from the meaning of *kōper* "ransom," the meaning of *kāpar* can be better understood. It means "to atone by offering a substitute." The great majority of the usages concern the priestly ritual of sprinkling of the sacrificial blood thus "making an atonement" for the worshipper. There are forty-nine instances of this usage in Leviticus alone and no other meaning is there witnessed.... It seems clear that this word aptly illustrates the theology of reconciliation in the Old Testament. The life of the

---

[545] Labeled by some the "Good Friday of the Old Testament." For a good treatment of the salient exegetical and theological data of Leviticus 16, see Averbeck, *NIDOTTE*, 2:699ff.
[546] *TDNT*, 3:306–310. Regarding Herrmann's last point, Maass asserts: "God is the decisive actor, the grantor of atonement" (*TLOT*, 2:632).
[547] *TDNT*, 3:304.

sacrificial animal specifically symbolized by the blood was required in exchange for the life of the worshipper. Sacrifice of
animals in Old Testament theology was not merely an expression of thanks to the deity by a cattle raising people. It was the
symbolic expression of innocent life given for guilty life. This
symbolism is further clarified by the action of the worshipper in
placing his hands on the head of the sacrifice and confessing his
sins over the animal (cf. Leviticus 16:21; 1:4; 4:4, etc.) which
was then killed or sent out as a scapegoat.[548]

Now, returning to an Old Testament truth sometimes dodged or,
even worse, theologically manipulated by too many systematicians, we
must acknowledge that the Old Testament data points to the efficacy of
these divinely prescribed sacrifices.[549] Herrmann puts it this way:

> The theological interpretation of these rites has often been in-
> fluenced by partisan doctrinal considerations which do not de-
> rive from the actual material and which incline our evaluation of
> it either to the one side or to the other. By contrast, it is essen-
> tial to keep to the material itself.... There can be no doubt that
> Yahweh has provided and ordained blood as a means of atone-
> ment, and that blood is suitable and effective as such in virtue of
> the נֶפֶשׁ, the soul or the life, which is contained in it.[550]

Another issue that has given rise to a heated debate is whether these
theologically relevant occurrences of כפר (*cpr*) are characterized best, as to
accomplishment, by the word "expiation" or the term "propitiation."[551]

---

[548] *TWOT*, 1:453.

[549] I.e. in their historical context within that juncture of progressive revelation. The sins of a rightly motivated, believing Israelite would be atoned for by the offering of a substitutionary animal sacrifice. That was guaranteed by God's Law. However, not one of these sacrifices was the ultimate one which would take care of the Old Testament sinner's sin *fully and finally*. As a member of the theocracy, he would need to come back at the prescribed times for corporate sacrifice, and as an individual sinner, he was to come and offer a sin and/or guilt offering as often as necessary.

[550] *TDNT*, 3:310. For another general survey, see Gordon J. Wenham, "The Role of Sacrifice," *The Book of Leviticus*, NICOT (Grand Rapids: Eerdmans, 1979), 25–29. On the specific hot-potato issue of the *efficacy* of these Old Testament sacrifices, see: Hobart Freeman, "The Problem of Efficacy of Old Testament Sacrifices," *Bulletin ETS* (1962); and especially John S. Feinberg, "Salvation in the Old Testament," *Tradition and Testament* (Chicago: Moody, 1981), 59–75.

[551] Averbeck warns: "The issue of 'expiation' versus 'propitiation' is more complex. The debate has generally been overwrought with false dichotomies and a lack of willingness to see the broader picture, apparently because of previous doctrinal commitments" (*NIDOTTE*, 2:708). For a good survey of this controversy, see Brown, *NIDNTT*, 3:151–160.

How hot and heavy this war can get is exemplified in Morris' intense challenge of C. H. Dodd's preference of expiation.[552] One thing agreed upon by all is the importance of the ἱλάσκομαι (*hilaskomai*) word group in the LXX as the family of choice for the rendering of corresponding members of כפר (*cpr*).[553] Obviously, this choice constitutes yet another important semantical-theological bridge to New Testament occurrences of this word group.[554] I would like to say that Dodd had *a* point in preferring the term expiation. It seems that he may have been motivated *at times* by a desire to separate Yahweh, the only true, living God, out from any association with pagan deities which are regularly pictured as blood thirsty (i.e. for more and more sacrifices to be offered up to them). But the term "expiation" too often exhibits a tendency to de-emphasize the righteous wrath of the supremely holy God against all sin and sinners. In biblical contexts, "the words of the *hilaskomai* group do not denote simple forgiveness or cancellation of sin, but that forgiveness or cancellation of sin which includes the turning away of God's wrath."[555] A paragraph from Brown's article well summarizes the views and shows the necessity for the propitiatory appeasement of Yahweh's righteous wrath:

> To sum up the discussion so far, it is clear that the authors of the Hebrew Old Testament and the LXX translators are far removed from the crude pagan idea of propitiating a capricious and malevolent deity. On the other hand, the evidence that we have examined does not suggest that these writers shared a common quasi-mechanistic view of life in which the effects of sin could be nullified by resorting to the appropriate rite as an antidote. There is a personal dimension which affects both the offending and the offended parties which means that, even where an offense has to be expiated, the action has to be taken because the personal relationships between the parties requires it. What C. K. Barrett says of Paul's teaching in Romans might also be applied to those passages in the Old Testament con-

---

[552] Cf. Leon Morris, *The Apostolic Preaching of the Cross* (Grand Rapids: Eerdmans, 1965), chapters 5–6, *passim*. Dodd's view is detailed in his "*hilaskesthai*, its Cognates, Derivatives and Synonyms in the Septuagint," *JTS* 32 (1931): 352–360. For a non-polemical presentation of pertinent data, see Hill, *GWHM*, chapter 2.

[553] For specific correspondences from word group to word group, see Lang, *TDOT*, 7:291.

[554] However, for the sake of inductivity when it comes to the Old Testament data, it might be wise to try to keep this a one-way bridge so that the fully developed notions of propitiation or appeasement are not read back wholesale into Old Testament occurrences.

[555] Leon Morris, "Propitiation," *Baker's Dictionary of Theology*, 425; once again, for the more extensive argument of his thesis, see *APC*, chapters 5–6.

cerning the expiation of man's sin: "It would be wrong to neglect the fact that expiation has, as it were, the effect of propitiation: the sin that might have excited God's wrath is expiated
(at God's will) and therefore no longer does so" (*The Epistle to
the Romans, BNTC*, 1957, 78).[556]

Needless to say, the כפר (*cpr*) word group of the Old Testament,
along with the LXX's renderings of it with members from the
ἱλάσκομαι (*hilaskomai*) family, constitute a solid foundation upon
which the New Testament writers build the marvelous superstructure of
the work of Christ. And one very important facet of His work is the propitiatory nature of His sacrifice upon the cross.

## The Concept of 'Atonement' in the New Testament[557]

I would like to survey the key New Testament terms and prepositions that develop this concept of atonement. It will prove to be helpful[558] to organize the word groups logically into categories of common
background (i.e. of imagery), i.e. those that are *commercial* in nature,
the one that speaks of *appeasement,* and finally the one that emphasizes a
*changed relationship.*

Two prominent word families fall in under the heading of "commercial terminology," the ἀγοράζω (*agorazō*) group and the λυτρόω (*lutroō*)
group. The ἀγοράζω (*agorozō*) group, as to background, speaks of buy-
ing in a market place, a *general* market place (cf. our malls and
superstores, modern counterparts of the historic general store.)[559]
Soteriologically significant occurrences of this word group include forms

---

[556] Brown, *NIDNTT*, 3:157. It should be noted that Brown's next paragraph begins like this: "The
element of propitiation is further supported by a closer examination of the significance of blood in
the Old Testament" (ibid.).

[557] Very technically speaking, the words "atonement," "to atone," etc. do not occur in the New
Testament; however, the AV has mistranslated the τὴν καταλλαγὴν (*tēn katallagēn*; literally "the
reconciliation") of Romans 5:11 as "the atonement," and the NIV (probably in deference to Old
Testament background) prefers to render members of the ἱλάσκομαι (*hilaskomai*; i.e. "to propiti-
ate") family by the *interpretive* words "atonement," "atoning sacrifice," etc. The reason I bring this
up and use the word "concept" in the heading is due to the systematic theological debate of unlimited verses limited "atonement" (cf. my critique later). This warfare almost always prematurely and
heatedly engages without a careful examination of the various word groups which all make nuanced
contributions to the basic idea of Christ's 'atonement' as it is richly developed in the New Testament.

[558] Especially later when we jump into the systematic theological war over the atonement.

[559] In comparison and contrast with the next word group, the background of which would support
the idea of purchasing in a specialty store, i.e. the specialty store of the ancient slave market.

of the simple verb ἀγοράζω (*agorozō*) and forms of the compound verb ἐξαγοράζω (*exagorazō*). The preposition ἐκ (*ek*), whether glued right on to the compounded form or occurring separately in a context with the simple verb (cf. Revelation 5:9), has a "root meaning" of "from out of."[560] Most of these occurrences likely intimate a purchasing that carries away the purchase (not merely some kind of money down for things left in lay away[561]). A very similar result occurs when ἀγοράζω (*agorozō*) is complemented by the preposition ἀπό (*apo*; cf. Revelation 14:3–4). Now, with minimal comment, I would like to cite the passages from this word group that make their market place contribution to our understanding of Christ's atonement. Note occurrences of the simple verb form in the following passages:

> For you were purchased (ἠγοράσθητε [*ēgorasthēte*]) with a price (1 Corinthians 6:20a).

> You were purchased (ἠγοράσθητε [*ēgorasthēte*] with a price (1 Corinthians 7:23a).[562]

> But there were also false prophets among the people, just as there will be false teachers among you. They will secretly introduce destructive heresies, even denying the sovereign Lord who bought them [τόν ἀγοράσαντα αὐτοὺς δεσπότην (*ton agorasanta autous despotēn*[563])]—bringing swift destruction on themselves (2 Peter 2:1; NIV).

---

[560] Metzger, *LASNTG*, 82. Harris adds, "Therefore, it naturally came to be used to denote origin, source, derivation, or separation" (*NIDNTT*, 3:1188). It is interesting that in Galatians 3:13 the compounded form ἐξηγόρασεν (*exēgorasen*) is immediately followed by ἐκ (*ek*).

[561] To extend this last theological metaphor, things which ultimately may or may not be picked up!

[562] It is interesting that this occurrence of ἀγοράζω (*agorazō*) is couched in a context that employs slavery imagery (vv. 21–23); therefore, because of this setting ἀγαράζω (*agarazō*) seemingly functions like the more specific verb λυτρόω (*lutroō*).

[563] This participial phrase very literally reads "the having purchased them 'despot'" (i.e. sovereign owner). The secular background of this terminology has to do with "masters" who have purchased and thereby own slaves (cf. Spicq, *TLNT*, 1:27–28). For some commentary, see: Richard Bauckham, *Jude, 2 Peter*, WBC, 50 (Waco: Word, 1983), 240, 243; and especially Simon J. Kistemaker, *New Testament Commentary Exposition of the Epistles of Peter and of the Epistle of Jude* (Grand Rapids: Baker, 1987), 282–283. To me, the uniqueness of the combination of the simple ἀγαράζω (*agarazō*) of which Christ, as δεσπότης (*despotēs*), is subject should raise a caution flag so as not to infer too much nor too little theologically from this verse. At the very least, however, these false teachers should be looked upon as having been "professing Christians" (A. T. Robertson, *Word Pictures in the New Testament* [Nashville: Boadman, 1933], 6:160).

And they sang a new song, saying "You[564] are worthy to take the book[565] and to open its seals, since you were slain and You purchased (ἠγόρασας [ēgorasas]) for God with your blood (people) out of (ἐκ [ek]) every tribe and tongue[566] and nation" (Revelation 5:9).

And they sang[567] a new song before the throne and in the presence of the four living creatures and the elders; now no person was able to learn the song except the 144,000, the ones who had been purchased out from (οἱ ἠγορασμένοι ἀπό [hoi ēgorasmenoi apo]) the earth.[568] These are the ones who have not been defiled with women, for they are chaste men; these are the ones who follow the Lamb wherever He goes. These were purchased out from among (οὗτοι ἠγοράσθησαν ἀπό [houtoi ēgorasthēsan apo])[569] men as first fruits to God and to the Lamb (Revelation 14:3–4).

Now we need to turn to Galatians for the two occurrences of the compound verb ἐξαγοράζω (exagorazō):

Christ[570] bought us back from (ἡμᾶς ἐξαγόρασεν ἐκ [hēmas exagorasen ek]) the curse of the law by having become a curse for us (ὑπὲρ ἡμῶν [huper hēmōn]) (Galatians 3:13a).

...in order that He[571] might buy back (ἐξαγοράσῃ [exagorasē]) the ones under the law, in order that we might receive the adoption (Galatians 4:5).[572]

In almost all of the soteriologically significant occurrences of this word group (cf. above) in the New Testament, their immediate or near contexts suggest that these divine purchases were paid for and 'taken home.'[573]

---

[564] I.e. Christ, the *Lamb* (cf. v. 6).

[565] I.e. the scroll.

[566] I.e. language.

[567] Some manuscripts contain ὡς (hōs), "as," at this point.

[568] I.e. purchased out from earth's peoples.

[569] For all practical purposes, there is no significant difference in force between the occurrences of ἀπό (apo) in Revelation 14:3–4 and ἐκ (ek) in Revelation 5:9.

[570] I.e. Messiah.

[571] I.e. the incarnate Son (v. 4).

[572] Field rightly says, "*exagorazō* is...used with [the] special sense of 'redeem' in Galatians 3:13; 4:4, where the idea of escape from the consequences of breaking God's law is added" (*NIDNTT*, 1:268).

[573] For some excellent discussion on the phenomenon, see: Morris, *APC*, 53–59.

Now we may advance our thinking by pressing on to a word group that, as to its background, is nuanced by explicit *slave-market* imagery. The λυτρόω (*lutroō*) group exhibits simple verb forms (Titus 2:14; 1 Peter 1:19), a simple neuter noun form (Matthew 20:28), a compound neuter noun form (1 Timothy 2:6), simple feminine noun forms (Luke 1:68; Hebrews 9:12), and compound feminine noun forms (Romans 3:24; 8:23; 1 Corinthians 1:30; Ephesians 1:7, 14; 4:30; Colossians 1:14; Hebrews 9:15). I will cite them in that order:

> ...who[574] gave Himself on our behalf (ὑπὲρ ἡμῶν [*huper hēmōn*]) in order that He might redeem (or, ransom; λυτρώσηται [*lutrosētai*]) us from (ἀπό [*apo*]) all lawlessness and might cleanse for Himself a chosen people,[575] zealous for good works (Titus 2:14).

> ...since you know that, not with perishable things, like silver or gold, you were redeemed (or, ransomed) out of (ἐλυτρώθητε ἐκ [*elutrōthēte ek*]) your futile life-style handed down from your forefathers, but[576] with precious blood as of an unblemished and spotless lamb, (namely, the blood)[577] of Christ (1 Peter 1:18–19).[578]

> ...just as the Son of Man did not come to be served but rather to serve and to give His life a ransom in the stead of many (λύτρον ἀντὶ πολλῶν [*lutron anti pollōn*]) (Matthew 20:28; cf. Mark 10:45).[579]

---

[574] I.e. Christ (v. 13).

[575] BAG, 654.

[576] Obviously the former ἐλυτρώθητε (*elutrōthēte*), "you were ransomed," is elliptically supplied on this side of the antithetical equation.

[577] Another obvious elliptical construction adding even more impact to this Christological-soteriological affirmation.

[578] The issue of to whom this ransom is paid is not explicitly addressed in the Bible. It certainly was not paid to Satan as some interpreters during the history of the church believed (cf., e.g. Origen). Many have argued, based upon theological inferences, that it most likely had been paid to God (cf., e.g., D. Edmond Hiebert, *1 Peter* [Chicago: Moody, 1992], 102), but "Scripture gives no answer to this question and therefore we do well not to raise it.... Obviously then, the question *who receives the ransom?* ought not to be asked.... The biblical focus is on the price that is paid and the effects of deliverance; it is not on the one who demands or receives the ransom" (Kistemaker, *Peter and Jude*, 69).

[579] The clauses are identical, only their syntactical introductions are different. In Matthew the ὥσπερ (*hōsper*) links the words which follow it to the verses preceding it by simple analogy, while in Mark 10:45 the introductory καὶ γάρ (*kai gar*), "for even," with its respective combination of explanatory and ascensive forces, shockingly points to the corrective analogy (cf. context, Mark 10:35ff.).

For[580] (there is) one God, and (there is) one mediator (between) God and man, (the) man Christ Jesus, who gave Himself (as) a ransom on behalf of (ἀντίλυτρον ὑπέρ[581] [*antilutron huper*]) all,[582] the testimony in reference to its own times[583] (1 Timothy 2:5–6).

Blessed is the LORD, the God of Israel,[584] because He has visited[585] and has provided[586] redemption (λύτρωσιν [*lutrōsin*]) for His people; and He has raised up a horn of salvation for us in the house of David, His servant (Luke 1:68–69).

But when Christ,[587] a high priest of good things which are happening, made a public appearance[588] through the greater and more perfect tabernacle—not made by hand, that is, not of this creation, and not through (the) blood of goats and calves, but through His own blood, He entered once[589] into

---

[580] The contextual connection of this explanatory γάρ (*gar*) is exceedingly important. It plugs back into Paul's urging of prayers to be made on behalf of all people including those of the highest human rankings (1 Timothy 2:1–2). This ministry of prayer is identified as being "good and acceptable (or, pleasing) in the presence of our Savior, namely, God" (1 Timothy 2:3). Our God, Paul next describes as the One "who desires all men to be saved and to come to a (real) knowledge (ἐπίγνωσιν [*epignōsin*]) of (the) truth" (1 Timothy 2:4). The following explanation of vv. 5–6 is tied tightly to this context of vv. 1–4. Do these apostolic affirmations about God desiring all men to be saved (v. 4) and Christ's offering of Himself as a "ransom for all" (v. 6) demand that we adopt the unlimited atonement view? Not necessarily. Let me first offer some food for thought that should help to sharpen focus on 1 Timothy 2:4 just *a little*. By the way, the focus is not always definitively clear exegetically and theologically for either systematic camp on this important issue of the atonement and its application(s). I would like to place 1 Timothy 2:4 into its largest circle of theological context (cf., at this time, the excursus in APPENDIX G: A Brief Introduction to the Theological Discussion Pertaining to the Divine Decree(s)).

[581] "The prefixing of *anti* emphasizes the idea of substitution" (Homer A. Kent, Jr., *The Pastoral Epistles* [Chicago: Moody, 1958] 105); cf. Wallace, *GGBB*, 388; cf. also my survey of ἀντί (*anti*) and ὑπέρ (*huper*) to follow.

[582] I.e. "all men" or "all people." Of all the terms relating to the concept of atonement in the New Testament, and out of all the ones that come from the most consistently *particularly applied* ransom-redemption group, this occurrence of ἀντίλυτρον ὑπέρ πάντων (*antilutron huper pantōn*) certainly bears some kind of *general* freight. This "all" possibly, *though not necessarily*, might refer to people of all ranks (cf., e.g., vv. 1–2) rather then each and every person who has ever lived.

[583] I.e. at God's appointed time.

[584] Zacharias was obviously praising Yahweh-God for breaking centuries of silence and sending the Messiah to rescue His people from sin, and for the birth of his own son who would be the forerunner.

[585] The verb ἐπισκέπτομαι (*episkeptomai*), "to visit," picks up various occurrences of God's visitings (cf. the verb פקד [*pqd*] in the Old Testament). These divine "visits" were either for judgment or with blessings; contextually, the latter purpose is clear in Luke 1:67ff.

[586] Literally, "made"; cf. the NASB's "accomplished."

[587] I.e. Messiah.

[588] Cf., e.g., BAG, 619.

[589] I.e. once and for all, a major message of this great epistle.

the holy (places[590]), having obtained eternal redemption (αἰωνίαν λύτρωσιν [*aiōnian lutrōsin*])[591] (Hebrews 9:11–12).

... being justified freely by His grace through the redemption (ἀπολυτρώσεως [*apolutrōseōs*]) which is in Christ Jesus (Romans 3:24).[592]

Now not only this, but also we ourselves, having the firstfruits of the Spirit, (yes) even we ourselves are groaning within ourselves, while we are eagerly waiting for (our) adoption as sons, the redemption (τὴν ἀπολύτρωσιν [*tēn apolutrōsin*]) of our body (Romans 8:23).[593]

Now of Him[594] you[595] are in Christ Jesus, who has become for us wisdom from God, both righteousness and holiness and redemption (ἀπολύτρωσις [*apolutrōsis*]) (1 Corinthians 1:30).

In whom[596] we have redemption (ἀπολύτρωσιν [*apolutrōsin*]) through His blood, the forgiveness of the[597] transgressions, according to the wealth of His grace... Who[598] is (the) down payment of our inheritance, unto (the) redemption (ἀπολύτρωσιν [*apolutrōsin*]) of the[599] possession, unto the praise of His glory (Ephesians 1:7, 14).

... in Whom[600] we have the redemption (τὴν ἀπολύτρωσιν [*tēn apolutrōsin*]), the forgiveness of the[601] sins[602] (Colossians 1:14).

---

[590] The plural either is mentally referring to the holy of holies, or it is functioning intensively.

[591] The αἰωνίαν (*aiōnian*) in reference to Christ's accomplished redemption reinforces the once-and-for-all theme of Hebrews.

[592] The beneficiaries of this redemption were previously stipulated in v.22, "all the ones who believe."

[593] Note how this dimension of Christ's redemption applies to the consummation of our salvation at the time when we will receive our resurrection bodies.

[594] I.e. by God's gracious intervention.

[595] Emphatic ὑμεῖς (*humeis*).

[596] I.e. in the Beloved One (v. 6), Christ.

[597] I.e. our.

[598] I.e. the Holy Spirit.

[599] I.e. God's.

[600] I.e. in God's "beloved Son" (v. 13b).

[601] I.e. our.

[602] Cf. and contrast Ephesians 1:7 above.

And on account of this He[603] is mediator of a new covenant, in order that, since a death[604] has occurred for (the) redemption (ἀπολύτρωσιν [*apolutrōsin*]) of the transgressions (committed) under the first covenant, the ones who have been called[605] may receive the promise of the eternal inheritance (Hebrews 9:15).

This exceedingly important word group is the most consistently narrow family in reference to the *application* of Christ's vicarious atonement.[606]

Appeasement terminology is next on the exegetical-theological agenda. As already indicated, the semantical legacy of Old Testament כפר (*cpr*) is carried on by the ἱλάσκομαι (*hilaskomai*) word group in the New Testament. The Old Testament background is discernible in most of the occurrences of this particular word family in the New Testament. There are only two appearances of the verb in New Testament revelation:

But the tax collector,[607] standing far away, was not even willing to lift up his eyes unto heaven, but rather he was beating his breast, saying, "O God, be propitiated (ἱλάσθητι [*hilasthēti*]) in regard to me,[608] the sinner! (Luke 18:13).

Therefore, He[609] was obligated to become similar to His brothers according to all things, in order that He might become a merciful and faithful high priest (regarding) the things pertaining to God, so that He might make propitiation (εἰς τὸ ἱλάσκεσθαι [*eis to hilaskesthai*]) (for) the sins of the people (Hebrews 2:17).

---

[603] I.e. Christ (v. 14).

[604] Contextually, His death.

[605] I.e. a perfect passive participle from καλέω (*kaleō*), the primary New Testament word group for the effectual call of God (cf., e.g., Leon Morris, *Hebrews*, EBC, 12:88; Hughes, *Hebrews*, 368; and especially Homer A. Kent, Jr., *The Epistle to the Hebrews* [Grand Rapids: Baker, 1972], 174).

[606] For two excellent discussions of these commercial word groups, see: Hill, *GWHM*, chapter 3; and Morris, *APC*, 11–63.

[607] As opposed to the *self*-righteous religious hypocrite (vv. 9ff.).

[608] I.e. "be gracious to me"; or, "have mercy on me."

[609] I.e. the incarnate Christ (cf. the whole previous context of Hebrews to this point).

The rest of the soteriologically significant occurrences of this word group are noun and adjective forms (cf. respectively, two masculine noun forms, two neuter nouns, and one adjectival form):

My children, I am writing these things to you in order that you may not sin. But if any person should sin, we have an advocate[610] with the Father, Jesus Christ, (who is) righteous. Indeed, He Himself is a propitiation (ἱλασιμός [*hilasimos*]) concerning (περί [*peri*])[611] our sins, not only concerning (περί [*peri*]) our own (sins), but also concerning (περί [*peri*]) (those) of the whole world (1 John 2:1–2).[612]

In this is love (ἡ ἀγάπη [*hē agapē*]), not that we loved God, but rather that He[613] loved us and sent (ἀπέστειλεν [*apesteilen*])[614] His Son (as) a propitiation (ἱλασμὸν [*hilasmon*]) concerning (περί [*peri*]) our (ἡμῶν [*hēmōn*])[615] sins (1 John 4:10).

Whom[616] God set forth (as) a propitiation (ἱλαστήριον [*hilastērion*]), through faith,[617] by means of His[618] blood, for a demonstration[619] of His righteousness on account of the passing over of previously committed sins in the forbearance of God, for the demonstration of His righteousness in the present time so that He might be just and the One who justifies the (person who has) faith in Jesus (Romans 3:25–26).[620]

---

[610] I.e. a *paraklete*.

[611] Note that the preposition περί (*peri*) does not *innately* convey the idea of substitution (cf. ὑπέρ [*huper*] and ἀντί [*anti*] below); however, it (i.e. περί [*peri*]) was often used in the LXX to identify the "sin-offering" (cf. Harris, *NIDNTT*, 3:1203).

[612] At face value, 1 John 2:2b seems to support some kind of universal affect in connection with Christ's work of appeasing the wrath of God.

[613] Emphatic; cf., e.g., Lenski's "he on his part" (R. C. H. Lenski, *The Interpretation of the Epistle of St. Peter, St. John, and St. Jude* [Minneapolis: Augsburg, 1966], 502).

[614] I.e. with absolute divine authority; this is John 3:16 language.

[615] Notice the limitation of application of Christ's work of appeasement in this context to professing Christian recipients.

[616] I.e. Christ (v. 24b).

[617] Literally "through *the* faith" (cf. the context for "the faith" being referenced); this is the channel of human responsibility for appropriating the messianic appeasement.

[618] I.e. Christ's blood.

[619] Or, proof.

[620] On some of the suggested interpretations of ἱλαστήριον (*hilastērion*) in this context see: Douglas Moo, *Romans 1–8*, WEC (Chicago: Moody, 1991), 232–238. Although ἱλαστήριον (*hilastērion*) in Romans 3:25 may not be used in the sense of "mercy seat," it most definitely is in the next example (i.e. Hebrews 9:5).

Now above it[621] (there were) glorious[622] cherubim overshadowing the mercy seat (τὸ ἱλαστήριον [*to hilastērion*])[623] (Hebrews 9:5a).

For[624] I[625] will be merciful (ἵλεως [*hileōs*]) in regard to their unrighteousness,[626] and I will remember their sins never again[627] (Hebrews 8:12).

The prominence of this word group in the Epistle to the Hebrews should not come as a surprise to us since this very soteriologically significant book develops the complex theme of the absolute supremacy of Christ. Our Lord is presented as the Priest par excellence, even the great High Priest;[628] amazingly, He Himself also was the ultimate sacrifice. Because of the propitiatory sacrifice of Himself upon the 'altar' of the cross, the wrath of God is fully and finally appeased. Applications of this ultimate appeasement[629] may be inferred from the respective contexts[630] of occurrences of the ἱλάσκομαι (*hilaskomai*) word group.

Rounding off the word groups pertaining to the concept of atonement in the New Testament is the family built upon the Greek root ἀλλ (*all*), which most basically signifies "to change," etc.[631] Theologically, i.e. soteriologically, this word group in the New Testament has to do with a changed relationship, i.e. between a holy God and sinful men. This change was brought about by the death of Christ. I will cite two occurrences of the singly compounded verb in Romans 5:10, a couple of occurrences of the singly compounded noun found respectively in Romans 5:11 and 11:15, then occurrences of singly compounded verbs

---

[621] I.e. the ark (v. 4).

[622] Cf., e.g., in the sense of magnificent in appearance.

[623] I.e. "the place of propitiation" (BAG, 376).

[624] I.e. the causal basis for the response of the redeemed in v. 11.

[625] I.e. God.

[626] Hebrews 8:12a is a quote out of a prominent Old Testament revelation about the New Covenant. The part quoted here is found in Jeremiah 31:34: "For I will pardon (אֶסְלַח [*'eslaḥ*]) their iniquities and not remember their sins any more." Remember, however, that the author of Hebrews quite frequently utilizes the LXX; herein, cf. Jeremiah 38:34 (LXX).

[627] Literally "I will never ever again remember their sins" (bad English, but good Greek!).

[628] Based on the imagery of the ones who entered the holy of holies once a year on the great Day of Atonement.

[629] I.e. both general ones and most importantly the particular ones of eternal consequence.

[630] I.e. the immediate and larger circles of context, also sometimes taking into consideration the interpretive principle of the analogy of Scripture (especially when it involves the other data pertaining to the atonement). Cf. some good interactions with the data in Hill, *GWHM*, chapter 2; and Morris, *APC*, chapters 5–6.

[631] Cf. Büchsel, *TDNT*, 1:251.

*and* nouns functioning *together* in 2 Corinthians 5:18–20. Finally, at the end of the list will appear three occurrences of the *doubly* compounded form of the verb in Ephesians 2:16 and Colossians 1:20, 22:[632]

> For if, while we were enemies,[633] we were reconciled to God (κατηλλάγημεν τῷ θεῷ [*katēllagēmen tō theō*])[634] by means of the death of His Son, much more, since we have been reconciled καταλλαγέντες [*katallagentes*])[635] we shall be saved (σωθησόμεθα [*sōthēsometha*]) in connection with[636] His life. And not only (this), but also, glorying in God through our Lord Jesus Christ through whom we received the reconciliation (τὴν καταλλαγὴν [*tēn katallagēn*]) (Romans 5:10–11).[637]

> For if their[638] rejection (means) the reconciliation (καταλλαγὴ [*katallagē*]) of the world,[639] what will (their)[640] acceptance (mean), except life out from among dead ones (Romans 11:15).

> Now all things (are) from God[641] who has reconciled us (τοῦ καταλλάξαντος [*tou katallaxantos*][642])to Himself (ἑαυτῷ

---

[632] Once again, these are the soteriologically significant occurrences of words from this important family about *change*.

[633] Or, taking the participial phrase concessively, "although we were enemies" (i.e. of God). Cf. similar temporal or concessive phrases exposing our former state in vv. 6a and 8b. Notice how Romans 5:10, along with the contexts of Ephesians 2:16 and Colossians 1:20, 22 which speak about the resultant peace established by our Lord's death, portray the essence of biblical reconciliation. At the bottom-line, we are talking about Christ's peace-making work on the cross.

[634] This is most obviously a divine passive (i.e. we were reconciled by the Father through the death of His Son).

[635] The participle literally translates "having been reconciled," but a causal sense best fits Paul's "much more" point to follow.

[636] Especially compare the emphasis on union with Christ which follows; or, the ἐν (*en*) could be construed instrumentally, "by his *life*."

[637] Notice how these three occurrences from this changed-relationship word group in Romans 5:10–11 are focused *particularly* on those who have been justified (cf. 5:1ff.).

[638] I.e. the vast majority of Jews who were rejecting their Messiah-Savior.

[639] I.e. the benefits of Christ's peace-making work extending out and being received by Gentiles all over (cf., e.g., Paul in Ephesians, chapters 2 and 3).

[640] Literally, "the."

[641] Literally, "out of God" (ἐκ τοῦ θεοῦ [*ek tou theou*]); i.e. He is the *Source* of "all things." "All things" is comprehensive including every outworking, in time, space, and history, of His decree. The most immediate application in this context would be the connection to the "new things" He sovereignly brings about in reference to every person who is in Christ by grace through faith (i.e. v. 17). Better yet, the context is clearly developing a salvation-history contrast of aeons; cf. Martin's translation of 2 Corinthians 5:17b–18a: "the old order has gone, to be replaced by the new [in every way]. And this new order in all respects is God's doing" (*2 Corinthians, WBC*, 135).

[642] Very literally, Paul calls God "the having reconciled us (one)." Note that the objects of Christ's peace-making work are contextually looked upon as believers *in v. 18.*

[*heautō*][643]) through Christ (διὰ Χριστοῦ [*dia Christou*][644]) and who has given[645] to us (ἡμῖν [*hēmin*][646]) the ministry of reconciliation (τὴν διακονίαν τῆς καταλλαγῆς [*tēn diakonian tēs katallagēs*]): that[647] God[648] was in Christ (ἐν Χριστῷ [*en Christō*]) reconciling the world to Himself (κόσμον καταλλάσσων ἑαυτῷ [*kosmon katallassōn heautō*][649]), not reckoning to them their[650] transgressions, also having placed in reference to us the word of this reconciliation (τὸν λόγον τῆς καταλλαγῆς [*ton logon tēs katallagēs*][651]). Therefore, on behalf of Christ (ὑπὲρ Χριστοῦ [*huper Christou*]), we are ambassadors, as though God is urging through us; we beg on behalf of Christ, be reconciled to God (καταλλάγητε τῷ θεῷ [*katallagāte tō theō*])[652] (2 Corinthians 5:18–20)!

For He Himself is our peace,[653] the one who made[654] the both[655] one and destroyed the dividing wall of the barrier by abolishing in His flesh the enmity, the law of the commandments consisting in ordinances,[656] in order that He might cre-

---

[643] I.e. to God (in context, God the Father).

[644] "...Christ is the divinely appointed means...of reconciliation" (Harris, *NIDNTT*, 3:1182).

[645] The participle connected by the "and" goes back to "the having reconciled us" description of God which appeared earlier. Now God is being pictured as "the-having-given-us" Father. God, the great "Giver," is a common theme throughout Scripture.

[646] The first person pronoun, like the previous one, by context is to be regarded as a reference to believers. I will not deal with the various arguments, one way verses the other, concerning whether or not this "us" is exclusive (i.e. Paul and company) or inclusive (i.e. Paul, company and his believing readership); the latter seems most reasonable *in this verse* (cf. and contrast v. 20).

[647] On the pleonastic ὡς ὅτι (*hōs hoti*), cf. BAG, 593.

[648] Again, by context, God the Father.

[649] In v. 19 the object of divine reconciliation is said to be "(the) world" (literally an anarthrous noun, "world"). Needless to say, this apparently creates a tension with the more specific objects of Christ's peace-making work identified in vv. 18 and 20 (respectively, "us" and "you"). Later I will present a model suggesting an interrelationship of macrocosmic and microcosmic usages of "world." For now concerning 2 Corinthians 5:16–21, the comments of Martin pertaining to v. 19 in this context are helpful (*2 Corinthians*, WBC, 134ff., especially 146–148). In the midst of all his discussion he warns that v. 19 "says no more than that God in Christ has acted in such a way as to restore friendly relations between the world and himself" (148).

[650] Literally, "the transgressions."

[651] Or, more dynamically, "He has entrusted us with the message of reconciliation" (Martin, *2 Corinthians*, WBC, 135).

[652] This passive imperative is obviously intended to stir up the responsibility of the readership to appropriate the benefit of Christ's peace-making work.

[653] The language of Ephesians 2:14ff definitely reveals the essence of reconciliation (cf. "peace" again in vv. 15 and 17); contrast their former condition of "enmity" (v. 15).

[654] The antecedent is located by moving backwards through v. 14a to v. 13, namely, "Christ Jesus."

[655] I.e. Jew and Gentile (cf. 2:11–3:7).

[656] BAG, 200.

ate in Himself the two into one new man, making peace, and that He might reconcile (ἀποκαταλλάξῃ [*apokatallaxē*])[657] the both in one body to God through the cross, having put to death the enmity by means of it[658] (Ephesians 2:14–16).

...and through Him[659] to reconcile (ἀποκαταλλάξαι [*apokatallaxai*]) all things to Himself by making peace through the blood of His cross, (yes), through it, whether the things upon the earth or the things in heaven (Colossians 1:20).[660]

And you,[661] formerly being alienated and enemies in your[662] mind in connection with your[663] evil works, He has now[664] reconciled (ἀποκατήλλαξεν [*apokatēllaxen*]) (you)[665] in the body of his[666] flesh through his[667] death so as to present you holy and spotless, beyond reproach in His presence (Colossians 1:21–22).[668]

So, most fundamentally, the reconciliation dimension of Christ's atonement has to do with the establishment of peace between man and God. Concerning this particular operation of grace, "God is the subject, man is the object, Christ is the means."[669]

---

[657] The double compound possibly suggests "'to reconcile completely' ... 'to change from one condition to another,' so as to remove all enmity and leave no impediment to unity and peace" (Vine, *EDNTW*, 514).

[658] Here the application of Christ's peace-making work pertains to the relationship of the two major ethnic categories of humankind, Jews and Gentiles.

[659] I.e. Christ (vv. 13b ff.)

[660] This occurrence of the strengthened verb form for reconciliation possibly connotes "to change back" (cf., e.g., S. Lewis Johnson, Jr., "From Enmity to Amity," *B Sac* [April, 1962]:143). It sits in a context which applies it to the whole created order (i.e. τὰ πάντα [*ta panta*]). What Paul says here seems to be the basis for the groaning creation's ultimate restoration (cf. Romans 8:18ff.). Note: Johnson, ibid., 143–145, for some condensed conclusions.

[661] Structurally, Colossians 1:21–23 is similar to Ephesians 2:1–3 (cf. Colossians 1:21) followed by Ephesians 2:4–10 (cf. Colossians 1:22–23). The accusative ὑμᾶς (*humas*), indicating the objects of reconciliation is brought forward so as to introduce a B. C. description of them. A condensed description follows.

[662] Literally, "the."

[663] Literally, "the."

[664] The "now" flags their A. C. state.

[665] Here's where the ὑμᾶς (*humas*) of v. 21 fits.

[666] I.e. Christ's.

[667] Literally, "the."

[668] This context is explicitly soteric. The force of vv. 21–22 is captured by O'Brien: "The gravity of their previous situation serves to magnify the wonder of God's mercy. The past is recalled not because the emphasis falls upon it, but to draw attention to God's mighty action—here in the reconciling death of his son—on the readers' behalf" (*Colossians, Philemon*, WBC, 66).

[669] John Walvoord, "Reconciliation," *B Sac* 120 (Jan–Mar, 1963):3; cf. 3–12 for a fairly good systematic survey. Cf. also Roger Nicole, "The Nature of Redemption," *Christian Faith and Modern Theology*, ed. by C. F. H. Henry (NY Channel Press, 1964), 139ff.; and Morris, *APC*, 214–250.

Now is the appropriate time to bring into this picture of the atonement, as variously colored in by those strategic word groups, the contribution of two important prepositions. The first one, ἀντί (*anti*), is incontestably vicarious in soteric contexts. The second being ὑπέρ (*huper*), according to some scholars and interpreters, is contestably substitutionary.

Concerning the several occurrences of ἀντί in key soteric contexts, Dana and Mantey have correctly insisted that:

> there is conclusive proof now that the dominant meaning for ἀντί in the first century was *instead of*.... This statement refers to the papyri usage. Professor Whitesell (Chicago) made a study of ἀντί in the Septuagint and found thirty-eight passages where it is rightly translated *instead of* in the RV. Since ἀντί is used in two atonement passages in the New Testament, such a translation needs careful consideration. Notice the following: Genesis 22:13, *and offered him up for a burnt offering instead of* (ἀντί) *his son*; Genesis 44:33, *Let thy servant, I pray thee, abide instead of* (ἀντί) *the lad a bond-man to my lord*; Numbers 3:12, *I have the Levites from among the children of Israel instead of* (ἀντί) *all the first-born*. These sentences unmistakably deal with substitution.... Does it mean *instead of* in Mt. 20:28 and Mk. 10:45...? Either that, or else it means, *in exchange for*, and each implies substitution. The obscurity of this passage is not the result of linguistic ambiguity, but of theological controversy.[670]

As already intimated, the substitutionary nature of the preposition ὑπέρ (*huper*) in soteric contexts[671] has been challenged by many critics. This time, let me appeal to Erickson's conclusion after having walked through the mine-fields of negative critics:

> The other pertinent preposition is ὑπέρ.[672] It has a variety of meanings, depending in part upon the case with which it is

---

[670] *A Manual Grammar of the Greek New Testament* (Toronto: Macmillan, 1955), 100. For more support upholding such a conclusion as that of Dana and Mantey's, cf. William Hendriksen, "The Meaning of the Preposition ἀντί in the New Testament," unpublished dissertation (Princeton Seminary, 1948); Morris, *APC*, 34–38; Harris, *NIDNTT*, 3:1179–1180; Basil F. C. Atkinson, "The Theology of Prepositions," a transcript of a Tyndale New Testament Lecture (Cambridge: Trinity College, 1943): 6; Wallace, *GGBB*, 365–367; etc.

[671] See, e.g., Luke 22:19–20; John 6:51; 10:11, 15; 11:50–52; 15:13; 17:19; 18:14; Romans 5:6, 8; 8:32; 14:15; 1 Corinthians 11:24; 15:3; 2 Corinthians 5:14, 15, 21; Galatians 1:4; 2:20; 3:13; Ephesians 5:2, 25; 1 Thessalonians 5:10; 1 Timothy 2:6; Titus 2:14; Hebrews 2:9; 5:3; 6:20; 7:25, 27; 9:7; 24; 10:12; 1 Peter 2:21; 3:18; 1 John 3:16.

[672] Herein Erickson is referring to its comparison with ἀντί (*anti*).

used. It is the instances of ὑπέρ with the genitive case that are
of particular interest to us here. It has been asserted that ἀντί
literally means "instead of" and ὑπέρ means "in behalf of." G.
B. Winer, however, has said, "In most cases one who acts in
behalf of another appears for him, and hence ὑπέρ sometimes
borders on ἀντί, *instead of*." ...In the case of ostraca and papyri, the word ὑπέρ clearly means "instead of." In some biblical passages, for example, Romans 5:6–8; 8:32; Galatians 2:20;
and Hebrews 2:9, ὑπέρ may be taken in the sense of "in behalf
of," although it probably meant "instead of." In several other
passages, however, notably John 11:50; 2 Corinthians 5:15;
and Galatians 3:13, the meaning is more obvious. Regarding
these verses Robertson says, "ὑπέρ has the resultant notion of
'instead' and only violence to the context can get rid of it." It
is not necessary that the meaning "instead of" be overt in every instance. For there is sufficient scriptural evidence that
Christ's death was substitutionary.[673]

Besides these substitutionary prepositions and in addition to the major word groups pertaining to the issue of atonement, there are a host of
soteriological images in the New Testament. Most of these deal with
Christ's fulfillment of the Old Testament sacrifical system (e.g., Lamb,
Passover Lamb, the blood, death/die, slain, cup, baptism, delivered up,
offered up, gave Himself up, etc.). Especially relating to the language of
sacrifice and ritual, Nicole has astutely observed that

the sacrifical terminology is a most pervasive feature of the totality of Holy Writ. It is one of the great connecting features
between the two Testaments, perhaps most emphatically articulated in the Epistle to the Hebrews.[674]

Then, after referring to a few of the texts I have already cited, Nicole continues: "To the texts listed above may be added a multitude of others
where Christ is referred to as a priest, or as the Lamb, or where the emphasis is placed on His blood, or yet where the deliverance from sin is pre-

---

[673] Erickson, *Christian Theology*, 814; cf. also: Morris, *APC*, 62–64; Dana and Mantey, *Manual Grammar*, 111–112; Harris, *NIDNTT*, 3: 1196–1197; Atkinson, "Theology of Prepositions," 13–14; Wallace, *GGBB*, 383–389.
[674] Nicole, "The Nature of Redemption," 198.

sented as a purification or cleansing."[675] These are the kinds of data one must seriously consider *prior to* synthesizing a theology of atonement.

Therefore, a couple of warnings are necessary before we move into the next section. First, all of the traditional, historical theories of the atonement are either heretical, theologically eccentric, or lacking to *some* degree in reference to their integration of *all* the exegetical data. As Robertson put it:

> ...no one of the theories of the atonement states all the truth nor, indeed, do all of them together. The bottom of this ocean of truth has never been sounded by any man's plumb-line. There is more in the death of Christ for all of us than any of us has been able to fathom.... However, one must say that substitution is an essential element in any real atonement.[676]

Consequently, although the substitutionary theory is the best option, when it is viewed, *singularly and without qualification*, as the theological *box* into which the various verses pertaining to the atonement are put, we find even this container to be just a bit too small. Some of the Bible's exegetical data will not fit into it. Hermeneutical hammers and crowbars forged in the furnaces of theological presupposition should never be employed to force it. The balance of the Bible concerning any and every issue must not be violated because of human systems. Theological tensions keep cropping up. For example, on the one hand, is God requiring a double payment on the part of the non-elect?[677] On the other hand, what would be the significance of such passages as John 3:18, 36; 16:9; and 1 John 5:10 if *some sort of connection* to the non-elect is emphatically denied? Scaer summarizes the biblical challenges with these words: "The conflict concerning the nature and extent of the atonement arose in Christian theology because of apparently conflicting statements in the Holy Scriptures on the atonement and election."[678]

---

[675] Ibid. For a superb excursus that critiques the various historical interpretations of the blood of Christ, see Hughes, *Hebrews,* 329–354.

[676] Wallace, quoting Robertson, *GGBB,* 389.

[677] On this problem, John Owen's arguments have not been improved upon (cf. *The Death of Death in the Death of Christ* [London: Banner of Truth, 1959], *passim*).

[678] David Scaer, "The Nature and Extent of the Atonement in Lutheran Theology," *BETS* 10 (Fall 1967): 179. Obviously, the theological parameters that I will be sketching out in reference to this exceedingly vital issue will be informed by the meaning and significance of those biblical data that will be explored in the next section dealing with "The Divine Plan and Process" (e.g. election, effectual call; etc.). Once again, here is the point at which statements about a pre-temporal plan and a post-fall process surface periodical tensions. The analogy-of-Scripture principle must be applied *with great care*. It must not be abused by disallowing, e.g., the voice of a piece of data to speak, even if it statistically represents an exceedingly minor report. It is still a part of the Book!

## The Theology of Atonement

Having surveyed the various word groups which advance the concept of atonement in the New Testament, individual occurrences statistically range in application from those which are unequivocally particular by affirmation and/or by context to some which are more general. Generally speaking, the word groups based upon images from the commercial realm,[679] overwhelmingly but not exclusively, indicate, by their respective contexts, particular soteric applications. Most often, but not always, contextual indicators demand or intimate that soteric occurrences from the appeasement family[680] apply to the elect. Although a slightly higher percentage of occurrences from the changed-relationship group[681] seem to lend themselves to more general applications, in most places the contexts indicate applications which are soteriologically particular. Furthermore, beside the exceedingly great importance of contextual factors, the special nuances of each of the atonement word groups seem to have some bearing on their suitability to applications along a continuum from *overwhelmingly* particular in reference to the elect to *mostly* particular with a few broader applications.[682]

With this very brief review of the exegetical data in our minds, it is time to view the theological battle over "limited" versus "unlimited atonement." Before we proceed, however, notice how this *systematic-theological* war *historically* has presented itself as offering only two options, the particularistic camp versus the universalistic camp.[683] Almost always, Christ's atonement has been perceived as "limited" *or* "unlimited." Almost always, in theological skirmishes the *intentionality* of Christ's work on the cross has been logically presented as being *singular*.

This battle, which has raged quite consistently throughout church history, has exhibited many tactical errors. One of these tactical errors is semantic in nature; we have been leading up to it via an examination of the key word groups and prepositions which develop the *concept* of atonement in the New Testament. Remember, however, that technically the *word* "atonement" does not occur in New Testament revelation. So a

---

[679] I.e. the ἀγοράζω (*agorazō*) and λυτρόω (*lutroō*) families.

[680] I.e. the ἱλάσκομαι (*hilaskomai*) word group.

[681] I.e. the καταλλάσσω (*katallassō*) family which emphasized Christ's peace-making work on the cross.

[682] These broader applications even up to and including, e.g., the cosmic dimension of reconciliation (cf. Colossians 1:20), must also be examined in the light of their immediate and larger circles of context. Once again, their voice must not be silenced hermeneutically because of a system, but they must be listened to as one sound in a much larger chorus.

[683] I prefer not bringing into this analysis the "regiment" of the Amyraldians whose *logical* colors historically seemed to be both blue and gray, thereby drawing fire from both sides.

credible New Testament theology is obliged to deal with the whole data reservoir prior to arriving at systematic conclusions. Vernon Grounds has stated the point well:

> The atonement cannot be interpreted biblically unless we are prepared to examine our own presuppositions and retain those which undergird the apostolic concept. Hence it is highly encouraging to witness among scholars a sustained attempt to go "Back to the Bible" in formulating their theories about the atonement.[684]

May we not engage in hermeneutical manipulations which destroy the *balance* of the Bible! Furthermore, terminologically, the semantic, tactical error is not eased (at least not fully) by modifying the theological vocabulary, for example, from "unlimited" to "general" and/or from "atonement" to "redemption."[685]

In this warfare, there also exist other kinds of tactical errors. The most significant of these has to do with how the two camps and the various regiments within each of them have resorted to complex fabrications of the supposedly "logical order of the divine decrees" in order to substantiate each's view of the atonement.[686] For a presentation of just some of the problems characterizing such a methodology, see APPENDIX G: "A Brief Introduction to a Theological Discussion Pertaining to the Divine Decree(s)." I basically consider these logical constructs to be finite exercises in futility, and I applaud the boldness of Van Til when he urged:

> ... and how avoid extremes? How attain a balanced view? By not allowing our logic to dominate over the teachings of Scripture.... Supra-or infralapsarianism,[687] taken as some advocates of these views have taken them, were faulty in their imposing of the reach of human logic upon the data of revelation.[688]

---

[684] *BDT*, 75. Grounds is correct in pointing out the need to go "back to the Bible," but I do not see much of that going on in these two systematic-theological camps. For the most part, they have entrenched themselves deeply.

[685] Apart from minor considerations, the issues are not really completely clarified *biblically* by choosing one set of terms over another, but they would be by the easing of the "or" ultimatum in the presence and control of both sets of biblical data.

[686] For a good bird's-eye survey of the various orders, see Warfield's chart (B. B. Warfield, *The Plan of Salvation* [Grand Rapids: Eerdmans, 1935], 33).

[687] Or any of the other "'logical constructs'"!

[688] Cornelius Van Til, *Common Grace and the Gospel* (N. P.: Presbyterian & Reformed, 1973), 145–146.

Taking Van Til's words as a challenge, how can some sort of a truce be reached? Most simply, by commitments to hermeneutical honesty! A general, introductory statement by Steele and Thomas exemplifies the kind of exegetical integrity that historically has been in short supply:

> Some passages speak of Christ's dying for "all" men and of His death as saving the "world," yet others speak of His death as being definite in design and of His dying for particular people and securing salvation for them.[689]

Turner admirably jumps right into the front lines of this battle standing between the combatants:

> Arminian general redemptionists highly prize passages such as 2 Peter 2:1, but do not properly understand passages such as John 10:11; John 17:2; Acts 20:28; and Ephesians 5:25 which clearly teach that Christ's death had special reference to the elect.... Arminianism, which holds that Christ died only to make men savable, is rejected by this writer.... The plain sense of the Word of God cannot be distorted because of theological presuppositions. The Word of God must mold theology, not vice versa.... Men are condemned because they do not believe this truth (John 3:18; 16:9; 1 John 5:10). This truth does not contradict or deny the corollary truth, namely that Christ's death has a special reference to the elect. It not only provides a way of salvation for the elect, but also effectuates that salvation through the means of irresistible grace. The cross is not the sole saving instrumentality, but it does guarantee that God will draw His elect to Himself.... The first problem with general redemption regards the very nature of redemption. General redemptionists must posit some element of potentiality or conditionality in redemption.... A second problem with general redemption concerns double payment. Particular redemptionists argue that God could not send men to hell to pay for their own sins if Christ

---

[689] David N. Steele and Curtis C. Thomas, *Romans, An Interpretive Outline* (Phillipsburg: Presbyterian Reformed, 1967), 174; cf. also Edwin Palmer, *The Five Points of Calvinism* (Grand Rapids: Baker, 1972), 50–52. Also, a very interesting and profitable study would be to take all the passages with data pertaining to the atonement and look them up in Calvin's *commentaries* to see how he handled both sets of data. Although I do not agree with his every hermeneutical call (e.g., it seems to me that in a *few* places where he should have come down on the particular side, he ended up on the general side; and vice versa), I do so admire his basic commitment to exegetical inductivity.

had already paid for them on the cross.... This writer admits that this[690] was a purpose of the atonement, but he denies that this is the only purpose.[691]

Notice how Turner's view, as duly influenced by all the biblical data, exposes the fallacies of the major either/or alternatives. The exegetically eccentric alternatives[692] may be summarized respectively as to the crux of their difference like this:

The atonement is particular in its design and intention (note the singular "design"... "intention").

The atonement is general in its design and intention (again, note the singulars).

Besides Turner's more exegetically driven reasons for arguing for a both/and treatment of the biblical data, some individuals during the course of church history have issued calls for a more biblically balanced perspective on the atonement. Although their arguments basically have been more philosophical in nature,[693] they do point to the need for theological balance.

A scriptural watchword for a both/and view may be taken from 1 Timothy 4:10:[694] "For unto this[695] we are toiling and striving,[696] since we

---

[690] Exegetically, he leaves room for a dimension of redemption that is applicationally different from the eternally particular redemption of the elect.

[691] David L. Turner, "An Analysis of the New Testament Evidence Commonly Asserted in Favor of the Doctrine of General Redemption" (unpublished Th. M. thesis, Grace Theological Seminary, 1976), 50, 70, 118–119, 121, 122–123.

[692] These certainly are not all hermeneutically eccentric to the same degree. Indeed, the basic particularistic position could credibly muster *most* (but not all) of the scriptural data on its side. Nevertheless, when someone from either side of this theological fence insists on one versus the other of the seemingly theo-*logical* alternatives, he locks out either more or less of the exegetical data relating to the atonement.

[693] Cf., e.g., Augustine's famous statement *sufficienter pro omnibus, efficienter pro electis* (i.e. "sufficient for all; efficient for the elect"). Buswell claims that Calvin grudgingly tolerated this maxim (James Oliver Buswell, *A Systematic Theology of the Christian Religion* [Grand Rapids: Zondervan, 1962] 2:141). Speaking of Buswell, he outlines the points of agreement among "moderate Calvinists" as follows: 1) the atonement "is *sufficient* for all"; 2) "the atonement is *applicable* to all"; 3) "the atonement is *offered* to all"; 4) "the atonement is particular in its *ultimate results*" (ibid., 141–142). Minimally, I would want to qualify the second point with, e.g., the words "although in different senses."

[694] For our purposes, it is not necessary to engage in a protracted discussion as to whether the "trustworthy saying" of v. 9 is retrospective (cf., e.g., James Moffatt, "The First and Second Epistles to Timothy and the Epistle to Titus," *Expositor's Greek Testament* [Grand Rapids: Eerdmans, reprinted 1970], 4:124) or points to the maxim of v. 10 (cf., e.g., Henry Alford, *Alford's Greek Testament* [Grand Rapids; Guardian, 1976], 3:340).

[695] Most likely Paul is referencing the "godliness" of v. 8.

[696] I.e. ἀγωνιζόμεθα (*agōnizometha*), an athletic term which makes its way into English as "to agonize."

have set our hope upon the living God,[697] who is Savior (σωτήρ [*sōtēr*]) of all men (πάντων ἀνθρώπων [*pantōn anthrōpōn*]) especially (μάλιστα [*malista*][698]) of believers (πιστῶν [*pistōn*]).” God is clearly identified as the “Savior” of “all men” and of “ones who believe.” No matter how one interprets this statement, he must not deny or grossly distort this apostolic affirmation. However, it is apparent that God is not necessarily the Savior of both groups *in the same way or to the same degree*. For example, Moffatt, years ago, argued that “the *prima facie* force of μάλιστα certainly is that all men share in some degree in that salvation which the πιστοί enjoy in the highest degree.”[699] It seems at the bottom line of 1 Timothy 4:10 there is some sort of a macrocosmic application of salvation, *and* there is a special microcosmic application.

Now, concerning the atonement in its mega biblical setting, it seems to suggest different levels of divine intentionality which lead to different applications of it. There is an efficient dimension to the death of Christ, and there is also a sufficient dimension.[700] An exegetically based both/ and position sees in the Scriptures more than a single purpose to the cross-work of Christ, although most of the passages do contextually emphasize the preeminently particular intention of the atonement.[701] The ultimate purpose is especially related to the securing of the salvation of the elect. However, there seems to be a general dimension as well. For example, the death of Christ as propitiation and reconciliation apparently has provided the ultimate grounds for common grace. Furthermore, Christ’s atonement as couched in its broader contexts most likely affects the withholding of an immediate exercise of the divine wrath. In certain contexts (e.g. John 3:18, *et. al*), there also seems to be enough generality in the cross-work of Christ to place *all* hearers of Good News on a higher plane of accountability. Those who do not respond to the Gospel are therefore guilty of the ultimate rebellion. And yet, the Bible teaches that original sin and natural depravity will bring, apart from a sovereign intervention of saving grace, eternal condemnation.

Needless to say, a biblically balanced both/and view creates logical tensions, but the Scriptures must inform us, not we them. To review this

---

[697] Next follows the soteriologically strategic appositional description of our living God.

[698] I.e. “most of all, above all, especially, particularly” (BAG, 490).

[699] *EGT*, 4:125. The qualification “in some degree” is crucial. I would prefer “in some sense.” For a discussion of four historical views on how Paul might view God as Savior of both groups, see Homer A. Kent, Jr., *The Pastoral Epistles* (Chicago: Moody, 1958), 158–160.

[700] The latter dimension must never be regarded as a vicarious blank check that makes all men savable. Such a conception is utterly disallowed when the totality of biblical data is brought to bear on it.

[701] Humorously, when confronted by systematists who arrange themselves at different places along the “‘Calvinistic’” continuum, I have said that the *tulips* which abundantly grow in biblical soil seem to average about four and three-quarters petals!

both/and position regarding the atonement, see my diagram and brief explanatory notes in "APPENDIX H: Narrowing Specifications of God's Soteriological Provision."

# The Divine Plan and Process[702]

As already observed, the divine plan includes every stage of salvation from initial salvation[703] through the pathway of sanctification all the way "home" to glorification. But it all issues from the eternal plan of God. Furthermore, although His predetermined plan is cosmically comprehensive, when it comes to lost people its most foundational element is election.

# Election

## Terminology of Election[704]

In the Old Testament, the primary word for election is בָּחַר (bāḥar).[705] This verb means most basically "to choose" or "to select," and theologically, "to elect." Where the LORD is noted as subject, "God chooses a people (Ps 135:4), certain tribes (Ps 78:68), specific individuals (I Kgs 8:16; I Chr 28:5; I Sam 10:24; II Sam 6:21), and a place for his name (Deut 12:5; etc.)."[706] Most particularly, "the focus of the theological usage of bḥr lies on the discussion of the election of the people by God..., while the human choice of God or of the right path fades in significance."[707] Deuteronomy 7:6–8 stands as a primary text concerning the corporate election of Israel by God:

---

[702] As an introduction as to where we are going next, please see APPENDIX I: The Intricate Outworkings: A Biblical *Ordo Salutis*.

[703] Cf., e.g., the historical justification of an elect person in time, space, and history.

[704] The words and passages cited will not all directly pertain to election in the spiritually and eternally salvific sense. Nevertheless, the broader concept of divine choice will help to clarify the soteriological employments of these various terms throughout revelation.

[705] For a helpful distribution chart of the Qal occurrences of בָּחַר (bāḥar) with categories of common usages and theological usages both with God as Subject (67%) and with people as subject, see: Wildberger, *TLOT*, 1:211.

[706] Oswalt, *TWOT*, 1:100. On God's choice (and often rejection) of the theocratic kings of Israel note some continuities *and discontinuities* with other ANE nations (Wildberger, *TLOT*, 1:213–215).

[707] *TLOT*, 1:213. This tendency in principle seems to foreshadow Jesus' affirmation recorded in John 15:16. In comparison and contrast with this predominate Old Testament pattern, Nicole has well argued that "in some cases (about 12 percent) humanity is the subject of the verb. In this case, God is never the direct object.... This reticence does not reduce in any way human responsibility, but safeguards the transcendence of God, who cannot be the simple object of human, often poor, choices" (*NIDOTTE*, 1:639).

For you are a holy people to Yahweh, your God; Yahweh, your God, has chosen you (בְּךָ בָּחַר [b*e*kā bāḥar])[708] to be His personally prized property (לִהְיוֹת לוֹ לְעַם סְגֻלָּה [lihyôt lô l*e*ʿam s*e*gullâ]) out from among all the peoples who are on the face of the earth.[709] It was not that you were more numerous than all the peoples (that) Yahweh set His affection on you (בָּכֶם חָשַׁק יהוה [ḥašaq yhwh bākem]) and chose you (וַיִּבְחַר בָּכֶם [wayyibḥar bākem]), for you were the fewest of all peoples. But rather because Yahweh loved you (מֵאַהֲבַת יהוה אֶתְכֶם [mē'ah*a*bat yhwh 'etkem]) and kept the oath which He had sworn to your fathers; Yahweh brought you out with a strong hand and ransomed you from a house of slavery, from the hand of pharaoh, king of Egypt.[710]

Taking off from this very passage Vine has noted:

God's "choices" shaped the history of Israel; His "choice" led to their redemption from Egypt (Deut. 7:7–8), sent Moses and Aaron to work miracles in Egypt (Ps. 105:26–27), and gave them the Levites "to bless in the name of the Lord" (Deut. 21:5). He "chose" their inheritance (Ps. 47:4), including Jerusalem, where He dwelt among them (Deut. 12:5; 2 Chron. 6:5, 21). But "they have chosen their own ways, and... I also will choose their delusions, and will bring their fears upon them..." (Isa. 66:3–4).[711]

In application to individuals, but rarely ever restricted merely to individuals,[712] Nehemiah 9:7–8 is an exemplary passage:

You are Yahweh, the God, who chose Abram (אֲשֶׁר בָּחַרְתָּ בְּאַבְרָם [*a*šer bāḥartā b*e*'abrām,]) and brought him out from Ur of

---

[708] Quite consistently with בָּחַר (bāḥar), its object is indicated by the prefixed preposition בְּ־ (b*e*-).

[709] The מִכֹּל הָעַמִּים (mikkōl hāʿammîn) is significant for a proper understanding of election; as Seebass argues: "Everywhere that bḥr occurs in relationship to persons, it denotes choice out of a group (generally out of the totality of the people).... Thus throughout, bḥr includes the idea of separating.... The most important passages where bḥr is used in this sense are Dt. 4:37; 7:6f.; 10:14f.; 14:2; and 1 K. 3:8" (TDOT, 2:82–83).

[710] Note that the ultimate basis of Israel's election was that God loved and chose this nation *just because* God loved and chose them! Quell puts it this way: "The one thing which remains vital in the Old Testament concept of election is the element of the mysterious and the inexplicable which Dt. expresses in the words: 'He has loved you'" (TDNT, 4:168).

[711] EDOTW, 34.

[712] We are going to hear much more about *solidarity* in the discussions to come (this phenomenon is not merely restricted to Adam theology).

the Chaldees, and named him "Abraham." And you found his heart[713] faithful[714] before you, and you made a covenant with him to give the land of the Canaanites, the Hittites, the Amorites, the Perizzites, the Jebusites, and the Girgashites to his seed. Now You have upheld Your promise because You are righteous.

The function of בָּחַר (bāḥar) referring to the election of individuals and/or a particular group of people is perpetuated by this verb's primary semantical counterpart throughout the LXX and on into the New Testament (i.e. ἐκλέγομαι [eklegomai]). But prior to rushing to New Testament revelation, it must be stated, with great emphasis, that the *concept* of election in the Old Testament is not restricted to linguistic parallels of בָּחַר (bāḥar). Nicole makes this point when he observes:

In the Old Testament the concept of divine election (of Israel, of individuals within the people) is closely connected to the use of the verb *bḥr*, choose. It must, however, be borne in mind that such an important and encompassing theme cannot be understood in terms of a single Heb. word. The very fact of divine election is embedded in Israel's history from the patriarchs onwards, and the idea is conveyed by other words or expressions, such as the roots *yd'* I, know[715]..., *bdl*, separate[716] ..., *lqḥ*, take[717]..., *kwn*, establish[718]..., and *qr'*, call[719]..., and it underlies concepts such as "the people of the LORD" (Judg 5:11), "treasured possession" (Exod 19:5), "holy nation" (Exod 19:6), and "covenant" (Deut 5:2).[720]

Now moving on into the New Testament, it will be beneficial to sub-categorize the Greek terminology, beginning with *terms denoting choosing*. Obviously, the ἐκλέγομαι (eklegomai) word family statistically predominates within this theological sub-group. This is so primarily because the LXX preferred ἐκλέγομαι (eklegomai) as the rendering of

---

[713] לְבָבוֹ (l'bābô), the core of his being, i.e. him.
[714] I.e. נֶאֱמָן (ne'emān); cf. the אמן ('mn) verb for Abraham's *faith* in Genesis 15:6, which faith showed its fruit in the patriarch's *faithfulness* (cf., e.g., Genesis 22); cf. also the applicational truth of Habakkuk 2:4.
[715] Cf., e.g., Genesis 18:19; Jeremiah 1:5; Amos 3:2.
[716] Cf., e.g., Leviticus 20:24, 26; 1 Kings 8:53.
[717] Cf., e.g., Numbers 8:16; 2 Samuel 7:8; 1 Kings 11:37.
[718] Cf., e.g., 2 Samuel 7:24.
[719] Cf., e.g., Hosea 11:1.
[720] *NIDOTTE*, 1:638.

choice for    בָּחַר (*bāḥar*). Furthermore, in this same vein, "ἐκλέγεσθαι has great theological significance as the chief rendering of בחר due to a desire to speak theologically."[721]

Coenen panoramically surveys some of the important continuities exhibited by this word group throughout its history of usage:

> *eklegomai*...is the mid. of *eklegō*, pick out, choose out a person or thing (from a sizable number). The act. form does not occur at all in the NT and only occasionally in the LXX.... The verbal adj. *eklektos*, which is sometimes used absolutely..., denotes the person or thing upon whom the choice has fallen. The noun *eklogē*, derived from the vb.... and originally meaning exclusively the act of choosing, can be used with the vbs. *lambanō*, take, *poieomai*, do, or *ginomai*, here in the sense of arrive at. The words of this group are used in various contexts, but wherever they are found, it is evident that certain things common to them all are implied. First, there are several objects from which to choose; secondly, the person making the choice is not tied down by any circumstances which force his hand, but is free to make his own decision. Thirdly, the person making the choice—at least at the moment of choosing—has the person or thing to be chosen at his disposal.[722]

With these generalities in mind, we would do well to review the theologically conspicuous occurrences[723] of various members of this word group in the context of New Testament revelation (study the respective references listed in the chart found in APPENDIX J).

To this primary word group, I must add three more families which develop the concept of choosing in the New Testament. The first is the αἱρέομαι (*haireomai*) family. The verb αἱρετίζω (*haretizō*) occurs only in Matthew 12:18, a quote of Isaiah 42:1, applied to God's messianic choice of Jesus. The verb αἱρέομαι (*haireomai*) is used in Philippians 1:22 and Hebrews 11:25 to indicate human choices, seemingly between two options. However, this verb's usage in 2 Thessalonians 2:13 is exceedingly significant soteriologically: "But we ought to keep on giving thanks to God at all times concerning you, brothers, beloved by the Lord, because God chose you (εἵλατο ὑμᾶς ὁ θεὸς [*heilato humas ho theos*]) as firstfruits[724] for salvation (εἰς σωτηρίαν [*eis sōterian*], i.e. unto

---

[721] Quell, *TDNT*, 4:145.

[722] *NIDNTT*, 1:536.

[723] Most of these more particularly are *soteriologically* conspicuous.

[724] A viable textual option reads ἀπ' ἀρχῆς (*ap archēs*), "from the beginning."

His *goal* of salvation) by the sanctification of the Spirit and by faith in the truth...." In a paragraph that appeals both to 2 Thessalonians 2:13 and Ephesians 1:4, Murray has appropriately argued that "election on the part of God in eternity is the source from which the process of salvation springs and it is the ultimate reason for the salvation of man—they are chosen by God unto salvation (II Thess. 2:13)."[725] Rounding out the New Testament terms which develop this concept of choosing are two related verbs, προχειρίζω (*procheirizō*) and προχειροτονέω (*procheirotoneō*). The first is used three times with two applications, God's messianic and apostolic choices or appointments (Acts 3:20, and Acts 22:14, 26:16), while the second is used only once in Acts 10:41 of God's choice of special eye-witnesses (i.e. the apostolic circle).

Now, let's briefly turn our attention to *terms denoting appointing.* The τάσσω (*tassō*) word group comes to mind first, and there are many members in its family tree.[726] Yet the simple verb remains the most significant member when it comes to the doctrine of election. Besides indicating human determinations,[727] the verb τάσσω (*tassō*) is used more significantly of divine appointments (cf. Matthew 28:16; Acts 22:10; and Romans 13:1). However, its soteriological usage in Acts 13:48b rises above them all. In order to demonstrate the impact of this clause, allow me to diagram it rather than merely translating it:

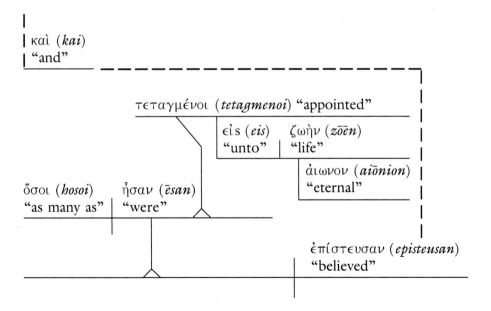

---

[725] John Murray, "Elect, Election," *BDT*, 179.
[726] Cf., e.g., Delling's family portrait, *TDNT*, 8:27–48.
[727] Cf., e.g., Acts 15:2; 28:23; and 1 Corinthians 16:15.

This indeed paints a graphic picture of who it is that believes, ultimately revealing also why it is that they believe, namely, because of the sovereign appointment of God.

A second word group, the τίθημι (*tithēmi*) group, also bears noteworthy freight for the doctrine of election viewed as appointment. Fairly regularly, "in the active voice it signifies God's destining someone for something,"[728] and "in the middle voice…God *fixes* times (Acts 12:18), appoints presbyters as overseers (Acts 20:28), and Christians to obtain salvation (1 Thess. 5:9)."[729] With immediate application to the eleven, our Lord closely associated this term of *appointment* with the primary word for *choosing* in John 15:16 a, b: "You[730] did not choose me but rather I chose you, and I have appointed (ἔθηκα [*ethēka*]) you that you should go and should bear fruit, and that your fruit should remain.…" Contrastingly, an awesomely dark (from the finite perspective) example of divine determination occurs in 1 Peter 2:8. Immediately after speaking of those who *responsibly* refuse to believe in Messiah Jesus (1 Peter 2:7b–8b), Peter goes on to affirm about the same group of people: "unto which (end) they were also appointed (ἐτέθησαν [*etethēsan*])."

Rounding off these terms denoting appointing, we finally come to the κεῖμαι (*keimai*) group. This family does not *directly* contribute to the doctrine of election; however, it does contain a few references that more indirectly provide a setting for the larger picture of divine determination. For example, in Luke 2:34 it is affirmed by Simeon that the Christ child "is appointed (κεῖται [*keitai*]) for the falling and rising of many people." Paul furthermore uses this verb to affirm one of the dimensions of his divine calling in Philippians 1:16, and in 1 Thessalonians 3:3, the apostle speaks more inclusively about the sufferings of servants of Christ as having been appointed or destined (κείμεθα [*keimetha*]) to that end by God.[731]

The next sub-category of terminology which develops the concept of election in the New Testament has as its common denominator *predestination*. The first term is found in some passages previously alluded to; it

---

[728] Packer, *NIDNTT*, 1:477; cf., e.g., Hebrews 1:2.

[729] Ibid.

[730] The first of two emphatic pronouns aiding in the making of His emphatic contrast (i.e. οὐχ ὑμεῖς με ἐξελέξασθε, ἀλλ᾽ ἐγὼ ἐξελεξάμην [*ouch humeis me exelexasthe all egō exclexamēn*]).

[731] Robertson argues that κείμεθα (*keimetha*) is a "present middle, used here as passive of *tithēmi*" (*WP*, 4:25); contextually and functionally, it should be regarded as a divine passive. Furthermore, the complementary prepositional phrases with εἰς (*eis*) found in all three of these examples identify the respective purposes of these various sovereign appointments.

is προορίζω (*proorizō*). Concerning the basic stem of this compound verb, "*horizō* is connected with *horos*, boundary, and *horion*, region. Originally it meant to set bounds, bound, and hence to establish, determine."[732] When the temporal πρό (*pro*) is prefixed to this stem ("before, beforehand," i.e. pre-), there develops a graphic picture of *pre*determination. This verb is used in the New Testament six times "in the sense 'to foreordain,' 'to predestinate.'"[733] All six of these occurrences are very formulative when it comes to biblical theology.

The occurrences of προορίζω (*proorizō*) in Acts 4:28 and in 1 Corinthians 2:7 speak more generally, respectively of God's predetermined arrangement of the chess-board of human history during passion week and to the time when the wisdom of God in the gospel of Christ was gloriously unveiled in history. The other four *directly* bear much freight when it comes to the doctrine of election.

Permit me first to re-emphasize Acts 4:28 and to cite 1 Corinthians 2:7. Along with Acts 2:22–24, verses 27 and 28 of the fourth chapter of Acts dramatically juxtapose statements about genuine human responsibility with exceedingly strong affirmations of divine sovereignty. Acts 4:27–28 reads:

> For of a truth both Herod and Pontius Pilate along with the Gentiles and the peoples of Israel were gathered together[734] in this city against Your holy child, Jesus, whom You anointed, to do (or, to accomplish) whatsoever Your hand and Your plan (ἡ βουλή [*hē boulē*]) predetermined to happen (προώρισεν γενέσθαι [*proōrisen genesthai*]).

The fulfillment of the predestined Suffering Servant made possible the launching of the historical proclamations of the Gospel. Paul reminds the Corinthians and us about the predetermined unveiling of that grand "mystery" when he says,

> But we[735] speak wisdom among the mature ones, however, not a wisdom of this age, neither of the rulers of this age who are off the scene; but we speak the wisdom of God in a mystery which has been hidden, which God predestined (προώρισεν [*proōrisen*]) be-

---

[732] Munzer, *NIDNTT*, 1:472.

[733] Schmidt, *TDNT*, 5:456.

[734] Contextually, most likely this leading verb should be taken as a divine passive, yet not to the exclusion of the human resolves that were also bound up in their assembling together.

[735] In context, the apostolic circle.

fore the ages for our glory, which not one of the rulers of this age understood, for if they had understood, then they would not have crucified the Lord of glory (1 Corinthians 2:6–8).

Now, putting the spotlight directly on election, we need to recall the second milestone of the five listed in the biblical *ordo salutis* of Romans 8:29–30: "Because whom He foreknew, He also predestined (προώρισεν [*proōrisen*]) (to be) conformed to the image of His Son, so that He might be firstborn among many brothers; and whom He predestined (προώρισεν [*proōrisen*]), these also He called…" (Romans 8:29–30a). Similar in application and force are the occurrences of προορίζω (*proorizō*) in Ephesians 1:5,11:

> just as He[736] elected us in Him[737] before the foundation of the world, that we should be holy and without blemish in His presence; in love having predestined us (προορίσας [*proorisas*]) to adoption, through Jesus Christ unto Himself, according to the good pleasure of His will, …in whom[738] also we were appointed (or, made a heritage), having been predestined (προορισθέντες [*prooristhentes*]) according to the purpose of the One who effectually operates according to the purpose of His will… (Ephesians 1:4–5, 11).

It is hard to imagine a stronger statement of sovereign determination as characterizing our election.

Equally significant are the theologically pregnant occurrences of the προγινώσκω (*proginōskō*) word group in the New Testament. Some have tried to place all the references into a temporal usage category (i.e. to know something about something or someone beforehand). But the only places in the New Testament that the προγινώσκω (*proginōskō*) family contextually denotes merely foresight (i.e. to know in advance) are Acts 26:5 and 2 Peter 3:17. In Acts 2:23, Romans 8:29a, 11:2, 1 Peter 1:2, 20 the members of this family are used in their theologically pregnant sense of foreordination. The verb indicates to "choose beforehand" and the noun means "predestination."[739] Bultmann summarizes this usage as follows: "In the NT προγινώσκειν is referred to God. His fore-

---

[736] I.e. God the Father; cf. v. 3a.
[737] I.e. in Christ; cf. v. 3b.
[738] I.e. in Christ; cf. v. 10.
[739] BAG, 710.

knowledge, however, is an election or foreordination of His people (R. 8:29; 11:2) or Christ (1 Pt. 1:20)."[740]

This usage is corroborated not only by these New Testament contexts but also by an important Old Testament precedent. Concerning this well attested phenomenon, Denney has rightly asserted that "we may be sure that προέγνω has the pregnant sense that γινώσκω (יָדַע) often has in Scripture."[741] On this connection of the stem verb γινώσκω (ginōskō) to those special uses of יָדַע (yāda‘) in the Old Testament, call to mind Genesis 18:19; Exodus 2:25; Psalm 1:6; 144:3; Jeremiah 1:5: Amos 3:2; and Hosea 13:5.[742] Now listen to how Cranfield correctly interprets the addition of the prefixed preposition προ- (pro-) to this special force of the stem: "The -εγνω is to be understood in the light of the use of yada‘ ... where it denotes that special taking knowledge of a person which is God's electing grace. The thought expressed by the προ- is not just that God's gracious choice of those referred to preceded their knowledge of Him, but that it took place before the world was created."[743] Furthermore, the pertinent New Testament texts do not speak of God's choice as predicated upon what He foresaw people would do (e.g. believe), but the contexts use this terminology to indicate His sovereign choice of *them*.[744]

With these preliminary exegetical insights before us, I'll simply translate the appropriate verses in their immediate contexts:

Men of Israel, listen to these words: Jesus, the Nazarene, a man attested by God to you by means of demonstrations of power, wonders, and sign-miracles, which God performed through Him in your midst—just as you yourselves know—

---

[740] *TDNT*, 1:715; he has also observed that the noun πρόγνωσις (*prognōsis*) "is found in the LXX at Jdt. 9:6 with reference to the predeterminative knowledge of God" (ibid., 716).

[741] Denny, "St. Paul's Epistle to the Romans," *EGT*, 2:652.

[742] For the uncompounded γινώσκω (*ginōskō*) bearing the sense of a special relationship of intimacy in the New Testament, cf. Matthew 7:23; John 10:14–15; 1 Corinthians 8:3; Galatians 4:9; 2 Timothy 2:19; 1 John 3:1; etc.

[743] *Romans*, 1:431.

[744] Cf., e.g., the repetitions of the relative pronoun οὓς (*hous*), "them," in Romans 8:29–30. Murray in commenting on Romans 8:29 has credibly concluded that "'foreknew' focuses attention upon the distinguishing love of God whereby the sons of God were elected" (*Romans* 1:318). For extended argumentation, cf. Steele and Thomas, *Romans*, 131–137. Also, Wallace rightly concludes after examining the syntactical options of Acts 2:23 that "God's decrees are not based on him simply foreknowing what human beings will do; rather, humanity's actions are based on God's foreknowledge and predetermined plan" (*GGBB*, 288).

this One, being delivered up by the predetermined purpose and foreknowledge (προγνώσει [*prognōsei*]) of God[745] you killed, having nailed Him to a cross by the hand of lawless people,[746] Whom God raised up after He loosed the pangs of death inasmuch as it was not possible for Him to be held by it (Acts 2:22–24).

Because whom He foreknew (προέγνω [*proegnō*]), He also predestined...(Romans 8:29a).

God has not rejected His people[747] whom He foreknew (προέγνω [*proegnō*]) (Romans 11:2).

Peter, an apostle of Jesus Christ to the elect,[748] to the scattered ones of the Diaspora in Pontus, Galatia, Cappadocia, Asia, and Bithynia, according to the foreknowledge of God the Father (κατὰ πρόγνωσιν θεοῦ πατρός [*kata prognōsin theou patros*]), by means of the sanctification of the Spirit, unto obedience and a sprinkling of the blood of Jesus Christ: Grace to you and peace be multiplied! (1 Peter 1:1–2).[749]

...live the time of your sojourn in fear,[750] since you know that, not with corruptible things, such as silver and gold, you were redeemed out of your empty lifestyle passed on down from your fathers, but with precious blood as of a lamb without blemish

---

[745] The collocation of βουλῇ (*boulē*) joined by καί (*kai*) to προγνῶσει (*prognōsei*) and governed by one article should be considered an extension of the Granville-Sharp rule.

[746] Note again, the overwhelming occurrence of the juxtaposition of sheer divine sovereignty and real human responsibility.

[747] I.e. Israel. God certainly has not rejected His people (cf., e.g., vv. 5, 7). As Murray has argued based upon the evidence from Romans 9–11, Israel's rejection because of unbelief is "not *total*," nor is it "final" (*Romans*, 2:xiv).

[748] As Hiebert notes, ἐκλεκτοῖς (*eklektois*) is a verbal adjective that "is passive, marking the readers as the objects of the electing action of God, who is the unnamed agent" (D. Edmond Hiebert, *1 Peter* [Chicago: Moody, 1992], 46).

[749] The syntax of these first two verses of 1 Peter is challenging and is potentially open to options. However, "most translators favor linking the word *elect* to three prepositional clauses: according to the foreknowledge of God the Father, through the sanctifying work of the Spirit, for obedience to Jesus Christ and sprinkling by his blood" (Simon J. Kistemaker, *New Testament Commentary. Exposition of the Epistles of Peter and the Epistle of Jude* [Grand Rapids: Baker, 1987], 35). So God's elect have been chosen "according to the foreknowledge of God the Father" unto (εἰς [*eis*]), *not* because of, obedience. In the words of Hiebert, "the third phrase, 'for obedience to Jesus Christ and sprinkling by His blood,' expresses the intended outcome of the work of God with His people" (*1 Peter*, 51).

[750] I.e. in the fear of the Lord (cf. v. 17a).

and spotless, namely Christ's, foreknown (προεγνωσμένου [*proegnōsmenou*]), on the one hand, before the foundation of the world, but on the other hand, manifested at the end of the times for your sake... (1 Peter 1:17b–20).

Hiebert neatly weaves together the two occurrences of προγινώσκω (*proginōskō*) in 1 Peter in the following fashion:

In his opening salutation, Peter assured his readers that they were included in the redemptive foreknowledge of God (1:1–2). Now their Redeemer is presented as central in that divine foreknowledge. "Was chosen" (*proegnōsmenou*) translates a perfect passive participle and designates the central place that Christ had, and continues to hold, in God's redemptive plan. The verb more literally means "was foreknown," but much more than mere prior knowledge is involved....God foreknew the whole program of redemption, and His foreknowledge rested with affectionate favor upon the Christ who had already been chosen as man's redeemer "before the creation of the world."... Before the establishment of the material universe, before there were human sinners to be redeemed, Christ, in the eternal counsel of God (cf. Acts 2:23), had already been chosen as man's Redeemer. Christ's work as Redeemer was no remedial afterthought.[751]

And I would add, based upon the same corpus of revelational data, nor is the predestination of the elect to belief and to eternal life an afterthought.

## The Theology of Election

The Bible is exceedingly clear on the basis of election. It is not found in man or what man does, but in Who God is and what He has done. Concerning the first part of this affirmation, we should at this time mentally review all that was surveyed regarding hamartiology (cf. chapter 4). At the same time, we must also remember that for finite (and fallen) minds there will always be a tension between biblical affirmations about the pretemporal divine decree of election and the historical orientations

---

[751] Hiebert, *1 Peter*, 104.

of descriptions about a post-fallen race. However, when those who have been sovereignly chosen by grace alone understand scripturally that they are to consider themselves as part of the "same lump" of filthy clay (Romans 9:22–24), that they were part of the macrocosmic, universally condemnable world, but by the mercy of God were taken out of it to become a microcosmic assembly for His glory, some of these tensions should surely ease. A respected mentor of mine put it this way, "Until we are willing to grant that there is no way that God could be unjust to fallen sinful creatures we will have serious difficulties with the doctrine of election."[752] He also wisely went on to say, "The doctrine of predestination, for one who accepts the biblical doctrine of depravity, is the only basis of hope of success in preaching the gospel. This belief should stimulate evangelism."[753] For a historical illustration of this point, note Acts 18:10b in its context.

Concerning the second part of the above affirmation, having to do with the fact that God must take the initiative in reference to both the plan and the process of salvation, the Bible, from cover to cover, documents this truth. The sole basis of election and its outworkings is the wondrous sovereign grace of God (e.g., Deuteronomy 7:8; Jeremiah 31:3; Hosea 11:8–9; 14:4–9; Romans 9:14ff; 11:5–6; 1 Corinthians 1:27–29; Ephesians 1:3–14; 2 Thessalonians 2:13–14; etc.). Obviously, the nature of this biblical presentation of election could well be described as being "unconditional." Coenen has summarized the scriptural perspective with these notations:

> If it be asked what are the principles which underlie God's choice, the only positive answer that can be given is that he bestows his favor upon men and joins them to himself solely on the basis of his own free decision and his love which is not dependent on any temporal circumstances....What is revealed of God's work of election runs right across all the usual human standards.[754]

In reference to the purposes of election it would be beneficial to categorize them as being immediate and ultimate. The purpose of election from the immediate perspective has to do with *our* initial, progressive,

---

[752] Charles Russell Smith, "Salvation and the Christian Life" lecture, Grace Theological Seminary, 1971.
[753] Ibid. For an excellent work that thoroughly upholds Smith's thesis see, J. I Packer's *Evangelism and the Sovereignty of God* (IVP, 1961); cf. also, my *Doing God's Business God's Way*.
[754] *NIDNTT*, 1:542.

and final sanctification. For example, after speaking of the fact of Israel's election in Deuteronomy 7:7–10, verse 11 goes on to sketch out the nation's responsibility in view of God's sovereign choice of them. This charge reads: "Therefore, take care to follow the commands, decrees and laws I give you today" (Deuteronomy 7:11, NIV).[755] In Romans 8:29–30 glorification is the goal of God's predestination. Furthermore, in Ephesians 1:4, a key passage on election as the sovereign choice of God made in eternity past, the target is progressive and final sanctification: "in order that you might be holy and blameless people in His presence" (Ephesians 1:4b).[756]

Looking at the purpose of election from an ultimate perspective, it points only in one direction, *God's* glory. For example, returning to Ephesians 1 and its awesome observations about God's work of grace in the lives of elect sinners, the chorus of praise to God in vv. 6, 12, and 14 is dedicated to bringing honor and glory to the merciful God who elects and saves.[757] Peter chimes in on this kind of chorus when he says,

> But you are a chosen people, a royal priesthood, a holy nation, a people belonging to God, that you may declare the praises of him who called you out of darkness into his wonderful light. Once you were not a people, but now you are the people of God; once you had not received mercy, but now you have received mercy (1 Peter 2:9–10; NIV).

Before we move on, I need to say a word about how we should teach election. An attitude controlled by biblical balance is prerequisite concerning this often touchy subject.[758] God indeed is sovereign throughout redemption;[759] however, He is never biblically viewed as outlawing all human means.[760] As a matter of biblical fact, human responsibility is scripturally associated with both the presentation (cf., e.g., Romans

---

[755] All such scenarios are examples of the indicative/imperative scenario which will be considered more extensively when we get to chapter 6 on sanctification.

[756] Cf. also how Ephesians 2:10 relates back to 2:1–9.

[757] Cf. also the emphasis of Ephesians 2:7 in its context (i.e. vv. 1–10).

[758] Once again, the words of my mentor, C. R. Smith, express this prerequisite very well: "We should always teach election in its biblical context. The method too often used is to lift the doctrine out of its biblical setting and connections, and make it the dominating principle of a logical system of theology. The result of this method too often turns a very precious truth into a cold and forbidding thing, paralyzing the spring of Christian joy and effort. Here of all places, our pedagogy must be that of the Bible itself" ("Salvation and the Christian Life," 1971). In my own years of teaching experience all too often I have witnessed how attitudinally imbalanced zealots have been so wrong in being essentially right.

[759] Again, there is no such thing as semi-sovereignty, at least not according to God's Word!

[760] And again, this is true even though His Word never allows a theology of "'partial'" total depravity.

10:14; 1 Corinthians 3:5–9; 2 Timothy 2:10; etc.) and the reception (cf., e.g., Matthew 11:28 in context; Romans 10:8–13; 2 Peter 1:5–11 in context; etc.) of the gospel.

Furthermore, although a few texts (cf. Exodus 9:16; Proverbs 16:4; Romans 9:17, 22; 1 Peter 2:8; Jude 4) express the flip-side of election (i.e. reprobation), the larger setting of all predestination passages puts the spotlight on God's grace and mercy in that He rescues some from the condemnation which we all deserve. For example, without denying the sober, sovereign reality of Romans 9:22, that truth is not Paul's final destination. Notice the progression of the apostle's argument exhibited in Romans 9:22–24:[761]

> But what if God endured vessels of wrath, prepared[762] for destruction, with much longsuffering, because he willed to show forth his wrath and to make known his power, and in order to make known the riches of his glory upon vessels of mercy, which he prepared beforehand for glory, whom he also called, even us, not only from among the Jews but also from among the Gentiles?

Indeed in this whole portion of Romans (i.e., chapters 9–11) which contains many juxtaposed affirmations of sheer sovereignty and human responsibility,[763] Paul's major burden seems to be that with which he capstones this mega section:

> For God has shut up all in disobedience[764] that He might show mercy to all.[765]

> Oh, the depth of the riches both of the wisdom and knowledge of God! How unsearchable are His judgments and unfathomable His ways! For WHO HAS KNOWN THE MIND OF THE LORD, OR WHO BECAME HIS COUNSELOR?

---

[761] The following translation is Cranfield's (*Romans*, 2:471).

[762] Although the participle κατηρτισμένα (*katērtismena*) is middle/passive in form, it *must* be interpreted as passive or else Paul's whole illustration of the sovereign potter falls to the ground. Note also that it simply reads "prepared" or "fitted" (cf. and contrast the προητοίμασεν [*proētimosen*], "prepared beforehand," in v. 23).

[763] For another biblical exhibit of such seemingly conflicting realities note how the New Testament writers apply Isaiah 6:9–10 differently so as to express one or the other of these twin truths held in biblical tension. Its usage in Matthew 13:13–15 and Acts 28:25–27 boldly highlights human responsibility, while its employments in Mark 4:11–12 and John 12:39–40 emphasize divine sovereignty.

[764] Cf. Romans 1:18–3:20.

[765] The context of this "all" applies ethnically to Jewish and Gentile believers.

OR WHO HAS FIRST GIVEN TO HIM THAT IT MIGHT BE PAID BACK TO HIM AGAIN? For from Him and through Him and to Him are all things. To Him *be* the glory forever. Amen (Romans 11:32–36, NASB).

We are called upon to preach the GOOD NEWS.[766] We are to be the human instruments of a *general* call. Speaking of calling, the appropriate time has arrived to move on to the *effectual* call of God.

# Effectual Call

In moving from election to the effectual call, we move from God's decree in eternity past to His efficacious drawings of predestined people to salvation in time, space, and history. As stated above the efficacious call of God differs from general callings. Biblical examples of general calls would include those mentioned in Isaiah 55:1; Matthew 22:14; Revelation 22:17; etc. In the case of God's elect, the general calls of the gospel will eventually lead to His effectual drawing of them to Christ. In other words, although most sinful people persistently resist the general calls, the effectual call will indeed succeed in bringing salvation to those whom God has chosen from the foundation of the world.

## *The Terminology of the Efficacious Call*

The primary word group used to convey the theology of God's effectual call in the New Testament is the καλέω (*kaleō*) group.[767] The writings of the Apostle Paul contain most of the theologically significant occurrences of this family. Coenen notes that

> Paul used the words *kaleō* (29 times), *klēsis* (8 times) and *klētos* (7 times) almost always with the sense of divine calling.... Paul

---

[766] Unlike the few eccentrics who claim they are called to preach with equal force and regularity the Gospel of BAD NEWS (i.e. reprobation). Of course, in order to faithfully preach the Good News, although we must not begin with the BAD NEWS of reprobation, we must humbly and clearly present the bad news of a universal culpability deserving of condemnation (e.g. Romans 1:18–3:20) before we outline God's merciful provision in Christ (e.g., Romans 3:21 ff.).

[767] Cf. occurrences of verbs, verbals, nouns, and adjectives of the καλέω (*kaleō*) family found, e.g., in: Romans 1:1,6,7; 8:28, 30; 9:11, 24; 11:29; 1 Corinthians 1:1–2, 24, 26; 7:20–24; Galatians 1:6, 15: 5:8, 13; Ephesians 1:8; 4:1, 4; Philippians 3:14; Colossians 3:15; 1 Thessalonians 2:12; 4:7; 5:24; 2 Thessalonians 1:11; 2:14; 1 Timothy 6:12; 2 Timothy 1:9; Hebrews 3:1; 9:15; 1 Peter 1:15; 2:9, 21; 3:9; 5:10; 2 Peter 1:3, 10; Jude 1; Revelation 17:14.

understands calling as the process by which God calls those, whom he has already elected and appointed, out of their bondage to this world, so that he may justify and sanctify them (Rom. 8:29f.), and bring them into his service....When Paul says that God's decision is not dependent on works but solely on him who calls (Rom. 9:11), he is stressing the unfettered choice of God, which is not influenced by human preconditions. It alone brings men to faith and is able to preserve them in it. Paul's language stresses the divine initiative in its participial constructions (cf. 1 Thess. 2:12 *kalountos*, "who calls"; Gal. 1:6 *kalesantos*, "who called"; cf. also 1 Peter 1:15 *ton kalesanta*, "who called").... God's call is mediated by the message of the Gospel (2 Thess. 2:14) which comes through the witness of men....Paul addresses church members as *klētoi*, called ones (Rom. 1:6f.; 8:28; and 1 Cor. 1:2, 24). In Rom. 1:7 and 1 Cor. 1:2 he addresses the *klētoi hagioi*, those called as saints. He desires to stress that both the existence of the church and individual membership in it are based solely on the will and work of God.[768]

Although the Apostle John does not use καλέω (*kaleō*) in this theologically pregnant sense, he does quote Jesus who employs the verb ἑλκύω (*helkuō*) to the same end. John 6:44 reads: "No person has the power to come to Me[769] unless the Father who has sent me draws him (ἑλκύσῃ αὐτόν [*helkusē auton*]), and I will raise him up on the last day." Concerning this particular word for the effectual calling of God, Kent has observed that

> it must not be imagined...that this "drawing" is a mere influence which may be wholesome and beneficial if followed, but is not always successful. The verb employed is a strong one, and is used of the actual dragging of a net (John 21:6, 11), dragging someone from the temple (Acts 21:30), and haling someone into court (James 2:6). In none of the uses where material objects are involved is there any suggestion that the "drawing" was not accomplished. This concept must not be

---

[768] *NIDNTT*, 1:275.

[769] I.e. to Jesus; furthermore this a is theologically freighted use of ἔρχομαι πρός (*erchomai pros*), i.e. a *spiritual* coming to Christ.

overlooked when the word is found in the figurative sense of
the divine pull on man's spirit as here and in 12:32.[770]

What Jesus said explicitly here in John 6:44, He already said implicitly
back at verse 37 wherein He taught that "a person cannot be saved unless he comes to Jesus; he cannot come unless he is given."[771] Morris
comments,

> The words stress the sovereignty of God. People do not come
> to Christ because it seems to them a good idea. It never does
> seem a good idea to natural man. Apart from a divine work in
> their souls (cf. 16:8) men remain contentedly in their sins.[772]

There are many other concepts and contexts which stress divine initiative and enablement (cf., e.g., Luke 8:10; 24:31–32, 45; John 6:65; Acts
16:14; 1 Thessalonians 1:5; etc.). Without God taking the initiative
through effectually drawing people to Christ no one would ever be saved.
During the Reformation there was a revival of the important implications
of this sovereign work of God. Most often these implications came to the
forefront in Luther and Calvin's treatments of the *Testimonium,* the inner,
secret witness of the Spirit.[773] The Holy Spirit persuades men of the truth
of the Gospel of God and pulls them to the God of the Gospel.

## The Theology of the Effectual Call

Among those who accept the pervasive teachings of Scripture on the
doctrines of sovereign grace, there sometimes is a slight parting of ways
when it comes to the questions of how effectual is the effectual call.
Some theological interpreters discuss the strategic importance of this
doctrine but stop seemingly inches short of its goal of bringing people *to*

---

[770] Homer A Kent, Jr., *Light in Darkness: Studies in the Gospel of John* (Winona Lake:BMIT, 1974),
107. By the way, the usage of this verb in John 12:32 does *not* speak of a universally effectual call,
since the "all men" of that verse is carefully defined by the context beginning at v. 20. Christ is telling his disciples that after His death, burial, and resurrection, God would draw people to Himself,
not just from among Jews but also from among Gentiles.

[771] William Hendriksen, *John*, NTC (Baker, 1953), 1:234.

[772] Leon Morris, *The Gospel According to John*, NICNT (Grand Rapids: Eidermans, 1971), 367.

[773] Cf., e.g., John Calvin, *Institutes* I. 7:4; 8:13; etc.; B. B. Warfield, *Calvin and Augustine* (Philadelphia: Presbyterian and Reformed, 1956), 31, 80–83; Bernard Ramm, *The Witness of the Spirit*
(Grand Rapids: Eerdmans, 1959); Theo Preiss, "The Inner Witness of the Holy Spirit," *Int* 7 (July
1953): 259–80; etc.

Christ. It is as if the effectual call is viewed as running an early lap in the relay race of salvation applied, but regeneration must somehow start out of the blocks seemingly on its own before salvation is historically initiated. But the biblical scenario seems to picture the effectual call as culminating its vital, final lap with an actual passing of the baton to regeneration. At that very instant of the passing of the baton from the 'hand' of the effectual call to the 'hand' of regeneration new life begins. The biblical *ordo salutis* seems to be the climaxing of the effectual call in regeneration at which time there is also a concurrent response of faith.[774] Buswell has well described the intricate interrelationship between the efficacious drawing of the Spirit and His work of regeneration with these words: "That regeneration is the *effect* or the *result* of effectual calling is an intelligible teaching; but to identify effectual calling as the same thing as regeneration, would cause great confusion."[775] With this clarification in mind we need to see how the Bible portrays regeneration.

# Regeneration

## The Terminology of Regeneration

The explicit terminology for "regeneration"[776] occurs very rarely in the New Testament; however, implicit terminology and metaphors for it occur throughout the pages of New Testament revelation. The Greek noun occurs only in Matthew 19:28, a passage that speaks of the historical setting up of a new, messianic order in the world,[777] and in Titus 3:5 which does speak of the soteriological regeneration of individuals. This might well be looked at, in view of Matthew 19:28, as the setting up of a new order in a person.[778] Furthermore, based upon the evidence of Titus 3:5 in its context along with many soteriological affirmations from other passages, it is obvious that regeneration and renewal are intimately interrelated. We might even view regeneration as the spiritual launching pad

---

[774] This is the *response*, a *re*action to the drawing work of the Spirit and also is concurrent with regeneration.

[775] James Oiver Buswell, *A Systematic Theology of the Christian Religion* (Grand Rapids; Zondervan, 1963), 2:167.

[776] The English term derives from the Latin rendering of the Greek noun παλιγγενεσία, "*palingenesia*...a compound noun from *palin* (again) and *genesis* (birth, origin)" (Guhrt, *NIDNTT* 1:184).

[777] Packer argues that "this echo of Jewish usage points to the larger scheme of cosmic renewal within which that of individuals finds its place" (*BDT*, 440).

[778] Cf., e.g., the establishment of a new world-and-life view (2 Corinthians 5:17b) as the result of the divine impartation of spiritual life (i.e., 5:17a).

for a process of renewal into the image of Christ. Or, carrying on our relay-race illustration, once new life is divinely implanted, renewal in the biblical *ordo salutis* scheme of things, takes the baton of new life and runs the sanctification lap.[779]

As already intimated, "although the literal term παλιγγενεσία is not found elsewhere in the New Testament, the idea is most certainly prominent."[780] For example, παλιγγενεσία (*palingenesia*) "is the noun which expresses the idea of the phrase, *gennethenai anothen*, 'to be born again.'"[781] It would serve us well at this time to examine the verb γεννάω (*gennaō*) and its compound form ἀναγεννάω (*anagennaō*) in soteriologically significant settings.

In John γεννηθῆναι is always used with a reference to the point of origin, mostly ἐκ τοῦ θεοῦ[782] or ἐξ αὐτοῦ[783] (1 John 2:29; 3:9; 4:7; 5:1, 4, 18; John 1:13); ἐκ πνεύματος[784] (John 3:5, 6, 8); ἐξ ὕδατος[785] (3:5); ἐκ τῆς σαρκός[786] (3:6) ἐκ θελήματος[787] (1:13); ἄνωθεν[788] (3:3, 7).[789]

Statistically and otherwise, John 3:1ff. is a primary passage on regeneration. Guthrie adequately outlines the nature of regeneration as illustrated by Jesus in John 3, rightly connecting the data of this pericope with an important affirmation from John's prologue:

The word of Jesus to Nicodemus about the need to be born of the Spirit, as well as the flesh (Jn. 3:4, 5), is parallel to John 1:13. Indeed the whole concept of regeneration is expressed in terms which assume the action of God.... In a physical sense no-one decides on his own birth, and the use of the analogy in a spiritual sense presupposes an act of grace.[790]

---

[779] Guthrie expressed it like this, "The processes of renewal which follow from regeneration are progressive and may be summed up as sanctification....Renewal cannot precede regeneration, but it does accompany it. The new born person has already experienced the first stage of renewal" (*NTT*, 587).

[780] Erickson, *Christian Theology*, 943.

[781] Buswell, *Systematic Theology of the Christian Religion*, 2:168.

[782] Lit. to be born "out of God."

[783] Lit. "out of Him."

[784] Lit. "out of Spirit."

[785] Lit. "out of water."

[786] Lit. "out of the flesh," i.e. a reference to physical birth.

[787] Lit. "out of will."

[788] Lit. "from above," most often rendered born "again."

[789] Buchsel, *TDNT*, 1:671.

[790] Guthrie, *NTT*, 610.

Moving on to the General Epistles, Buchsel briefly but succinctly summarizes Peter's usage of the compound verb from this same word group when he notes that "in 1 Pt. regeneration is God's act on man (1:3) or by the Word of God (1:23), i.e., the Gospel (cf. v. 25)."[791]

James adds a different word to the New Testament arsenal of terms for regeneration when he says, "Having willed (it), He[792] gave birth (ἀπεκύησεν [apekuēsen])[793] to us by means of the word of truth, so that we might be a certain first fruits from among His creatures" (James 1:18). This word for "creatures" introduces yet another word group that has relevance for regeneration, the κτίζω (ktizō) word family. I have already mentioned in connection with Titus 3:5 the significance of the noun κτίσις (ktisis) in the context of 2 Corinthians 5:17. When God spiritually produces a "new creature" (καινὴ κτίσις [kainē ktisis]), He inaugurates a new, theocentrically oriented outlook in that person: "behold, new things have arrived" (ἰδοὺ γέγονεν καινά [idou gegonen kaina])![794] In Ephesians 2:10 Paul speaks of the fruit of good works which necessarily and eventually evidences itself since we "have been created (κτισθέντες [ktisthentes]) in Christ Jesus" to that end. In this same context the origin of this new spiritual creation in Christ was previously identified by another metaphor for regeneration in v. 5: God the Father "made us alive together with Christ" (συνεζωοποίησεν τῷ χριστῷ [sunezōopoiēsen tō Christō]).

When turning our attention to occurrences of members from the νεόω (neoō) and καινόω (kainoō) word families, we are confronted yet again with the seemingly inextricable bond between regeneration and renewal. It would be wise for us to study, in their respectively immediate and larger circles of context, both now under soteriology and later under sanctification, ἀνανοέω (ananoeō) in Ephesians 4:23; καινότης (kainotēs) in Romans 6:4, 7:6; ἀνακαινόω (anakainoō) or ἀνακαίνωσις (anakainōsis) in Romans 12:2, 2 Corinthians 4:16, Colossians 3:10; and, once again, the occurrence of both "regeneration" and "renewal" in Titus 3:5.

---

[791] TDNT, 1:673.

[792] I.e. God the Father (cf. v. 17).

[793] Cf. and contrast our natural plight apart from God's intervention, i.e. sin gives birth (ἀποκύει [apokuei]) to death (James 1:15).

[794] In this important area of theology, Ladd really shines (cf., e.g., TNT, chapter 34).

## The Theology of Regeneration

Via review, regeneration "denotes a saving act of God, performed on man and in man, but not by man."[795]

> Regeneration is the "birth" by which this work of the new creation is begun, as sanctification is the "growth" whereby it continues.... Regeneration in Christ changes the disposition from lawless, God-less self-seeking... which dominates man in Adam into one of trust and love, of repentance for past rebelliousness and unbelief.... The use of the figure of new birth to describe this change emphasizes two facts about it. The first is its *decisiveness*.... The second fact emphasized is the *monergism* of regeneration. Infants do not induce, or cooperate in, their own procreation and birth; no more can those who are "dead in trespasses and sins" prompt the quickening operation of God's Spirit within them... Spiritual vivification is a free, and to man mysterious, exercise of divine power (John 3:8), not explicable in terms of the combination or cultivation of existing human resources (John 3:6), not caused or induced by any human efforts (John 1:12–13) or merits (Titus 3:3–7), and not, therefore, to be equated with, or attributed to any of the experiences, decisions and acts to which it gives rise and by which it may be known to have taken place.... In the Gospel (of John), Christ assures Nicodemus that there are no spiritual activities—no seeing or entering God's kingdom, because no faith in himself—without regeneration.... Conversely, in the Epistle,[796] John insists that there is no regeneration that does not issue in spiritual activities.[797]

---

[795] Guhrt, *NIDNTT* (1:185).
[796] I.e. 1 John.
[797] Packer, *BDT*, 440–441.

# Adoption

Metaphorically there is continuity and some discontinuity as we shift our focus from regeneration, (or, "new birth") to adoption. Vine crystallizes this word-picture phenomenon when he notes that "adoption is a term involving the dignity of the relationship of believers as sons; it is not a putting into the family by spiritual birth, but putting into the position as sons."[798] He also points out how the familial nuance of the Greek term for "adoption" is related to its etymological composition: "*huiothesia* (υἱοθεσία), from *huios*, 'a son,' and *thesis*, 'a placing,' akin to *tithēmi*, 'to place,' signifies the place and condition of a son given to one to whom it does not naturally belong."[799]

The semantical background of this exact term occurs in extra-biblical texts as early as the second century BC; however, a few idiomatic parallels go back much further.[800] All the New Testament occurrences of this term (i.e. Rom. 8:15, 23; 9:4; Galatians 4:5; and Ephesians 1:5) are found in the Pauline corpus. Concerning Romans 8:15, Vine has appropriately commented as follows: "In Romans 8:15, believers are said to have received 'the spirit of adoption,' that is the Holy Spirit who, given as the Firstfruits of all that is to be theirs, produces in them the realization of sonship and the attitude belonging to sons."[801] Then Romans 8:23 comes along and focuses on the last stage of adoption:

> An important point is that R. 8:23 can also describe υἱοθεσία as future.... This is not merely asserting that man can never possess this sonship, never have it in his hands, never be in a position where he no longer needs God.... God follows a uniform course in His dealings with believers, so that sanctification acquires its meaning from the goal of the perfect and definitive consummation in which our body...will be redeemed..., so that faith becomes sight.[802]

Concerning the third occurrence of υἱοθεσία (*huiothesia*) in Romans, i.e., in 9:4, "'the adoption' is stated to be one of the privileges of Israel

---

[798] EDNTW, 14.

[799] Ibid., 13–14.

[800] Cf., e.g., MM, 648; and Martitz, TDNT, 8:397; for an outline of the Graeco-Roman custom of adoption, see Rees, "Adoption," ISBE (1939), 1:58.

[801] EDNTW, 14.

[802] Schweizer, TDNT, 8:399.

in accord with the witness of the Old Testament (cf. Ex. 4:22; Deut. 14:1; Isa. 43:6; 63:16)."[803]

In Galatians 4:5 Paul employs υἱοθεσία (*huiothesia*) as a strategic point in his polemic:

> They are said to receive "the adoption of sons," i.e., sonship bestowed in distinction from a relationship consequent merely upon birth; here two contrasts are presented, (1) between the sonship of the believer and the unoriginated sonship of Christ, (2) between the freedom enjoyed by the believer and bondage, whether of Gentile natural condition, or of Israel under the Law.[804]

Turning to Ephesians 1:5 we see a focus upon the eternal roots of our adoption, "a reference to God's foreordination which rules out all the boasting of man with his natural or acquired qualities."[805] So on the spectrum of the actualization of God's sovereign plan, from its footing and foundation in eternity past through its final historical fulfillment, Ephesians 1:5 and Romans 8:23 respectively stand at the opposite ends of it. However, the basic theological definition of "adoption" applies to all of its occurrences no matter where they fall along this applicational continuum: "It is the all-transforming act of the Son that changes bondage into sonship."[806]

---

[803] Murray, "Adoption," *BDT*, 25. I would add Hosea 11:1, esp. because of its "'many'" and "'One'" association (cf. Matthew 2:15). The connection through Romans 9:4 opens up the door to the Old Testament; as a *conceptual* backdrop, it would be appropriate to examine the relationship between God and Israel as depicted through the metaphors Father/sons/children/firstborn, etc. See., e.g. Arnold, בכר (*bkr*), *NIDOTTE*, 1:658–59; and Haag, בֵּן (*bēn*), *TDOT*, 2:155. For theological interfacings of these important relational metaphors, see: J. Barton Payne, *Theology of the Older Testament* (Grand Rapids: Zondervan, 1962), 181–182, 416–417, 425. Concerning בכר (*bkr*) especially as it occurs in Exodus 4:22 and Jeremiah 31:9, Arnold has rightly asserted: "God's grace and sovereign rule over people and nations was demonstrated by his freedom to choose those who were not the firstborn by nature and treat them as firstborn" (*NIDOTTE*, 1:659).

[804] Vine, *EDNTW*, 14.

[805] Schweizer, *TDNT*, 8:399.

[806] Ibid. In the New Testament, generally related, metaphorical parallels are found in John's expression "children of God" and in usages of "abba, Father" (for discussions, see respectively, Murray, *BDT*, 25–26, and Guthrie, *NTT*, 554–555).

# Justification

## *The Terminology of Justification*

The Hebrew root צדק (*ṣdq*) which was used in the Old Testament to convey the concept of justification was part of a larger Semitic family that shares such ideas as being just, regarding as just, etc.[807] This phenomenon of semantic continuity is acknowledged by Hill, but he also rightly goes on to note a very important feature of usage elevation in the Old Testament:

> The צדק words do not appear in biblical Hebrew as new words.... Although the biblical Hebrew use of the צדק words was founded on the earlier usage which it inherited, the words were given a characteristic content by their particular association with the terminology of the covenant-relation.... The suggested threefold development in the history of the צדק words may be of guidance in the understanding and interpretation of other religious and theological terms. This development takes the word from an association with man and his life...to an association with Yahweh, and back again to man, with a richer content and colour drawn from its relation to deity.... The idea of conformity to a norm seems to be the basic significance of the root צדק which most satisfactorily accounts for its various developments.[808]

For the people of Yahweh the norm was obviously His covenant which itself was based upon His own character.[809]

Various stems of the verb, the essentially synonymous nouns צֶדֶק (*ṣedeq*, masculine) and צְדָקָה (*ṣᵉdaqâ*, feminine),[810] and the adjective צַדִּיק (*ṣadîq*) occur "523 x in the Hebr. OT (excl. proper names) plus 1x Aram. *ṣidqâ* (Dan. 4:24)."[811] It should be remembered that Hebrew is often semantically economic. In application to the צדק (*ṣdq*) word family,

---

[807] For a good survey of צדק (*ṣdq*) in comparative Semitics, see: Reimer, *NIDOTTE*, 3:744–746. Most importantly, Reimer notes that "the notions sketched out in the survey of ANE material suggest a natural gradation in the word group that comprises both active and stative meanings: one 'acts rightly,' one can be 'be righteous'" (*ibid.*, 745).

[808] Hill, *GWHM*, 96–97.

[809] Reimer briefly stated the general principle as follows: "*ṣdq* terminology indicates right behavior or status in relation to some standard of behavior accepted in the community" (*NIDOTTE*, 3:750).

[810] On the essential synonymy of the nouns, see Koch, *TLOT*, 2:1046–1047.

[811] Ibid., 1048; for the breakdown by books of these occurrences in handy chart form, see: ibid., 1048–1049. Note that over one-quarter of these occurrences is found in the Psalms.

"the ideas of *righteousness, justification,* and *acquittal* all cluster round one verbal root, and are seen to be parts of one whole."[812] Furthermore, the theologically conspicuous occurrences of this word group manifest themselves in one of two interrelated spheres of significance, the forensic[813] and the stative/ethical. Concerning the first and prerequisite sphere of justification, the occurrence of the Hiphil verb הִצְדִּיק (*hiṣdîq*) in the last part of Isaiah 53:11 is both Christologically and soteriologically paradigmatic: "My righteous Servant (צַדִּיק עַבְדִּי [*ṣadîq ʿabdî*]) will justify (יַצְדִּיק [*yaṣdîq*]) the many, and their iniquities He[814] will bear."[815] Employing a different verb but in connection with the feminine noun צְדָקָה (*ṣᵉdaqâ*), "righteousness," another theologically laden verse reads: "And he[816] believed in Yahweh, and He[817] reckoned it (וַיַּחְשְׁבֶהָ [*wayyaḥšᵉbeha*]) in reference to him[818] as righteousness (צְדָקָה ([*ṣᵉdaqâ*])" (Genesis 15:6). It is very likely that this text about God's acquittal of Abraham was in the mind of Habakkuk when he penned God's oracle containing that key dictum about the nature and lifestyle of all people who have been graciously acquitted by the LORD: "But[819] a righteous person (וְצַדִּיק [*wᵉṣaddîq*]) by his faithfulness[820] shall live" (Habakkuk 2:4b).

Murray does a good job of surveying the ground over which we have quickly moved, especially reviewing the ultimate biblical pattern for "righteousness." He appropriately notes that צדק (*ṣdq*):

> is frequently used in the Old Testament to denote the quality of righteousness or justice and is preeminently predicated of God. As applied to God it refers to his attribute of righteous-

---

[812] Girdlestone, *Synonyms of the Old Testament*, 159.

[813] Cf., e.g., Genesis 15:6; Exodus 23:7; Deuteronomy 25:1; 1 Kings 8:32; 2 Chronicles 6:23; Job 13:18; 27:5; Psalm 106:31; Proverbs 17:15; Isaiah 5:23; Isaiah 45:25; Isaiah 53:11; etc. The majority of these occurrences involve the usage of the so-called "declarative *Hiphil*"; cf. the *Hiphil* delocutive, e.g., in Bruce K. Waltke and M. O'conner, *An Introduction to Biblical Hebrew Syntax* (Winona Lake: Eisenbrauns, 1990), 438–439.

[814] An emphatic "He."

[815] I.e. as a heavy load (cf. BDB, 687).

[816] I.e. Abraham (cf. 15:1ff.).

[817] I.e. the LORD God, the juxtaposed antecedent.

[818] I.e. Abraham, as the one who believed in the LORD.

[819] I.e. in contrast with any and all who are prideful and wicked.

[820] Note how this noun from the root אמן (*'mn*) picks up the same root for Abraham's exercise of faith in Genesis 15:6, and how the pronounced righteousness of Genesis 15:6 here in Habakkuk becomes a descriptive of any individual so acquitted by God. Furthermore, it is assumed, as illustrated by the life of Abraham and by the burden of Habakkuk, that such people will exhibit an ethical lifestyle commensurate with their positional status. For a more thorough discussion of the theology of the Genesis 15:6–Habakkuk 2:4 connection, see my "Interpretive Challenges Relating to Habakkuk 2:4b," *GTJ*, 1:1 (Spring 1980): 43–69, *passim*.

ness or justice. It is also predicated of men and describes their character or conduct or both as upright or just or righteous.[821]

Human character and conduct when judged as genuinely "just" by biblical norms is built theologically on an antecedent, forensic foundation of God. Consequently, Murray goes on to make this important connection between divine acquittal and ethical righteousness: "In connection with this justifying act of God we must reckon with the possibility that the justifying act, though strictly forensic in character, might still have respect to a righteousness of character and behavior predicable of the persons justified, after the analogy of I Kings 8:32."[822] As a matter of fact, God expects and even demands that the ethical fruit of His not-guilty declaration be subsequently displayed in the life of justified people.

Once again, the LXX has helped, semantically and theologically, to connect the Old Testament teachings about justification and righteousness to corresponding New Testament explanations and expansions. Statistically, "the *dikaios* word-group translates words belonging to the Heb. *ṣdq* word-group on 462 out of a possible 476 times."[823] Hill has done an admirable job in outlining the importance of the fact that in the LXX:

> the δίκαιος-words underwent considerable expansion and change of meaning through being consistently used to render the Hebrew root צדק.... In the classical Greek usage of the terms the idea of conformity to a standard was present and the standard was primarily that of social obligation. In the Old Testament use of צְדָקָה the standard implied possesses divine authority and often is the demands of the covenant law.... The words were employed to refer to God's character, attitude and actions. In Classical Greek usage, δίκαιος, etc., were not terms used of the divine, except at a very early date.[824]

Furthermore, "the verb δικαιόω is not found with its secular Greek meaning in the LXX: it has to be interpreted in terms of the Hebrew roots it renders. When it translates the root צדק..., the forensic sense is almost always present."[825] In this same vein, Hill also importantly stresses that "the *Hiph'il* (הִצְדִּיק), in which the declaratory and forensic connotation is dominant, is without exception translated by the active of

---

[821] Murray, *Romans*, 1:336.
[822] Ibid., 1:342–343.
[823] Seebass, *NIDNTT*, 3:354.
[824] *GWHM*, 108, 109.
[825] Ibid., 109.

δικαιόω."[826] Such are some of the providential preparations for the significance of the δικ (*dik*)[827] word-group in the New Testament.

Adjectives, adverbs, nouns, and verbs of this δικ (*dik*) word family occur throughout the New Testament.[828] Paul's writings contain about half of this group's occurrences in the New Testament. The apostle's employments of the verb δικαιόω (*dikaioō*), for example, in Romans 3:20, 24, 26, 30; 4:2, 5; 5:1, 9; 8:30, 33; 1 Corinthians 4:4; Galatians 2:16ff; 3:8, 11, 24; and Titus 3:7 are especially formulative when it comes to the doctrine of justification by grace through faith. His corollary theological references which utilize the combination of a λογίζομαι (*logizomai*) verb form, i.e. "to count, reckon, regard," etc.,[829] with the noun δικαιοσύνη (*dikaiosunē*), i.e. "righteousness" (note Romans 4:3–6, 8–11, 22–24 and Galatians 3:6[830]) also emphasize forensic justification. And even beyond these references, the Pauline doctrine of justification is highlighted by the antithetical parallelisms he draws in connection with the κατάκριμα (*katakrima*) word group[831] (cf. Romans 5:16–17; 8:33–34). Overall, Hill very capably condenses Paul's usages of the various members of the δικ (*dik*) word family:

(1)The verb δικαιόω does not seem to be used in the Epistles (not, in fact, in any of the New Testament documents) in either of the senses normally attaching to it in non-biblical Greek.[832]...Its use in the active form is the same as that of δικαιόω in the LXX where it translates the Hebrew הִצְדִּיק, with the meaning "to cause to be in the right," "to put someone in the right" by giving judgment in his favor.... Consequently, we may say that the verb is primarily and predominantly a forensic term, a word of the law-court, describing a relation to, or a status before God, the judge of all men....(2) The words "righteous"[833] and "righteousness"[834] also possess a wide area of

---

[826] Ibid., 107.

[827] I.e. the most basic Greek root of this word complex (cf. Metzger *LASNTG*, 54). Based mostly upon secular Greek usage, Spicq (*TLNT*, 1:318) says that δίκη (*dikē*), "custom, justice," etc., is "the basic term in this group."

[828] For a brief but accurate survey, see: Vine, *EDNTW*, 338–340, 534–535; for a much more thorough survey concentrating heavily on this word-group's theological impact, see: Morris, *APC*, 270–290.

[829] Cf., e.g., BAG, 476–477.

[830] I.e. the latter is a quote of Genesis 15:6; the Greek verb λογίζομαι (*logizomai*) renders the Hebrew verb חָשַׁב (*ḥašab*), and the Greek noun δικαιοσύνη (*dikaiosunē*) translates the Hebrew noun צְדָקָה (*ṣᵉdāqâ*).

[831] I.e. "judgment, condemnation"; "to judge, to condemn."

[832] I.e. "to deem right" or "to treat right" according to merely human standards.

[833] I.e. the adjective.

[834] I.e. the noun.

meaning which is strange to Greek usage, but closely related to the Hebrew צְדָקָה and the LXX δικαιοσύνη. When the noun is used with reference to man's salvation, it means "the *status* of being in the right" graciously given by God.... (3) In a manner akin to Greek usage, both δίκαιος and δικαιοσύνη are used in an ethical or qualitative sense. This is the case when they refer to that "righteousness" which must characterize Christian living in obedience to the will of God.... We may claim then with confidence that Paul's use of the group of words is firmly rooted in biblical Greek usage, rather than in that of Classical Greek writers. Awareness of this fact has provided us with an essential clue to the interpretation of Paul's language of "justification."[835]

## The Theology of Justification

Very briefly, in reference to justification, I would like to remind us of (1) the need for it in man, (2) its grounds in God, (3) its relationship to faith, and also (4) its relationship to works. At the risk of being repetitive, it would indeed behoove us at this time to review the nature and consequences of human sin. Everywhere we turn in God's Word, the Scriptures inform us that in and of ourselves we stand condemned, not acquitted, in the presence of the Righteous Judge. Passages like Job 4:17; 15:14; Psalm 143:2; Romans 3:21ff. compared with 1:18–3:20; etc. are especially exemplary. Consequently, if a man is to be just before God, the grounds of such an acquittal must be in and of the Lord Himself. The truth of this wonderful act of mercy raises a logical tension. Packer refers to this tension when he notes that "Paul's deliberately paradoxical reference to God as 'justifying the ungodly' (Romans 4:5)—the same Greek phrase as used by the LXX in Exodus 23:7; Isaiah 5:23, of the corrupt judgment that God will not tolerate—reflects his awareness that this is a startling doctrine."[836] After stating this seemingly irresolvable tension, Packer goes on to show how God amazingly resolved it in the person and work of Christ:

> Paul's thesis is that God justifies sinners on a just ground, namely, that the claims of God's law upon them have been fully satisfied. The law has not been altered, or suspended, or flouted for their justification, but fulfilled—by Jesus Christ.... On the ground of Christ's obedience, God does not impute

---

[835] *GWHM*, 160–161.
[836] *BDT*, 305.

sin, but imputes righteousness to sinners who believe (Rom. 4:2–8, 5:19).[837]

Consequently, His righteousness is reckoned as our righteousness (cf. Jeremiah 23:6; 1 Corinthians 1:30) by grace through faith.

Faith (cf. a fuller treatment in the sub-section to follow) plays a responsible role in reference to justification. Illustratively, it is important to compare the seminal response of Abraham, for example, as referenced in Genesis 15:6. Throughout the Scriptures, this eminently prominent patriarch provides a special paradigm for justification by grace *through faith*. More broadly, the ground-level necessity of faith is historically surveyed in the material contained between the bookend statements of Hebrews 11:2 and 39.[838] Indeed the necessity of faith is conspicuous throughout salvation history. However, it becomes crystal clear that

> believers are justified *dia pisteōs* (Rom. 3:25), *pistei* (Rom. 3:28), and *ek pisteōs* (Rom. 3:30). The dative and the preposition *dia* represent faith as the instrumental means where by Christ and his righteousness are appropriated; the preposition *ek* shows that faith occasions...our personal justification. That believers are justified *dia pistin*, on account of faith, Paul never says, and would deny. Were faith the ground of justification, faith would be in effect a meritorious work, and the gospel message would, after all, be merely another version of justification by works—a doctrine which Paul opposed in all forms as irreconcilable with grace, and spiritually ruinous (cf. Rom. 4:4; 11:6; Gal. 4:21–5:12).[839]

Paul, nevertheless, does not depreciate works *per se*. First, works may be viewed as a subsequent demonstration of genuine faith in the Old Testament. Preliminarily,[840] compare Genesis 15:6 and 22:1–19 with James 2:14–24; and Genesis 15:6 and Habakkuk 2:4 with Hebrews 10:38 in its context of human responsibility. Also, throughout the New Testament, good works are looked upon as the expected issue from people who have been justified by God in Christ (cf., e.g., Romans

---

[837] Ibid.

[838] For a good discussion of "The Place of Faith" in the Old Testament, consult Morris, *APC*, 263–266.

[839] Packer, *BDT*, 306–307.

[840] "Faith" will be discussed more thoroughly in the next section, including a section on its relationship to good works.

6:13–18; Ephesians 4:24; Philippians 1:11).[841] This certainly does not mean that one is justified by faith and sanctified by works, but it does point to the fact that there is an ethical dimension which must be carefully acknowledged in both testaments.[842]

# Faith

## *The Terminology of Faith*

There are two primary word groups relating to faith in the Old Testament. As we will see shortly, this observation also will hold true for the New Testament. Regarding the terminology of believing in Old Testament revelation, the root אמן (*'mn*) is most semantically equivalent with the English denotations of "to believe, belief, faith," etc. Verb forms of אמן (*'mn*) in the *Qal* stem are not significant soteriologically. However, as background, the *Niphal* participle is of some significance concerning the fidelity of God (cf., e.g., Deuteronomy 7:9; Isaiah 49:7; Jeremiah 42:5). This form of אמן (*'mn*) may also be used to indicate human faith, or better, faithfulness (cf. the affirmation about Abraham in Nehemiah 9:8).[843] However, it is the *Hiphil* verb that carries the most soteriological freight in the Old Testament:

> The *Hiphil* finds an analogous use as an expression for man's relation to God. Here...it has declarative rather than causative significance.... האמין can undergo further deepening and extension. In particular, it can come to embrace the total relation between God and man.... For Isaiah [הֶאֱמִין is] a particular form of existence of those who are bound to God alone....[844]

Concerning a sampling of the distribution of הֶאֱמִין (*he'emin*) in the Old Testament[845] by syntactical packages, Jepsen has observed:

> *he'emin* appears in the following constructions: with *be*,[846] "in, on": Gen. 15:6; Ex. 14:31; 19:9; Nu. 14:11; 20:12; Dt. 1:32;

---

[841] This important issue will come up again when I sketch out the nature of true discipleship, and in chapter 6 which will deal with sanctification.

[842] Cf., e.g., Morris, *APC*, 269–270; Hill, *GWHM*, 160–161; Guthrie, *NTT*, 501.

[843] Weiser rightly notes the connection of this statement about the faithfulness of Abraham with the declaration about his faith in Genesis 15:6 (*TDNT*, 6:185; cf. also Jepsen, *TDOT*, 1:295–298).

[844] Weiser, *TDNT*, 6:187, 189.

[845] For the bigger picture of the distribution of all forms of this word group at a glance, see: Wildberger, *TLOT*, 1:137.

[846] I.e. the prefixed preposition בְּ (*b'-*) pointing to the object of belief.

28:66; 1 S. 27:12; 2K. 17:14; Jer. 12:6; Jonah 3:5; Mic. 7:5; Ps. 78:22, 32; 106:12; 119:66; Prov. 26:25; Job 4:18; 15:15, 31; 24:22; 39:12; 2 Ch. 20:20; with *le*[847] "in": Gen. 45:26; Ex. 4:1, 8 (twice), 9: Dt. 9:23; 1 K. 10:7; 2 Ch. 9:6; Isa. 43:10; 53:1; Jer. 40:14; Ps. 106:24; Prov. 14:15; 2 Ch. 32:15; with an inf.: Ps. 27:13; Job 15:22; with a *ki* clause: Ex. 4:5; Job 9:16; 39:12; Lam. 4:12; absolutely[848]: Ex. 4:31; Isa. 7:9; 28:16; Hab. 1:5; Ps. 116:10; Job 29:24; 39:24.[849]

From this data reservoir, Jepsen correctly concludes that

> *he'emin* above all affirms that its subject gains confidence, i.e., ...in a person or a message.... In most cases the text indicates in whom or in what confidence is placed. Thus *he'emin* contains a judgment about what deserves or does not deserve confidence. Perhaps the best paraphrases that have been suggested to convey the meaning of *he'emin* are: "to gain stability, to rely on someone, to give credence to a message or to consider it to be true, to trust in someone."[850]

Prior to considering some other significant members of this word group, another brief excursus on the "faith" of Abraham seems appropriate at this juncture. Payne assembles the major pieces relating to Abraham's believing in God like this:

> The patriarch Abraham believed in Yahweh, and He reckoned it to him for righteousness (Gen. 15:6; cf. Rom.4:18). The Hebrew root of this verb "believe" is *āman*, "to be steady, firm, or trustworthy, trust in." The basic idea is therefore that of "confirming," of causing oneself to find support.[851]... [The] object, in Scripture's discussion of Abraham's faith, was none other than God Himself.... The translation that best brings out this idea of "relying upon," or of "fastening one's confidence upon," is simply this: "Abraham trusted in God." ... Faith may therefore exhibit a quantitative development, but not a qualitative one. It does not evolve from doubt to trust.

---

[847] I.e. the prefixed preposition ־לְ (*lᵉ־*), also pointing to the person or thing believed "in."
[848] I.e. by itself.
[849] Jepsen, *TDOT*, 1:300.
[850] Ibid., 1:307–308.
[851] For a supplemental discussion on the basic common denominators of the root אמן (*'mn*), cf. Wildberger, *TLOT*, 1:134–137.

A man either has committed himself to the historical God of salvation or he has not.... Faith in the Person, if sincere, will be followed by a faith in (that is, an assent to) His propositional declarations.... Abraham's faith included both the negative renunciation of his own ability and his positive reliance upon God.... Abraham's faith involved both a subjective and an objective side.... In both of these respects, then, Abraham became the "father of the faithful." Subjectively, he establishes the pattern for our attitude of faith (Gal. 3:7; Rom. 4:16); and objectively, he serves as an example recipient both of the God-given righteousness that comes through faith and of a divinely granted heirship to the world (Gal. 3:29; Rom. 4:11, 13).[852]

Some may have wondered above why I put the faith of Abraham in quotes (i.e. "faith"). The semantical reason for this will become more obvious as we press on to two important nouns from the אמן (᾽mn) word-group.

Both אֱמֶת (᾽ᵉmet) and אֱמוּנָה (᾽ᵉmûnâ) really signify "faithfulness" not "faith." The former term, אֱמֶת (᾽ᵉmet), "has acquired the meaning 'truth'"; however, this meaning "cannot constitute the starting point for the semantics of ᾽ᵉmet."[853] אֱמֶת (᾽ᵉmet) as attributed to persons conveys "faithfulness," just as does אֱמוּנָה (᾽ᵉmûnâ), its nearest synonym."[854] אֱמוּנָה (᾽ᵉmûnâ) when used impersonally emphasizes "steadiness,"[855] but "in all other passages where ᾽emunah appears, it refers to the conduct of persons, about the same number of times of God and of man."[856] Ethically, it speaks of "sincerity, faithfulness, reliability, and stability," qualities which relate to a person's "inner attitude and the conduct it produces."[857] It is not surprising therefore to read, for example, in Habakkuk 2:4, "but a righteous person should live by means of His faithfulness" (בֶּאֱמוּנָתוֹ [beᵉmûnatô]). Speaking about אֱמוּנָה (᾽ᵉmûnâ) in such passages as Habakkuk 2:4, Moberly has well argued that this particular term

conveys the attractiveness of moral living. Although the great Old Testament (and biblical) words "righteousness" and "ho-

---

[852] *Theology of the Older Testament*, 304–307.

[853] Wildberger, *TLOT*, 1:151.

[854] Ibid., 1:152–153; Wildberger appeals to the couplet חֶסֶד וֶאֱמֶת (*ḥesed weᵉ᾽met*), "grace and faithfulness" (cf., e.g., reference to God in Genesis 24:27 then relatively to a man in v. 49).

[855] Moberly, *NIDOTTE*, 1:427.

[856] Jepsen, *TDOT*, 1:317.

[857] Ibid.; in the same vein, Jepsen goes on to argue that "᾽emunah conveys the idea of inner stability, integrity, conscientiousness, soberness, which is essential for any responsible service" (ibid.).

liness" have through misuse become problematic and unattractive for many (e.g., "self-righteous," "holier-than-thou"), "faithfulness," in the sense of integrity, trustworthiness, and dependability, has no such negative overtones. It may, therefore, be a particularly important concept for conveying central Old Testament and biblical truths in a modern context.[858]

So, in the study of the אמן ('mn) word group, we encounter yet another example of a theological continuum from salvation to sanctification, in this case, from the attitude and "'act'" of faith to its fruits of "faithfulness." "To sum up, it may be said that he'emîn and 'emûnâh describe a living act of trust in the Old Testament, and also the dimension of human existence in a historical situation."[859]

Conceptually paralleling the אמן ('mn) word group in the Old Testament is the family of terms derived from the Hebrew root בטח (bṭḥ).[860] "The derivatives of the root bṭḥ first of all have the meaning 'to feel secure, be unconcerned,' or, specifying the reason for the security, 'to rely on something or someone.'"[861] Indeed, "bṭḥ can describe secure circumstances or a secure frame of mind."[862] Furthermore, Gerstenberger goes on to note that "as a rule one states the basis or direction of this feeling of security, esp. through prepositional usages (bṭḥ bᵉ/ 'el / 'al)."[863] Unfortunately, in many places in the Old Testament, "a negative evaluation...is dominant: men trust in false security (Hab. 2:18), or set their hope on something false (Hos. 10:13)."[864] Moberly does a good job of briefly summarizing this biblical phenomenon that exposes false "trusting," hopefully so as to encourage true "trusting":

> Trust can be placed in a large number of different people or things and can often be misplaced. God is the supreme object of trust, and some of the things in which people put their trust are substitutes for God, however naturally worthy of trust they may appear to be in themselves. Thus, people can often put

---

[858] NIDOTTE, 1:430–431.

[859] Michel, NIDNTT 1:597.

[860] On the Semitic root and some suggested cognates of בטח (bṭḥ), see Gerstenberger's brief survey, TLOT, 1:226–227. His distribution chart provides a handy, at-a-glance, survey of Old Testament usage (ibid., 227).

[861] Jepsen, TDOT, 2:89.

[862] Gerstenberger, TLOT, 1:228.

[863] Ibid.

[864] Michel, NIDNTT, 1:596. Very interestingly, the LXX "rendered bṭḥ in the negative sense predominately by pepoithenai, 'to trust in, believe in, put confidence in,' but when a text used bṭḥ to convey the idea of relying on God, they ordinarily used elpizein, 'to hope'" (TDOT, 2:89).

their trust in riches (Job 31:24; Ps. 49:6 [7]; 62:10 [11]; Prov. 11:28), in powerful people (Ps. 146:3), in strongly fortified cities (Deut. 28:52; Jer. 5:17), or in their own cleverness (Prov. 3:5; 28:26)—all in contexts where the writer views these as negative things, alternatives to trusting in God.... The contrast between misguided trust in human ways and expedients and true trust in God is well encapsulated in a poem elsewhere in Jeremiah: "Cursed is the one who trusts in man,[865] who depends on flesh for his strength and whose heart turns away from the LORD. He will be like a bush in the wastelands; he will not see prosperity when it comes.... But blessed is the man who trusts in the LORD,[866] whose confidence[867] is in him. He will be like a tree planted by the water..." (Jer. 17:5-8).[868]

A good example of true "trusting" is found in the accounts about Hezekiah's confidence and hope in God in the face of the terrorizing threats of Assyria and its armies (cf. 2 Kings 18–19; Isaiah 36–37; 2 Chronicles 32).[869] In these historical passages verb forms from the root בטח (btḥ) occur 17 times. Quite often the verb is used "for the whole attitude of faith"[870] (cf., e.g., occurrences in Psalms 4:6 [v. 5, Eng.]; 22:5–6 [vv. 4–5, Eng.]; 25:1–2; 28:7; 37:3; 62:9 [v. 8, Eng.]; 86:2; 115:9–11; 118:8–9; 119:42; 143:8;[871] Proverbs 3:5; 16:20; Isaiah 26:4; etc.). As one can glean from these and other passages where this important verb occurs, it may express "the beginning of the act of trust, which increases in a secure area of life or which aims at the creation of this area."[872] Nevertheless, "whether it describes circumstances or states confidence of various durations, frequencies, and magnitudes, it always envisions an object of confidence."[873] Consequently, soteriologically speaking:

One can successfully place confidence only in Yahweh, ... no other entity can be an ultimate object of trust. This restriction

---

[865] I.e. יִבְטַח בָּאָדָם (yibṭaḥ bā'ādām).

[866] I.e. יִבְטַח בַּיהוה (yibṭaḥ bayhwh).

[867] I.e. מִבְטָחוֹ (mibṭaḥô); i.e. "the object of confidence" or trust (BDB, 105).

[868] NIDOTTE, 1:645, 646.

[869] For some commentary on the significance of Hezekiah's trust, see: Ibid., 646–648.

[870] Weiser, TDNT, 6:192.

[871] About 40% of the verbal occurrences of בטח (btḥ) are found in the Psalms.

[872] Gerstenberger, TLOT, 1:228.

[873] Ibid.

applies to almost all texts in which *bṭḥ* occurs; it is thus an eminently theological term.... This evidence means that Israelite tradition recognizes and demands[874] an absolute, exclusive devotion to Yahweh; this trust in Yahweh includes *hope* of salvation (Job 11:18) and *faith* in the God of the fathers (Psa. 22:4f).[875]

Besides believing (אמן [*'mn*]) and trusting (בטח ([*bṭḥ*]), some other important Hebrew roots relating to the concept of faith in the Old Testament are ירא (*yr'*), "to fear"[876]; יחל (*yḥl*), "to wait for" or "to hope in"[877]; the graphic imagery of חסה (*ḥsh*), "to seek refuge, flee for protection"[878]; the pictorial שען (*š'n*), "to lean" or "to depend on"[879]; and some less significant roots such as קוה (*qwh*) and חכה (*ḥkh*).[880]

Turning our attention to the New Testament, when it comes to the ideas of "believing" and "faith," the πιστεύω (*pisteuō*) word group immediately arrests our attention. Semantically, this word group generally corresponds to the אמן (*'mn*) family from the Hebrew Old Testament. In addition, this πιστεύω (*pisteuō*) word group in the New Testament perpetuates associations with trust, obedience, hope, etc.[881] Most basically, the verb πιστεύω (*pisteuō*), "to believe, also to be persuaded of, and hence, to place confidence in, to trust, signifies in this sense of the word, reliance upon, not mere credence."[882] Consequently, in places the con-

---

[874] From the conservative vantage point, "'God Himself recognizes and demands....'"

[875] Ibid., 229, 230; it is therefore no wonder that "Jewish and Christian theologians included the meaning 'confidence in God' in their considerations of the total sphere of 'faith, obedience, hope'" (ibid., 230).

[876] Cf., e.g., Genesis 20:11; 2 Kings 17:32–34; Ecclesiastes 12:13; concerning ירא (*yr'*), Payne has briefly characterized it as follows: "'Fear' is faith, as it submits to His will" (*Theology of the Older Testament*, 307).

[877] Cf., e.g., Job 13:15; Psalms 33:18; 42:6 [v. 5, Eng.]; 71:14; Micah 7:7; Gilchrist says of this term: "*yaḥal* is used of 'expectation, hope' which for the believer is closely linked with 'faith, trust' and results in 'patient waiting'" (*TWOT*, 1:860).

[878] Cf., e.g., 2 Samuel 22:3; Nahum 1:7; this figuratively boils down to 'putting one's trust in (God),' to 'confide' or 'hope in (him)' (cf. Wiseman, *TWOT*, 1:700).

[879] Cf., e.g., Job 8:15; 24:23; Proverbs 3:5; Isaiah 30:12; 50:10; Harman supplies some salient observations about שען (*š'n*) in the Old Testament: "The vb. occurs 22x..., always in the ni. It has the general meaning of leaning on something or someone, but in contexts dealing with persons it moves into the semantic field of relying on or trusting in.... Over half of the occurrences of *š'n* are in passages in which reference is made to trust in someone, especially in the Lord" (*NIDOTTE*, 4:202, 203).

[880] On such terms, see Wiser for brief notations (*TDNT*, 6:183, 193–196).

[881] Or, as Bultmann puts it, this family evidences "the continuation of the Old Testament and Jewish tradition.... πιστεύω as to believe.... as to obey..... as to trust.... as to hope.... as faithfulness" (*TDNT*, 6:205–208).

[882] Vine, *EDNTW*, 61.

notations of the New Testament verb reach back not only semantically to the Hebrew root אמן (*'mn*) but also conceptually to the nuances of בטח (*bṭḥ*), *et. al.* Soteriologically significant New Testament passages almost always emphasize trusting in God and/or believing what He has said or promised (cf., e.g., Matthew 9:28; Mark 1:15; 9:23;[883] Luke 1:20; 24:25; John 1:12; 2:11, 22–25; 3:15, 16, 18, 36; 5:46–47; 6:35, 47, 64; 8:24, 30, 31, 45–46; 9:35–38; 14:1; 17:8; Acts 4:4; 13:39, 48; 16:31; Romans 4:3, 5, 11, 17, 18, 24; 10:4, 9–11, 14; Galatians 2:16; 3:6; 1 Timothy 3:16; 2 Timothy 1:12; Hebrews 11:6;[884] James 2:19, 23; 1 Peter 2:6–7; 1 John 3:23; 4:1; 5:1; etc.). Even though this is a random sampling of verbs and verbals of πιστεύω (*pisteuō*) in the New Testament, it shows clearly the heavy concentration of them in John's Gospel. Interestingly, John never used the noun πίστις (*pistis*) in his gospel, but employs verb forms almost 100 times. Sometimes, πιστεύω (*pisteuō*) stands by itself, sometimes it occurs with a noun in the simple dative case, at other times we see it with an accusative of thing (i.e. what is believed). It also occurs with prepositions: 1) with ἐπί (*epi*) emphasizing the basis of belief; 2) with ἐν (*en*) in a general sense; and 3) 34 times with εἰς (*eis*), usually, but not always, signaling genuine committal.[885]

As we move on to the noun πίστις (*pistis*) and the adjective πιστός (*pistos*), it is important to recognize that these words are used with either active or passive senses in their various settings.[886] The semantical spectrum of the noun therefore exhibits various colorings, for example, "faith, confidence, fidelity," "what can be believed, trust, trustworthiness, Christian faith, doctrine, promise,"[887]etc. So, in its passive sense the noun πίστις (*pistis*) signals "that which is believed, *body of faith*, or *belief*, doctrine" (cf., e.g., Galatians 1:23; 1 Timothy 4:1; 6:21; 2 Timothy 4:7; Jude 3).[888] For right now we want to focus soteriologically on this noun's active sense of "believing" in the New Testament[889] (cf., e.g., Mark 2:5; Luke 7:9, 50; 17:5–6; 22:32; Acts 14:27; 20:21; Romans

---

[883] Note the noun for "faith" with an alpha-privative (i.e. ἀπιστία [*apistia*]) in the next verse (i.e. Mark 9:24).

[884] The verbal is joined by the noun "faith" (i.e. πίστεως [*pisteōs*]) in this verse.

[885] Concerning this particular construction, the two exceptions to true saving faith will be mentioned in my forthcoming discussion on "True Discipleship." On these various constructions and their theological impact see Morris, *The Gospel According to John*, NICNT, 335–337; also note Buswell, *Systematic Theology of the Christian Religion*, 2:175–184. Regarding the bigger picture of both πιστεύω (*pisteuō*) and πίστις (*pistis*) in combination with various prepositions *throughout* the New Testament, see Harris, *NIDNTT*, 3:1211–1214.

[886] Spicq, *TLNT*, 3:110.

[887] Louw and Nida, *GELSD*, 2:198.

[888] BAG, 669.

[889] Cf. ibid., 668.

3:22, 25–28, 30–31; 4:5, 9, 11–14; 16, 19–20; 5:1–2; 9:30; 10:6; 1 Corinthians 2:5; Galatians 2:16; 3:2, 6, 7–9, 11–12, 14, 22–26; 5:5–6; Ephesians 1:15; 2:8; Philippians 3:9; Colossians 1:4; 2:12; 1 Thessalonians 1:3, 8; 3:5–7; 2 Thessalonians 2:13; 1 Timothy 4:12; 6:11–12; 2 Timothy 1:5; 2:22; Hebrews 11, *passim*; James 2:1, 5, 14, 17–18, 20, 22, 24, 26; 5:15; 1 Peter 1:5, 7, 9, 21; 5:9; 2 Peter 1:1, 5; 1 John 5:4; Revelation 2:19; 13:10; 14:12). Consider Vine's general synopsis of such occurrences with an active sense: "*pistis* (πίστις,...), primarily, 'firm persuasion,' a conviction based upon hearing (akin to *peithō*, 'to persuade'), is used in the New Testament always of 'faith in God or Christ, or things spiritual.'"[890]

Although as I have already stated that the adjective πιστός (*pistos*) also may exhibit passive and active categories of usage,[891] its passive senses overwhelmingly predominate.[892] As a matter of fact, it is difficult to set forth cases in the New Testament wherein descriptive adjectival and substantive appearances of πιστός (*pistos*) function *indisputably* actively.

Now I want to add to the discussion the weight of the verb πείθω (*peithō*). As Becker notes, "The stem *peith- (pith-, poith-)* has the basic meaning of trust."[893] The perfect tense of this verb is soteriologically significant:

> The prefix always denotes a situation in which the act of examining and weighing up has been concluded, and where a firm conviction has already been reached (cf. Lk. 20:6; Rom. 8:38; 14:14; 15:14; 2 Tim. 1:5, 12; Heb. 6:9). This can refer to convictions concerning facts or people (e.g. that John was a prophet, Lk. 20:6), as well as to the all-embracing, unshakable certainty that has been attained in faith (Rom. 8:38).... The 2nd perf. *pepoitha* with the prep. *epi* always means to depend on, trust in, put one's confidence in.[894]

Analogically, one is reminded of Old Testament בָּטַח (*bāṭaḥ*) and בְּ־ בָּטַח (*bāṭaḥ bᵉ-*) when surveying most usages of πείθω (*peithō*) in the New Testament. And, just as in the Old Testament, New Testament

---

[890] *EDNTW*, 222.
[891] Cf., e.g., BAG (670): "1. pass. *trustworthy, faithful, dependable,...* 2) act. *trusting, cherishing faith* or *trust...*also *believing, full of faith, faithful.*"
[892] Ibid., 670–671.
[893] *NIDNTT*, 1:588.
[894] Ibid., 591, 592.

πείθω (*peithō*) is used of people believing in wrong things,[895] or of those who believe in God and demonstrate their confidence in His sovereign providence.[896]

## The Theology of Faith

We can learn much about this theology first by studying some important parallelisms and/or close associations with believing/faith. As I will show in the next section, faith often teams up as a twin with repentance. Faith and obedience are also inextricably related in the New Testament. For example, "There is unity between John and Paul in the fact that for both faith has the character of obedience."[897] On even a broader scale, Michel, based upon the evidence found throughout the New Testament, concludes that "faith, and the act of believing, assume the character of fidelity."[898] The testimony of James in this vital area is exceedingly relevant; he

> is conscious of the need to prove faith (1:3; cf. 1 Pet. 1:7). He demands renunciation of all conduct that conflicts with living faith and confession (1:6ff). For him, faith and obedient conduct are indissolubly linked. . . . It would seem that James is replying to those who have taken Paul's doctrine of justification by faith out of context, assuming that Paul's repudiation of works as the ground of justification relieved them of the need for good works and a changed life. Thus they may have taken Rom. 4:3 and Gal. 3:6 (=Gen. 15:6) and ignored Rom. 6:1ff.; 12:1ff.; Gal. 5:15–26.[899] It is striking that James also quotes Gen. 15:6 in James 2:23. He also illustrates his argument by referring to the example of Abraham. But whereas Paul appeals to Abraham's belief in the promise of God which was the occasion of the verdict of justification in Gen. 15, James appeals to the story in Gen. 22 which shows Abraham's willingness to sacrifice Isaac. James 2:22 draws the conclusion: "You see that faith was active along with his works, and faith was completed by works."

---

[895] E.g., trusting in wealth, protective devices, themselves, etc. (cf. respectively, Mark 10:24; Luke 11:22; 18:9).

[896] Cf., e.g., Matthew 27:43 (predicated of Christ); Acts 17:4; 28:24; Philippians 2:24 (contrast distrust in the flesh, 3:3–4); 2 Timothy 1:12. Also when, e.g., Paul expresses confidence in reference to people, it is always ultimately grounded in God (cf., e.g., Galatians 5:10; Philippians 1:6; 2 Thessalonians 3:4; 2 Timothy 1:5; Philemon 21; Hebrews 6:9).

[897] Bultmann, *TDNT*, 6:225.

[898] *NIDNTT*, 1:603.

[899] They needed also to have remembered, e.g., that Ephesians 2:10 complements and does not contradict vv. 1–9.

... The thesis which James wishes to argue is that "faith by it-self, if it has no works, is dead" (2:17).[900]

Fear and faith are also closely associated in New Testament revela-tion.[901] Of course, the combination of fear with faith is not

> the anxiety which lies behind all the efforts of the natural man to win salvation in his own strength. The believer has not re-ceived a πνεῦμα δουλείας πάλιν εἰς φόβον[902] but a πνεῦμα υἱοθεσίας[903] (R. 8:15). Nevertheless, the divine imperative is not set aside. The appropriate φόβος [phobos, "fear"] is simply awareness that man does not stand on his own feet. It is the concern not to fall from χάρις [charis, "grace"], whether in frivolity or the pride of supposed security.[904]

Faith is also paired up with "hope,"[905] with "love,"[906] "life,"[907] etc. Furthermore, turning to a theological antonym of faith, it stands in stark contrast with self-anything. This New Testament emphasis picks up the watchwords of God through Jeremiah:

> Thus says the LORD, "Let not a wise man boast of his wisdom, and let not the mighty man boast of his might, let not a rich man boast of his riches; but let him who boasts boast of this, that he un-derstands and knows Me, that I am the LORD who exercises lovingkindness, justice, and righteousness on earth; for I delight in these things," declares the LORD (Jeremiah 9:23–24, NASB).

Faith indeed "contradicts all human boasting and undermines any at-tempt to base man's relationship with God on doing the law."[908] Guthrie corroborates:

---

[900] Ibid., 605–605.

[901] Remember that this reality is built upon a solid Old Testament foundation (cf., e.g., Job 28:28; Psalm 111:10; Proverbs 1:7; 9:10; Ecclesiastes 12:13).

[902] I.e. "a slavery spirit again unto fear."

[903] I.e. "a full sonship spirit."

[904] Bultmann, TDNT, 6:221. We will return to this theologically significant combination of faith and fear, addressing the issue more fully in chapter 6 on sanctification.

[905] Michel notes, "Since faith contains the element of being sustained...as well as trust..., it merges into hope (Rom. 8:24; 1 Cor. 13:13)" (NIDNTT, 1:601); for other documentation of this fact, Bultmann adds Romans 4:18; 1 Thessalonians 1:3; Hebrews 11; 1 Peter 1:21 (TDNT, 6:207–208).

[906] I.e. a demonstrated love which makes it an analogue of obedience (c.f., e.g., John 14:15, 21, 23; 15:10; 1 John 5:3; 2 John 6).

[907] Michel, e.g., legitimately argues that "faith and life are intimately connected. He who believes in the Son has the promise that he will not perish but have eternal life (John 3:16ff; 11:25)" (NIDNTT, 1:603).

[908] Ibid., 1:601.

Faith is...the negation of self-confidence. It says "no" to pride in human achievement. It involves throwing oneself unreservedly on the mercy of God.... The mission of Jesus was based on the conviction that what God expected of people was impossible through human effort, but became a viable proposition when faith linked them to God's way of doing things, i.e. to his redemptive plan.[909]

Now we can back up and take some wide-angle pictures with our theological camera. From the array of data previously surveyed, it should be obvious that it is difficult to synthesize a comprehensive definition of faith. Even if we restricted the corpus of the data to our Lord's teachings relating to faith in the Gospels, "it must not be forgotten that every summons and statement of Jesus contained the elements of faith, trust, knowledge, decision, obedience and self-direction. The preaching of Jesus cannot be understood apart from the many-sided aspects of faith...and trust."[910] Yet someone might say that this quest for a definition of "faith" is unnecessary since God has already provided one in Hebrews 11:1; nevertheless, "this is not a comprehensive summary of all the elements in faith, but of those which were fundamental for a church under persecution: assurance of what is hoped for and conviction of being led by what cannot be seen."[911]

Having recognized the limitations of all simple definitions, does not mean, however, that descriptive attempts at summarizing the basics of biblical faith should be abandoned. Some of these attempts, as a matter of fact, put an illuminating spotlight on the various characteristics and associations of faith in the Bible. Let me offer just a few of these definitions. Buswell defines saving faith as "an act of total commitment."[912] Guthrie says that faith is "the act of believing.... The specifically Christian use of the word 'faith' is in the sense of committing oneself to Christ."[913] Erickson includes in his definition a comparison with repentance, saying, "As repentance is the negative aspect of conversion, turning from one's sin, so faith is the positive aspect, laying hold upon the promises and the work of Christ."[914] A common denominator concerning faith seems to be a dependent response to God and/or His promises.

It is important to remember that faith does not become unemployed after justification. For example, Michel rightly begins to build a faith

---

[909] *NTT*, 576, 577.
[910] Michel, *NIDNTT*, 1:600–601.
[911] Ibid., 604.
[912] *Systematic Theology of the Christian Religion*, 2:176.
[913] *NTT*, 575.
[914] *Christian Theology*, 938.

bridge from initial justification to sanctification when he offers this definition: "'Faith' means receiving the message of salvation and conduct based on the gospel."[915] Concerning faith as being essential in reference to both initial salvation and progressive sanctification, Bultmann has aptly argued that "the saving faith denoted by πίστις and πιστεύειν, whether in the abs. or with some qualification, can be considered either in respect of its origin or in respect of its continuation."[916] Passages like Genesis 15:6; Romans 4; Galatians 3; etc., focus on faith and initial salvation. Indeed, the example of Abraham alone teaches us that "the type of faith necessary for salvation involves both believing that and believing in, or assenting to facts and trusting in a person.... Our view of revelation leads us to stress the twofold nature of faith: giving credence to affirmation and trusting in God."[917] These elements of faith were not only essential to the justification of this paradigm patriarch but also to his walk by faith (e.g. Genesis 22 with James 2). Faith is absolutely essential for the whole life of a justified person. When it comes to sanctification, Paul's watchword in 2 Corinthians 5:7 knows no exceptions or limitations: all believers must continue to "walk by faith."[918] So from beginning to end, faith is characterized by a totally dependent entrustment, and it is demonstrated through a persistent commitment to obedience.

Permit me to mention and to interact very briefly with a volatile theological controversy pertaining to faith as "*the* gift of God.'" This systematic skirmish has led to some eccentric views (e.g., all the way from faith being "all mine" at one end of the pole to it being like a "zap" totally out of Heaven's blue at the other end of the pole). A good way to ease into a quest for biblical balance in this area is to call to mind the exclamation and plea of the father of the demoniac boy in Mark 9. As Guthrie rightly reasons, "The seeming paradox of the man's desperate cry in Mark 9:24 ('I believe...help my unbelief') brings out an essential feature of Christian faith—that belief is possible only with the help of one who is himself the object of faith."[919] Yet faith *is man's response* to God's initiative and enablements.[920]

---

[915] *NIDNTT*, 1:601.

[916] *TDNT*, 6:212.

[917] Erickson, *Christian Theology*, 940.

[918] This prerequisite of faith and the Christian life will be picked up again in chapter 6 on sanctification. Faith is a navigational necessity when it comes to walking the balance beam of the Christian life. As we will see later, "the life of faith"... is "characterized by the tension between the indicative and imperative" (Michel, *NIDNTT*, 1:602).

[919] *NTT*, 576, n.11.

[920] We need to remember, e.g., that "regeneration and faith must be simultaneous" (Buswell, *Systematic Theology of the Christian Religion*, 2:183); however, this biblical concurrence in no way supports salvation as being any kind of synergistic phenomenon.

Too many interpreters have tried to manipulate the exegetical data of Ephesians 2:8 into their own theological box. The antecedent of the pronoun "that" in this verse is not "faith" alone. Buswell handles the syntax of this verse very credibly when he says, "The word 'that' refers not only to the 'grace' and not only to the 'faith' but to the whole manner expressed in these words. Both grace and faith are feminine nouns, but the word 'that,' *touto*, is neuter, showing that it is not merely grace, and not merely faith, but the entire concept of grace accepted by faith, which must be regarded as the gift of God."[921] Listen, therefore, to Chafer's carefully balanced treatment of this strategic passage from Ephesians 2:

> God alone is able to accomplish the marvelous transformations which enter into the eternal salvation of the sinner. Therefore, it is reasonable to the highest degree, that He must reserve every feature of that transaction to Himself. On this aspect of truth, the Apostle declares (verses 8 and 9), that it is "by grace are ye saved," and "not of works lest any man should boast." Salvation is God's unrecompensed gift (John 10:28; Romans 6:23), and therefore, although it is a thing in which the saved one may delight forever, he cannot boast as one who has added any feature to it. Even the faith by which it is received is itself a *gift* from God.[922] As to this fact, each saved person will freely confess that he would not have turned to God had it not been for the drawing, calling and illuminating power of the Spirit.[923] As to who will thus turn to God, God alone must determine; for we are chosen in Him before the foundation of the world (1:4). There is no after-thought with God. The Gospel is to be preached to every creature, and it is the divine responsibility, through that preaching, to execute the eternal purpose. This God has done, is doing, and will to the end.[924]

---

[921] Ibid., 2:182.

[922] Note he does not say it is *the gift* of God in an exclusive sense, but more importantly notice how Chafer goes on to describe it as "a gift of God."

[923] I.e. saving faith is man's response to the Spirit's efficacious call which culminates in regeneration.

[924] L. S. Chafer, *The Ephesian Letter* (Findly, Ohio: Dunham, 1935), 79.

# Repentance

Having already acknowledged the close association of the responsibilities of "faith" and "repentance" in the Bible (cf., e.g., Acts 20:21[925]), it is time to sketch out what special nuance the latter contributes to the broader soteriological picture. Repentance is an ongoing demand that God places before sinful people. In order to understand this responsibility better, I will begin as usual with the semantics of repentance.

## *The Terminology of Repentance*

The Old Testament background relating to repentance is conveyed primarily through two Hebrew word groups and a variety of picturesque images. The first word group derives from the Hebrew root נחם (*nḥm*). This root sometimes carries the concept of comfort,[926] but its other semantical field explicitly pertains to the topic of repentance. In this domain of meaning, the Niphal verb conveys the following meanings: "to feel pain (about something), regret something,"[927] to "be sorry, repent, change one's mind."[928] Kromminga's brief survey of this sphere of usage is helpful:

> In the Old Testament the verb "repent" (*niph'al* of *nāḥam*) occurs about thirty-five times. It is usually used to signify a contemplated change in God's dealings with men for good or ill according to his just judgment (I Sam. 15:11, 35; Jonah 3:9–10) or, negatively, to certify that God will not swerve from his announced purpose (I Sam. 15:29; Ps. 110:4; Jer.

---

[925] Acts 20:21 concisely captures this important relationship when Paul characterizes his own ministry of preaching and teaching with these words, "bearing solemn witness to both Jews and Gentiles about repentance unto God and faith in our Lord Jesus." This verse contains two tightly packed couplets, Ἰουδαίοις τε καὶ Ἕλλησιν (*Ioudaiois te kai Hellēsin*) and τὴν εἰς θεὸν μετάνοιαν καὶ πίστιν εἰς τὸν κύριον ἡμῶν Ἰησοῦν (*tēn eis theon metanoian kai pistin eis ton kurion hēmōn Iēsoun*) which respectively associate the two major ethnic categories of spiritually bankrupt humanity and the twin responsibilities necessary for the appropriation of salvation. Whether one is a Jewish sinner or a Gentile sinner, God requires both responses in connection with His gracious rescue.

[926] Cf., e.g., Stoebe's analysis (*TLOT*, 2:734–737).

[927] Ibid. 2:738.

[928] Butterworth, *NIDOTTE*, 3:82.

4:28).[929] In five places *nāḥam* refers to human repentance or relenting.[930] The LXX translates *nāḥam* with *metanoeō* and *metamelomai*.[931] Either Greek verb may occur designating either human repentance or divine "relenting" (so the RSV in some places).[932]

*Turning* (pun intended) to the other Old Testament term, "the word most frequently employed to indicate man's repentance is *shûb*."[933] This root's most basic meaning is "to return," and "as with other verbs of movement...usages of *šûb* are numerous in both lit. and fig. meanings."[934] Some of the denotations and connotations of שׁוּב (*šûb*) are: "repent, turn; return, go back; go back and forth; revert; turn back, change one's mind; withdraw;" etc.[935] Often the term is used to picture all kinds of "turnings away" or "turnings back," most often describing various scenarios of apostasy.[936] Consequently, it is fitting that God commands sinful people "to turn around," i.e. to repent. As Thompson and Martens have noted,

> the word *šwb* is a central word for the concept of repent. The imagery is one of a person doing a turnabout. Critical in this turnabout, if it is to be repentance, is the direction toward

---

[929] Although this application of נחם (*nḥm*) is not relevant for our consideration of issues relating to soteriology, it has stimulated much discussion and led to theodicies pertaining to these references about God "repenting." Briefly in passing, His "repenting" is "an anthropomorphic way of expressing God's dissatisfaction with human conduct...or most frequently God's withdrawal of a threatened punishment" (Dunn, *Romans* 2:686). Speaking of such contexts, Stoebe well renders the theologically challenging part of Exodus 32:12, 14, "'then Yahweh regretted the disaster with which he had threatened his people,'" commenting "*nḥm* ni. is never sorrowful resignation but always has concrete consequences. Consequently, 'and he regrets the evil' can elaborate 'he is gracious and merciful' (Joel 2:13; Jonah 4:2; cf. in the broad sense also Psalm 106:45)" (*TLOT*, 2:738). Addressing the seeming contradiction of 1 Samuel 15:11, 35 with v. 29, Butterworth argues that "the explanation seems to be that God does not capriciously change his intentions or ways of acting. It is the change in Saul's behavior that leads to this expression of regret" (*NIDOTTE*, 3:82; the rest of Butterworth's points are also quite balanced hermeneutically).
[930] See Exodus 13:17; Judges 21:6, 15; Job 42:6; Jeremiah 8:6; 31:19; notice also that in the last passage (cf. vv. 18–20) נחם (*nḥm*) is found in parallelism with שׁוּב (*šûb*).
[931] Another indication of the LXX's role in the building of semantical/theological bridges.
[932] Kromminga, *BDT*, 443–444.
[933] Wilson, *TWOT*, 2:571; for a distribution chart of this high frequency root in the Old Testament, see Soggin, *TLOT* 3:1312–1313.
[934] *TLOT*, 3:1313; cf. Soggin's subsequent survey which is quite helpful (ibid., 3:1313–1317).
[935] Thompson and Martens, *NIDOTTE*, 4:55.
[936] Cf., e.g., ibid., 56–57.

which one turns, namely, to Yahweh. The moves in this turning process are delineated clearly in Jeremiah 3:22–4:2, a veritable liturgy of repentance: acknowledging God's lordship (3:22); admitting wrongdoing (3:23) including the verbal confession, "We [I] have sinned" (3:25); addressing the shame (3:25); and affirming and adhering to new conduct (4:1–2).[937]

The LORD especially used His mouthpieces, the prophets, to deliver His exhortations to turn back.[938] "2 Kings 17:13 summarized the message 'by all prophets and seers of Israel and Judah.' It was simply 'repent' (*šubû*): 'turn back (*šubû*) from your evil ways and observe My commandments and statutes strictly according to the instructions which I gave to your fathers and which I send to you by My servants the prophets.'"[939]

Concerning this particular Old Testament term for repentance, Kromminga importantly has pointed out its conceptual link to the New Testament, observing that

the background of the New Testament idea of repentance lies…primarily…in forms of *šûb* meaning "to turn back, away from, or toward" in the religious sense. The LXX consistently translates *šûb* with forms of *epistrephō* and *apostrephō*. Repentance follows a turning about which is a gift of God (Jer. 31:18–20; Ps. 80:3, 7, 19).[940] Isaiah 55:6–7 gives the typical Old Testament call to repentance and conversion.[941]

It is important to note that the Old Testament apparently does not differentiate between the concepts of repentance and conversion as the New Testament frequently does. As we will see, in the New Testament the στρέφω (*strephō*) word group relates particularly to *conversion*; while μεταμέλομαι (*metamelomai*) and μετανοέω (*metanoeō*) respectively emphasize *regret* and *repentance*.

---

[937] Ibid., 57. They also point to the paradigmatic importance of the Hosea 14:1–3 (2–4) passage.

[938] Ibid.

[939] Walter C. Kaiser, Jr., *Toward an Old Testament Theology* (Grand Rapids: Zondervan, 1978), 137–138.

[940] Herein I would add the abbreviated version of the truth expressed in Jeremiah 31, i.e., Lamentations 5:21. Jeremiah understood very well that if rebellious people were to do a spiritual 180, God would need to take the initiative.

[941] Kromminga, *BDT*, 444.

Besides שׁוּב (*šwb*) and נחם (*nḥm*),

> the Bible is rich in idioms describing man's responsibility in the process of repentance. Such phrases would include the following: "incline your heart unto the Lord your God" (Joshua 24:23); "circumcise yourselves to the Lord" (Jeremiah 4:4); "wash your heart from wickedness" (Jeremiah 4:14); "break up your fallow ground" (Hosea 10:12) and so forth. All these expressions of man's penitential activity, however, are subsumed and summarized by this one verb *shub*.[942]

The theology of repentance in the New Testament, as I mentioned above, is advanced by two associated word groups. Kromminga introduces their interrelationship as follows: "In the NT *metanoia* (noun) occurs twenty-three times and *metanoeō* (verb) thirty-four times. *Metamelomai* occurs seldom and is used almost exclusively in the sense of 'regretting, having remorse.'"[943] This comparison and contrast is taken up more fully by Michel who, based upon the evidence from classical Greek, notes that "μετανοεῖν means a change of heart either generally or in respect of a specific sin, where as μεταμέλεσθαι means 'to experience remorse.' μετανοεῖν implies that one has later arrived at a different view of something (νοῦς), μεταμέλεσθαι that one has a different feeling about it (μέλει)."[944] Although the μεταμέλομαι (*metamelomai*) word group occurs only eight times in the New Testament, there is enough evidence to conclude that these two word groups are not being used as theological synonyms. "When 'remorse' is ascribed to man, there is an obvious difference from repentance.... Remorse does not have to be pleasing to God. It can simply be a change in mood...."[945] Two contexts illustrate the basic difference between these two sometimes related but not identical word groups. Laubach, utilizing these two New Testament settings, makes this point very well:

> The example of Judas makes it clear that *metamelomai* and *metanoeō* do not have identical meanings in the New Testament.... Judas recognized that Jesus had been wrongly con-

---

[942] Hamilton, *TWOT*, 2:909.

[943] *BDT*, 444. Concerning the second word group, Laubach refers to the adjective with alpha-privative: "The adj. *ametamelētos*, not to be regretted, only occurs in Rom. 11:29 and 2 Cor. 7:10. It refers to something of which God (Rom. 11:29) or a man (2 Cor. 7:10) will not repent, and hence means irrevocable" (*NIDNTT*, 1:356).

[944] Michel, *TDNT*, 4:626.

[945] Ibid., 627.

demned. He regretted his betrayal (Matt. 27:3), but he did not find the way to genuine repentance. We find the same differentiation in 2 Cor. 7:8–10. Paul did not regret that he had written a sharp letter to the Corinthians, for the sorrow caused to its recipients had led them to true repentance (*metanoia*), to an inner turning to God. There is no need to regret such a repentance, for it always serves only our salvation.[946]

So, most generally speaking, the μεταμέλομαι (*metamelomai*) word group in the New Testament indicates a feeling of concern or regret which may or may not lead to complete repentance.

Having some insight into the difference between "'after-regret'" (i.e. the μεταμέλομαι [*metamelomai*] words) and a "'change of mind/heart'" (i.e. the μετανοέω [*metanoeō*] words) will allow us to examine and to appreciate more the special theological contribution of the later group.[947] Some excerpts from Goetzmann go a long way toward identifying the special focus of this μετανοέω (*metanoeō*) group in the New Testament:

> The NT does not follow LXX usage but employs *metanoeō* to express the force of *šûb*, to turn round.... This change...in the choice of words—*metanoeō* instead of *epistrephō*—shows that the NT does not stress the concrete physical concept implied in the OT use of *šûb*, but rather the thought, the will, the *nous*.... For all that, the change of words has not merely intellectualized the concept of *šûb*.... Rather the decision by the whole man to turn round is stressed.... The closest link with the prophetic call to repentance is undoubtedly found in John the Baptist, who called the people to repentance and to "bear fruit that befits repentance" (Matt. 3:2, 8 par.).... Repentance is regarded both as an act open to men and as a duty.... The preaching of Jesus resembled that of the Baptist. Matt. 3:2 and 4:17 record the identical call, "Repent, for the kingdom of heaven is at hand."[948]

So, somewhat like we found in the case of biblical "faith," "repentance" can be characterized initially as an attitude, but that attitude

---

[946] *NIDNTT*, 1:356.

[947] Incidentally, in the case of these two word groups, the etymologies of their respective base stems provide insights into their semantical and theological differences (cf., e.g., Spicq, *TLNT*, 2:472ff.). For example, Spicq notes that "*metanoeō* is literally 'know after,'" then he concludes, "*metanoeō* has to do first of all with a change of mind..." (Ibid., 472).

[948] Goetzmann, *NIDNTT*, 1:357–358.

needs to be documented more and more consistently by a 180° lifestyle for it to be considered true "repentance" (i.e. some subsequent changes in habit are required to corroborate a "change of mind"). Furthermore,

> primitive Christian preaching...linked with the call for repentance all the elements we have already met, the call to faith (Acts 20:21; cf. Acts 26:18; 19:4), the demand to be baptized (Acts 2:38), the promise of the forgiveness of sins (Luke 24:47; Acts 3:19; 5:31), and of life and of salvation (Acts 11:18; 2 Cor. 7:9f.). Conversion is turning from evil (Acts 8:22; 2 Cor. 12:21: Rev. 2:21f.) to God (Acts 20:21; 26:20; Rev. 16:9). In Acts 3:19 and 26:20 *metanoeō* and *epistrephō* are placed side by side. This shows that the two concepts are related.[949]

Paying careful attention to the continuities and discontinuities of these various terms and concepts (esp. in reference to faith, repentance, and conversion) is, for example, a prerequisite for understanding "'Lordship salvation'" in its biblical context.[950]

## The Theology of Repentance

First and foremost, μετανοέω (*metanoeō*) can never be clearly comprehended biblically without keeping in mind mankind's noetic (i.e. νοῦς [*nous*]) predicament as outlined by such texts as Genesis 6:5; Romans 1:28; etc. The unsaved sinner needs a radical redirection of mind (i.e. μετα+νοέω [*meta+noeō*]); he needs a 180° correction in his mindset regarding both himself and his sin in view of God and the things of God (cf., e.g., Ephesians 4:17–18; Colossians 1:21, etc.). And since μετανοέω (*metanoeō*) describes the particular "change of mind" demanded by God as a prerequisite for a right relationship with Himself (e.g., Luke 15:7; 24:47; Acts 17:30; 2 Peter 3:9; etc.), repentance must be preached and taught along with the demand of belief:

> As we examine this matter of repentance, we cannot avoid being impressed with its importance as a prerequisite for salvation. The large number of verses and the variety of contexts in

---

[949] Ibid., 359.
[950] A forthcoming consideration of "True Discipleship" will serve as a climax to this chapter which has mainly been dedicated to initial salvation.

which repentance is stressed make clear that it is not optional but indispensable. That people in many different cultural settings were urged to repent shows that it is not a message only for a few specific locations. Rather repentance is an essential part of the Christian gospel.[951]

Secondly, as in the case of faith, repentance is viewed biblically from two different, but complementary, angles: it is both the duty of man and "'the gift of God.'" Man must indeed repent (cf., e.g., Luke 13:3; Acts 3:19, etc.), but that responsibility does not negate the fact that God enables people to repent (cf., e.g., Acts 11:18; 2 Timothy 2:25; etc.). Because of man's hard-mindedness, divine enablements are necessary if there are to be proper human responses in the spiritual realm. This reality pertains not only to initial repentance but also to progressive "'repentance'" (i.e. that renewal of mind which expresses itself in holy living; cf., e.g., Romans 12:1–2; Ephesians 4:23; Revelation 3:19).[952]

# Conversion

As already mentioned, the Hebrew root שׁוּב (šûb) does double duty. It expresses both of the ideas of repentance and conversion. Broomall's survey provides a good distillation of the significance of שׁוּב (šûb) as conversion:

> Conversion is described in the OT as a turning from evil (Jer. 18:8) unto the Lord (Mal. 3:7). Because of man's evil nature (Hos. 5:4), this change is resisted (II Chron. 36:13). God is the primary mover (Jer. 31:18), although man appears to have a subordinate part (Jer. 24:7). Individuals (II Kings 23:25) and nations (Jonah 3:10) are subjects of conversion. God used the prophets as secondary agents in effecting conversion (Neh. 9:26; Zech. 1:4). Those who refuse to turn to the Lord are punished with such evils as chastisement (Amos 4:6–12), captivity (Hos. 11:5), destruction (I Kings 9:6–9), death (Ezek. 33: 9,11); those who return to the Lord receive such blessings as forgiveness (Isa. 55:7), freedom from punishment (Jonah

---

[951] Erickson, *Christian Theology*, 937; "repentance" indeed crystallizes a proper response to the gospel.

[952] This important issue will be taken up more thoroughly in chapter 6 which deals with sanctification.

3:9f.), fruitfulness of service (Ps. 51:13; Hos. 14:4–8), life (Ezek. 33:14f).[953]

Such ambivalence is not to be found in the New Testament. Although the LXX's use of the στρέφω (*strephō*) word complex to render שׁוּב (*šûb*) seems to muddy the biblical waters, the usage of this same word group in the New Testament is clear. Concerning the semantical thrust of the στρέφω (*strephō*) word complex in New Testament revelation, Laubach has observed that

> *strephō*,[954] *apostrephō*,[955] and *epistrephō* ... share the meaning of turn, turn to, turn oneself, turn around.... They describe a largely intentional turning of the body, or thoughts, to a person or thing. *Strephō* is used more in the sense of turn over, turn round, transform, and later turn towards. *Epistrephō* means turn towards, turn round, return, both trans. and reflex., and then derivatively be converted, i.e. change one's mind and behavior.[956]

Already becoming obvious is the fact that ἐπιστρέφω (*epistrephō*) is the most soteriologically significant member of this family. It

> is found 36 times in the NT, and in addition in variant readings in Lk.10:6 (D), Acts 15:16 (D), 2 Pet. 2:21 (TR)....18 times it has its secular meaning of turning, returning, turning away, etc. ..., and 18 times with its theological meaning of conversion especially in Acts and the Epistles (cf. Mk. 4:12 par., Lk. 1:16f.; 22:32; Acts 15:19; 2 Cor. 3:16; Jas. 5:19f.)[957]

Although in the latter settings it may "often be synonymous with *metanoeō*,"[958] it is more regularly documented by *evidences* of a turn about face from sin to God. Laubach goes on to stress this very point when he says,

> When men are called in the NT to conversion, it means a fundamentally new turning of the human will to God, a return

---

[953] *BDT*, 139.
[954] Cf. Matthew 18:3.
[955] Cf. Acts 3:26.
[956] *NIDNTT*, 1:354.
[957] Ibid., 355.
[958] Ibid.

home from blindness and error to the Savior of all.[959]...Such a conversion leads to a fundamental change of the whole life (Acts 26:20). It receives a new outlook and objectives.... *epistrephō* is used for the conversion of a man which involves a complete transformation...of his existence under the influence of the Holy Spirit.[960]

Paul seemed to hold up the Thessalonian believers as a preeminent example of biblical conversion. Those around them who witnessed their faith and its fruit reported that these believers from Thessalonica "turned (from ἐπιστρέφω [*epistrephō*]) to God from their idols so as to serve the living and true God" (1 Thessalonians 1:9b). Once again, "a change of one's beliefs" was documented by a "change of one's ways."[961]

These twin emphases hold true not only for the στρέφω (*strephō*) and μετανοέω (*metanoeō*) word families but also for many of the other soteriological terms of responsibility we have briefly visited. Therefore, such complementary emphases lead us to a transitional topic on our way to a discussion of sanctification. This important topic which immediately follows asks the crucial question, "By biblical standards, who is a genuine Christian?"

# True Discipleship

In addressing this issue, two extremes must be avoided: 1) the extreme of Gospel reductionism (sometimes more polemically labeled "easy believism"); and 2) the extreme of an unbiblical level of initial moral maturity (e.g. arguing that faith *plus* some corroborative work or works, like lifestyle changes, must be present at the very time of justification).

Let me begin by revealing the exegetical and theological errors that characterize the first of these extremes. According to the New Testament data, Christianity *is* discipleship (and *vice versa*). The so-called "Great Commission" is a good place to begin. Our Lord Jesus Christ says:[962]

---

[959] On respectively turning *from* sin to God, cf., e.g., Acts 26:18; 1 Peter 2:25; etc.

[960] Ibid.

[961] Cf. Louw and Nida's summary of the two practical domains of the noun ἐπιστροφή (*epistrophē*) (*GELSD*, 2:102; cf. 1:373–374, 510).

[962] This commission from Matthew's account seems to be the only "commission" not restricted in some sense to the eleven gathered in the upper room (contra. the contexts of Mk. 16:15–18 [note the textual problems besides] and Luke 24:46–49 [note the emphasis on them being eye-witnesses; cf. Acts 1 also]). The commission recorded in Matthew was apparently directed towards a larger audience, the whole nuclear core of believers at that time (cf. Matthew 28:10–16 with 1 Corinthians 15:5–6).

All authority has been given to Me in heaven and upon the earth. Therefore, when you go,[963] disciplize (μαθητεύσατε [*mathēteusate*]) all the nations, baptizing them into the name of the Father and of the Son and of the Holy Spirit, teaching[964] them to keep on keeping[965] all things whatsoever I have commanded you. And behold I[966] am with you always[967] until the full consummation of the age (Matthew 28:18b–20).

Christ's previous teachings as recorded throughout all four gospels allowed no misunderstandings as to what He meant in this commission when He commanded, "Make disciples!" He certainly did not mean that the original core of His followers were to go out and enlist people who make lip-service professions to a watered-down gospel. After all, in Matthew 28:20a the content is spelled out as being comprehensive in scope.

The paradigm parable of the seed, sower, and soils, from early on, also makes the issue clear (cf. Matthew 13:2ff.; Mark 4:1ff.; Luke 8:4ff.). As Guthrie well notes from this masterful piece of our Lord's teaching:

"Believing" is equated to "receiving the Word" in a permanent, not simply temporary way (cf. Lk. 8:13).... Since the parable reflects the various responses to Jesus' ministry, the vital function of faith is vividly seen and the good soil hearers show their faith by hearing and holding fast to the word and working it out in practice (Lk. 8:15).[968]

---

[963] I prefer to take this aorist participle temporally due to the slight time delay between the giving of the commission and the logical implementation of it immediately *after Pentecost* (i.e. Christ's "wait" order came before His "go" order). Yet, as long as this wait-go sequence is paid due credence, I have no problem understanding it as an aorist participle of attendant circumstance (i.e. "go...make disciples!"); the leading imperative does contribute its impact and urgency to the subordinate participle.

[964] The present participles, "baptizing" and "teaching," obviously emphasize on-going attendant responsibilities in relationship to the command "disciplize" (i.e. "make disciples"). These participles furthermore seem to be used respectively with iterative and modal functions (e.g., "make disciples, baptizing them *whenever the occasion calls for it*," and "make disciples *by* on-goingly teaching them..."). Some interpreters, however, prefer to take both of these present participles as conveying the means of making disciples (cf., e.g., Wallace, *GGBB*, 645).

[965] Paraphrasing the force of this present infinitive. Seemingly secondary exegetical details are really not secondary; they speak loudly against those who argue for any kind of an "'easy believism'" Christianity.

[966] An emphatic "I" referring to the Christ who possesses "all authority."

[967] Literally, "all the days."

[968] Guthrie, *NTT*, 577.

That Christ in His preaching of the Good News stressed commitment along with confession is obvious throughout the gospel accounts. This truth is *explicitly* expressed by our Lord in a number of settings; note especially the following ones:

> Then he said to them all: "If anyone would come after me, he must deny himself and take up his cross daily and follow me. For whoever wants to save his life will lose it, but whoever loses his life for me will save it. What good is it for a man to gain the whole world, and yet lose or forfeit his very self? If anyone is ashamed of me and my words, the Son of Man will be ashamed of him when he comes in his glory and in the glory of the Father and of the holy angels" (Luke 9:23–26; NIV).

> As they were walking along the road, a man said to him, "I will follow you wherever you go." Jesus replied, "Foxes have holes and birds of the air have nests, but the Son of Man has no place to lay his head." He said to another man, "Follow me." But the man replied, "Lord, first let me go and bury my father." Jesus said to him, "Let the dead bury their own dead, but you go and proclaim the kingdom of God." Still another said, "I will follow you, Lord; but first let me go back and say good-bye to my family." Jesus replied, "No one who puts his hand to the plow and looks back is fit for service in the kingdom of God" (Luke 9:57–62; NIV).

Although this last passage has been restricted by many to *service* that may or may not follow salvation, its stress on Christ having top priority applies both to salvation and to an *expected* obedience attendant to it.

The important principle of priorities, along with a corollary principle of "counting the cost," speak directly to the issue of true Christianity as it is carefully characterized by our Master. In this regard, Luke 14:25ff. is a paramount passage. Christ structures these tests of true commitment in arresting and sometimes shocking ways. Using masterfully illustrated scenarios, Jesus measures true discipleship (i.e. genuine Christianity) with the "yardsticks" of spiritual priorities, total commitment, and personal sacrifice. If one should "come" to Him in the salvific sense,[969] certain indications of commitment *must* be present. If there is no seed of commit-

---

[969] Cf., e.g., the calls of the Spirit and the bride to "come" to Christ in Revelation 22:17.

ment planted in the heart of a claimer, that person, as affirmed by Christ Himself, "cannot be my disciple."[970]

It is vitally important to note, according to these illustrative scenarios, that Christ meant that such kinds of people cannot be genuine Christians. Very informingly, from the hand of Luke himself, the same penman who recorded these strong words of Jesus, we also have received this important historical notation recorded in Acts 11:26: "The disciples were first called Christians at Antioch" (NIV). So there was absolutely no confusion in the early church about the salvific synonymity of "disciple" and "Christian."

All of this means that some degree of initial commitment must be present in the heart[971] along with a confession of the lips if initial salvation has truly occurred. If it has occurred, the fruits of faith *will eventually* manifest themselves *to various degrees* (cf. again, e.g., Matthew 13:8).

Expressed inversely, a mere profession of faith does not indicate a true possession of salvation. A couple of historical episodes illustrate this point quite well. When we were recently exploring biblical faith, I mentioned that some interpreters have taken profession of belief to mean that genuine salvations have indeed taken place. The combination of the πιστεύω (*pisteuō*) plus εἰς (*eis*) as found in John's Gospel is often their supreme court of appeal. However, this combination does not, in and of itself, assume that *genuine* saving faith is present. This truth is sadly documented by the contexts of John 2:23 and 8:30. Concerning the "many" who "believed in His name" (i.e. πολλοὶ ἐπίστευσαν εἰς τὸ ὄνομα [*polloi episteusan eis to onoma*]) in John 2:23, it goes on to say in vv. 24–25 that "Jesus, on His part, was not entrusting Himself to them,"[972] for He knew all men, and because He did not need anyone to bear witness concerning man for He Himself knew what was in man" (John 2:24–25; NASB). He could x-ray men's hearts to see if their professions were genuine or false.

With this in mind, let us press on to John, chapter 8. Verse 31 is the theological crux of the whole passage. But in order to understand its great punch even better, a brief survey of the larger context is in order. Another large, mixed crowd had gathered to listen to Jesus' teaching. Among them there were some of the religious leaders of the people whose hatred for Christ and His authoritative proclamations had been growing hotter and hotter. Indeed, John 8 turns out to be yet another

---

[970] The threefold repetition of οὐ δύναται εἶναί μου μαθητής (*ou dunatai einai mou mathētēs*) connected to the corresponding scenarios of measurement painfully exposes a superficial, non-salvific "'coming'" to Christ.

[971] I.e. as evaluated by God's infallible MRI's of the spiritual cores of people.

[972] Literally, "but Jesus...did not believe (ἐπίστευεν [*episteuen*]) them."

episode of controversy fueled by their animosity. Now especially concerning verses 30–31, Hendriksen is right on target when he insists that "no transition of any kind from one group of men to another sharply contrasted group is apparent to the ordinary reader of the Greek text or of the English translation."[973] So, among those who *appeared* to have "believed in Him" (ἐπίστευσαν εἰς αὐτόν [*episteusan eis*]; v. 30) were some who later were ready to kill him (cf. vv. 37ff.) and who also tried to do so (v. 59). Christ said of this particular constituency that they had not believed Him (vv. 45–46). Schroam has well capsulized this whole context with these words: "In response to him they demonstrated the difference between themselves and disciples.... The discourse develops actual disbelief and the refusal of the label 'disciple.'"[974]

Now is the appropriate time to place our Lord's didactic "gem" into this setting: "Therefore Jesus was saying to the ones who had believed Him,[975] 'If you should remain in My word, truly you are disciples of me.'" I need to make a few exegetical observations about Christ's words before pulling the pieces together hermeneutically. Beginning with the apodosis of our Lord's affirmation,[976] the tense of this verb "to be" is present, not future. He is not saying, if you shall do such and such then you "shall be" such and such, but rather if this be true about you, you *are* this. Secondly, apparently to avoid any misunderstanding, especially about the word "disciples" (a term which may exhibit a range of semantic applications as it manifests narrower or larger circles of inclusion[977]), our Lord carefully qualified His words "you are my disciples" with the adverb ἀληθῶς (*alēthōs*), "truly, really, actually."[978] In doing this we can be sure that His punch-line apodosis pertains to "genuine disciples."[979]

---

[973] William Hendriksen, *Exposition of the Gospel According to John*, 2:51; cf. Kent, *Light in the Darkness*, 126.

[974] T. L. Schroam, "The Case of *Ioudaios* in the Fourth Gospel" (unpublished Th. D. dissertation, Rijksunwersiteit te Uerecht, 1974), 99.

[975] The "faith" construction now becomes a substantive perfect participle plus the simple dative case: τοὺς πεπιστευκότας αὐτῷ (*tous pepisteukotas autō*), "the ones/those who had believed Him."

[976] I.e. the punch-line, the logical "then" part of this "if ...then" construction.

[977] E.g., in the New Testament ranging from curious followers to converted followers, from the 12 "disciples" Jesus names as "apostles" to all believers in Him, etc.

[978] BAG, 36. Centuries ago, John Owen rightly identified the importance of ἀληθῶς (*alēthōs*): "The word *indeed*, is plainly opposed to spurious discipleship, of which the world has seen much from the days of Christ to the present time" (*A Commentary, Critical, Expository, and Practical, on the Gospel of John* [New York: Scribner, 1869], 196).

[979] Morris, *John*, 456; (at this juncture see also his excursus on "true discipleship" in *The Gospel According to St. John*, TNTC [Grand Rapids: Eerdmans, 1957], 117).

Now moving back to the "if" part of Jesus' statement, this "if" protasis is a third class conditional statement. It "says nothing about whether the condition is fulfilled or not, but explains what would be the case were it realized."[980] The verb in this conditional element is one that by inherent meaning denotes continuance.[981] Therefore, "*obedience* is the same thing as abiding in the word."[982]

Now, what do we make of Christ's carefully constructed conditional statement in this context of John 8? Well, for one thing, the proof of true faith, genuine believing, is "in the pudding." Here, it did not take a long time as the context advances to show that the people under consideration were *not genuine* disciples. They were *not true* believers. Their practice denied their original profession. Harrison put it this way, "It is the old story of pseudo faith. In this case, they did not *abide* in his word—which opens the way to knowing the truth more fully—to the point of being set free through it (v. 32)."[983] Robertson takes this central teaching from John 8 and applies it to our day, saying, "As then, so now. We accept church members on *profession* of trust in Christ. Continuance in the word...proves the sincerity or insincerity of the profession. It is the acid test."[984]

Another relevant text that affirms "Lordship salvation" as defined properly in its *biblical* context is one that rightly shows up again and again in evangelistic presentations, Romans 10:9–10:

> ...if you confess with your mouth Jesus as Lord and believe in your heart that God raised Him from the dead, you shall be saved; for with the heart man believes, resulting in righteousness, and with the mouth he confesses, resulting in salvation (NASB).

The parallelisms and even the chiastic arrangement[985] emphasize the fact that these are two complementary constituents of salvation/justification.[986] Dwelling on the twin responsibilities of *confessing* that "Jesus is

---

[980] Ibid. In other words, it functions quite generally as a measuring rod by which to gauge genuine Christianity.

[981] The basic meanings of μένω (*menō*) are "to remain, abide, continue, persist," etc. (cf., e.g., BAG, 504–505).

[982] Hendriksen, *John*, 2:52.

[983] E. F. Harrison, "John," *Wycliffe Bible Commentary* (Nashville: Southwestern, 1962), 1091.

[984] *WP*, 5:149.

[985] Notice how the chiasm highlights these essential responsibilities; i.e., confess/mouth...believe/heart (v. 9)...heart/believe...mouth/confess (v. 10).

[986] Note yet another parallelism within v. 10: literally "unto righteousness" (i.e. εἰς δικαιοσύνην [*eis dikaiosunēn*]) and "unto salvation" (i.e. εἰς σωτηρίαν [*eis sōtērian*]).

Lord" and *believing* in the resurrected Savior, Bultmann rightly concludes, "Since ὁμολογεῖν [*homologein*, "to confess"] and πιστεύειν [*pisteuein*, "to believe"] are obvious equivalents in the synonymous parallelism…, it is apparent that acknowledgment of Jesus as Lord is intrinsic to Christian faith…."[987] At initial salvation there must be present not only an understanding and acceptance of Christ as Savior but also a recognition and acknowledgment of Christ as Lord over one's life.

But some on the other side of this theological fence might say, "But, what about 'carnal Christians'?" Well, first and foremost, concerning the presence of "brothers"[988] who are said to be acting in a carnal (i.e. fleshly) manner (cf. 1 Corinthians 3:1–3), this does not mean that the Bible is presenting "'Carnal Christianity'" as a *normative* class within or alongside of true Christianity. In 1 Corinthians 3:1–3, Paul was not condoning them but confronting them on this very issue. To condone such a condition would be an affront to the Living Word and the written Word.

Let me offer two more examples to show that the Scriptures never recognize as normative this so-called category of "carnal Christians." The first one is another negative example. It comes from Hebrews 5:11–13:

> Concerning Whom[989] we have much to say although it is hard to explain, since you have become sluggish in reference to your hearing.[990] For, you see, although, on account of the time, you ought to be teachers, you again have need for someone to teach you the A, B, C's of the beginning of the word of God. Indeed you have come to have need of milk and not of solid food, for everyone who always uses[991] milk is unaccustomed to the word of righteousness, since he is an infant.[992]

However, the apostle refuses to leave them in the complacency of spiritual infancy. He immediately challenges them with a contrasting condition which is to be normative: "But solid food is for mature people, the ones, who on account of practice, have their faculties trained for the

---

[987] *TDNT*, 6:209.

[988] I will speak more to the issue of such designations, for example, in contexts containing exhortations and warnings (cf. chapter 6 on sanctification). For one thing, we need to remember that when the writers of the New Testament were writing to "the brethren," "the saints," etc., they were addressing their spiritually mixed audiences by their common *profession*.

[989] Referring back to Christ, especially functioning in His highly priestly role as further illustrated by Melchizedek.

[990] Cf., the NIV: "you are slow to learn."

[991] Cf., *NASB*: "for everyone who partakes *only* of milk…."

[992] I.e. a spiritual baby.

discernment of both good and evil" (Hebrews 5:14). Furthermore, the author immediately issues another exhortation that directly ties back into what he has just said: "Wherefore, leaving behind the word about the first thing about Christ,[993] let us be moved along to maturity..." (Hebrews 6:1a).

The norm is always shown to be one of an ever maturing Christian, not a "carnal Christian." Now consider Paul's more positively expressed description of true Christianity in Ephesians 4:11–16. He begins by affirming that the ascended Lord Jesus Christ "gave some to be apostles, some to be prophets, some to be evangelists, and some to be pastors and teachers" (Ephesians 4:11; NIV). Then he offers a longer explanation of God's *intentions* in reference to the giving of these gifts to the church:

> for the equipping[994] of the saints unto a work of service unto the building up of the body of Christ,[995] until we all attain to the unity[996] of the faith and of the full knowledge of the Son of God, unto a mature man, unto a measure of stature of the fullness of Christ, in order that we might no longer be infants, tossed here and there by waves and being driven around by every wind of teaching[997] by the craftiness of men, by cunning in reference to deceitful scheming; but being truthful in love, let us grow up, in all things, to Him, who is the Head, even, Christ, from whom the whole body being joined together and being held together by every ligament of supply according to the operation in connection with the measure of each individual part, makes the growth of the body for the edification of itself in love (Ephesians 4:12–16).

Genuine Christianity assumes a continuing maturity, not stagnation nor retardation.

Now, turning to the other extreme (as sometimes exhibited to various degrees in a few defenses of "Lordship Salvation"), although saving faith is never merely a lip-service profession and although biblical believing initially contains seeds of commitment to Christ, one must never leave the impression that salvation is pictured in any way as a faith-*plus*-works phenomenon. Biblical faith is a faith *that works*. However, some-

---

[993] Cf., NIV: "Therefore let us leave the elementary teachings about Christ...."
[994] And/or mending.
[995] I.e. the Church.
[996] Literally, "oneness"; "one" is a key word in 4:1ff.
[997] Or, "doctrine."

times in overly zealous presentations of genuine Christianity (i.e. true discipleship) a biblical faith-that-works is depicted errantly as though it were faith-plus-works. When this happens, the gravest of theological errors has occurred (cf., e.g., Galatians 1:6ff.). Sometimes *initial* repentance is defined too concretely. If initial repentance is characterized as being essentially a change of life style rather than an initial change in attitude and outlook as prompted by the operations of the Spirit,[998] then some kind of meritorious work is being added to faith, thereby denying a biblical salvation, namely, one that comes only by grace through faith.

Furthermore, we need to remember that we must also "walk by (biblical) faith." The error of works sanctification is no less serious than that of works salvation (cf., e.g., Galatians 3:3). At every stage of this graciously wonderful salvation process a faith that works is central.[999] Any form of unbiblical perfectionism at any stage of this process runs counter to the whole Word of God. Indeed, the Bible is transparently clear about sin whether it be the sin of a sinner about to be justified or the sins of saved sinners in the process of being sanctified. On these issues, the Scriptures are perfectly balanced. Compare, for example, Cooke's relevant comments based upon John's transition from chapter one to chapter two of his first epistle: "In the light of I John 1:10, the presence of personal sin in the Christian life is undeniable...and in the light of 2:1 the presence of personal sin is undesirable."[1000] Growth in the grace and knowledge of our Lord Jesus Christ is assumed, but at no stage of this process, outside of the final "booster-rocket" stage of glorification, do we "arrive." True disciples are in process (cf., e.g. Romans 6–8; 12:1–2; 2 Corinthians 3:18; Ephesians 4:23; Philippians 3:12–14; Colossians 3:10; 2 Peter 1:2–3 with vv. 4–11; 3:18 etc.). Indeed, the first stage of that process (i.e. *initial* sanctification, salvation proper) and every step along the way come about by grace through faith, a faith, however, that must be defined very carefully by intricately balanced biblical standards.

---

[998] Who is also prompting the person to respond in faith.

[999] This important truth will be discussed more fully in the next chapter.

[1000] W. Robert Cooke, "Hamartiological Problems in First John," *B Sac* 123 (July–Sept. 1966):252.

# CHAPTER 6

# SANCTIFICATION

## *The Basic Terminology of Sanctification*

### Old Testament Terms

*The Primary Root* קָדַשׁ *(qdš)*[1001]

Quite typically of this particular Hebrew root, we read something like this: "Its fundamental force seems to be to set apart an object from ordinary usage for a special (religious) purpose or function, and in particular to set apart for God."[1002] Technically, however, "the often-accepted basic meaning 'set apart' (cf., e.g., Eichrodt 1:270–272) may only be inferred."[1003]

This root "occurs in several dialects of Akkadian with the basic meaning 'to be clean, pure, consecrated.' In the Canaanite texts from Ugarit, the basic meaning of the word group is 'holy,' and it is always used in a cultic sense."[1004] Consequently, when it comes to the significance of קָדַשׁ *(qdš)*, we need to try to extrapolate its basic essence before pressing on to key associations and applications. However, this is an exceedingly challenging task, since as Müller puts it, the ancient Semitic root קָדַשׁ *(qdš)* "describes the status or character of holiness; it indicated...a conception of numinous quality *sui generis*."[1005] In other words, it is sort of like the dilemma a young child faces in school when he is urged to define a new word by synonyms or by descriptive combinations of other words besides the new term being learned. After straining over קָדַשׁ *(qdš)*, we are hard pressed to say any more than that the basic meaning of noun forms (i.e. holiness) is "holiness," the essence of the

---

[1001] For a distribution chart of the occurrences of the root קָדַשׁ *(qdš)* in its various forms throughout the Old Testament, see: Müller, *TLOT*, 3:1106–1107.
[1002] Hughes, *BDT*, 470.
[1003] Müller, *TLOT*, 3:1104.
[1004] McComiskey, *TWOT*, 2:787.
[1005] Müller, *TLOT*, 3:1104.

adjective "holy" is "holy," the force of the verb "to be holy" is "to be holy," etc. McComiskey, therefore, concludes that "it seems best to see the root *qdsh* as serving to delineate the sphere of the 'holy.'"[1006]

Biblically, this tendency should not surprise us that much in that Yahweh God is the pure essence of and the perfect paradigm for קֹדֶשׁ (*qdš*).[1007] He is extolled as being superlatively "holy" (cf., e.g., Isaiah 6:3). Therefore, relationally "God is considered to be the source of holiness."[1008] Here is where the cultic significance of קֹדֶשׁ (*qdš*) plays a significant role.[1009] Indeed, as Procksch emphasizes, "From the very first קֹדֶשׁ is very closely linked with the cultic. Anything related to the cultus, whether God, man, things, space or time, can be brought under the term קֹדֶשׁ."[1010] A good example of this cultic connection occurs in Numbers 17:3 [16:38, Eng.]:

> The censers of the Korahites were regarded as holy because they had been devoted to the Lord.... The devotion of the censers seems to have created a condition of inviolable holiness that could not allow for their being treated in a common way.[1011]

Although it is technically true that in קֹדֶשׁ (*qdš*), "there is nothing implied...as to moral character,"[1012] the Scriptures do strongly emphasize ethics when it comes to applications of this root to personal beings. This prevalent phenomenon makes קֹדֶשׁ (*qdš*) a primary building block for biblical sanctification. Nevertheless, such applications are part of the bigger picture, the common denominator of which is "relation or contact with God."[1013]

---

[1006] *TWOT*, 2:787.

[1007] Cf., e.g., Naude's discussion (*NIDOTTE*, 3:879ff.).

[1008] Ibid., 3:879.

[1009] Naude (*NIDOTTE*, 3:878) correctly observes that "by far the most extensive occurrences of the word group are to be found in the cultic and ritual texts...."

[1010] *TDNT*, 1:89.

[1011] McComiskey, *TWOT*, 2:787.

[1012] Rall, *ISBE* (1939), 4:2682; he goes on to suggest an example: "It is this formal usage without moral implication that explains such a passage as Genesis 38:21. The word translated 'prostitute' here is from the same *kādash*, meaning lit., as elsewhere, the sanctified or consecrated one (...cf. Dt. 23:18, 1 K 14:24; Hos. 4:14)" (ibid.).

[1013] Girdlestone, *Synonyms*, 176; note Girdlestone's helpful sample applications of קֹדֶשׁ (*qdš*) (ibid., 175–76).

## The Secondary Roots בדל *(bdl) and* נזר *(nzr)*

These two roots share a common emphasis on separation. They thereby also parallel the important applicational force of קדשׁ *(qdš)* in many of its contexts. Consider, for example, the force of בדל *(bdl)* in the following passage:

> Now keep all My statutes and all my ordinances and do them so that the land to which I am bringing you to dwell in it might not vomit you out. Indeed you must not walk according to the Gentile nations which I am going to send away from your presence, because they have done all these things;[1014] therefore I have abhorred them. However, I have said to you,[1015] "You will possess their land since I will give it to you in order that you might possess it, a land flowing with milk and honey." I am Yahweh, your God, who has separated (הִבְדַּלְתִּי [*hibdaltî*]) you from (מִן [*min*]) the peoples. Consequently you are to make a distinction (וְהִבְדַּלְתֶּם [*wᵉhibdaltem*]; i.e. to separate) between a clean and unclean beast and between a clean and unclean bird; so you must not make yourselves detestable by beast or by bird or by anything that moves about the ground which I have separated (הִבְדַּלְתִּי [*hibdaltî*]) for you as unclean. Therefore, you must be holy people (קְדֹשִׁים [*qᵉdôšîm*]) to Me, since I, Yahweh, am holy (קָדוֹשׁ [*qadôš*]); indeed, I have separated (וָאַבְדִּל [*wā'abdil*]) you from מִן [*min*] the peoples to be mine[1016] (Leviticus 20:22–26).

This paradigm passage helps to understand other occurrences of key verb forms derived from this root throughout the Scriptures. McComiskey, for example, appropriately concludes that

> this verb, used only in the Niphal and Hiphil, has the basic connotation "to be separated" or "to separate," "to divide." ...The concept of separation inherent in *bādal* was used to

---

1014 Cf., the previous context for samples of such wicked behavior.

1015 I.e. "I have promised you...."

1016 The parallelism of the roots קדשׁ *(qdš)* and בדל *(bdl)* is designedly striking. Statements about the separation of Yahweh's people from the pagan nations are quite common in Scripture; Otzen rightly notes that "*bdl* is used several times to denote Israel's separation from the heathen" (*TDOT*, 2:2); cf., e.g., Ezra 6:21; Nehemiah 9:2; 10:29 [v. 28, Eng.]; etc. This work of grace is all the more amazing in view of the sin of God's people which naturally separates them from the LORD (cf., e.g., the impact of בדל [*bld*] in Isaiah 59:2).

describe God's special activity in setting apart Aaron to the consecration of the holy things (I Chr. 23:13) and the setting apart of the Levites (Num. 16:9; Deut. 10:8). Israel was set apart to be God's heritage(I Kgs. 8:53).[1017]

When we turn to the root נזר (*nzr*), the example of the Nazirite (i.e. נָזִיר [*nāzîr*]) immediately comes to mind (cf. Numbers 6). And, once again, separation proves to be the most basic feature of this root: "*nazir* referred originally to something removed from everyday life, elevated above the customary and set aside for something special, dedicated."[1018] Therefore, McComiskey rightly concludes:

> The basic meaning of *nāzar* is "to separate."... With the preposition *min* it has the meaning "keep oneself away from."[1019]... When the word occurs with the preposition *le* in either the Niphal or Hiphil it connotes "separation to." It is used in this way of consecration to Yahweh on the part of the Nazirites...and of the consecration of the Israelites to Baal (Hos. 9:10).[1020]

As we have seen based upon usages of קָדֵשׁ (*qdš*), בדל (*bdl*), and נזר (*nzr*), the focus of sanctification in the Old Testament is ultimately on separation. This emphasis on a separation *from* the profane *to* the pure will be perpetuated to a significant degree in the New Testament, although its cultic colorings will largely pale away into the background.

## New Testament Terms

### *The Primary Word Group* ἅγιος *(hagios)*

Concerning the background of the ἅγιος (*hagios*) family in ancient Greek literature, Seebass has observed that "there is no certain etymology for *hagios*. It is related to *hazomai* (from *hagiomai*) which is not found in the LXX or the New Testament, meaning to stand in awe of the gods or one's parents."[1021] Much more importantly, as we move into

---

[1017] *TWOT*, 1:91. Van Dam makes the common denominator of בדל (*bld*) even more specific when he characterizes the main force of this root with these words: "...separating what does not belong together and separating for a specific task" (*NIDOTTE*, 1:604); it should be noted that Van Dam treats quite paradigmatically the five occurrences of בדל (*bdl*) in Genesis 1.
[1018] Kühlewein, *TLOT*, 2:729.
[1019] Cf., e.g., Leviticus 15:31; 22:2; Numbers 6:3; Ezekiel 14:7.
[1020] *TWOT*, 2:567.
[1021] *NIDNTT*, 2:224.

biblical Greek, specifically the LXX, "the word-group serves predominately to translate Heb. *qādôš* and its derivatives. In addition, there are the (rare) occurrences of *nāzîr*, Nazirite, to be considered."[1022] Procksch rightly stresses, in application to the translators of the LXX, that they did not "allow the Hebrew קדשׁ to be coloured by the Greek meaning of ἅγιος, but impressed ἅγιος wholly into the service of the Hebrew קדשׁ."[1023] As we have seen so many times already in connection with a variety of terms, this semantical/theological tendency builds a linking bridge to the New Testament.[1024]

When we get into the New Testament itself, we find the adjective ἅγιος (*hagios*) referring to the holiness of God or of Christ in general, the Spirit in particular, to members of Christ's Body, the Church, to the Christian life, etc.[1025] Concerning the verb ἁγιάζω (*hagiazō*), it is used of:

> (a) the gold adorning the Temple and of the gifts laid on the altar, Matt. 23:17–29; (b) food, I Tim. 4:5; (c) the unbelieving spouse of a believer, I Cor. 7:14; (d) the ceremonial cleansing of the Israelites, Heb. 9:13; (e) the Father's name, Luke 11:2; (f) the consecration of the Son by the Father, John 10:36; (g) the Lord Jesus devoting Himself to the redemption of His people, John 17:19; (h) the setting apart of the believer for God, Acts 20:32; cp. Rom. 15:16; (i) the effect on the believer of the Death of Christ, Heb. 10:10, said of God, and 2:11; 13:12, said of the Lord Jesus; (j) the separation of the believer from the world in his behaviour—by the Father through the Word, John 17:17, 19; (k) the believer who turns away from such things as dishonour God and His gospel, 2 Tim. 2:21; (l) the acknowledgment of the Lordship of Christ, I Pet. 3:15.[1026]

Finally, in reference to the noun ἁγιασμός (*hagiasmos*), "sanctification," it "is used of (a) separation to God, I Cor. 1:30; 2 Thess. 2:13; I Pet. 1:2;" "(b) the course of life befitting those so separated, I Thess. 4:3, 4, 7; Rom. 6:19, 22; I Tim. 2:15; Heb. 12:14."[1027]

---

[1022] Ibid.; for a discussion of particular categories of occurrences, survey Seebass' subsequent treatment (ibid., 2:225–227).

[1023] *TDNT*, 1:95.

[1024] Shortly I will say a bit more about this phenomenon as it pertains to the biblical development of the doctrine of sanctification.

[1025] For an adequate survey see Procksch, *TDNT*, 1:100–110.

[1026] Vine, *EDNTW*, 546.

[1027] Ibid., 545.

*The Secondary Terms* ὅσιος  *(hosios) and* εὐσέβεια *(eusebeia)*

The first of these two terms does not follow the semantical precedent of the LXX. As Seebass notes:

> In the NT *hosios* is a rare word (8 occurrences, of which 5 are in quotations; *hosiotēs* [holiness] twice; *anosios* [unholy] twice). The most important OT use (*hosioi*, the congregation) does not appear. The members of the Christian community are not *hasîdîm* but chosen ones (*ekletoi;* ...) and saints (...*hagios*); ... Eph. 4:24 mentions *hosiotēs* as one of the qualities of the new man.[1028]

Concerning the second term εὐσέβεια (*eusebeia*), Vine highlights the term's etymological make up, noting that it comes "from *eu*, well, and *sebomai*, to be devout," then he extrapolates its significance arguing that this word group "denotes that piety which, characterized by a Godward attitude, does that which is well-pleasing to Him."[1029] Occurrences of εὐσεβής (*eusebēs*), "devout, godly, pious, reverent,"[1030] and εὐσέβεια, "devoutness, piety," etc.[1031] in the LXX render a variety of Hebrew words and are often found in parallelisms with several different antonyms.[1032] Moving on into the New Testament, this word group appears quite frequently in Paul's later epistles (cf., e.g., 1 Timothy 2:2; 3:16; 4:7, 8; 6:3, 5, 6, 11; 2 Timothy 3:5; Titus 1:1).[1033] It is also used by Peter (cf., e.g., Acts 3:12; 2 Pet. 1:3, 6, 7; 3:11). Quite obviously, "godliness" and sanctification go together. Günther even describes "godliness" as "the Christian manner of life."[1034]

## A Basic Theology of Sanctification

Foundationally, it is exceedingly important to remember that in the Old Testament "God Himself was regarded as holy, i.e. as a Being who from His nature, position, and attributes is to be set apart and revered as distinct from all others; and Israel was to separate itself from the world and the things of the world because God was thus separated;

---

[1028] *NIDNTT*, 2:237.

[1029] *EDNTW*, 272.

[1030] BAG, 326.

[1031] Günther, *NIDNTT*, 2:91.

[1032] For a brief survey, see Foerster, *TDNT*, 7:179.

[1033] Louw and Nida interestingly render 1 Timothy 2:2 "as 'to live as God would have us live' or 'to live as God has told us we should live'" (*GELSD*, 1:532).

[1034] *NIDNTT*, 2:95.

they were to be holy, for He was Holy (Lev. 11:44, 19:2, 20:7, 26, 21:8)."[1035] It is not at all coincidental that the New Testament picks up this same ethical demand for holiness (cf., Peter's reference to Leviticus 11:44–45 in 1 Peter 1:16). As a matter of fact, it builds a massive ethical superstructure on this solid Old Testament foundation. In reference to the noun ἁγιασμός (*hagiasmos*), "sanctification" *per se*, Procksch has well captured its ethical essence in the New Testament reasoning that

> ἁγιασμός is the will of God (1 Thes. 4:3), and it consists again in purity. . . . The opposite of ἁγιασμός is ἀκαθαρσία (4:7),[1036] except that ἀκαθαρσία is a moral state which cannot possibly be linked with calling (οὐ . . . ἐπί ἀκαθαρσίᾳ), whereas ἁγιασμός is the moral form in which it is worked out. The body is to be serviceable to δικαιοσύνη εἰς ἁγιασμόν (R. 6:19), so that ἁγιασμός is again the moral goal of purity (cf. R. 6:22...). In Christ is made possible δικαιοσύνη τε καὶ ἁγιασμός καὶ ἀπολύτρωσις (1 C. 1:30), and it is by Him or by the Spirit (2 Th. 2:13; 1 Pt. 1:2...) that it comes into effect in Christians, so that the ἁγιασμός or sanctifying effected by the Spirit is the living form of the Christian state.... If atonement is the basis of the Christian life, ἁγιασμός is the moral form which develops out of it and without which there can be no vision of Christ. The term ἁγιασμός is always distinguished from ἅγιος and ἁγιάζειν by the emphasis on the moral element.[1037]

## A Brief Survey of the Phases or Stages of Sanctification

### Initial Sanctification

Sanctification is positional before it becomes progressive. Ladd does a good job in correcting a common misconception about sanctification when he says,

> a widely prevailing view is that justification is the term designating the beginning of the Christian life, while sanctification designates development of that life through the internal work of the Spirit. This, however, is an oversimplification of the

---

[1035] Girdlestone, *Synonyms*, 176.
[1036] I.e. "impurity."
[1037] *TDNT*, 1:113.

New Testament teaching and it obscures an important truth. In fact, the idea of sanctification is soteriological before it is a moral concept.[1038]

First Corinthians 6:11 stands as Exhibit A in this regard: "and such were some of you;[1039] but[1040] you were washed, but[1041] you were sanctified,[1042] but[1043] you were justified in the name of the Lord Jesus Christ and in the Spirit of God." In view of this positional reality, "since every believer is sanctified in Christ Jesus, 1 Cor. 1:2, cp. Heb. 10;10, a common New Testament designation of all believers is 'saints,' *hagioi*, i.e., 'sanctified' or 'holy ones.' Thus sainthood, or sanctification, is not an attainment, it is the state into which God, in grace, calls sinful men, and in which they begin their course as Christians, Col. 3:12; Heb. 3:1."[1044] "Because believers do belong to God—because they have been sanctified—they are called upon to experience sanctification and to shun uncleanness."[1045] The relationship of positional sanctification to progressive sanctification is another scenario of the theological indicative/imperative motif.[1046]

## Progressive Sanctification

Progressive sanctification (i.e. sanctification proper; cf., e.g., John 17:17; Hebrews 2:11; 10:14; etc.) is therefore

> the continuing work of God in the life of the believer... Sanctification is a process by which one's moral condition is brought into conformity with one's legal status before God.... It designates not merely the fact that believers are formally set apart, or belong to Christ, but that they are then to conduct themselves accordingly. They are to live lives of purity and goodness.[1047]

We should progressively be becoming more conformed into the ethical image of our Lord Jesus Christ (cf., e.g., 2 Corinthians 3:18; 4:16; Ephesians 4:11–16; Colossians 3:10; etc.).

---

[1038] *TNT*, 519.

[1039] Cf., the characteristics of unrighteous people in vv. 9–10.

[1040] I.e. ἀλλά (*alla*) introducing a strong antithesis.

[1041] Another ἀλλά (*alla*).

[1042] I.e. ἡγιάσθητε (*hēgiasthēte*), an aorist passive indicative pointing to the reality of an initial, positional sanctification accomplished by God at the time of justification (see the very next affirmation).

[1043] Yet a third ἀλλά (*alla*).

[1044] Vine, *EDNTW*, 546.

[1045] Ladd, *TNT*, 520.

[1046] Cf., the third of the "Topics" discussed below.

[1047] Erickson, *Christian Theology*, 967–969.

## Final Sanctification

Finally, there is the ultimate phase of sanctification, more commonly labeled glorification (cf., e.g., 1 Thessalonians 3:13; 5:23; etc.; also cf. the concept undergirding Philippians 1:6). Historically, there has been a controversy between progressionists versus perfectionists in reference to sanctification. Erickson briefly sketches out these two perspectives on perfection when he says,

> One major issue over which there has been disagreement throughout church history is whether the process of sanctification is ever completed within the earthly lifetime of the believer. Do we ever come to the point where we no longer sin?... Our conclusion is that while complete freedom from and victory over sin are the standard to be arrived at and are theoretically possible, it is doubtful whether any believer will attain this goal within this life.... Although we may never be perfectly sanctified within this life, we shall be in the eternity beyond and hence should presently aim to arrive as close to complete sanctification as we can.[1048]

Although *God's* "divine power has given us everything we need for life and godliness" (2 Peter 1:3, NIV), *our* indwelling sin (cf., e.g., Romans 7:14ff; 1 John 1:8–10; etc.) short-circuits a perfectly consistent application of these divine provisions. For these and other reasons, the New Testament brims with exhortations and commands to live more consistently sanctified lives (cf., e.g., Romans 12:1–2; 2 Corinthians 7:1; Ephesians 4:17ff.; Philippians 3:12ff.; Colossians 3:5ff.; 2 Peter 3:18; etc.).

## *Some Specific Topics and/or Tensions Pertaining to Sanctification*

### The Role of Fear and Faith

"The Fear of the LORD is the beginning of wisdom" (Psalm 111:10a). It is correspondingly "the beginning of knowledge" (Proverbs 1:7). Furthermore, in a context of both suffering and accusation, Job reiterated the words of God saying, "Now He said to mankind, 'Behold, the fear of the Lord—it is wisdom, and to turn away from evil

---

[1048] Ibid., 971–974; for a more extensive discussion see Guthrie, *NTT*, 661–675.

is understanding'" (Job 28:28).[1049] The fear of God is not something that is designed to function only as an impetus for salvation; it is to play a primary role in sanctification also. Consequently, the fear of the LORD should be an active motivating force right from the "beginning" of the salvation process to its end. Its presence is the earmark of a true believer (cf., e.g., Genesis 22:12; Deuteronomy 6:13; 10:12; Psalm 85:10 [v. 9, Eng.]; 103:11, 13, 17; 119:63; 147:11; Proverbs 14:26–27; etc.); its absence the indication of an infidel (cf., e.g., Psalm 36:1; Romans 3:18).

This intended ethical impact closely associated with the fear of God moves on into and through the pages of the New Testament. For example, in the midst of a context saturated with exhortations to holy thinking and living, Paul writes these words to his beloved Philippians: "work out your own salvation[1050] with fear and trembling!" (Philippians 2:12b). What should we make of this universal biblical preoccupation with the fear of the LORD? It is hard to improve upon Murray's answer to this important question:

> The fear of God is the soul of godliness.... We are advised that what the Scripture regards as knowledge or wisdom takes its inception from the apprehension and emotion which the fear of God connotes. If we are thinking of the notes of biblical piety none is more characteristic than the fear of the Lord. ... Lest we should think that the religion of the Old Testament *is in this respect* on a lower level, and that the New Testament rises above that which is represented by the fear of the Lord, we need but scan the New Testament to be relieved of any such misapprehension....[1051] The fear of God in us is the frame of heart and mind which reflects our apprehension of who and what God is, and who and what God is will tolerate nothing less than totality commitment to him.[1052]

Consequently, genuine disciples of Christ ought to be "perfecting holiness in the fear of God" (2 Corinthians 7:1b, NASB). Since "it is a

---

[1049] The words "wisdom" (חָכְמָה [hokmâ]), "knowledge" (דַּעַת [daʿat]), "understanding" (בִּינָה [bînâ]), etc. are preeminently significant as ethical terms rather than merely intellectual words in the Old Testament (for some good discussions, see Schmitz, *NIDNTT* 2:395–396; and Goetzmann, *NIDNTT*, 2:1027–1029).
[1050] Again, the context indicates that Paul is speaking of *sanctification* proper.
[1051] Some of the passages Murray appeals to are Matthew 10:28; Luke 12:4–5; Acts 9:31; Romans 11:20–21; Colossians 3:22; Hebrews 4:1; 1 Peter 1:17; 2:17 (*Principles of Conduct*, 229–242).
[1052] Ibid.

dreadful thing to fall into the hands of the living God" (Hebrews 10:31, NIV), let us "pursue peace with all men, and the sanctification without which no one will see the Lord" (Hebrews 12:14, NASB).

At salvation and throughout the lives of disciples, **faith** is the primary channel of dependent appropriation of the absolutely essential resources of God. The relationship of faith to sanctification in 2 Corinthians 5:7 is just as essential and vital as it is when it applies to justification, for example, in Romans 3:28. Berkouwer, with great balance discusses this important issue:

> We must be thoroughly aware that in shifting from justification to sanctification we are not withdrawing from the sphere of faith.... Christian activity is certainly not to be excluded, or belittled, or condemned: but if this activity is to be sound it must never be severed from its relation to the mercy of God.... The doctrine of the work of the Holy Spirit is designed precisely to prevent us from viewing man as an independent, dynamistic unit. This doctrine does not make man self-sufficient but rather underlines his perpetual and inherent lack of self-sufficiency.... All views which end up with some simplistic theory of regeneration will deprive us of the wonderful mystery of the work of the Holy Spirit—wonderful because it turns man from a study of his own condition to the life of faith in which he feeds on God's grace alone and seeks to continue in the sanctification he has received.... Faith is the pivot on which everything revolves. Faith, though not of itself creative, preserves us from autonomous self-sanctification and moralism.... For progress in sanctification never meant working out one's own salvation under one's own auspices; on the contrary, it meant working out one's own salvation with a rising sense of dependence on God's grace.[1053]

So, "successful ethics cannot exist independently of faith in the redeemer-God."[1054] And yet, at the same time, "genuine faith cannot long exist independent of ethical commitment."[1055] We must continue to "walk by faith," namely a biblically vital faith that evidences itself in the production of the fruits of holiness.

---

[1053] Berkouwer, *Faith and Sanctification*, 20, 27, 83, 87, 93, 112.
[1054] Payne, *Theology of the Older Testament*, 316.
[1055] Ibid.

## The Importance of Love

Like the fear of the Lord, love for the Lord is also an earmark of genuine believers. In this regard, love includes much more than emotion; it most often is associated with expected obedience (cf., e.g., Deuteronomy 5:10; 6:5; 10:12; 11:1, 22; Psalm 31:24 [v. 23, Eng.]; Micah 6:8; John 14:21, 23–24; 15:10–14; 1 John 4:10, 19; etc.). In the Old Testament, the root אהב ('hb) very regularly occurs with emphases on the LORD's gracious exercise of "love" in application to His elect people and His expectation that such a beloved people would reciprocate in their love for Him and for one another.[1056] By synthesizing Deuteronomy 6:4–5 and Leviticus 19:18, Jesus boiled down the whole law to this intended significance: first loving the LORD and then loving one's neighbor (Matthew 22:37–40).

John, the so-called "apostle of love," extensively developed this major theological theme of our Lord in the New Testament. As Guthrie notes:

> The theme of love is particularly characteristic of the Johannine literature. As a desirable Christian virtue it has its roots in God's love for his Son.... On many occasions he [i.e. Jesus] pointed out that love for himself was to be a motive for ethical behavior.... There can be no doubts that the new life as Jesus conceived it centered on love.... Moreover, man's love for God comes more to the fore in the epistles than in the gospel as a motive for the Christian life.... They [i.e. the love passages in 1 Jn] set a high target, but are not expected for that reason to deter people from reaching towards it. Indeed, for Christians, loving is not an option but an obligation.[1057]

One should not think that only John is interested in developing this important love theme. As Ridderbos points out:

> The context of the new obedience, in the epistles of Paul too, finds its most central and fundamental expression in love.... This central significance of love in Paul's preaching of the new life can be shown in various ways. Just as faith can be called

---

[1056] Cf., discussions in Jenni, *TLOT*, 1:50–52; Wallis, *TDOT*, 1:104–117; Els, *NIDOTTE*, 1:278–291.

[1057] Guthrie, *NTT*, 664–666.

the mode of existence of the new life, so can love....[1058] In the first place love derives its central significance from the fact that it is the reflection of the love of God in Jesus.... In the second place this love constitutes the vital element of the church. It is in love that the body of which Christ is the Head, is built up (Eph. 4:15, 16), in which believers together are rooted and grounded (Eph. 3:17). For this reason love can be called the bond of perfection (Col. 3:14)[1059]; indeed in its own way it forms the unity of the church (Col. 2:2). The application of the commandment of love consequently has in Paul the clear effect of stirring up the strong awareness in the church of mutual responsibility.... Here again there is the clear relationship between love and sanctification. As a fellowship sanctified and appropriated by God to himself, the church is bound together and set apart by love.[1060]

Would that Christ's church display the badge of love[1061] more transparently and consistently in a world known for its hatred.

## The Indicative/Imperative Motif

The terminology of indicative and imperative is being used herein more in a theological sense than a grammatical sense although most of the New Testament scenarios that employ this motif will also follow suit with their respectively corresponding Greek moods. The *fact* of what God *has done* or what He *has promised to do* becomes the basis and/or the incentive for us to exercise our responsibility *to do*, namely, to make progress in holy living.

### Based upon God's Past 'Done'

Looking backward over our shoulders at salvation history, the Scriptures again and again appeal to what God has accomplished salvifically.

---

[1058] Ridderbos appropriately appeals to such passages as Romans 13:10ff; 15:30; 1 Corinthians 13; Galatians 5:5ff; 6:2, 15; Ephesians 3:17; Colossians 1:4; 2:7; 1 Thessalonians 1:3; 1 Timothy 6:11; 2 Timothy 3:10; Titus 2:2; etc.

[1059] The imagery in this context most likely looks upon "love" as the *belt* that binds together the other virtues of this wardrobe which is to characterize holy living.

[1060] Ridderbos, *POT*, 293–294; cf. also Ladd, *TNT*, 522–524; Leon Morris, *Testaments of Love: A Study of Love in the Bible* (Grand Rapids; Eerdmans, 1981), *passim*.

[1061] Francis Schaeffer well branded love in the New Testament *The Mark of the Christian* (Downers Grove: InterVarsity Press, 1970).

Most often these affirmations of fact are not just thrown out as tidbits of salvation history but are designed to goad His people on to be, or to keep on becoming ethically, who, by His grace, positionally they are.

A good example of this motif in the Old Testament is found in Deuteronomy 7:6–11. Verses 6–10 emphasize the indicative of God's done while v. 11 follows with the consequential *imperative* for the people to do:

> For you are a people holy to the LORD your God. The LORD your God has chosen you out of all the peoples on the face of the earth to be his people, his treasured possession. The LORD did not set his affection on you and choose you because you were more numerous than other peoples, for you were the fewest of all peoples. But it was because the LORD loved you and kept the oath he swore to your forefathers that he brought you out with a mighty hand and redeemed you from the land of slavery, from the power of Pharaoh king of Egypt. Know therefore[1062] that the LORD your God is God; he is the faithful God, keeping his covenant of love to a thousand generations of those who love him and keep his commands. But those who hate him he will repay to their face by destruction; he will not be slow to repay to their face those who hate him. Therefore, take care to follow the commands, decrees and laws I give you today (Deuteronomy 7:6–11, NIV).

When we come to the New Testament, a special focus of God's *done* involves union with Christ. The Apostle John develops the picture of this union and the productivity that should come from it in John 15. Erickson summarizes this important passage as follows:

> It is clear that our continued walk in the Christian life, our sanctification, is dependent on union with him. Jesus made this quite evident in his imagery of the vine and the branches.... Jesus viewed union with him, which is closely

---

[1062] Technically, vv. 6–10 are not purely a divine theological indicative since the responsibility to "know" darts in at the beginning of v. 9. It anticipates the main, punch-line imperative of v. 11. Also, note how properly thinking about the God of this indicative (v. 9) implicitly becomes a prerequisite for living holy lives in His presence (v. 11). This responsibility of proper thinking is generally related to the next topic I will bring up, i.e., the centrality of the mindset in salvation and sanctification. Furthermore, notice how conceptually parallel Romans 6:1–14 is with Deuteronomy 7:6–11, esp. herein how the priority of the mindset is picked up both in Deuteronomy 7:9 and Romans 6:11.

linked to keeping his commandments (v. 10), as the key to the believer's whole Christian life. Fruit-bearing (v. 5), prayer (v. 7), and ultimately joy (v. 11) depend upon it.[1063]

In John, "abiding" in Christ (cf., e.g., John 15:4–7) is the crucial responsibility out of which all other ethical "imperatives" flow. Based upon the union graciously established by God, the believer-branch needs to remain dependently tapped into the vital Vine who is Christ.[1064]

The concept of abiding in Christ carries over into John's first epistle which has so much to say about the ethical life-style of *true* believers. Guthrie sketches out the implicit indicative/imperative developments within 1 John when he argues that

> the man who abides in Christ has an obligation to walk as Christ walked (1 John 2:6). He must, moreover, keep his commandments (1 John 3:24). Abiding in Christ issues in love of the highest kind, for it is nothing less than God's own love in us (1 Jn. 4:12).... So closely linked is the idea of the indwelling God with its ethical effect that John can say "he who abides in love abides in God and God abides in him" (1 Jn. 4:16). The great frequency of the idea of "abiding" in 1 John (cf. 1 Jn. 2:6, 24, 27, 28; 3:6, 24; 4:12–13, 15–16), shows that John sees a special need to stress the source of power for the new life.[1065]

Paul transparently develops the indicative/imperative motif in several places. I will appeal to two of the most prominent ones which are found respectively in Romans 6 and Colossians 3.

It is generally accepted that the two basic divisions of Paul's Epistle to the Romans are chapters 1–11 having to do with "doctrine" and 12:1–2ff. having to do with "duty." Although the break between chapters 11 and 12 does seem to separate the more distinctly theological part of Romans from its more characteristically ethical portion, there are some indications of ethical emphases in the first part of this epistle and of doctrinal points in its final portion. Furthermore, in a few places doctrine and duty intermingle. The most important of the passages which

---

[1063] *Christian Theology*, 974–975.

[1064] Ladd argues that the Johannine concept is "somewhat similar to the Pauline idiom of being in Christ, and Christ being in the believer; but the Pauline idiom is eschatological while the Johannine idiom involves more of the idea of personal fellowship" (*TNT*, 278).

[1065] *NTT*, 642–643.

bounce back and forth between the indicative and imperative of sanctification is Romans 6:1–14. This text provides the indicative basis for the
imperative obligations of holy living. This passage's moral mandates,
based upon the divine realities stemming from union with Christ, antici-
pate the more detailed ethical applications of 12:1–2ff.

Logically, the passage contains four essential demands on how to
turn our union with Christ (i.e. the divine indicative) into dynamic daily
living (i.e. our ethical imperative).[1066] Theologically, we need to remember that this text does not unfold by giving us so many verses of indicative followed by the remaining verses being devoted to the ethical imperative. Throughout these 14 verses, indicative and imperative alternate
evidencing how important the interrelationship of position and practice
really is to biblical sanctification. For an emphasis on the theological indicative, examine carefully vv. 2b, 3–4a, 5a, 6a–b, 7, 8a, 9–10, 14b; and
for emphases on the moral imperative study vv. 2a, c, 4b, 5b, 6c, 8b, 11–
13, 14a.

Turning our attention to Colossians 3:1ff., the indicative realities we
have by grace through our union with Christ constitute the grounds of
and the goads for holy living in the here and now. Colossians 3 is especially interesting in that Paul appeals to certain salvation-history
indicatives anchored in the past along with a guaranteed future one (i.e.
v.4). Both of these divine "dones" are designed to prompt purity on the
pathway of the Christian life. First, look carefully at the indicatives of vv.
1a, 3, 4 (i.e. the future one), 9b–11, 12a, etc., then at the imperatives of
vv. 1b, 2, 5–9a, 12b, etc. Paul's overall burden is clear; it may be theologically paraphrased as follows: "In view of what God has already accomplished in saving us, our mindset and manner of life need to be
dedicated wholeheartedly to becoming, in reference to our behavior,
who we are in Christ."

## Based upon God's Future 'Done'

The addition of God's guaranteed future 'done' (cf. again, e.g.,
Colossians 3:4) sometimes becomes the primary motive for Christian
morality in other New Testament passages. It is highly profitable to
study 1 Corinthians 15:58 in its context; 2 Corinthians 5:10 in its con-

---

[1066] Cf. my more detailed outline in APPENDIX K. For some helpful discussions on the larger
context of Adam theology and aeon theology, see Moo, *Romans 1–8*, 367ff., who speaks of two
realms and two eras; and Dunn, who says of the indicative realities contained in Romans 6:1ff.,
"For Paul, evidently, *the character of daily conduct is actually determined by these deeper realities....* The proof of such deeper realities is not some profound mystical experience but the daily
decisions of everyday relationships and responsibilities" (*Romans 1–8*, 330).

text; 2 Peter 3:10–14; 1 John 2:28–3:3; etc.[1067] In view of the divine promise of what we shall one day be in Christ (i.e. morally perfect), we ought to be exercising our moral muscles all along the pathway of sanctification.

> In summary, we conclude that union with Christ in his death and resurrection, the indwelling of Christ in the Spirit, and the blessing of eternal life are different ways of describing the same reality: the situation of the man of faith who has become a new creation in Christ and entered the new era of salvation and life.... The practical outworking of this new life is, however, one of tension—the tension between the indicative and the imperative. [1068] Because the man of faith *is* a new creation and has entered the new aeon of salvation, he has died with Christ (Rom. 6:5); he has been crucified with Christ (Gal. 2:20); the old man has been crucified with him (Rom. 6:6); the flesh has been crucified (Gal. 5:24); the body of flesh has been put off in circumcision of the heart (Col. 2:11). This is the indicative. This is not something subjective and automatic and spontaneous; it indicates a new state of existence that must manifest itself in a new life.... The important thing to note is the tension between the indicative and the imperative: the old man..., the old self has been put to death—it has been put off in principle; yet believers are exhorted to do in practice what has already been done in principle.[1069]

Furthermore,

> the imperative rests on the indicative and...this order is not reversible.... The imperative is grounded on the reality that has been given with the indicative, appeals to it, and is intended to bring it to full development.... The execution of the impera-

---

[1067] By the way, this phenomenon is not restricted to the New Testament; cf. the primary purpose of prophecy (i.e. holy living in the here and now), e.g., in: Isaiah 1:16–20 in context; Hosea 1:2–9; also chapters 4–5 in balance with 1:10–2:1; 6:1–3; 14:1–9; Joel 1:2–7, 15–18; 2:1–11 with 1:8–14; also Joel 2:12–17 with 2:18ff.; Amos 5–9 with 9:9–15; 2 Samuel 12:1–15a with 2 Samuel 2:16 (cf., also Psalms 51 and 32); Jonah 1:2; 3:4 with 3:5–9, 10; Micah 3:12 with Jeremiah 26:18–19; cf. 2 Chronicles 32:24–26; Jeremiah 25:1–11 with Daniel 9:1–2ff; Habakkuk 1:5–11 with 1:12–2:1; then 2:2–20 with 3:16–19; etc.

[1068] For a good article that explores this indicative/imperative tension more deeply, see C. F. D. Moule, "'The New Life' in Colossians 3:1–17," *Review and Expositor*, 70 (Fall 1973): 481–493.

[1069] Ladd, *TNT*, 492–493.

tive is not in the power of man himself, but is no less a matter of faith. Indicative and imperative are both the objects of faith, on the one hand in its receptivity, on the other in its activity. For this reason the connection between the two is so close and indissoluble. They represent two "sides" of the same matter, which cannot exist separate from each other.... By way of conclusion we may say that the imperative is grounded on the indicative to be accepted in faith once and for all and time and again anew.[1070]

## "Old Man"/ "New Man"

More often than not in the New Testament, occurrences of the indicative/imperative motif as based upon past salvation history contain references to the designations "old man" and/or "new man." Preliminarily, these two designations are biblical metaphors with more of a corporate/eschatological significance than an individual/anthropological significance. For example, as mentioned previously, Romans 6:1ff., a key text appealing to the *positional* demise of the "old man" (i.e. the indicative reality) as a basis for the new life of the new man (i.e. the imperative responsibility), is tied in tightly to the Adam theology of Romans 5:12ff.[1071] Nevertheless, a genuine believer does feel significant tension throughout the Christian life. However, this tension is not between two co-existing, personal entities within him.[1072] The terms "old man" and "new man" pertain essentially to an eschatological "already"/ "but not yet" tension, not to two individual anthropological ontologies at war with one another. Also preliminarily, the designations "old 'nature'" and "new 'nature'" are theological terms not found in the Bible. They were obviously coined and have been employed to try to characterize individual believers who, although on the pathway of sanctification, are yet experiencing the pangs of personal sin.[1073]

---

[1070] Ridderbos, *POT*, 254–257.

[1071] Cf., e.g., Ridderbos, *POT*, 62–64; Murray, *Principles of Conduct*, 211–221; etc.

[1072] The Scriptures do not make us out to be schizophrenics on the pathway of sanctification. For some exegetical-theological clarifications, see Roy A. Harrisville, "Is the Coexistence of the Old or New Man Biblical?" *Lutheran Quarterly*, 8 (1956): 20–32.

[1073] Since, at various times during the course of church history, the term "nature" has been applicationally substantized (i.e. practically viewed as a synonym for "person"), it would be more appropriate to choose a different word if one insists on speaking of this theological tension in a similar vein (cf., e.g., "capacity," "disposition," "propensity," etc.).

Now let me try to sharpen the focus a bit with some attempts at defining respectively "old man" and "new man" within their biblical settings. Cranfield boils down the "old man" simply to "the whole self in its fallenness."[1074] Haarbeck's synthesis of ὁ παλαιὸς ἄνθρωπος (*ho palaios anthropos*, "the old man") "is the autonomous man under sin."[1075] Showers argues that "the 'old man' is the human person viewed ethically in his unregenerate state as characterized by the position of slave to the sinful disposition and by the sinful way of life."[1076] More carefully yet, Meyer argues that "the *terminus ante quen* for παλαιός is the adoption of Christianity, so that, ...the whole expression ὁ παλαιὸς ἄνθρωπος, generically the collective *pre-Christian condition* in a moral respect, is presented as personified."[1077] Contrastingly, by corollary definition, "the new man" refers to "the collective new Christian ethical condition, conceived as personified and set forth objectively, so that it appears as becoming individually appropriated by the putting on."[1078] At the same time we must remember that

> the idea of newness is distinctly eschatological.... The Pauline statement that in Christ the old has passed away and the new has come is an eschatological statement.... The underlying idea is that while believers live in the old age, because they are in Christ they belong to the new age with its new creation (indicative) and they are to live a life that is expressive of the new existence (imperative).[1079]

It is as if, with the dawning of the soteriological reality of 2 Corinthians 5:17, we step into an eschatological-positional/ethical-practical time warp. Moule meanders through some of its tensions when he comments:

> The strange thing about the new life claimed by Christians is that they have it and have it not; they have yet to become what, as they claim, they already are. Not surprisingly, this causes tension within and criticism without.... The Christian claim, if taken seriously, means perplexity for the historian, disturbance for the ethicist, and pain for the believer. He has

---

[1074] *Romans*, 1:309.

[1075] *NIDNTT*, 2:675.

[1076] Renald Showers, "The New Nature" (*GTS*: Th. D. dissertation, 1975), 130.

[1077] H. A. W. Meyer, *Critical and Exegetical Handbook to the Epistles to the Philippians and Colossians, and to Philemon* [Winona Lake: Alpha, 1979], 353.

[1078] Ibid.

[1079] Ladd, *TNT*, 479–480; cf. also 481–483 for some good commentary.

been delivered from the dominion of darkness and transferred to the Kingdom of God's beloved Son (Col. 1:13); and yet, ... he remains vulnerable to what in Galatians, is called "the present evil age" (Gal. 1:4). So he is torn in two directions. The preacher tells him that what he could not do for himself has already been done for him by God; and that he has only to accept with gratitude the finished work of Christ. And yet, the same preacher is always exhorting him to do better, and telling him that his performance does not match up to his calling. In a nutshell, the Christian command is a perplexing one: "Become what you are!"... It is paradoxical. It is tension-causing.... If the growth-pains are never felt, it is doubtful whether the new life has begun.[1080]

This is not only a quite accurate theological synopsis of the exegetical tension, for example, between Colossians 3:9b in its own context of 3:1–4:6 but also between the positional reality of Colossians 3:9b (cf. the indicative affirmations of Romans 6:3ff.) and the ethical demands of Ephesians 4:22–24. We are to strip off the remnant dirty rags of the "old man" (e.g., Colossians 3:8–9a; Ephesians 4:22, 25, etc.) and get dressed up in the ethical clothes of the "new man" (e.g., Colossians 3:12ff.; Ephesians 4:23–24; etc.).

## The Centrality of the Mindset

### Concerning Initial Salvation: A Review

We need to remember that the key anthropological terms of both testaments, more often than not, function rationally and volitionally.[1081]

---

[1080] "'The New Life' in Colossians 3:1–17," 481–482.

[1081] Cf., e.g., לֵב (*lēb*) in Exodus 35:5, 22, 29; Numbers 24:13; Deuteronomy 8:5; Judges 5;15; 1 Kings 8:18, 2 Kings 12:5 [v. 4, Eng.]; 2 Chronicles 24:4; 29:10; Job 10:34; Proverbs 6:32; 7:7; 9:4, 16; 10:13, 21; 11:12; 12:11; 16:1; Isaiah 6:10; 10:7; 65:17; etc.; cf., e.g., רוּחַ (*rûaḥ*) in Proverbs 16:2, 18, 19, 32; Ezekiel 11:5; 20:32; etc.; cf., e.g., נֶפֶשׁ (*nepeš*) in Genesis 23:8; 2 Kings 9:15; Esther 4:13; etc.; cf., e.g., יֵצֶר (*yēṣer*) in Genesis 6:5; 8:21; Deuteronomy 31:21; Isaiah 26:3; etc. In certain New Testament settings these noetic nuances also pertain respectively to καρδία (*kardia*; cf., e.g. Matthew 9:4; Mark 2:6–8; Luke 1:51; 2:19; etc.), πνεῦμα (*pneuma*; cf., e.g., 1 Corinthians 2:11) and ψυχή (*psuchē*; cf., e.g., Acts 14:2; Ephesians 6:6; Philippians 1:27; 2 Peter 2:14; etc.). More consistently and definitively, the following New Testament word families are dedicated to thinking and planning: the νοῦς (*nous*) word group (cf., e.g., Mark 7:18; 13:14; John 12:40; Romans 1:28; Ephesians 2:3; 4:17; Colossians 1:21; 2:18; Hebrews 4:12; etc.), the φρεν (*phren*) word group (cf., e.g., Matthew 16:23; Ephesians 4:2; Philippians 2:2–3, 5; 3:15, 19; 4:2; 1 Peter 5:5; etc.), and the λεγ (*leg*) word group (cf., e.g., Matthew 5:19; Mark 2:6, 8; 7:21; Luke 5:22; 12:17; Romans 1:21; 1 Corinthians 3:20; etc).

Furthermore, a high percentage of these occurrences also are situated in hamartiologically significant settings. Man's spiritually terminal "heart trouble" is generally summarized in passages like Jeremiah 17:9 and Mark 7:20–23. Indeed humanity's noetic depravity (cf., e.g., Genesis 6:5; 8:21; Romans 1:28; Ephesians 4:17–19; Colossians 1:21; etc.) is observed to be a theological "given" throughout the Scriptures. This noetic depravity often manifests itself in an apostate mindset. The mind of man is pictured quite regularly as turning away, as departing from God and/or the things of God.[1082]

Since the natural man is sinful and selfish, the initiative for deliverance from his heart apostasy must come from God. The LORD is both the heart-knower (cf., e.g., 1 Kings 8:39; Psalm 44:22 [v. 21, Eng.]; Jeremiah 17:10; Acts 1:24; 15:8; etc.) and the heart-transplanter (cf., e.g., Jeremiah 24:7; Ezekiel 36:26; etc.). Therefore, it is He who grants 'change of mind,' i.e. "repentance" (cf. Acts 11:18). Yet, from the human side there is responsibility in reference to repentance. The Scriptures brim with admonitions "to return" (i.e. שׁוּב [šûb]) or "to repent" (cf., e.g., Deuteronomy 30:1–3; Joel 2:12–13; Matthew 3:2, 8; 4:17; Luke 24:47; Acts 2:28; 3:19; 8:22; 17:30; 26:20; etc.).

## Concerning Progressive Sanctification

An initial 180° reorientation of a man's mindset through repentance does not mean that he is once and for all cured of sinfully selfish preoccupations. For this reason, a continuing process of renewal must issue from a prerequisite repentance. In the arena of sanctification, we need to recognize that the Lord is the ultimate heart-incliner (cf., e.g., 1 Kings 8:57–58; Psalms 119:36; 141:4, etc.). Yet, once again, from the human side there is a corollary responsibility of heart-orientation. In the Old Testament, it is helpful in this regard to compare, for example, Joshua 24:23[1083]; 1 Chronicles 22:19[1084]; 2 Chronicles 19:3; Ezra 7:10[1085]; Psalm 119:112[1086];

---

[1082] In the Old Testament man's לֵב (lēb), "heart," is found in revealing combinations with a number of verbs connoting all kinds of spiritual departures and declensions (cf. הָלַךְ [hālak], e.g., Ezekiel 20:16; רָחַק [rāḥaq], e.g., Isaiah 29:13; שִׂים [śîm] with a negative, e.g., Exodus 9:21; שִׁית [šît], e.g., Psalm 62:11 [v. 10, Eng.]; סוּר [sûr], e.g. Jeremiah 5:23; פָּנָה [pānâ], e.g. Deuteronomy 30:15–18; נָטָה [nāṭâ], e.g., 1 Kings 11:2, 4, 9; כּוּן [kûn] with a negative, e.g., 2 Chronicles 12:14). In the New Testament this spiritual apostasy is generally labeled "the mindset of the flesh," i.e. an anthropocentric mindset unsubmissive to God (cf., e.g., Romans 8:5a, 6a, 7; see a manifestation of it in Matthew 16:23).

[1083] I.e. לֵב (lēb) with the verb נָטָה (nāṭâ).

[1084] I.e. לֵב (lēb) with the verb נָתַן (nātan).

[1085] Both texts employ לֵב (lēb) with the verb כּוּן (kûn).

[1086] I.e. לֵב (lēb) with the verb נָטָה (nāṭâ); cf.; Joshua 24:23.

Daniel 1:8[1087]; Daniel 10:11–12[1088]; etc. When we get to the New Testament, this priority of noetic renewal (cf., e.g., Romans 12:2; Ephesians 4:23) involves both a prerequisite for it and the practice of it. Its prerequisite of "lowliness of mind" (AV) is boldly highlighted by the occurrence of ταπεινοφροσυνή (*tapeinophrosunē*) in Philippians 2:3.[1089]

The practice of aiming the mind as a key to godly living[1090] in the personal realm is developed in such passages as Colossians 3:2 in its immediate context and Romans 8:5–13 in its mega setting of chapters 6–8. The former passage simply reads: "Set your minds on the things above,[1091] not on the things upon the earth" (Colossians 3:2). This command calls for a theocentric focus of our minds as a basis for the exhortations to holy living which follow (cf. Colossians 3:5ff.).

Romans 8:5–13 is a theologically complicated passage which uses a variety of motifs to develop its main message of living dependently upon God, not independently by relying upon self. Within this section the indicative/imperative phenomenon returns; we are *to be* (cf., e.g., v. 12) who we *are* in Christ via reliance upon the Spirit (cf., e.g., vv. 9a, 11a). It is, therefore, important to pay careful attention to the statements about *being* "in" or "according to" the flesh (cf., e.g., vv. 5a, 5b, 8, 9) and those which speak of *walking* or *living* "according to" the flesh or the Spirit (cf., e.g., v. 4b, 12–13). A consistent life-style of operating according to the flesh experientially denies that someone is "in the Spirit." Furthermore, these radically different operations of people are driven by opposite mindsets, i.e. by a mindset on the Spirit, an orientation towards dependence, versus a mindset on the flesh, an orientation indicating a rebellious independence. Listen to how all of this flows back and forth as Paul develops his ethical exhortation:

> For the ones who are according to the flesh (κατὰ σάρκα [*kata sarka*])[1092] set their minds (φρονοῦσιν [*phronousin*]) on the things of the flesh;[1093] however, the ones who *are* according to the Spirit[1094] *set their minds* on the things of the

---

[1087] I.e. לֵב (*lēb*) with the verb שִׂים (*śit*).

[1088] I.e. לֵב (*lēb*) with the verb נָתַן (*nātan*); cf. 1 Chronicles 22:19.

[1089] Note the highly informative context which begins back in 1:27 and then proceeds to use our Lord in His incarnation as the ultimate example of such humility.

[1090] For a fuller treatment of the centrality of the mind and sanctification, see my article in *GTJ*, 5:2 (Fall 1984): 205–227.

[1091] Informed by the immediately preceding context as being "where Christ is, seated at the right hand of God" (Colossians 3:1b, NASB).

[1092] I.e. their whole being is characterized by a sinfully selfish independence from God.

[1093] I.e. they are habitually intent on sinfully selfish things.

[1094] I.e. these are contrastingly characterized by a dependence upon the Spirit of God.

Spirit.[1095] For the mindset of the flesh (τὸ φρόνημα τῆς σαρκὸς [*to phronēma tēs sarkos*])[1096] is death; however, the mindset of the Spirit (τὸ φρόνημα τοῦ πνεύματος [*to phronēma tou pneumatos*])[1097] is life and peace, since the mindset of the flesh (τὸ φρόνημα τῆς σαρκὸς [*to phronēma tēs sarkos*]) is enmity toward God, for it does not submit itself to the law of God, for it does not have the ability to do so[1098]; now the ones who are in the flesh are not able to please God. However, you are not in the flesh but in the Spirit, if indeed the Spirit of God is dwelling among you.[1099] (Now if someone does not have the Spirit of Christ this (person) is not His.) However, if Christ is among you, on the one hand the body is dead on account of sin, but on the other hand the spirit is life on account of justification. Now if the Spirit who raised up Jesus from the dead dwells among you, the one who raised up Christ from the dead shall also give life to your mortal bodies through His Spirit which dwells among you. So then, brothers, we are debtors not to the flesh to live according to the flesh, for if you are living according to the flesh,[1100] you are going to die, however, if, by the Spirit, you are putting to death the practices of the body, you will live (Romans 8:5–13).

There is also a corporate realm of application concerning the priority of the mindset in the sanctification process. Occurrences of the νουθετέω (*noutheteō*) word family convey this obligation to the church. Spicq has nicely outlined the basic meanings and the applications of νουθετέω (*noutheteō*) as follows:

A compound of *nous* and *tithēmi*, the verb *noutheteō* basically means "put something in someone's mind," hence "instruct, lecture," sometimes by way of refreshing the memory, sometimes by way of making observations or giving warnings.... St. Paul...never ceased warning or reprimanding with tears each

---

[1095] Cf., the focused intent upon "the things above" in Colossians 3:2.
[1096] I.e. the flesh's selfish way of thinking.
[1097] I.e. a submissive and dependent way of thinking as influenced by the Spirit of God.
[1098] Simply phrased οὐδέ δύναται (*oude dunatai*).
[1099] Or, metaphorically/corporately depicted "in you" (cf. vv. 9b, 11a, 11b).
[1100] I.e. consistently living as characterized by the autonomous self.

Ephesian[1101] or Corinthian Christian: "I write these things not to shame you, but as to beloved and respected children, to set your minds aright.... You do not have many fathers."[1102] All apostolic pastoral care can be summed up in these warnings-admonitions: "Warning every person and instructing every person in all wisdom, in order to make every person perfect in Christ."[1103] In brotherly life, after all, reciprocal warnings waken the conscience of the delinquent and lead back to the right path those who have gone astray.... The exact nuance varies from case to case: "Teach each other in all wisdom, admonishing one another" (*didaskontes kai nouthetountes heautous*, Col. 3:16); "Rebuke those who are disorderly" (1 Thess. 5:14); ... Brotherly correction presupposes that Christians are spiritual adults and are, like the Roman Christians, "able to warn each other" (Rom. 15:14).[1104]

This is how biblical counseling is to operate in Christ's churches. It reinforces right patterns of thinking and scripturally exposes wrong patterns. When the mind is biblically back on track, then the observable evidences of a moral lifestyle should follow.

## Law/Liberty[1105]

The perennial tension of law and gospel, or more applicationally and polemically expressed, law and/or liberty, has been cutting across theological "party" lines throughout the course of Church history. It is not always easy to predict who will come down more on the side of continuity over discontinuity or vice versa. Furthermore, if we start at the poles and proceed along a continuum in between them, various degrees of this theological tension exist.[1106] However, during the past twenty to twenty-five years, fruitful discussions on the crucial issues pertaining to this

---

[1101] See Acts 20:31.

[1102] See 1 Corinthians 4:14.

[1103] See Colossians 1:28.

[1104] *TLNT*, 2:548, 550–551.

[1105] This section is not intended to address the issue of restrictions and liberties in application to relationships within the Body of Christ. For an excellent synopsis of that important topic, see Steele and Thomas' excursus on Romans 14:1–15:13, "Note 12: Christian Liberty" (*Romans* 112–118).

[1106] On the contemporary scene, theonomists would very closely hug the continuity pole while some Lutherans, many "easy believists" (cf., the discussion above on "True Discipleship"), and stringently dispensational antinomians would station themselves next to the discontinuity pole.

tension have taken and are taking place.[1107] We must keep on pursuing biblical balance in this strategic area that is so vitally related to sanctification. As we do this, it would be wise to follow the channel markers of Murray: "We must guard grace from the adulterations of legalism and we must guard law from the depredations of antinomianism."[1108]

Theological inductivity is hard to come by not only because of the preunderstandings of Christian interpreters of the Law but also because of some tensions that arise from the exegetical data *per se*. For example,

> Paul's thought about the Law is difficult to understand because he seems to make numerous contradictory statements.[1109] He asserts that those who do the Law shall be justified (Rom. 2:13) and shall find life by the Law (Rom. 1:5; Gal. 3:12); but at the same time he affirms that no man shall be justified by the Law (Rom. 3:20) but is only brought to death by the written code of the Law (II Cor. 3:6), for the Law cannot give life (Gal. 3:21). He claims that he was blameless in his obedience to the Law (Phil. 3:6) and yet asserts that no man can perfectly submit to the Law (Rom. 8:7).[1110]

A first step in easing such biblical tensions is to understand that "law," be it תּוֹרָה (*tôrâ*) in the Old Testament or νόμος (*nomos*) in the New Testament, exhibits a wide variety of usages in Scripture. For example, it is wrong to restrict תּוֹרָה (*tôrâ*) blanketly to the commandments of the Decalog, or to Judaism's so-called 613 apodictic and casuistic regulations, or even to the Jewish canonical designation of the whole Pentateuch. In various settings, תּוֹרָה (*tôrâ*) may exhibit such primary usages as "direction, instruction, law." [1111] As Harley asserts, coming from the Hebrew root ירה (*yrh*), "the word *tôrâ* means basically 'teaching.'"[1112] More fully, Girdlestone argues:

---

[1107] For example, ever since the 1981 meeting of the Evangelical Theological Society in Toronto, the major issues of continuity and discontinuity have been conspicuously laid out on the table for discussion. This, in turn, has spawned the "Dispensational Study Group" which has become an open forum for the discussion of many important continuity-discontinuity issues, and even beyond this group, a new study group has arisen dedicated specifically to the relationship of the Christian to the Law of God.

[1108] *Principles of Conduct*, 182; cf. also, e.g. William Hendriksen, *New Testament Commentary: Exposition of the Gospel according to Mark* (Grand Rapids: Baker, 1975), 394–395.

[1109] I.e. *seemingly* "contradictory statements."

[1110] Ladd, *TNT*, 495.

[1111] BDB, 435.

[1112] *TWOT*, 1:404.

The verb (ירה) whence it[1113] is derived signifies...to point out or teach. The law of God is that which points out or indicates His will to man. It is not an arbitrary rule, still less is it a subjective impulse; it is rather to be regarded as a course of guidance from above. The verb and the noun are found together in Exod. 24:12, "I will give thee a law, and commandments which I have written, that thou mayest teach them." It is generally, though imperfectly, represented in the LXX by the word νόμος.[1114]

The semantical choice of νόμος (*nomos*) to render the occurrences of תּוֹרָה (*tôrâ*) throughout the Old Testament has often led to legalistic misconceptions. And this fact, in turn, has led to antinomian responses to many of the appearances of νόμος (*nomos*) in the New Testament.[1115] However, some of those reactionary responses to "law" as LAW are partially defused when it is recognized that in some settings תּוֹרָה/νόμος (*tôrâ/nomos*) indicates "the entire Old Testament canon."[1116] For example, the Book of Deuteronomy often broadens the meaning of תּוֹרָה (*tôrâ*), making it "a comprehensive designation for the entire body of legislation deriving from Yahweh and given through Moses."[1117] Beyond Deuteronomy occasions of the broader usage of תּוֹרָה/νόμος (*tôrâ/nomos*) are observed in reference to other books of the Old Testament. Allen sketches out this phenomenon as follows: "'Torah' seems to embrace not only the Pentateuch but also at least Isaiah and Jeremiah and Proverbs as canonical Scriptures in which God has made known his character and purpose for his people. It is hailed as Yahweh's communication of moral truth and demonstration of his grace and guidance."[1118] Such Old Testament conceptions hardly picture the law as God's "Sword of Damocles."

---

[1113] I.e. תּוֹרָה (*tôrâ*).

[1114] *Synonyms*, 206.

[1115] For an adequate discussion of this problem along with some hermeneutical resolutions, see C. H. Dodd, *The Bible and the Greeks* (London: Hodder and Stoughton, 1935), 25–40.

[1116] Cf., e.g., Liedke and Petersen on this semantical expansion (*TLOT*, 3:1422).

[1117] William Michael Soll, "Psalm 119: The Hermeneutic of an Acrostic Lament," unpublished Ph.D. dissertation (Nashville: Vanderbilt, 1982), 69–71.

[1118] Leslie C. Allen, *Psalms 101–150*, WBC (Waco: Word, 1983), 141–142. No wonder "the 'law' which the poet describes in Psalm 119 is not a yoke which 'neither our fathers nor we have been able to bear' (Ac. 15:10). To the Psalmist the *torāh* is a gift of God, which was both preceded and followed by divine grace" (A. A. Anderson, *Psalms 73–150*, NCBC [Grand Rapids: Eerdmans, 1981], 2:808).

So תּוֹרָה (*tôrâ*) sometimes refers to "Scripture as a whole."[1119] But what about νόμος (*nomos*) in the New Testament? Yes, sometimes it also reaches beyond "law" as LAW and signifies a scripture or the Scriptures in their totality.[1120] Indeed, it would not have been impossible for Paul to substitute νόμος (*nomos*) in *its broadest sense* for γραφή (*graphē*) in 2 Timothy 3:16–17.[1121]

Another, more significant understanding that helps to ease the most difficult occurrences of "law" in the New Testament is what I call the polemical usage of νόμος (*nomos*). The settings of these challenging appearances of νόμος (*nomos*) reveal that the law *per se* is not being denigrated; what is severely attacked are all misunderstandings and misuses of it.

Take for example, what Jesus says in Matthew 5:21ff. Each case scenario[1122] goes something like this: "You have heard that it was said" (Matthew 5:21a),[1123] followed by a short quote from the Pentateuch, then followed by an authoritative supplement by Messiah Himself (i.e. "But I am saying to you…"). Jesus herein is setting the law into its attitudinal and ethical context, the context wherein God has always intended it to operate. In so doing, our Lord was indirectly but strongly rebuking the religious leaders of His day. They specialized in externalism, even adding their own man-made ordinances to God's good revelation. Matthew 5:20, addressed primarily to the crowd of common people, is so crucial for a proper understanding of the polemical atmosphere of what is going on in 5:21ff.; it shockingly reads: "For I tell you that unless your righteousness surpasses that of the Pharisees and the teachers of the law, you will certainly not enter the kingdom of heaven" (Matthew 5:20, NIV). They needed to understand what true spirituality is. A right heart is the source of right habits, and right habits are revealed and evaluated by the instructions and directions of God as couched in their largest circles of biblical context. No humanistic perversions or additions are allowed.

---

[1119] Derek Kidner, *Psalms 73–150* (Downers Grove: IVP, 1980), 418.

[1120] Cf., e.g., the reference to Psalm 82:6 in John 10:34, also noting the parallels with "word" and "Scripture" in John 10:35; the quote of Psalm 35:19 in John 15:25; quotes from the Psalms and Isaiah in Romans 3:10b–18 which are referred to as "law" in Romans 3:19; a quote of Isaiah 28:11 cited as νόμος (*nomos*), "law," in 1 Corinthians 14:21; etc.

[1121] The sense would be "all *divine instruction* is God-breathed and profitable...." No matter if one does not substitute νόμος (*nomos*) for γραφή (*graphē*), the πᾶσα γραφή (*pasa graphē*) of 2 Timothy 3:16 refuses to leave out any portion of the Old Testament in reference to both its inspiration *and* its valuable guidance as applied to a "man of God" in the New Testament era.

[1122] Cf. vv. 27ff., 33ff., 38ff., and 43ff.

[1123] Note that this is not one of the normal introductory formulas that was used when quoting a portion of Scripture directly.

In order to preempt any potential misunderstandings that He was about to junk or to degrade the law *per se* in vv. 21ff., the Lord Jesus authoritatively affirmed its continuing role in vv. 17–19:

> Do not assume[1124] that I have come to do away with (καταλῦσαι [*katalusai*])[1125] the law (τὸν νόμον [*ton nomon*]) or the prophets[1126]; I did not come to do away with but to fulfill (πληρῶσαι [*plērōsai*]). For truly I am telling you, until heaven and the earth come to an end, in no way shall one *iota*[1127] or one projection *of a letter*[1128] be done away with, until all things come to pass. Consequently, whoever should break one of these commandments, *even* the least of them, and should teach men so, he will be called least in the kingdom of heaven; however, whoever practices and teaches *them*, this person shall be called great in the kingdom of heaven (Matthew 5:17–19).

Our Lord, quite obviously, was anything but an antinomian. Therefore, in the verses which follow (i.e. vv. 21ff.) "Jesus makes it clear…that his claim was not leveled against the law…, but against man's self-righteous attitude to the law…."[1129]

Paul's seeming depreciation of the law is also directed against anthropocentric misuses (i.e. abuses) of the law (cf., e.g., Romans 2:17–3:8; 9:31–32; Galatians 2:21; 3:2–3; 5:4; Philippians 3:9; etc.). Paul in such passages is arguing against works-justification and/or works-sanctification. He understood that the problem with the law is not inherent and objective but hamartiological and subjective (i.e. in man). In this important area Romans 8:1–4 provides some great insight:

> There is therefore now no condemnation for those who are in Christ Jesus. For the law of the Spirit of life in Christ Jesus has

---

[1124] Cf., e.g., νομίζω (*nomizō*) and its other semantical relatives in Louw and Nida, *GELSD*, 1:369. Besides being an appropriate semantical choice of words herein, Jesus may have also used νομίζω (*nomizō*) paronomastically in anticipation of νόμος (*nomos*).

[1125] To "destroy, demolish, tear down, abolish, annul, make invalid" are some of the meanings of this verb (BAG, 415). Jesus did not come to give the law its "pink slip" sending it to the "unemployment line."

[1126] Sometimes Jesus used this twofold combination to designate the whole Old Testament canon, and sometimes He used a threefold combination with the same intent (cf., e.g., Luke 24:44).

[1127] Cf. the tiny Hebrew letter ׳ (*y*).

[1128] I.e. a tiny "projection" found on several of the Hebrew consonants. Jesus is obviously using hyperbole to make His point about no part or parcel of the Old Testament Scriptures ever being junked during the full course of earth and human history as we know it.

[1129] Esser, *NIDNTT*, 2:443. For some good commentary on this point, see Guthrie, *NTT*, 675–680.

set you[1130] free from the law[1131] of sin and death. For what the Law[1132] could not do, weak as it was through the flesh,[1133] *God did*: sending His own Son in the likeness of sinful flesh[1134] and *as an offering* for sin, He condemned sin in the flesh, in order that the requirement of the Law might be fulfilled in us, who do not walk according to the flesh, but according to the Spirit (Romans 8:1–4, NASB).

Also, like his Lord, Paul anticipated Jewish opposition to what he was saying, so he too attempted to preempt their accusation that he was an antinomian. Therefore, he inserted important clarifications at strategic places throughout his heavy duty polemic against legalism (cf., e.g., Romans 3:31 and 7:7–14).

Since there is so much in the Pauline corpus about this vital issue, it may be best to select one good example as a key text where the law-versus-liberty battle lines have traditionally been drawn, Romans 10:4.

At the beginning of his monograph on Romans 10:4, Badenas has aptly observed that "there are few Pauline statements more used and abused than this one.... This passage is far more eagerly used than explained."[1135] Antinomians of all stripes have excised out of its immediate and larger circles of context the shorter statement "Christ is the end of the law," making it their banner in warfare. Granted, the interpretive factors relating to Romans 10:4 can get quite complicated,[1136] but exegetically credible rebuttals to the radically discontiguous view are not in short supply. First, the antinomian's motto for marching conveniently leaves out the crucial prepositional phrase which modifies it, namely, εἰς

---

[1130] Some textual evidences reads "me"; other pieces of evidence support the reading "us."

[1131] Note that interpretively but correctly the NASB renders both of the occurrences of νόμος (*nomos*) in v. 2 as "law" using the lower case to indicate spiritual realities or principles.

[1132] The "Law" in upper case as Old Testament Law *per se*.

[1133] Here is the key qualifier that identifies the problem with the Law which in reality is our problem. It is a problem of the "flesh," i.e. not a physical problem but one seated in our prideful independence and self-efforts (see the discussion of בָּשָׂר/σάρξ [*bāśār/sarx*] in chapters 2 and 3).

[1134] Vincent well says, "Not *in the flesh of sin*, which would have represented Him as partaking of sin. Not *in the likeness of flesh*, since He was really and entirely human; but *in the likeness of the flesh of sin*" (Marvin R. Vincent, *Word Studies in the NT* [NY: Scribner's Sons, 1908], 3:85). Ridderbos correctly concludes about this phrase, "' Flesh' and 'sinful flesh' need not coincide. But sin in the nature of the case takes place in the flesh and stamps the human mode of existence as 'the sinful flesh.' It is in 'the likeness' of this that God sent his Son, a phrase with which Paul elsewhere expresses the difference between correspondence and identity (cf: Rom. 6:5). Christ came, therefore, in the weak transitory human state, without sharing in the sin of the human race" (*POT,* 65).

[1135] Robert Badenas, *Christ the End of the Law: Romans 10:4 in Pauline Perspective* (Sheffield: JSOT, 1985), 1, 5.

[1136] Cf. ibid., *passim*.

δικαιοσύνην (*eis dikaiosunēn*), "unto righteousness." From the polemical angle of Paul's argument, he once again states that Christ and His
Crosswork constitute the ultimate and final death-blow to a legalistic
conception of salvation.[1137] In reference to this important point, Guthrie
hits the bull's-eye of the hermeneutical target when he says,

> The key is found in the words *eis dikaiosunēn*...which literally
> mean "unto righteousness."... In the passage in which the
> statement comes, it is not the function and status of law which
> is under discussion, but the Israelites' attempts to seek a righ-
> teousness of their own.[1138]

But the word τέλος (*telos*) in Romans 10:4 may connote, besides
"end, termination, cessation, abrogation," etc., "purpose, aim, object,
goal, fulfillment, climax, plenitude," etc.[1139] In view of Paul's parallel
lines of argumentation throughout Romans, it is quite feasible that the
apostle not only used τέλος (*telos*) polemically in the sense of "end"
against the legalists but also pedagogically in keeping with the main topic
of this epistle, the Gospel of God's sovereign grace. Consequently, one of
the positive points he is making with Romans 10:4 would be that "Christ
brings to the believer the righteousness promised in Scripture."[1140]

Before leaving Romans 10:4, it is enlightening to note the significance of the verses which immediately follow it. Paul documents "the
righteousness based on faith" by quoting from Deuteronomy.[1141] This
would hardly be the tactic of an antinomian!

A word needs to be said about the primary purpose of the Law. Its
primary, although not exclusive, purpose has always been to expose the
sinfulness of sin. In so doing, it becomes a condemning instrument of
God especially concerning all prideful attempts to attain self-righteous-
ness and/or self-sanctification. Paul conveys the law's primary purpose
both through clear teaching (cf., e.g., Romans 3:20; 5:13–14, 20;
Galatians 3:19, 21–22, 24) and by personal testimony (cf., e.g., Romans

---

[1137] I.e. the Person and work of Christ supremely demonstrate the futility of having as one's goal the attainment of a righteous standing before God through law-keeping.

[1138] *NTT*, 694.

[1139] Cf. Badenas, *Romans 10:4*, 35–37.

[1140] Ibid., 148.

[1141] Cf. Payne, *Theology of the Older Testament*, 320–321; Walter C. Kaiser, Jr., *The Uses of the Old Testament in the New* (Chicago; Moody Press, 1985), 197–201; 233–235; etc. Kaiser, citing over 20 sample scenarios of New Testament references to the Old Testament, correctly concludes: "There are some clear cases where what most allege as being the distinctly high ethic of the New Testament actually is nothing more than a direct citation of the Old Testament" (ibid., 200).

7:7ff.; Galatians 2:19; Philippians 3:9 in its context; etc.). So the Law functions predominately as a "death notice."[1142]

Nevertheless, this primary purpose does not negate the Law's most basic secondary purpose, even in application to New Testament believers. We have already observed that תּוֹרָה/νόμος (*tôrâ/nomos*) often signifies the totality of divine revelation as a guide for life. And, furthermore, even when "law" is used in its more restricted sense as LAW, it remains a vital part of πᾶσα γραφή (*pasa graphē*), not only being "God breathed" but also "profitable." This reality however raises an important hermeneutical issue. Are Christians to apply every part of the LAW in a regulative way to their lives (as most theonomists would argue)? Or, should the Law be logically subdivided, e.g., into the traditional categories of moral, civil, and ceremonial? Although objections have been raised from various quarters that the Old Testament never subdivides the Law into such categories, there are legitimate reasons for doing so. The New Testament does provide some important hints as to why the Law, especially as it reveals the moral character of God, should be applied to New Testament disciples. This continuity pertains to "the more important matters of the law" (Matthew 23:23, NIV). However, ceremonial and governmental continuities are prohibited or, at the very least, sharply challenged (cf., e.g., 1 Corinthians 7:19; Colossians 2:16; The Epistle to the Hebrews, *passim*).

Where does all this leave us? With some discontinuities but with one very significant factor of continuity. Consider some of the following attempts at expressing the balance of the biblical data as it pertains to Law and Gospel and/or law and liberty:

> The law and promise aspects of God's covenant relationships with his people do not violate each other.[1143]

---

[1142] Even in the Old Testament, when periodically the theocratic community was exhorted to obey the Law and live (cf., e.g., Deuteronomy 30:11ff.), the contexts of such challenges show that these urgings were not intended to solicit from the people a self-attained, salvific justification. Barker appropriately reminds us "that the Law was given to the redeemed people of God as a means of expressing their love to God as well as a means of governing their relationship to God and to each other. It was not a way of salvation but a way to enjoy an orderly life and God's fullest blessing within the covenantal theocratic arrangement" (Ken Barker, "False Dichotomies Between the Testaments," *JETS* 25:1 [March 1982], 7). Furthermore, God's laws and commandments are frequently interspersed with His gracious provisions for dealing with His people's attitudes and acts of disobedience (consider, e.g., the whole sacrificial system; on the bigger picture of the inevitability of sin and repentant cries before the LORD, cf. Solomon's prayer in 1 Kings 8:31ff., especially vv. 46ff.).

[1143] Smick, *TWOT*, 1:129.

Law and grace are not opposing concepts. Faith and legalism are.[1144]

The New Testament uses the Old Testament Law for exhortation and for application of eternal truths and principles, particularly in the area of morality and ethics.[1145]

The quest for a *sine qua non*, a fundamental principle or an epitome of the law, was illustrated in two or three situations in the life of our Lord: Mark 12:28–34; Matt. 22:34–40; and Matt. 23:23–24.... Jesus respond[ed] to the lawyer's question by linking Deut. 6:4–5 with Lev. 19:18: love for God was first, and this was to be followed by love for one's neighbors.... The lawyer recognized the truthfulness of the answer just given to him by Jesus. But the most remarkable thing was that this lawyer went on to link Deut. 6:4 and Lev. 19:18 with 1 Sam. 15:22; Hosea 6:6; and Micah 6:6–8: loving God and one's neighbor was "much more than all the whole burnt offerings and sacrifices" (Mark 12:33). And did Jesus rebuke this attack on the unified character of the law? Quite the reverse, he commended the man for his wisdom and said, "You are not far from the Kingdom of God," i.e. from being converted.... The case for a single, monolithic law of God, which refuses to recognize Jesus' ranking of the "weightier" and "the least" within that law, must now be totally re-evaluated. Further, the claim that the law of the Lord, in all its parts, has now been ended *en toto* due to Christ's perfect fulfillment of that one (i.e. ceremonial) law and due to Paul's allegedly unequivocal statement that even the Ten Commandments have been abrogated (2 Cor. 3) (?), must now itself be abandoned in light of Paul's teaching in that very passage and elsewhere.[1146]

Wherever reading of the law is preceded by true conversion, and proper priorities are observed in one's own life, there is no more bondage to the "letter," but great liberty in the

---

[1144] Thomas McComiskey, *The Covenants of Promise* (Grand Rapids: Baker, 1985), 223; cf. also 78, 80, 94–137.

[1145] Barker, "False Dichotomies," 10.

[1146] Walter C. Kaiser, Jr., "The Weightier and Lighter Matters of the Law: Moses, Jesus, and Paul," *Current Issues in Biblical and Patristic Interpretation*, ed. by Hawthorne (Grand Rapids: Eerdmans, 1975), 183–184, 191; for his exegetical insights regarding 2 Corinthians 3:1–17, cf. 185–192.

"word" of the Lord (2 Cor. 3:17), even the perfect law of liberty (Jas. 1:25; 2:12).[1147]

Consequently, "Biblical law and the gospel of God's grace are not archrivals but twin mercies given by the same gracious Lord who did not wish his people in any age to be impoverished but to enjoy life to the fullest."[1148]

## Eternal Security/Assurance

Eternal security and assurance, although related, are not identical. Eternal security is absolutely objective since its reality is grounded in God. However, assurance involves *a* subjective evaluation on our part. So, from the divine perspective the issue is black and white—*genuine* believers are eternally secure; and yet, from the human perspective the issue may be somewhat gray—assurance has *a* subjective dimension in reference to personal human evaluation along the pathway of life. A good caption verse that respectively illustrates both dimensions of this biblical tension is 2 Timothy 2:19: "Nevertheless, God's solid foundation stands firm, sealed with this inscription: 'The Lord knows those who are his,' and, 'Everyone who confesses the name of the Lord must turn away from wickedness.'" (2 Timothy 2:19, NIV).

Consequently, God's word to us in some places carries the comfort of passages such as John 10:27–29:

> My sheep hear my voice, and I know them, and they follow Me; and I give eternal life to them, and they shall never perish;[1149] and no one shall snatch them out of My hand. My Father, who has given them to Me, is greater than all; and no one is able to snatch them out of the Father's hand (John 10:27–29, NASB).

However, that same Word of God in other places more soberly brings challenges similar to the one found in 2 Corinthians 13:5: "Put

---

[1147] Ibid., 192.

[1148] Walter C. Kaiser, Jr., "God's Promise Plan and His Gracious Law," *JETS* (Sept. 1990):302.

[1149] The Greek is exceedingly strong: οὐ μὴ ἀπόλωνται εἰς τὸν αἰῶνα (*ou mē apolōntai eis ton aiōna*).

yourselves to the test (Ἐαυτοὺς πειράζετε [*heautous peirazete*][1150]) *to see* if you are in the faith; examine yourselves (ἐαυτοὺς δοκιμάζετε [*heautous dokimazete*][1151]). Or, do you not realize this *about* yourselves that Jesus Christ is among you,[1152] unless perhaps you are unapproved (εἰ μήτι ἀδόκιμοί ἐστε [*ei mēti adokimoi este*][1153])." It will not do, at least not in God's eyes, to choose one set of passages at the expense of the other in order to uphold the polarized position with which one feels most comfortable. So, we find ourselves in the midst of yet another area that calls us to be as biblically balanced as possible. Therefore, in order to sharpen our theological focus on security/assurance it will be necessary to avoid the polar extremes: 1) We must not overemphasize the warnings or contingencies passages[1154] to the neglect of the didactic passages dealing with security;[1155] and 2) We must never ignore or manipulate the warnings or contingencies passages in the light of the many clear passages on the security of the believer. To be biblical in our theology, we need to live in the constructive tension between both sets of complementary data.

There are several things which must be remembered in this quest for balance. First and probably foremost as already intimated, the passages on eternal security constitute *an* important basis for assurance; however, arrogance and presumption are uncharacteristic of persevering saints. Erickson puts it this way:

> The practical implication of our understanding of the doctrine of perseverance is that believers can rest secure in the assurance that their salvation is permanent; nothing can separate them from the love of God.... On the other hand, however, our understanding of the doctrine of perseverance allows no room for indolence or laxity.[1156]

Secondly, attitudinal and behavioral norms like those found, for example, in 1 John place before us some concrete scenarios as biblical yard-

---

[1150] Note the present tense imperative: "Keep on examining yourselves!"

[1151] Another present tense imperative: "Keep on testing yourselves!"

[1152] Or, picking up the many-members-*one Body* metaphor, "in you."

[1153] I.e. "'unless, when tested, you flunk.'"

[1154] Such as, e.g., 1 Corinthians 11:32; 15:2; Colossians 1:22–23; 1 Timothy 1:19–20; 4:1; 2 Timothy 2:11–12, 16–18; 4:10; Hebrews 6:4–6; 10:26–27; 2 Peter 1:10; 2:1–2; etc.

[1155] Such as e.g., John 5:24; 6:35–40; 17:11–12, 15; Romans 5:8–10; 8:1, 29–30, 35–39; 1 Corinthians 1:7–9; 10:13; Ephesians 1:5, 13–14; 4:30; Philippians 1:6; Colossians 3:3–4; 1 Thessalonians 5:23–24; 2 Timothy 4:18; Hebrews 9:12, 15; 10:14; 1 Peter 1:3–5; 1 John 5:4, 11–13 [in the context, however, of 1 John], 20; Jude 1, 24–25; etc.

[1156] Erickson, *Christian Theology*, 996.

sticks to help us in the subjective evaluation of our lives (i.e., in order to see if our "walk" is matching our "talk"). Thirdly, the Spirit of God uses His Word through the warnings passages applicationally to accomplish different things in reference to different hearers within common audiences.[1157] This important recognition calls for further explanation.

It is exceedingly important to note that the epistles containing these warnings passages were written to bodies of *professing* Christians. Permit me to excerpt some very significant observations from a paper written years ago by Caneday:

> The writers of the New Testament wrote their books to people—ones who had attached themselves to the church by a profession of faith. They were not so naive as to presume that all who would come into contact with their letters were regenerate individuals. However, they did not question or disparage the professed faith of their readers. The apostles addressed the church according to its profession and in this manner included tests, exhortations, and admonitions to depend solely upon grace, and warnings against apostasy by which the readers could measure their own profession and ascertain their status.... Exhortations in Scripture have at least a threefold purpose: 1.) to reveal the spurious professor of faith, 2.) to cause the believer to strive for holiness of life, and 3.) to drive the believer to his only source of enablement—the preserving grace of God.[1158]

Compare the words of A. A. Hodge, especially in reference to a primary function of the warnings passages in the Word:

> That he [i.e. God] does secure the final perseverance of his people in a manner perfectly consistent with their free agency is...clear. He changes their affections and thus determines the will by its own free spontaneity. He brings them into the

---

[1157] I have often told my students that when the Holy Spirit goes "hunting" applicationally, He does not use His Word like a 22 caliber plinking rifle but like a sawed-off shotgun. Often many applicational targets are represented in a given audience, and He is capable of hitting every one of them "dead-on."

[1158] Ardel B. Caneday, "Reciprocal Vital Union and Perseverance of the Saints in Johannine Literature," unpublished post-graduate seminar paper (Grace Theological Seminary, March 17, 1977), 1–2, 24. Cf. Berkouwer who really did not jump the reformed theological "ship" when he said, "Final perseverance is set before believers as a goal coupled with a warning" (G. C. Berkouwer, *Faith and Perseverance* [Grand Rapids: Eerdmans, 1958], 84).

position of children by adoption, surrounding them with all of the sources and instruments of sanctifying influence, and when they sin he carefully chastises and restores them.... The outward word necessarily comes to all men alike, addressing them in the class in which they regard themselves as standing; and as professors, or "those who think they stand," are many of them self-deceived, this outward word truly implies the uncertainty of their position (as far as man's knowledge goes), and their liability to fall.... God secures the perseverance in holiness of all his true people by the use of means adapted to their nature as rational, moral, free agents. Viewed in themselves they are always, as God warns them, unstable, and therefore, as he exhorts them, they must diligently cleave to his grace. It is always true, also that if they apostatize they shall be lost; but by means of these very threatenings his Spirit graciously secures them from apostasy.[1159]

Such biblically balanced syntheses provide a key for understanding, for example, the major burden of the Epistle to the Hebrews. Consider its opening, launching-pad warning:

We must pay more careful attention, therefore, to what we have heard, so that we do not drift away. For if, the message spoken by angels was binding, and every violation and disobedience received its just punishment, how shall we escape if we ignore such a great salvation? This salvation, which was first announced by the Lord, was confirmed to us by those who heard him (Hebrews 2:1–3, NIV).

Indeed, eternal security and assurance constitute but one facet on God's grand soteriological gem, a gem for which we are privileged to offer our perpetual praises to the Lord, since, as Westcott has noted, "It can be said of the believer, σώζεται [sōzetai; 'he is being saved'], σωθήσεται [sōthesetai; 'he shall be saved'], ἐσώθη [esōthē; 'he was saved'], σέσωσται [sesōstai; 'he is saved']."[1160]

---

[1159] A. A. Hodge, Outlines of Theology (Carlisle, PA: Banner of Truth Trust [Reprinted 1983]), 543–545.

[1160] B. F. Westcott, St. Paul's Epistle to the Ephesians: The Greek Text with Notes and Addenda ([London: Macmillian, 1906], 32).

# CONCLUSION

We must allow the Apostle Paul, that great champion of the doctrines of sovereign grace, to offer concluding words from God's Word on the terms and topics highlighted in this treatise. As previously intimated, Titus 3:3–8 is quite comprehensive:

> At one time we too were foolish, disobedient, deceived and enslaved by all kinds of passions and pleasures. We lived in malice and envy, being hated and hating one another. But when the kindness and love of God our Savior appeared, he saved us, not because of righteous things we had done, but because of his mercy. He saved us through the washing of rebirth and renewal by the Holy Spirit, whom he poured out on us generously through Jesus Christ our Savior, so that, having been justified by his grace, we might become heirs having the hope of eternal life. This is a trustworthy saying. And I want you to stress these things, so that those who have trusted in God may be careful to devote themselves to doing what is good. These things are excellent and profitable for everyone (Titus 3:3–8, NIV).

SOLI DEO GLORIA

# APPENDICES

## APPENDIX A:
## AN EXCURSUS ON THE INVIOLABILITY
## OF THE "ONE-FLESH" RELATIONSHIP
## OF MARRIAGE

Genesis 2:18–24 fills in the details of chapter one, verses 26–28. Concerning "the man" (הָאָדָם [hā'ādām])[1] about whom it is affirmed that it was "not good"[2] for him to be alone (i.e. by himself), the LORD revealed that He would graciously intervene by making "a helper suitable for him." In the compound prepositional phrase כְּנֶגְדּ (kᵉneged), found only in Genesis 2:18, 20 and usually translated as "suitable for" (cf., e.g., NASB, NIV), the second constituent of it derives from a root whose basic force is "to communicate."[3] נֶגֶד (neged) as a substantive connotes "that which is opposite, that which corresponds."[4] In conjunction with the prefixed כְּ- (kᵉ-), the following compounded nuances have been suggested for this prepositional package: "like his opposite," "proper for him,"[5] "according to what is in front of" him, "corresponding to" him,[6] etc. God was going to remedy Adam's, i.e. "the man's," lonely condition by creating a female image-bearer who would complement the male image-bearer and communicate with him on the horizontal level.[7] This valuable piece of revelational data helps to illumine the rest of the Genesis 2 account, especially the man's naming of his bride from God "woman" and the Scripture's designation of the male-female union as "one flesh."

---

[1] In the context of Genesis 2:18, הָאָדָם [hā'ādām] denotes that male image-bearer, i.e. Adam, who was created first.

[2] This "not good" (לֹא־טוֹב [lo' ṭob]) is particularly arresting in view of all the "goods" capstoned by the "exceedingly good" of chapter 1.

[3] Cf. Westermann, TLOT, 2:714–718.

[4] Cf. KB, 2:666. Note the force and significance of this preposition. Each of the relational partners in the design of God is to complement the other in all areas of being. This is a primary reason why the sin of homosexuality is "against nature" (Romans 1:26). It violates the original order; therefore, all who *practice* it stand under the condemnation of God. The only remedy, as in the case of all sin and sins, is God's gracious salvation appropriated by biblical repentance as corroborated by the fruit of obedience (1 Corinthians 6:9–11).

[5] Ibid.

[6] BDB, 617.

[7] Vertical communication with God, as we shall see, is also a vital part of the significance of mankind having been created in the image and likeness of the Creator.

Concerning the creation of the female image-bearer out of the male image-bearer, Genesis 2:22 affirms: "and the LORD God fashioned[8] into a woman the rib which He had taken from the man, and brought her to the man" (NASB). This verse about the creation of the woman out of the man functions apparently as a sequel to the forming or shaping of the man out of the dust of the ground (cf. Genesis 2:7). It is imperative to note that it is Yahweh-God who not only creates the woman for the man but who also gives the bride away and performs the marriage. And indeed, as indicated by the man's responses, Adam was exceedingly grateful. His immediate outburst as he awakened from God's anesthesia was זֹאת הַפַּעַם (zōt happaʿam), literally "this is the time." Idiomatically, this exclamation could be expressed in contemporary language by something like, "Wow! This one is right on target!"[9] The man also recognized that the woman had come *from him* according to the plan and provision of God (cf. v. 22 with the "of's" or "out of's" of v. 23).[10]

Much ink has been spilt over Adam's naming of the female image-bearer "woman."[11] Most familiar is Luther's seemingly canonized interpretation based upon the word אִישׁ (ʾîš), "man." Since the word for "woman" in Genesis 2:23 is אִשָּׁה (ʾiššâ), Luther translated it into German as "männin" which connotes 'a female man.'[12] It is also possible that the Hebrew word for "woman" may have come from a different root (e.g., אנשׁ [ʾnš]).[13] This Semitic root exhibits at least three basic semantical fields, "to be weak," "to be friendly, social," "and to be soft delicate."[14] All three of these could well pertain quite generally to female image-bearers. Furthermore, each of these nuances potentially illustrate how the female image-bearer complements the male image-bearer. In any event, Adam immediately recognized and appreciated this female love-gift from God.

Now taking off on the word "flesh" (i.e. בָּשָׂר [bāśār]) in vv. 21 and 23, the scriptural precedent for the inviolable marriage of a man and a

---

[8] A new creation word is added to the stock pile of such terms in Genesis 1–2. This word (i.e. בָּנָה [bānâ]) most basically conveys the meaning of "to build." It seems to have been the best choice of vocabulary, especially in view of Adam's ecstatic response at the outset of v. 23!

[9] Contrast the animals that Adam had observed and named in vv. 19–20, but with which there was no intimate fellowship.

[10] Note the four occurrences of מִן (min) in vv. 22–23. On the headship significance of this fact, remember Paul's allusion to it in 1 Corinthians 11:8–9.

[11] This was obviously her generic name, not her individual personal name "Eve" (i.e. חַוָּה [hawwâ] in Genesis 3:20).

[12] Cf., e.g., KD, 1:90.

[13] Cf. BDB, 60–61.

[14] Ibid.

woman is published: "consequently" or "therefore"[15] a man (i.e. אִישׁ ([*'is*]) will leave [16] his father and mother and will cling to[17] his wife, and they will become one flesh." Concerning the introductory compound conjunction of this verse (i.e. עַל־כֵּן [*'al kēn*]), BDB, using Genesis 2:24 as one of their examples, suggest that what follows it would "regularly" indicate "the origin of a name, or custom, or proverb." Our Lord Jesus obviously took it as a divinely established precedent for all times when, after quoting Genesis 2:24, He added, "So they are no longer two, but one. Therefore what God has joined together, let not man separate" (Matthew 19:6, NIV). As we will see later, "flesh" in the Bible *rarely* refers to the physical stuff of human beings (however, note its predominantly physical connotation in Genesis 2:21), but rather, "flesh" most frequently is a synecdochical term referring to man's whole being (i.e. his physical aspect + his metaphysical aspect = "flesh"). Therefore, the joining of a man and a woman together, as far as God is concerned, results in an indissoluble one-flesh union. Like "body" and "spirit" (cf., e.g., James 2:26), the ordained bond of marriage in God's eyes may be broken only by death (cf., e.g., Romans 7:2–3; 1 Corinthians 7:39).

This "one-flesh" metaphor for the *inviolability* of marriage is further corroborated by the fact that God regards marriage as "a divinely protected covenant between husband and wife."[18] Although immediately applied to the rebellious priests of the prophet's day, God's perspective revealed in Malachi 2:14 also applies across the board: "... The Lord has been a witness between you and the wife of your youth, against whom you have dealt treacherously,[19] though she is your companion and *your wife by covenant*"[20] (NASB). Any violation of this one-flesh covenant brings on the following divine assessments, affirmations, and admonitions (Malachi 2:15–16, NIV[21]):

Has not the LORD made them one? In flesh and spirit they are his. And why one? Because he was seeking godly off-spring. So

---

[15] Cf. "For this reason" and "for this cause" in the NIV and NASB respectively.

[16] עָזַב (*'āzab*) is normally a strong term of separation.

[17] דָּבַק (*dābaq*) is normally a strong word for adherence (cf. glue to).

[18] This is Hugenberger's excellently defended thesis in: Gordon P. Hugenberger, *Marriage as a Covenant: Biblical Law and Ethics as Developed from Malachi* (Grand Rapids: Baker, 1994).

[19] The Hebrew root בגד (*bgd*), "to act faithlessly, treacherously, perfidiously" (Wakely, *NIDOTTE*, 1:582), occurs as a condemning chorus throughout chapter 2 of Malachi (cf. vv. 10, 11, 14, 15, 16) exposing how exceedingly serious this breaching of the marital covenant was in the eyes of the LORD God.

[20] Emphasis added.

[21] Although the Hebrew text is translationally and interpretively challenging, the dynamically interpretive rendering of the NIV seems to be quite reliable.

guard yourself in your spirit, and do not break faith with the wife of your youth. "I hate divorce," says the LORD God of Israel, "and I hate a man's covering himself with violence as well as with his garment," says the LORD Almighty. So guard yourself in your spirit, and do not break faith.

But what about passages like Deuteronomy 24, Ezra 10, Matthew 5, and Matthew 19? Don't they seem to contradict the Almighty's affirmation of "I hate divorce" in Malachi 2:16? Not necessarily! For example, Ezra 10 had to do with so-called "marriages" to foreign wives, a practice that had been condemned by God throughout the Old Testament. And concerning the nearly thirty-five hundred years of Jewish and Christian interpretive history of Deuteronomy 24:1–4, most have avoided admitting that the passage does *not* deal with divorce *in general*.[22] Furthermore, the phrase עֶרְוַת דָּבָר in Deuteronomy 24:1 (i.e. *'erwat dābār;* lit, "the nakedness of a thing," rendered as "some indecency" [NASB], "something indecent" [NIV], etc.) has not yet precisely been nailed down. As Murray rightly concedes, "It has to be admitted that it is exceedingly difficult if not precarious to be certain as to what the 'unseemly thing' really was."[23]

Complicating this all the more are the interpretive traditions concerning the "exception clauses" of Matthew 5:32 and 19:9 as they allegedly tie back into Deuteronomy 24:1 ff. Not enough attention is paid to the settings of Jesus' interactions in Matthew 5 and 19. In chapter 5, our Lord is primarily dealing with rabbinical accretions to and interpretations of the Law (notice how carefully He phrases His entrees to these various ethical issues in Matthew 5:21a, 27a, 33a, 38a, 43a). In chapter 19, the whole discussion began when Pharisees with their interpretive agendas tried to put our Lord on the spot.

Jesus' seeming concessions in Matthew's Gospel were couched within these quite similar settings. Also, it seems to be more than merely a matter of synoptic interest that our Lord in Mark (i.e. Mark 10:11–12) and Luke (i.e. Luke 16:18) unconditionally rules out divorce. Besides those significant factors comes the challenge of trying to specify what πορνεία (*porneia*) refers to in the two "exception" clauses (i.e. παρεκτὸς λόγου πορνείας [*parektos logou porneias*] in Matthew 5:32 and μὴ ἐπὶ πορνείᾳ [*mē epi porneiā*] in Matthew 19:9). It is unfortunate that too

---

[22] Cf. the compounded protasis of vv. 1–3 with the apodosis in v. 4; both the NASB and the NIV do a good job of rendering the syntax of the Hebrew text. By the way, for a commendably inductive historical and exegetical examination of this passage and the other key passages to follow, see: David C. D'Amour, "What God Has Joined Together ..." unpublished Th. M. thesis, The Master's Seminary, 1994.

[23] John Murray, *Divorce* (Philadelphia: Presbyterian and Reformed, 1961), 9.

many Christians have built their doctrine of divorce primarily upon the shifting hermeneutical sands of Deuteronomy 24:1, Matthew 5:32, and Matthew 19:19. This is especially disconcerting in view of our Lord's expectation for New Testament disciples: "For I tell you that unless your righteousness surpasses that of the Pharisees and the teachers of the law, you will certainly not enter the kingdom of heaven" (Matthew 5:20, NIV). The ethics of followers of Christ should not be patterned after the loop-holer legalists of Jesus' day but should be driven by the motivation to please their Lord in all things. And what pleases our Master in reference to marriage and divorce is clear, not hermeneutically fuzzy: "... have you not read, that He who created *them* from the beginning MADE THEM MALE AND FEMALE, and said 'FOR THIS CAUSE A MAN SHALL LEAVE HIS FATHER AND MOTHER, AND SHALL CLEAVE TO HIS WIFE; AND THE TWO SHALL BECOME ONE FLESH'? Consequently they are no more two, but one flesh. What therefore God has joined together, let no man separate" (Matthew 19:4–6, NASB).[24]

---

[24] Consequently, the pursuit of a divorce is not an option for one who earnestly desires to honor God's will. He or she, if the partner is seeking a divorce, has only one option and that is to pursue reconciliation. However, should the other partner succeed in his or her legal attainment of a "divorce," the child of God is to remain single ( 1 Corinthians 7:8–16). Death alone truly breaks the marital bond allowing for remarriage: "A woman is bound to her husband as long as he lives. But if her husband dies, she is free to marry anyone she wishes, but he must belong to the Lord" (1 Corinthians 7:39, NIV).

# APPENDIX B:
# A TABLE OF THE OLD TESTAMENT TERMS
# FOR "IMAGE" AND "LIKENESS"

| The Hebrew masculine noun צֶלֶם (ṣelem) | | The Hebrew feminine noun דְּמוּת (dᵉmût) | |
|---|---|---|---|
| OCCURRENCE | CONNECTION | OCCURRENCE | CONNECTION |
| Genesis 1:26–27 | God's "image" in man | Genesis 1:26 | God's "likeness" in man |
| Genesis 5:3 | God's "image" in man | Genesis 5:1, 3 | God's "likeness" in man |
| Genesis 9:6 | God's "image" in man | 2 Kings 16:10 | the pattern of the altar |
| 1 Samuel 6:5, 11 | "images" of tumors and mice | 2 Chronicles 4:3 | brazen figures in the temple |
| 2 Kings 11:18 | idols | Psalm 58:5 (v. 4 Eng.) | an idiom of comparison: "like" |
| 2 Chronicles 23:17 | idols | | |
| Psalm 39:7 (v. 6, Eng.) | "phantom" (NASB, NIV)?; "shadow" (NRSV)? | Isaiah 13:4 | " |
| Psalm 73:20 | "form" (NASB)? "fantasies" (NIV)? | Isaiah 40:18 | " |
| | | Ezekiel 1:5, 10, 13 16, 22, 16, 28 | "form, shape" |
| Ezekiel 7:20 | statues, idols | Ezekiel 10:1, 10, 21, 22 | "form, shape" |
| Ezekiel 6:17 | statues, idols | | |
| Ezekiel 23:14 | statues, idols | | |
| Amos 5:26 | "image of pagan deities" | | |
| The Aramaic noun צְלֵם (ṣᵉlēm) | | Ezekiel 23:15 | an idiom of comparison with a concrete association |
| Daniel 2:31–32, 34–35 | statue | | |
| Daniel 3:1, 2, 3, 5, 7, 10, 12, 14, 15, 18 | statue | Daniel 10:16 | a vision, but Daniel saw someone "who looked like a man" (NIV) |
| Daniel 3:19 | "(facial) expression" (NASB) | | |

# APPENDIX C:
# TRADUCIANISM OR CREATIONISM:
# WHAT MODEL ALIGNS BEST WITH
# THE BIBLICAL DATA?

This systematic-theological "call" is by no means an easy one.[25] Historically, both sides have armed themselves with their favorite proof-texts. Some favorite ones of traducianists have been Genesis 5:1–3, Genesis 46:26, John 1:13, and Hebrews 7:9–10. The arsenal of most creationists normally includes Ecclesiastes 12:7, Isaiah 57:16, Zechariah 12:1 and Hebrews 12:9.

Critiquing these positions in reverse order, most creationists assume that their texts demand a direct creation of the metaphysical aspect of human offspring by God Himself (i.e. "hands-on" creations of their spirits). However, each of these "'creationist texts'" could well be taken as conveying the mediate, not immediate, involvement of God. In other words, this is another scenario of His sovereign providence, involving the employment of secondary means,[26] rather than direct acts of creation on His part.[27] If parents produce only the material aspect of their offspring, when and how does God directly produce the metaphysical aspect?[28] Furthermore, in view of the fall and the Bible's copious and clear teaching on natural depravity, it would seem that God would need not only to create billions of spirits throughout the course of human history, but also He would need to create them fallen.

Traducianism's basic thesis seems to interpret the majority of the biblical data more consistently.[29] Consider, for example, Genesis 5:1–3:[30]

---

[25] Especially since, as Berkouwer reminds us, "nowhere in Scripture is the origin of the soul spoken of as a separate theme" (*Man: The Image of God*, 295).

[26] Cf., e.g., the theology of passages like Psalms 119:73; 139:13–16; Jeremiah 1:5; Galatians 1:15; etc.

[27] As a matter of fact, the suggestion that God goes on creating just like He did in Genesis 1 seems to run counter to such affirmations as those found in Genesis 2:1–3 and Exodus 20:11.

[28] Needless to say, the "when" part of this question impinges upon the abortion issue. However, there is no possibility of any potential time lag in reference to the traducian model. Both aspects, the physical and the metaphysical begin together at conception. A *person, not* merely some*thing* physical, begins to develop when sperm meets egg (cf. Psalm 51:5–6 [vv. 7–8, Hebrew]).

[29] It should not be assumed from the following line of argument, however, that every traducianist must necessarily be a seminalist when it comes to Romans 5:12ff. As we will see later, Romans 5:12ff is overwhemingly representational in its focus. See Berkouwer for a good exposure of how hamartiological preunderstandings have often adversely affected anthropological conclusions in this arena of creationism vs. traducianism (*Man: The Image of God*, 283–84, 288–89).

[30] The proximity and semantic parallels of Genesis 5:1–2 with 1:26–28 make the analogy of 5:3 all the more conspicuous and significant.

This is a written record of the generations (or descendants, i.e. תּוֹלְדֹת [*tôlᵉdôt*][31]) of Adam (אָדָם [*'ādām*][32] ). On the day God created man (אָדָם [*'ādām*]), in the likeness (בִּדְמוּת [*bidmût*]) of God He made him. Male and female He created them; then he blessed them, and named them "man" (or mankind, i.e. אָדָם [*'ādām*]) on the day he created them. Now after Adam (*'ādām*) had lived one hundred thirty years, he begot (or brought forth, or fathered; i.e. from יָלַד [*yālad*]) *a son* or *a person*)[33] in his likeness, according to his image (בִּדְמוּתוֹ כְּצַלְמוֹ [*bidmûtô kᵉṣalmô*]), and he named him "Seth."[34]

The inference is that human beings, both body and "'soul'"[35] are brought into individual existence through the processes of procreation.

---

[31] A very appropriate term derived from the root יָלַד (*yld*), essentially conveying "to bear, bring forth, beget." The plural of this term as found here in 5:1 also shows up in 2:4; 6:9; 10:1, 32; 11:10, 27; 25:12, 13, 19; 36:1, 9; and 37:2. Besides its semantical contributions, it is also regarded by many as an organizational hinge throughout the first book of the Bible.

[32] By context, this ocurrence of אָדָם (*'ādām*) indicates the first man "Adam." But notice the fluid movement from the one to the anthropological many as the passage progresses.

[33] There is no stated object of the verb; however, it is easily supplied by virtue of the last clause of v. 3 wherein "Seth" is named.

[34] Analogically, notice not only the production of an image and likeness bearer but also the naming of him.

[35] "Spirit" is a better term for designating the strictly immaterial dimension of a human being, since "soul" in the Bible is an overwhelmingly wholistic designation. Nevertheless, "soul" has been theologically (not exegetically) canonized as a metaphysical term.

# APPENDIX D:
# DICHOTOMY, TRICHOTOMY, OR WHAT?

Even though the systematic-theological discussions about dichotomy and trichotomy detract from the primarily wholistic emphasis of biblical anthropology, a few words need to be said about them. We find dogmatic representatives holding to one or the other of these positions, each camp claiming to have *the* biblically correct perspective on man.

Furthermore, each group of adherents brandishes sets of favorite proof-texts. For example, dichotomists often refer to Genesis 2:7,[36] 2 Corinthians 5:1–10,[37] and 2 Corinthians 12:2.[38] Virtually all trichotomists appeal to 1 Thessalonians 5:23 and Hebrews 4:12 in defense of their viewpoint. However, separate enumerations, no matter how many,[39] do not necessitate separate parts of man's being. The same individual may be characterized by many labels (e.g., "soul," "spirit," "heart," "mind," "will," "bowels," etc.). But the biblical usages of such designations when they focus more on the immaterial side of man are employed perspectivally rather than substantivally.

The terms "spirit" and "soul"[40] are most often used interchangeably when referring to the immaterial nature of man. These terms are quite often functional in nature: "spirit" is an appropriate designation for man's non-physical aspect as viewed in close association with the spiritual or immaterial realm or sphere of existence, while "soul" is an appropriate designation for man's metaphysical aspect as viewed in the natural or material realm or sphere of existence. Either word, ψυχή (*psuchē*) or πνεῦμα (*pneuma*), may refer to the whole metaphysical nature of man. Consider, for example, the following parallelisms:

> "both *soul* and body" (Matthew 10:28)
> "both in body and *spirit*" (1 Corinthians 7:34)

---

[36] I. e. the divinely shaped material of dust from the ground (the physical constituent) plus the breath (נְשָׁמָה [*nišmâ*]) that God breathed (נָפַח [*nāpaḥ*]) into man (the metaphysical constituent).

[37] Cf. the brief discussion on the "intermediate state."

[38] The personal, metaphysical, conscious core of Paul's being could potentially exist and function apart from his bodily dimension.

[39] For example, Mark 12:30, according to the *assumption* of most trichotomists, might suggest a quadrachotomy! Similarly, a synthesis of just a few passages might lead some to posit a sexochotomy or more!!

[40] I.e. when ψυχή (*psuchē*) is used *infrequently* in the New Testament to signal man's immaterial side (cf. chapter 1 above).

Furthermore, although rarely occurring in this scenario, either term may designate the disembodied metaphysical conscious core of a person. Compare, for example,

"receive my *spirit*" (Acts 7:59)
"the *souls* of those who had been slain" (Revelation 6:9)

In addition, the adjectives related to ψυχή (*psuchē*) and πνεῦμα (*pneuma*), ψυχικός (*psuchikos*) and πνευματικός (*pneumatikos*), expecially as used in the context of 1 Corinthians 15:44, show a major difference of the resurrection body by stressing its adaptability to a different realm. In other words, the soulish body is one which is adapted for life in this material world; the resurrected body is described as "spiritual," being one especially adapted for life in the spiritual world. So, the basic metaphysical aspect of man may be referred to by different terms which may in turn bend themselves to the highlighting of special functions or relationships, but they do not signal different parts in man.

Now concerning the supposed evidence for trichotomy coming from 1 Thessalonians 5:23, consider the following series of corrective comments:

> Since in this passage Paul is concerned with the preservation of the whole man, it would seem reasonable to suppose that the piling up of terms is for emphasis rather than for definition.[41]

> "...and may your spirit and soul and body be preserved in entirety, free from blame." This is another way of expressing the desire for their complete sanctification.... It is precarious to try to construct a tripartite doctrine of human nature on the juxtaposition of the three nouns πνεῦμα, ψυχή, and σῶμα. The three together give further emphasis to the completeness of sanctification for which the writers pray, but the three together add but little to the sense of ὑμῶν τὰς καρδίας ("your hearts") in 3:13.[42]

> So important is this sanctification that Paul repeats the prayer in another form, this time praying that the whole man may be preserved entire and without blame. There are some who see in the reference to spirit, soul, and body an indication that man is a threefold being.... But this is probably to press the language beyond what is warranted. Paul is not at this point giving a

---

[41] Guthrie, *NTT*, 165.
[42] F. F. Bruce, *1 and 2 Thessalonians*, WBC (Waco: Word Books, 1982), 129–130.

description of the nature of the human constitution, but engaging in prayer. He uses this graphic form by way of insisting that the whole man, and not some part only, is involved.... In different ways, Paul emphasizes that sanctification applies to the whole of man, and is not to be restricted to any segment.[43]

In this verse, Paul is thus "speaking rhetorically, making no essential distinction between spirit and soul."[44]

Concerning Hebrews 4:12, advocates of trichotomy assume that the sword-like cleaving by the Word of God is *between* the "soul" and the "spirit," thereby demanding a tripartite anthropology.[45] However, "what the author is saying is that God's Word can reach to the innermost recesses of our being."[46] In other words,

our author is not concerned to provide here a psychological or anatomical analysis of the human constitution, but rather to describe in graphic terms the penetration of God's word to the innermost depth of man's personality.... The point is ... that no separation could be more intimate than that between soul and spirit or between joints and morrow.... The mention of soul and spirit and of joints and marrow, then, serves to convey effectively the notion of the extreme power of penetration of the word of God, to the very core of man's being.[47]

So in the few passages where some sort of distinction is being made concerning the most basic aspects common to all humanity, man from the systematic-theological perspective is a dichotomous entity.[48] Biblical anthropology is overwhelmingly synthetic rather than analytically compartmentalized.

---

[43] Leon Morris, *The First and Second Epistles to the Thessalonians,* NICGNT (Grand Rapids: WM. B. Eerdmans Publishing Co., 1984), 180–181.

[44] Charles M. Horne, *The Epistles to the Thessalonians,* Shield Bible Study Series (Grand Rapids: Baker, 1961), 53.

[45] That this is an *assumption* is obvious, for example, because of the challenges of construing Greek genitives, especially as they are linked up in series as here. It is possible, although not probable, that the "division" spoken of in Hebrews 4:12 pertains to each of the four terms (i.e. *of* soul and *of* spirit, both *of* joints and *of* marrow"). However, the two couplets, the first having a metaphysical affinity and the second sharing physical commonality, do seem to imply some sort of a separation within these doublets. Nevertheless, it certainly does not demand that the "soul" and "spirit" are distinct anthropological parts. The point of these selective illustrations is that the Word of God can separate what is normally perceived to be inseparable.

[46] Leon Morris, *Hebrews, EBC* (Grand Rapids: Zondervan, 1981), 12:44.

[47] P. E. Hughes, *A Commentary on the Epistle to the Hebrews* (Grand Rapids: Eerdmans, 1977), 165–166.

[48] Remember Erickson's terminology: "conditional unity"; "contingent monism" (*Christian Theology,* 536–537).

# APPENDIX E:
## SOME SELECTED DIRGES ON SIN IN THE OLD TESTAMENT

Here are just a few among many cacophonic dirges about sin in the Old Testament.

Blessed[49] is the one whose rebellion (root פשע [pš']) is forgiven[50], whose sin (root חטא [ḥṭ']) is covered![51] Blessed is the man[52] whose iniquity (root עוה [ʿwh]) Yahweh does not count against him, and in whose spirit there is no deceit!

When I kept silence my bones wasted away through my groaning all day long. For by day and by night Your hand was heavy upon me; my moisture was turned into the droughts of summer. Selah. My sin (root חטא [ḥṭ']) I made known to You, and my iniquity (root עוה [ʿwh]) I did not cover up; I said, "I will confess against myself[53] my rebellions (i.e. rebellious deeds or acts; root פשע [pš']) to Yahweh and You[54] forgave[55] the iniquity (root עוה [ʿwh]) of my sin (root חטא [ḥṭ']). Selah (Psalm 32:1–5).

Be gracious to me, O God, according to Your loyal love;[56] according to the abundance of Your tender mercies[57] blot out my rebellions (i.e. rebellious acts or deeds; root פשע [pš']). Thoroughly wash me from my iniquity (root עוה [ʿwh]), and cleanse me from my sin (root חטא [ḥṭ']).[58] For I[59] know my re-

---

[49] "'O the happinesses, joys, etc. of...'"; or, from the perspective of the covenant community, "How admirable is the one who...." This introductory word is the primary beatitude term of the Old Testament.

[50] Literally, "is lifted up," i.e. "is carried, borne" (by context a *divine* passive).

[51] Another divine passive belonging to the realm of Part III of this book on the doctrines of sovereign grace.

[52] אָדָם ('ādām); if taken with an *ultimate* generic application, the *person*.

[53] Accepting the variant vocalization.

[54] Emphatic.

[55] The active form of the verb "is forgiven" in v.1.

[56] חֶסֶד (ḥesed) has been brought over into English with various renderings. The term is much greater than any or even the aggregate of its translations. It functions basically as the conceptual counterpart of New Testament χάρις (charis), "grace" (cf. Part III).

[57] The plural noun of the רחם (rḥm) word group, stressing God's tender loving care in the Old Testament.

[58] Actually, this line unfolds chiastically with the two terms for sin emphatically juxtaposing in the middle of it.

[59] Emphatic.

bellions (i.e. rebellious acts or deeds; root פֶּשַׁע [*pš'*]),[60] and my sin (root חטא [*ḥt'*]) is in front of me always. Against You, and You only, I have sinned (root חטא [*ḥt'*]), and I have done that which is evil (root רעע [*r''*])[61] in Your eyes,[62] so that You are righteous when You speak and You are pure when You judge. Indeed, in iniquity (root עוה [*'wh*])[63] I was brought forth,[64] and in sin (root חטא [*ḥt'*]) my mother conceived me (Psalm 51:3–7; vv. 1–5, English).

Hear, O heavens, and give ear, O earth! For Yahweh has spoken: "Sons I have reared and raised up, but they[65] have rebelled (root פֶּשַׁע [*pš'*]) against Me. An ox knows its owner and an ass (knows) its master's manger; (however[66]), Israel does not know[67]; My people do not understand."[68] Woe, sinning (root חטא [*ḥt'*]) nation, a people heavy with iniquity (root עוה [*'wh*]), seed of evildoers (root רעע [*r''*]), sons acting corruptly (root שחת [*šḥt*])! They have forsaken (root עזב [*'zb*])[69] Yahweh; they have spurned (or despised; root נאץ [*n'ṣ*]) the Holy One of Israel;[70] they have turned backwards (probable root נזר [*nzr*]).[71] Upon what (part) will you be struck again? You keep on adding apostasy (root סור [*swr*]).[72] Every head is for a wound, and every heart is sick. From the sole of the foot even to the head, there is no soundness (root תמם [*tmm*]) in it—bruise and blow and fresh stripe—they have not been pressed out nor bound up nor softened with oil (Isaiah 1:2–6).

---

[60] This term for his sin emphatically stands first in this line.

[61] This term for his sin also emphatically stands first in its clause.

[62] I.e. of God's righteous and holy evaluation.

[63] Both this prepositional phrase speaking about David's sinful estate and the one in the next clause are, once again, placed first for emphasis.

[64] A term of parturation (i.e. from the womb); for some excellent commentary on this verse, see Edward R. Dalgish, *Psalm Fifty-one in the Light of Ancient Near Eastern Patternism* (Leiden: Brill, 1962), 91ff.

[65] An *emphatic* contrast.

[66] An occurrence of asyndetonic antithetical parallelism.

[67] I.e. persistently does not acknowledge.

[68] I.e. they have consistently shown themselves to be lacking spiritual perception. The last two lines of v. 3 illustrate the noetic consequences of being settled in sin.

[69] A term of apostasy.

[70] I. e. treated their LORD with contempt.

[71] This portion of the text is challenging. If taken as turning back or away from God, it is another word picturing defection and apostasy. It is also possible that it may read: "'they have dedicated themselves to another (god)'" (see W. L. Holladay, "The Crux in Isaiah 1:4–6," VT, 33 [1983]: 235–237). If so, idolatry is obviously in view.

[72] Yet another term for withdrawal, defection.

Therefore, I prayed to Yahweh, my God, and confessed and said, "Now, O Sovereign Lord, the great and awesome[73] God who keeps the covenant and (His) loyal love[74] with the ones who love Him and who keep His commandments, we have sinned (root חטא [ḥt']); we have acted perversely (root עוה ['wh]); we have acted wickedly (root רשע [rsʿ]); we have re-volted (root מרד [mrd]), turning aside (i.e. departing; root סור [sur]) from Your commandments and ordinances. Nor have we listened to Your servants, the prophets, who spoke in Your name to our kings, our princes, and our fathers, and to all the people of the land" (Daniel 9:3–6).[75]

---

[73] I.e. the one-to-be-feared God.

[74] I.e. חֶסֶד (ḥesed).

[75] The holy standard that exposed all this sin was God's law. For an admonition to pray and to con-fess as Daniel did in these verses, cf. Solomon's urgings in 1 Kings 8:31ff., see esp. vv. 46ff. For a post-exilic edition of such a prayer of confession, see Ezra 9, esp. vv. 6–7: "O my God, I am ashamed and I feel ashamed to lift up, O my God, my face to You because our iniquities (root עוה ['wh]) have multiplied over (our) head, and our guilt (root אשם ['šm]) has grown great even to the heavens. From the days of our fathers we (have lived) with great guilt (root אשם ['šm]) even until this day, and because of our iniquities (root עוה ['wh]), we, our kings, (and) our priests have been given into the hand of the kings of the lands, by sword, by captivity, both in plunder and in shame of face, just as it is this day."

# APPENDIX F:
# SOME SELECTED DIRGES ON SIN IN
# THE NEW TESTAMENT

A good place to begin is with the teachings of Jesus on mankind's spiritual heart disease. For example, in Matthew 12:34a our Lord said this to a resistant group of Pharisees:

> You brood of vipers, how can you being evil (πονηροὶ ὄντες [ponēroi ontes][76]), speak good things?

Similarly, but to an audience of His followers, He said this in Luke 11:13a:

> If you then, being evil (πονηροὶ ὑπάρχοντες [ponēroi huparchontes][77]), know to give good gifts to your children,...

More fully in Matthew 15 and in its parallel passage in Mark 7 our Lord exposed the true source and symptoms of sin. Getting to the "heart" (pun intended!) of the matter, listen to Hendriksen's translation of Mark 7:20–23:[78]

> He [i.e. Jesus] continued, "What comes out of [ἐκ (ek)[79]] a man, it is that which defiles a man. For it is from inside, from men's hearts [ἐκ τῆς καρδίας (ek tēs kardias)] that the evil schemes [οἱ διαλογισμοὶ οἱ κακοὶ (hoi dialogismoi hoi kakoi)[80]] arise [ἐκπορεύομαι (ekporeuomai)[81]]: sexual sins, thefts, murders, adulteries, covetings, malicious acts [πονηρίαι (ponērioi)], deceit, lewdness, envy, abusive speech, arrogance, folly. All these evil things [πάντα ταῦτα τὰ πονηρὰ (panta tauta ta ponēra)] proceed from inside and defile a man."

---

[76] The present participle of the most common verb for "being" in combination with the anarthrous adjective magnifies the characterizing condition of these people.

[77] The same anarthrous adjective as that found in Matthew 12:34 is used but with a different, and possibly more concrete, state of being participle. For example, Godet comments, "Ὑπάρχειν denotes the actual state as the starting-point for the supposed activity" (Frederick L. Godet, *Commentary on the Gospel of Luke*, Classic Commentary Library [Grand Rapids: Zondervan, n.d.], 2:58–59).

[78] William Hendriksen, *Exposition of the Gospel According to Mark*, NTC (Grand Rapids: Baker, 1975), 282, 289; bracketed Greek words and phrases added.

[79] Cf. the ἔσωθεν (esōthen), "from within," vv. 21 and 23, and contrast the ἔξωθεν (exōthen), "from without," v. 15 (i.e. the latter pointing to the externalists' feeble and false view of the source of defilement).

[80] A strong statement about *noetic* depravity.

[81] I.e. (characteristically) *come out from*.

Hendriksen's comments on these verses are also very helpful when it comes to understanding Jesus' hamartiology:

> The introductory term "the evil schemes," "designs," or "devisings" is literally "those bad dialogizings." In his own mind a person frequently carries on a dialogue. See Psalm 14:1; 39:1; 116:11; Daniel 5:29, 30; Obadiah 3; Mark 2:6–7; 5:28; Luke 12:17f.; 15:17–19; 16:3, 4; Revelation 18:7. In three of these instances of talking to oneself—namely, Psalm 39:1; Mark 5:28; Luke 15:17–19, such a "dialogue" or "deliberation" can be described as being good. One—Luke 16:3, 4—is half good, half bad, as the context shows. All the rest are wicked. This holds also in such cases where the very word "dialogue" or "dialogizing" is used. In nearly every instance— Luke 2:35 is a possible exception—the deliberations, inner reasonings, or devisings are of a definitely sinful nature. In addition to Matthew 15:19; Mark 7:2; see Luke 5:22; 6:8; 9:46, 47; 24:38; Romans 1:21; 14:1; 1 Corinthians 3:20; Philippians 2:14; 1 Timothy 2:8; James 2:4....One of the reasons why such dialogizings are so important is that they give rise to actions and stimulate inner drives. They also reveal themselves in spoken words. These several items are now enumerated by means of examples: 6 plurals are followed by 6 singulars; 6 kinds of actions are followed by 6 items that represent drives (or states) of the heart...and speech.... In the present context, which pictures Jesus in the act of describing what it is that defiles or pollutes a person, all the twelve items are naturally of an evil nature.[82]

Paul, throughout his epistles, picks up this hamartiological baton. For example, before he reveals the provisions of the Good News of salvation in Romans 3:21ff., he clearly reviews the bad news of sin in 1:18–3:20.[83] Excerpts from Dunn's quite consistently good translation will be used to characterize the foundations of Pauline hamartiology:[84]

---

[82] Ibid., 286.

[83] Although this section obviously applies to the *whole* of our fallen race (especially in view of its main punch-lines found in 3:19–20), the historical inception of sin in the garden (i.e. original sin) is implied (cf. Romans 1:18–32 with Genesis 3). Therefore, Romans 1:18–3:20 reviews the situation of *the many __and__* the one (i.e. the one=Adam). It anticipates the situations of *the one __and__* the many in Romans 5:12–21. For some substantiations of this phenomenon, see especially D. J. W. Milne, "Genesis 3 in the Letter to the Romans," *RTR*, 39 (Jan–Apr 1980): 10–18.

[84] Dunn, *Romans*, 1:52–53, 77–78, 94, 108, 118–119, 128–129, 144–145.

For the wrath of God is being revealed from heaven against all impiety [ἀσέβειαν (*asebeian*)] and unrighteousness of men [ἀδικίαν ἀνθρώπων (*adikian anthrōpōn*)] who suppress the truth[85] in unrighteousness [ἀδικίᾳ (*adikiā*)], because what can be known about God is evident to them. For God has shown it to them. For his invisible attributes from the creation of the world are perceived rationally in the things which have been made, both his external power and deity, so that they are without excuse. Because though they knew God they did not glorify him as God or give him thanks, but became futile in their thinking,[86] and their foolish hearts were darkened.[87] Claiming to be wise they became fools,[88] and changed the glory of the incorruptible God for the mere likeness of corruptible man, birds, beasts and reptiles. Wherefore God handed them in the desires[89] of their hearts to uncleanness [ἀκαθαρσίαν (*akatharsian*)[90]] to the dishonoring of themselves: they exchanged the truth of God for falsehood and worshipped and served the creature rather than the Creator, who is God blessed forever. Amen.

For this reason God handed them over to disgraceful passions. For their females changed natural relations into what is contrary to nature.[91] Likewise also the males gave up natural relations with the female and were inflamed with desire for one another, males with males committing what is shameless and receiving back in themselves the appropriate penalty for their error. And as they did not think God qualified for continued recognition, God gave them over to a disqualified mind [ἀδόκιμον νοῦν (*adokimon noun*)[92]], to do what is improper[93]—filled with all unrighteousness

---

[85] This is probably the key description of mankind in Romans 1:18–23. Humankind continuously incarcerates the truth about the Sovereign Creator so that natural revelation cannot convert them; it only condemns them. Because of their persistent refusal to accept the theology of this grand display of God's handiwork, they end up defenseless (cf. ἀναπολογήτους [*anapologētous*] at the end of v. 20).

[86] I.e. another expression for man's noetic catastrophe; cf. Ephesians 4:17.

[87] Cf. Ephesians 4:18.

[88] I.e. *moral* morons.

[89] Or, lusts.

[90] The context here emphasizes moral impurity, although the Old Testament *background* most often focuses on ceremonial or ritual impurity.

[91] Both lesbianism and homosexuality are divinely indicted as being "against nature" (παρά φύσιν [*para phusin*]) in vv. 26–27.

[92] Yet another affirmation of noetic depravity.

[93] A mind that flunks God's moral test manifests all kinds of depravity (cf., e.g., the excerpts from Matthew 15 previously cited).

[ἀδικίᾳ (*adikiā*)], wickedness [πονηρίᾳ (*ponēriā*)], greediness [πλεονεξίᾳ (*plonexiā*)], badness [κακίᾳ (*kakiā*)]—full of jealousy [φθόνου (*phthonou*)], murder [φόνου (*phonou*)], rivalry [ἔριδος (*eridos*)], deceit [δόλου (*dolou*)], spite [κακοηθείας (*kakoētheias*)⁹⁴] rumor-mongers [ψιθυριστὰς (*psithuristas*)], slanderers [καταλάλους (*katalalous*)], God-haters [θεοστυγεῖς (*theostugeis*)], insolent [ὑβριστὰς (*hubristas*)], arrogant [ὑπερηφάνους (*huperēphanous*)], braggarts [ἀλαζόνας (*alazonas*)⁹⁵], contrivers of evil [ἐφευρετάς κακῶν (*epheuretas kakōn*)], disobedient to parents [γονεῦσιν ἀπεθεῖς (*goneusin apetheis*), senseless [ἀσυνέτους (*asunetous*)]⁹⁶, faithless [ἀσυνθέτους (*asunthetous*)], loveless [ἀστόργους (*astorgous*)], merciless [ἀνελεήμονας (*aneleēmonas*)]. Although they have known the just decree of God, that those who practice such things deserve death, they not only do the same but approve of those who practice them.

For this reason you are without excuse, you sir, each one of you who passes judgment.⁹⁷ For in that you pass judgment on the other you condemn yourself; for you practice the very things on which you pass judgment. And we know that the condemnation of God is in accordance with truth against those who practice such things.... For there is no partiality with God.

For as many as have sinned without the law shall also perish without the law; and as many as have sinned within the law shall be condemned through the law....

For we have now charged both Jews and Greeks as all alike under sin [ὑφ᾽ ἁμαρτίαν εἶναι (*huph hamartian einai*)⁹⁸ ], as it is written,

"There is none righteous, not even one." "There is none who understands.⁹⁹ There is none who seeks out God. All¹⁰⁰ have turned

---

⁹⁴ I.e. "malice, malignity" (Spicq, *TLNT*, 2:236); from its usages outside of the New Testament, Spicq concludes that "the word refers to perverse intentions, innate malice..., an inclination to evil...that cannot be rooted out..." (*ibid.*, 237).

⁹⁵ Cf. 1 John 2;16, ἡ ἀλαζονεία τοῦ βίου (*hē alazoneia tou biou*), "the boastful pride of life" (NASB).

⁹⁶ This and the next three descriptives are un-words, i.e. each has the alpha privative represented in the "-less" portions of Dunn's renderings.

⁹⁷ In Romans 2:1–3:9a, although general applications may be made to every category of human beings, Paul especially carries on a strong polemic against Jewish legalists.

⁹⁸ Literally this phrase reads "to be under sin," i.e. "to be under the dominion of sin" (John Murray, *The Epistle to the Romans*, NICNT [Grand Rapids: Eerdmans, 1965], 1:102).

⁹⁹ A moral noetic condition.

¹⁰⁰ Notice how Paul's Old Testament quotes move from "none" to "all," fitting expressions of *total* depravity.

aside,[101] they have together become worthless [ἠχρεώθησαν (ēchreōthēsan)[102]]; there is none who does good, there is none, not so much as one."[103] "Their throat is an open grave, they use their tongues to deceive." "The venom of asps is under their lips." "Whose mouth is full of curses and bitterness." "Their feet are swift when it comes to shedding blood, ruin and wretchedness are in their ways, and the way of peace they have not known." "There is no fear of God before their eyes."[104]

Now we know that whatever the law[105] says it says to those within the law, in order that every mouth might be stopped and all the world become liable [ὑπόδικος (hupodikos)] to God's judgment.[106] For by works of the law shall no flesh be justified before him, for through the law comes the knowledge of sin (Romans 1:18–32; 2:1–2, 11–12; 3:9b–20).

Two passages in Ephesians further illustrate Paul's main-stream hamartiology. In Ephesians 2:1-3 he writes:

> And you[107] being[108] dead in reference to your transgressions (παραπτώμασιν [paraptōmasin]) and sins (ἁμαρτίαις

---

[101] One of many ways to express apostasy.

[102] Or, have "become depraved" (BAG, 128); cf. Murray's illustrative comments (*Romans*, 1:103–104).

[103] No fallen human being can slip through such a finely screened hamartiological sieve.

[104] For some helpful observations on this catena (Romans 3:10–18) of Old Testament quotations, cf. Keck's analysis (Leander A. Keck, "The Function of Romans 3:10–18: Observations and Suggestions," *God's Christ and His People*, ed. By Jewell and Meeks [Oslo: Universitelsforlaget, 1977], 141 ff.). Logically these 14 Old Testament indictments against all fallen humanity break down into the following categories: character (vv. 10–12); communications (vv. 13–14); conduct (vv. 15–17); contempt (v. 18).

[105] Notice that "the law" in the context of this catena refers to Scripture in general.

[106] All men are ὑφ᾽ ἁμαρτίαν (*huph hamartian*), "under sin" (v. 9); therefore, πᾶς ὁ κόσμος (*pas ho kosmos*), "the whole world" (v. 19), has become ὑπόδικος (*hupodikos*), "*liable to judgment* or *punishment, answerable, accountable*" (BAG, 852). Being culpable, humanity stands condemned before the righteous Judge.

[107] The syntax of Ephesians 2:1ff. is eye-catchingly bold and very informative theologically. The "you" (i.e. ὑμᾶς [*humas*] ), is later joined by a "we" (i.e. ἡμᾶς [*hēmas*]), also an accusative plural, in v. 5a. Both constituencies combine as the objects or beneficiaries (i.e. the recipients) of God's salvation in Christ. In particular, it says in vv. 5–6 that "you" (i.e. the Ephesian audience) along with "us" (i.e. Paul and company) were 1) "made alive together with Christ"; 2) "raised up with" (Him); and 3) "seated with" (Him). Furthermore, it should be noted how the "you," "we too all," and the "even as the rest" (i.e. respectively, vv. 1a, 3a, 3b) make the descriptions of vv. 1–3 absolutely universal in scope. Consequently, vv. 1–3 depict the totality of humanity apart from and/or prior to (i.e. in the case of the Christian, as here) a sovereign application of divine grace through Christ.

[108] This literal translation of the present participle of being captures the continuous condition of the recipients before God wonderfully rescued them. More smoothly, we could render these opening words concessively in view of what is to come: "…although you were dead…God made you alive together with Christ…."

[*hamartiais*] ), in which you formerly walked[109] according to the age of this world, according to the ruler of the authority of the air,[110] of the spirit which is currently working among the sons of disobedience; among whom we also all once lived in the lusts of our flesh, doing the desires of the flesh and of the imaginations, and we were[111] children of wrath by nature[112] as also the rest.

Now moving on to Ephesians 4:17–19, the apostle writes:[113]

This, therefore, I say[114] and testify in the Lord, that you no longer walk[115] just as the gentiles[116] indeed walk in the vanity[117] of their mind (i.e. νοῦς [*nous*]), being darkened[118] in their thinking (διάνοια [*dianoia*] )[119] alienated from the life of God on account of the ignorance (ἄγνοια [*agnoia*])[120] that is in them, on account of the hardening of their heart; which very ones, having become callous, have given themselves over to debauchery unto the working of every kind of impurity with a desire for more.

---

[109] A common comprehensive metaphor for living life.

[110] A reference to Satan.

[111] Notice how these verses launched with a focus on *being*, then *being* manifested itself in doing and thinking. Now Paul's exposures come full circle back to *being*.

[112] For a good treatment of these words as solidly supporting the doctrine of original sin, see: David L. Turner, "Ephesians 2:30 and *Peccatum Originale*," *GTJ* (Fall 1980): 195–219.

[113] Notice again how Paul moves from living or doing (v. 17a, b) to its basis in thinking (vv. 17c, 18a) and being (vv. 18b–19a) then back to live-style once again (v. 19b). However, there is an applicational contrast of these verses when compared to Ephesians 2:1ff. In the former passage, the divine initiative in salvation broke the positional reality of being dead in our sins. Here in Ephesians 4:17ff. the focus is upon our human responsibility in the sanctification process, namely, not to think and act like B. C. people.

[114] I.e. in the sense of apostolic command.

[115] A consistent pattern of the immediately following life-style is proscribed.

[116] Herein the reference is to non-Christians.

[117] Or, emptiness, pointlessness, purposelessness, futility, etc.

[118] A periphrastic perfect passive participle: "*being darkened* is something that took place in the past but has a continuing effect. The 'understanding' or power of discursive reasoning had been affected by sin" (William Hendriksen, *NTC: Exposition of Ephesians*, NTC [Grand Rapids: Baker, 1967], 210.

[119] Or "'understanding, intelligence, mind' as the organ of νοεῖν"(BAG, 186).

[120] Salmond well comments, "The term ἄγνοια again is not a term merely of intellect. It denotes an ignorance of Divine things, a want of knowledge that is inexcusable and involves moral blindness....a culpable ignorance in their own nature or heart" (S.D.F. Salmond, *The Epistle to the Ephesians*, EGT [Grand Rapids: Eerdmans, reprinted 1970], 3:339–340).

One more dirge should prove sufficient to round out our brief listing of New Testament passages concentrating on sin. Titus 3:3–7 is another B. C. / A. C. reminder. The B. C. part reads like this:

For we, yes even we, were[121] formerly[122] foolish (ἀνόητοι [anoētoi][123]), disobedient (ἀπειθεῖς [apeitheis]), going astray (πλανώμενοι [planōmenoi][124]), being enslaved (δουλεύοντες [douleuontes][125]) to various kinds of lusts and pleasures (ἡδοναῖς [hēdonais][126]), living[127] in malice (κακίᾳ [kakiā]) and envy (φθόνῳ [phthonō] ), hateful (στυγητοί [stugetoi] ) and abhoring one another.

---

[121] Our characterizing state of life.

[122] The B.C. marker.

[123] An un-word from the νοέω (noeō) word group, connoting people who are spiritually and ethically without understanding.

[124] A present participle stressing people who are always *going astray* (BAG, 671).

[125] I. e. a habitual estate of being enslaved to sin (cf. Romans 6:17–18).

[126] This word family gives its name to the licentious philosophy of Hedonism.

[127] I.e. διάγοντες (*diagontes*), another present participle depicting our former life-style.

# APPENDIX G:
## A BRIEF INTRODUCTION TO A THEOLOGICAL DISCUSSION PERTAINING TO THE DIVINE DECREE(S)

I prefer to speak of the divine *decree* in order to emphasize its unity. There was apparently only one "time" of divine decision in eternity past although there are many facets to it.[128] It is even bigger than election, the atonement, and its applications, although these facets are primary. Indeed, its outworkings are comprehensive,[129] including, for example, all history,[130] circumstances of life,[131] duration of life,[132] manner of death,[133] the good acts of men,[134] the evil acts of men,[135] the salvation of sinners,[136] the perdition of ungodly men,[137] the most seemingly trivial of things,[138]etc.

The greatest mystery of this sovereign plan has to do with the origin of evil, especially the entrance of sin into God's sinless creation. The mind of man is quickly bankrupted by this greatest of conundrums. We know from Scripture that there is no sin in God and that this Holy (and wholly), sinless God hates all sin. Yet, based upon other truths from *His* infallible Word, we must deduce that His eternal plan included sin. There certainly was no *eternal* dualism of good and evil.

Two more mysteries related to this ultimate one about the origin of evil being part of the eternal decree involve: 1) the nature of *who God is* and the interrelationship of His attributes to *what He does*, and 2) the theological tensions that arise from the biblical data about predestination and election in that these data come to us from affirmations that *perspectivally* originate from *both* eternity past *and* from this side of time, space and history.[139]

---

[128] Cf. some of its facets in APPENDIX I.

[129] Generally, e.g., cf. Psalm 33:11; 103:19; 135:6; Isaiah 14:24–27; Daniel 4:31–32 (vv. 34–35, English); Romans 8:28; Ephesians 1:11; 3:11; etc.

[130] Cf., e.g., Daniel 2:20–21; Acts 17:26; Romans 13:1; etc.

[131] Cf., e.g., Genesis 20:6 in the context of the whole chapter; James 4:13–15; etc.

[132] Cf., e.g., Job 14:5.

[133] Cf., e.g., John 21:18–19.

[134] Cf., e.g., Genesis 20:6, again; Isaiah 44:28–45:7; 46:10–11; Ephesians 2:10; etc.

[135] Cf., e.g., Genesis 45:4–8; 50:20; Acts 2:23; 4:27–28; etc.

[136] Cf., e.g., 2 Thessalonians 2:13–14; *et.al.*

[137] Cf., Proverbs 16:4; Romans 9:22; 1 Peter 2:8; Jude 4.

[138] Cf., e.g., Proverbs 16:33 (however, see the Book of Esther, especially the casting of the pur and how the 'dice' fell in Chapter 3); Matthew 10:29–30; etc.

[139] Esp. post-*fall* history.

Permit me first to say just a word about the second of these consequential conundrums. Man's circuit breakers either pop or burn up when
dealing with the logical tensions that the biblical data bring to us. When
we explore the exegetically based truths about a pretemporal decree
which includes predestination, election, etc.,[140] most frequently set historically in contexts of post-fall applications pertaining to eternal salvation or eternal condemnation, no human system can pack every piece of
the data neatly into a logical box. Don't misunderstand me; we must do
our best on every theological topic to systematize as much of the total
revelational data as possible. However, we must humbly recognize that
our infinite, all-wise God has set some definite limits on how far we can
go in our syntheses. Every exegetical theologian must pay due respect to
divinely placed boundary markers such as those generally identified in
Deuteronomy 29:29; Isaiah 55:8–9; Romans 11:33–36; etc. These governing realities must also control us as we carefully consider the first issue
raised, having to do with the God who *is* and the God who *acts*.

Concerning God's being and His deeds, logical tensions sometimes
arise. Nevertheless, there seems to be a precedent substantiated by the
teachings of the Bible. *Generally* speaking, God's nature determines
whatever He does, and vice versa, whatever He does correspondingly exemplifies His nature. Yet, there are places in biblical revelation, take for
an example 1 Timothy 2:4, that tend to challenge the universal validity
of this seeming precedent. Handling this small handful of texts including
1 Timothy 2:4 certainly tests the inductive fibers of sovereign grace
theologians. When approaching this verse, biblicists must not allow it to
say too much (as many *theological freedom*-fighters do); however, neither
may true biblicists presuppositionally dismiss its voice or bend it through
hermeneutical manipulations.

Nonetheless, there *may* be an interpretive insight which indicates
that this verse is not necessarily a death trap to sovereign grace advocates.
This insight has to do with the possible nuancing of the verb "to desire,"
i.e. θέλω (*thelō*), herein. Although most contemporary scholars consider
the two word groups for "to will" (verb) and "will" (noun) to be "almost entirely interchangeable" by New Testament times,[141] θέλω (*thelō*)
historically has often been nuanced as *desire*, while βούλομαι (*boulomai*)
has more consistently been nuanced as *purpose*.[142] It is not outside the

---

[140] The biblical data undergirding these theological verities is forthcoming.

[141] Müller, *NIDNTT*, 3:1016.

[142] Cf. ibid., 1017 (where the βούλομαι [*boulomai*] group is associated theologically with "irrefragable
determination"), and 1019 (where the θέλω [*thelō*] group is sometimes associated with a "general willing, desiring") [however, Müller dubs this "a quite secular sense"]—[I say not necessarily "a secular
sense"]; note interspersed allusions to these nuanced meanings in Vine, *EDNTW*, 162, 676–677; and
Richard Trench, *Synonyms of the New Testament* (Grand Rapids: Baker Book House, 1989).

realm of probability, and certainly not outside the realm of semantical possibility, that θέλω (*thelō*) in 1 Timothy 2:4 is referencing the more emotionally colored *desire* of God as differentiated from the deliberative *design* of God. In other words, the emphasis may be on an attribute of God rather than on an act of God. Contextually, the point may be that the sovereign God is not some kind of mean autocrat that gets His "kicks" from the perdition of the non-elect. In order to ponder this possible interpretive nuancing of θέλω (*thelō*) in 1 Timothy 2:4, I am simply going to list in two columns the verses wherein some verb and noun occurrences of these two word groups are located in the New Testament:

The verb βούλομαι (*boulomai*); e.g.:
  Matthew 11:27
  Luke 10:22
  Hebrews 6:17 (ptc. + noun)
  James 1:18
  2 Peter 3:9[143]

The verb θέλω (*thelō*); e.g.:
  Matthew 23:37[144] 26:39
  Luke 5:12–13
  Romans 7:15–21, *passim*
  1 Timothy 1:7
  1 Timothy 2:4
  2 Timothy 3:12
  Revelation 22:17

The noun βουλή (*boulē*); e.g.:
  Acts 2:23; 4:28; 13:36
  Ephesians 1:11 (with θέλω [*thelō*])
  Hebrews 6:17 (noun + ptc.)

The noun θέλημα (*thelēma*); e.g.:
  Matthew 6:10; 7:21; 12:50;
    18:14
  Luke 12:47
  John 5:20; 6:38–40
  Romans 12:2
  Ephesians 1:11 (with βούλομαι
    [*boulomai*]); 2:3; 5:17
  1 Thessalonians 4:3; 5:18
  1 Peter 2:15
  1 John 2:17

---

[143] If this nuancing is applicable, this verse may show that these suggested colorings of θέλω (*thelō*) and βούλομαι (*boulomai*) turn out to be a double-edged sword theologically. Yet, there may be a contextual factor in the Peter passage that prevents it from being theologically wounded by this two-edged semantical sword. In 1 Timothy 2:4 the object of θέλω (*thelō*) is πάντας ἀνθρώπους (*pantas anthrōpous*), "all men" [I'll say more about this "all men" when it comes up again as "all" (people) at the end of 1 Timothy 2:6a]; however, the object of βούλομαι (*boulomai*) is most likely Peter's *readership*; cf. the τινας (*tinas*), "any," as informed by the ὑμᾶς (*humas*), "you," the guaranteed recipients of the Lord's patience.

[144] This occurrence seems to focus clearly upon an emotionally changed *desire*.

Whatever anyone may think about this suggested "'clarification,'" everyone who respects the Bible needs to acknowledge the general theological tension that is generated by the following non-negotiable truths:

> The wonderfully balanced attributes of God.
> The absolute sovereignty of God.[145]
> The wretched sinfulness of man and yet, the genuine responsibility of man.[146]

---

[145] The Word of God knows nothing about a semi-sovereignty or a contingent sovereignty; that would not be sovereignty at all.

[146] Genesis 20 and Acts 2:22–24; 4:27–28 wonderfully illustrate this humbling tension.

# APPENDIX H:
## NARROWING SPECIFICATIONS OF GOD'S SOTERIOLOGICAL PROVISION

The truth of 1 Timothy 4:10 is corroborated when all of the soteriological data is surveyed. Concerning the controversy over the "atonement" (i.e. general *or* particular), exegetical theologians must acknowledge *both/and* perspectives. Insisting on an either/or solution does violence to at least some of the Scriptural evidence.

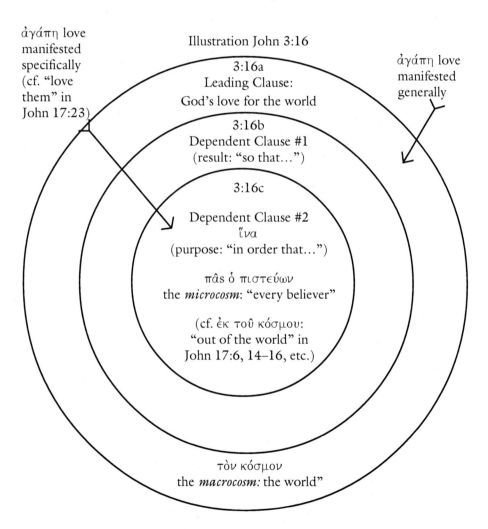

ἀγάπη love manifested specifically (cf. "love them" in John 17:23)

Illustration John 3:16

ἀγάπη love manifested generally

3:16a
Leading Clause:
God's love for the world

3:16b
Dependent Clause #1
(result: "so that...")

3:16c
Dependent Clause #2
ἵνα
(purpose: "in order that...")

πᾶς ὁ πιστεύων
the *microcosm*: "every believer"

(cf. ἐκ τοῦ κόσμου:
"out of the world" in
John 17:6, 14–16, etc.)

τὸν κόσμον
the *macrocosm:* the world"

Many passages point to a *particular* ransom, reconciliation, propitiation. Cf. the implications of John 17:2 in context (=the *particular intention* of the Cross-work of Christ).

Consequently: a *genuinely* Vicarious (substitutionary) "Atonement" (i.e. no "double payment"): He bore *our* sins.

A *few* passages (i.e. 1 Timothy 2:6; 2 Peter 2:1) apparently speak of Christ's ransoming in general, and some contexts intimate a broader reconciliation and propitiation (e.g. 2 Corinthians 5:19; 1 John 2:2).

Consequently: This sphere of perspectival data indicates that there are some general intentions in reference to the Cross-work of Christ.

Purposes (?): An appeasement preventing immediate retribution, the dogmatic proclamation of the "Good News," an escalation of accountability at judgment (e.g. John 3:18), etc.

# APPENDIX I:
## THE INTRICATE OUTWORKINGS:
## A BIBLICAL ORDO SALUTIS

The terminology of *ordo salutis*, meaning "order of salvation," usually refers to the supposedly "logical" sequence of the divine decrees.[147] However, the various advocates of different theological schools line the particular matters of salvation up in different ways, obviously in conformity with their respective systems.[148] Historically, many seemingly erudite constructs have been offered in defense of "*the* proper order.'" At the risk of being ridiculed by some of my theological friends, may I suggest that the better part of biblical wisdom beckons us to junk all such "logical" orders authored and defended by finite men and spend more time with the scriptural data, once again allowing the balance of the Bible to humble us.[149] We need to remember that God has indeed blessed us with much to explore theologically; however, He has also drawn some boundaries that the minds of men should not cross (cf., once again, e.g., the statements and implications of Deuteronomy 29:29; Isaiah 55:8–9; Romans 11:33–36; etc.). We need to be very careful when it comes to finite speculations, especially in this highly vulnerable area dealing with a *pretemporal* plan involving the death of Christ applied to the elect who are, however, almost always depicted in their post-fallen, *historical* condition.

With this warning in mind, as we begin to move from the divine plan to the divine process pertaining to salvation, I would urge us to call to mind a biblical *ordo salutis*. It is not an exhaustive one since it contains only five salvific truths out of the scores of realities which make up the various aspects of our redemption. Notwithstanding, these five important constituents of our wondrous salvation representatively span the whole scope of the divine plan and process which moves from eternity past through time, space, and history to eternity future. My textual target is probably obvious by now, namely, Romans 8:29–30.

---

[147] For a more technical description and discussion, see L. Berkhof, *Systematic Theology* (Grand Rapids: Eerdmans, 1941), 415ff.

[148] For samples at a glance, see once again, Warfield's chart (B. B. Warfield, *The Plan of Salvation* [Grand Rapids: Eerdmans, 1935],33).

[149] Exegetical theology, being superior to philosophical theology, will eventually yield more *genuine* fruit.

Picking up the passage one verse back, I would simply like to outline its impact since the particulars contained in these verses will be dealt with more extensively under the discussions pertaining to election, effectual call, justification, *et.al.*

Romans 8:28–30 surveys some of the important essentials of salvation:

    I.  Romans 8:28 provides a bird's-eye view of salvation as God's business.

   II.  Romans 8:29–30 selects some significant milestones along salvation's way:[150]

      A.  In eternity past, God set His special love upon us (v. 29a).

      B.  In eternity past, God also lovingly marked us out for salvation (vv. 29b–30a).

      C.  In history, God effectually summoned us to salvation (v. 30b, c).

      D.  In history, God acquitted us in Christ (v. 30d, e).

      E.  In eternity future, God has already proleptically consummated us (v. 30f).[151]

In other places throughout the scriptures the pieces to salvation's wondrous puzzle are not laid out sequentially. Therefore, we must restrain ourselves from lining them up in a certain order so as to substantiate (i.e. seemingly so) our theological presupposition(s).[152] As we encounter the many aspects of salvation biblically, they should be viewed more like facets of a precious gem. Each facet reflects a nuance of color; however, there is only one diamond of divine deliverance. In other words, this gem legitimately may be turned to view its many splendored reflections of redemption, but it always remains one divinely fashioned stone of salvation.

---

[150] Cf. Steele and Thomas' links-in-a-chain chart with brief comments (i.e. "The Unbreakable Chain" [*Romans*, 70]).

[151] All five verbs are aorist indicatives; each, including our future glorification, is affirmed to be a divine done deal.

[152] A good example of limited inclusion comes from the two basic systematic camps which have arisen in reference to regeneration and faith. One camp argues that regeneration must precede faith. If this be so, even for a "logical" milli-second, one is confronted with a spiritual anomaly, a regenerate unbeliever. Vice versa, for those who just as strongly argue that faith must precede regeneration, the anomaly of a believing unregenerate rises up against them. As we will see later, after discussing the effectual call, regeneration, and faith, the scriptures most likely view the later two aspects of salvation as happening concurrently.

# APPENDIX J:
## THEOLOGICALLY SIGNIFICANT OCCURRENCES OF MEMBERS OF THE ΕΚΛΕΓΟΜΑΙ (EKLEGOMAI) WORD GROUP IN THE NEW TESTAMENT

| The Verb ἐκλέγομαι (eklegomai): | The Adjective ἐκλεκτός, ή, ον (eklektos, -ē, -on): | The Noun ἐκλογή (eklogē): |
|---|---|---|
| *Mark 13:20 | Matthew 20:16 | Acts 9:15 |
| Luke 6:13 | Matthew 22:1 | Romans 9:11 |
| John 6:70 | Matthew 24:22,24,31 | Romans 11:5 |
| John 3:1 | *Mark 13:20 | Romans 11:7 |
| John 15:16 | Mark 13:22, 27 | Romans 11:28 |
| John 15:19 | Luke 18:7 | 1 Thes.1:4 |
| Acts 1:2 | Luke 23:35 | 2 Peter 1:10 |
| Acts 1:24 | Romans 8:33 | |
| Acts 13:17 | Romans 16:13 | |
| Acts 15:7 | Colossians 3:12 | |
| 1 Cor. 1:27,28 | 1 Timothy 5:21 | |
| Ephesians 1:4 | 2 Timothy 2:10 | |
| James 2:5 | Titus 1:1 | |
| | 1 Peter 1:2 | |
| | 1 Peter 2:4, 6, 9 | |
| | 2 John 1 | |
| | 2 John 3 | |
| | Revelation 17:14 | |

*Both the verb and adjective occurring in the same verse.

# APPENDIX K:
## THE INDICATIVE/IMPERATIVE MOTIF:
## ROMANS 6:1–14

Four essential demands are reflected in Paul's message on how to turn our union with Christ into dynamic daily living:

I. (vv. 1–3) Paul's Introduction to this Union with Christ Demands our Responsibility.
   A. (v. 1) Paul's crucial question regarding this responsibility.
   B. (vv. 2–3) Paul's critical answers regarding this responsibility.
      1. (v. 2a) His forceful answer.
      2. (vv. 2b–3) His common-sense answer.
         a. (v. 2b) The logic of it.
         b. (v. 3) The reality of it.

II. (vv. 4–10) Paul's Explanation of this Union with Christ Demands our Understanding.
   A. (v. 4) We must understand God's purpose for this union with Christ.
   B. (vv. 5–10) We must understand our involvement in this union with Christ.
      1. (vv. 5–7) We must understand our death to sin.
      2. (vv. 8–10) We must understand our resurrection life.

III. (v. 11) Paul's Application of the Union with Christ Demands our Mindset.[153]

IV. (vv. 12–14) Paul's Exhortation concerning this Union with Christ Demands our Total Commitment.
   A. (vv. 12–13a) The negatives of this commitment.
   B. (v. 13b) The positives of this commitment.
   C. (v. 14) The illustration of this commitment.

---

[153] Cf. the next topic to be discussed, i.e. the centrality of the mindset in salvation and sanctification.